The Tlingit Encounter with Photography

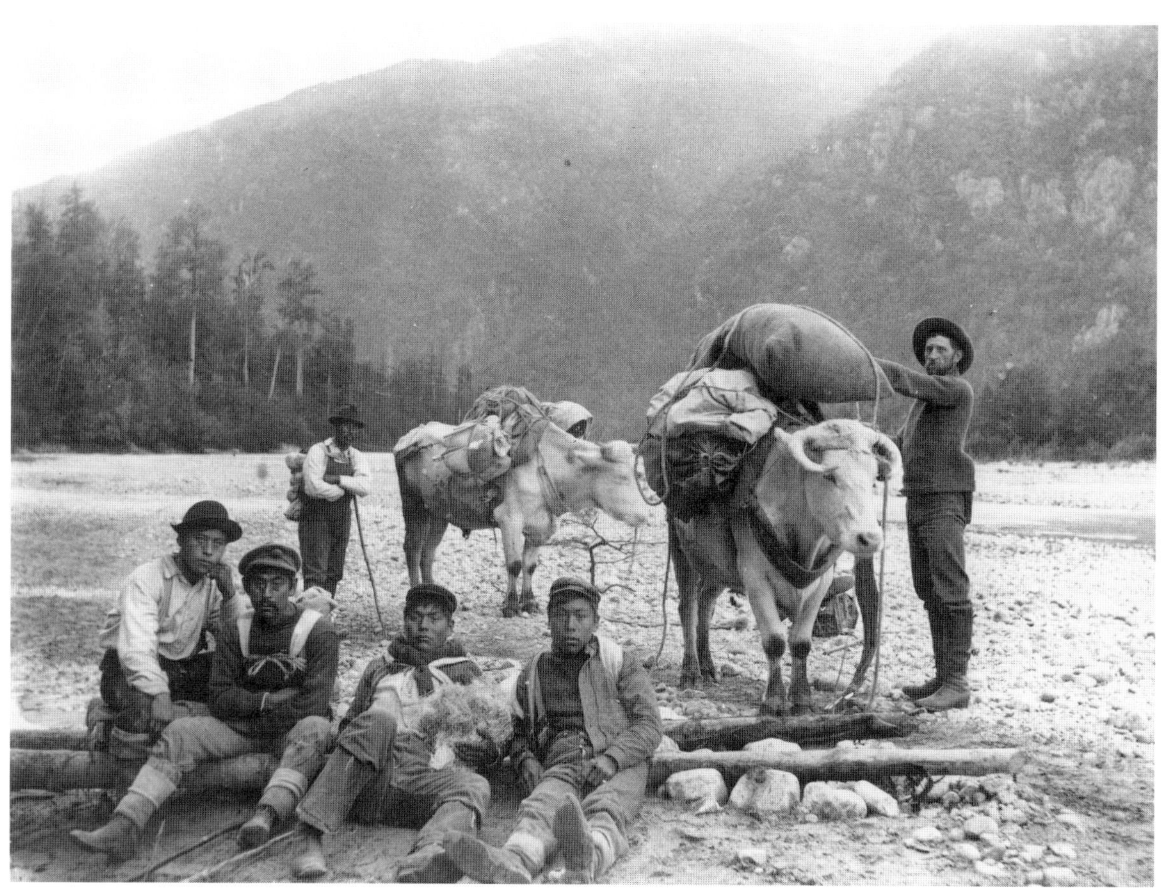

Chilkat men with pack oxen on Chilkoot Trail, Alaska, 1897. Photographed by Frank La Roche. By permission of the University of Washington Libraries, Seattle, WA. Special Collections. (NA 938)

Sharon Bohn Gmelch

THE
TLINGIT ENCOUNTER
WITH PHOTOGRAPHY

University of Pennsylvania Museum of Archaeology and Anthropology

LIBRARY OF CONGRESS CATALOGING-IN-PUBLICATION DATA

Gmelch, Sharon
  The Tlingit encounter with photography / Sharon Bohn Gmelch.
      p. cm.
  Includes bibliographical references and index.
  ISBN 978-1-934536-10-0 (hardcover : alk. paper)
  1. Tlingit Indians—Social life and customs. 2. Photography in ethnology—Alaska--History. 3.
Photography in ethnology—History. 4. Alaska—Social life and customs. 5. Alaska—History. I.
University of Pennsylvania. Museum of Archaeology and Anthropology. II. Title.
  E99.T6G64 2008
  979.8004'9727—dc22
                            2008031086

SHARON BOHN GMELCH *is Professor of Anthropology at the University of San Francisco and Union College. She is the author or editor of six other books and the co-producer of an ethnographic film on the Tlingit.*

Printed in the U.S. on acid-free paper.

To my parents,
Patricia Enright Bohn and Harold Owen Bohn,
for introducing me to Alaska at such an early age and for giving me the gifts
of love and curiosity.

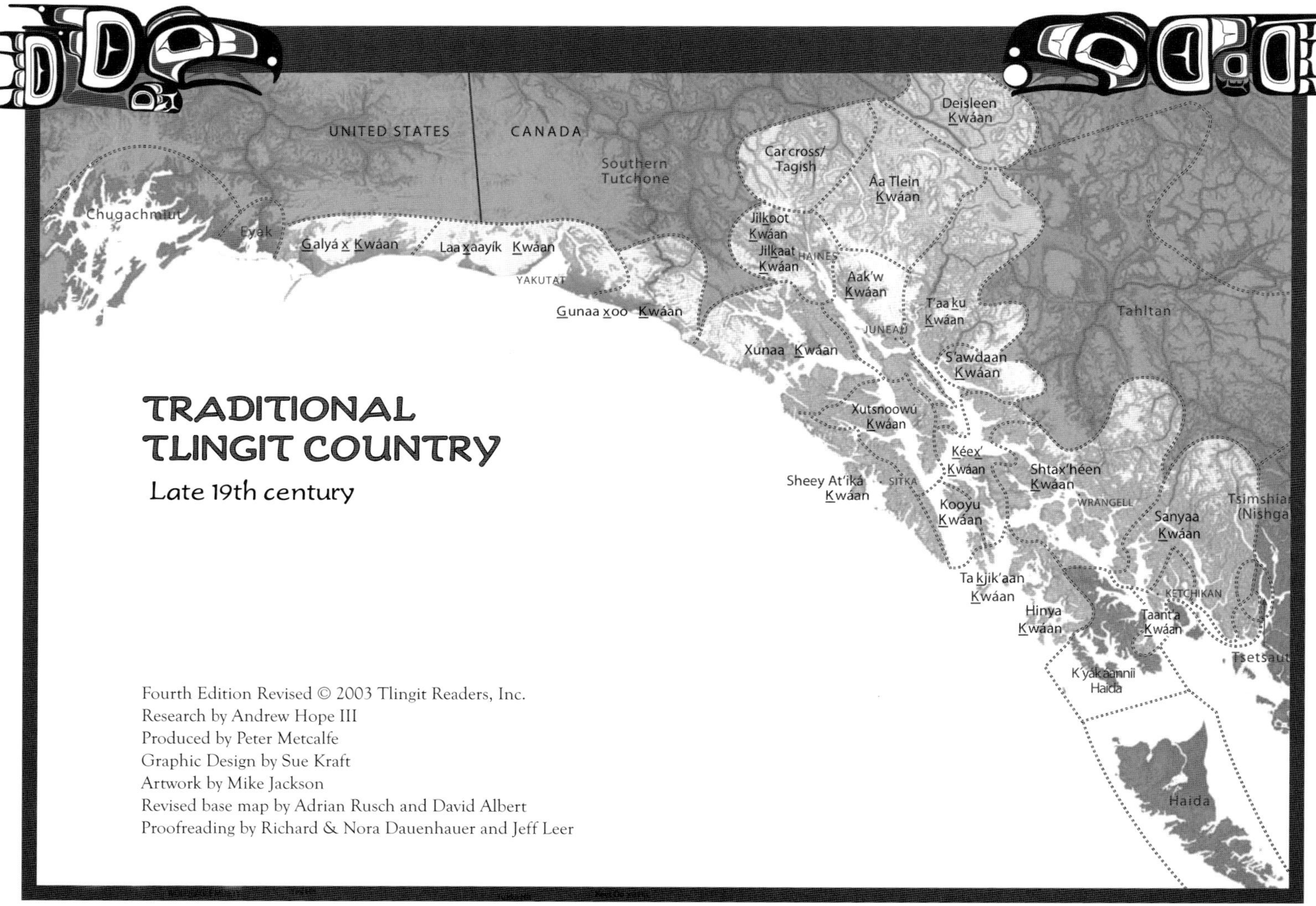

Map of Tlingit country in the late 19th century, showing their named Kwáans or territories by which the Tlingit who resided there were also known.

＋ CONTENTS ＋

❖ PREFACE & ACKNOWLEDGMENTS ❖

In 1982 I spent a summer in the "bush" in the northernmost part of Tlingit territory on the Alsek River in Dry Bay and, occasionally, in the village of Yakutat. My husband George was conducting research for the National Park Service there and I was taking the summer off to enjoy Alaska and being pregnant. The following year, we both returned to Sitka to conduct a study of subsistence for the Alaska Department of Fish and Game. These experiences reinforced my attachment to Alaska first formed when I lived in Fairbanks as a child. They also brought home the deep significance of the land and its resources—both natural and spiritual—to the Tlingit and to many non-Natives living there.

It was at the close of my Sitka research that I learned of Elbridge W. Merrill's photographs of the Tlingit, thanks to a chance conversation with Peter Corey, the director of the Sheldon Jackson Museum. At his suggestion, I looked through two collections of Merrill's work located in the Stratton Library of Sheldon Jackson College (which closed in 2007) and at the Sitka National Historical Park. It was clear that Merrill's little-known images, taken between 1899 and 1929, were significant historical documents. I also found them uncommonly compelling, a reaction that was only strengthened when I learned how little was known about Merrill's own life.

This knowledge, combined with my interests in visual anthropology and inter-ethnic relations and my attachment to Alaska launched me on a long research odyssey. It has been interrupted many times by other research and writing, including the making of an ethnographic film in Sitka about Tlingit identity and cultural revitalization with filmmaker Ellen Frankenstein—which itself was sparked by Merrill's images. Over the years, the research evolved from a narrow biographic study of Merrill and an examination of his work to a broader exploration of the Tlingits' photographic colonization by Euro-Americans and their own early reactions to and use of photography.

* * *

Many Alaskans have helped me along the way. Robert "Bob" Sam generously shared his knowledge of Tlingit culture, Merrill, and Sitka's history with me. The late Mark Jacobs, Jr., Tlingit historian and at his death in 2005 the leader of the Killerwhale clan, provided me with valuable assistance on many occasions beginning with my subsistence research in Sitka in 1983. Historian

Robert DeArmond, Jr., who grew up in Sitka, and the late Joe Ashby, member of the Sitka Historical Society, shared my interest in learning more about Merrill's life and work and dug up facts and sources for me. I am deeply grateful to all four of these individuals' for their companionship and insights.

I also wish to thank—in some cases posthumously—those members of the Tlingit community who allowed themselves to be interviewed over the years: Roy Bailey, Bill Brady, Isabella Brady, Albert Davis, Ellen Hope Hays, Laurie Cropley Hill, Dave Galanin, Steve Johnson, Daisy Jones, Bertha Karras, Ester Littlefield, John Littlefield, Roby Littlefield, Jessie Price, and Gill Pruitt. Many non-Tlingit residents and former residents of Sitka were also interviewed, including Neill Andersen, the Very Rev. Eugene Bourdukofsky, Louise Brightman, Margo Britch, Al Brookman, John Buchanan, Afton Coon, Henry Kyllingstad, Margaret Osbakken, Chuck Petersen, Charlie Nick Trierschild, and Leslie Yaw. Professional colleagues who looked at samples of Merrill's work and discussed aspects of it with me include Martin Benjamin, Ellen Frankenstein, George Gmelch, David Ogawa, Joanna Scherer, Bill Schneider, Rod Slemmons, Victoria Wyatt, and the late Lydia Black and Daniel Robbins. Their comments and suggestions have been very helpful, as have those of anonymous readers of the manuscript, although I must take responsibility for the shortcomings that remain. Patricia Roppel tracked down some archival information for me on the ship Elbridge W. Merrill likely took to Sitka. Linguist Jeff Leer of the University of Alaska provided me with Tlingit translations.

The list of archives I have visited in my search for information and images is lengthy, and includes the Stratton Library of Sheldon Jackson College, Sitka National Historical Park, the Kettleson Library, the Isabel Miller Museum and Sitka Historical Society, in Sitka, AK; the Alaska State Historical Library, Juneau, AK; the Rasmuson Library at the University of Alaska, Fairbanks, AK; the Bancroft Library of the University of California, Berkeley, CA; the Suzzallo Library of the University of Washington, Seattle, WA; the Field Museum, Chicago, IL; the Peabody Institute Library and Danvers Historical Society, Danvers, MA; the University of Pennsylvania Museum of Archaeology and Anthropology and the Presbyterian Historical Society, Philadelphia, PA; the Library of Congress and the National Anthropological Archives of the Smithsonian Institution, Washington, DC; the British Columbia Provincial Archives, Victoria, BC; and the George Eastman House Photographic Archives, Rochester, NY. Without fail, the archivists and staff members at these institutions were courteous and helpful. Lynn Wallen and Judy Hauck provided me with important information about the collection of Tlingit artifacts Merrill bequeathed to the Alaska State Museum and Library. Richard Trask of the Peabody Institute Library found Merrill's early photographs of Danvers for me. I especially wish to thank Evelyn Bonner, Nancy Ricketts, and Henry Kyllingstad, then at the Stratton Library of Sheldon Jackson College, and Gary Candaleria, Marilyn Knapp, and Robert Woolsey, then at the Sitka National Historical Park, for their time and patience in earlier stages of my research. On-line archives consulted include the Glenbow Museum in Calgary, AB; the George Johnston Museum, Teslin, YU; and the National Archives and Records Administration, Washington, DC.

Institutions and funding agencies that have supported this work in one capacity or another include: Union College (through faculty research grants and a publication subvention), the National Park Service (Herbert Kahler Fellowship), the National Endowment for the Humanities, and the Alaska Humanities Forum. I was also privileged to hold two writer's residencies from the Island Institute in Sitka and Hedgebrook in Bellingham, WA. Former student Sarah Bittleman accompanied me to Sitka one summer and with patience and good humor examined Merrill's photographs and helped dig out archival materials. Kathy DeLorenzo, Joyce Bazar, and former student Amanda Haag helped enormously at various stages with manuscript preparation. Mary Marr gave an early version of the manuscript a close and valuable reading. Sue Thorsen of the Sitka National Historical Park helped with information about the 1904 potlatch and Merrill's collection of photographs. Walda Metcalf, director of publications at the University of Pennsylvania Museum, deserves special thanks for her enthusiasm and careful attention to all aspects of turning the manuscript into a book; senior editor Jennifer Quick did a wonderful job with design. I also wish to thank Union College librarians David Gerhan, Bruce Connelly, and Donna Burton for their cheerful and professional help on many occasions.

Good friends Richard K. Nelson and Nita Couchman made my many stays in Sitka especially fun and rewarding. To my son Morgan Gmelch, who was first in Sitka as a baby but is now in graduate school in environmental policy in Washington, DC, thank you for the pleasure you have always given me. Thanks, too, to my colleague and husband, George Gmelch, for his steady encouragement and patience. And finally, I'd like to thank my parents, Patricia Enright Bohn and Harold Bohn, for their never-failing support and for introducing me to Alaska at the tender age of five. I'll never forget the terrorizing winter drive we made up the Alcan Highway on our way to Fairbanks or my bundled-up walks to school in temperatures so cold the snow squeaked like rubber bands. Many years later Morgan also braved the elements to attend kindergarten in Fairbanks while George and I taught at the University of Alaska during a sabbatical from Union College in balmy upstate New York.

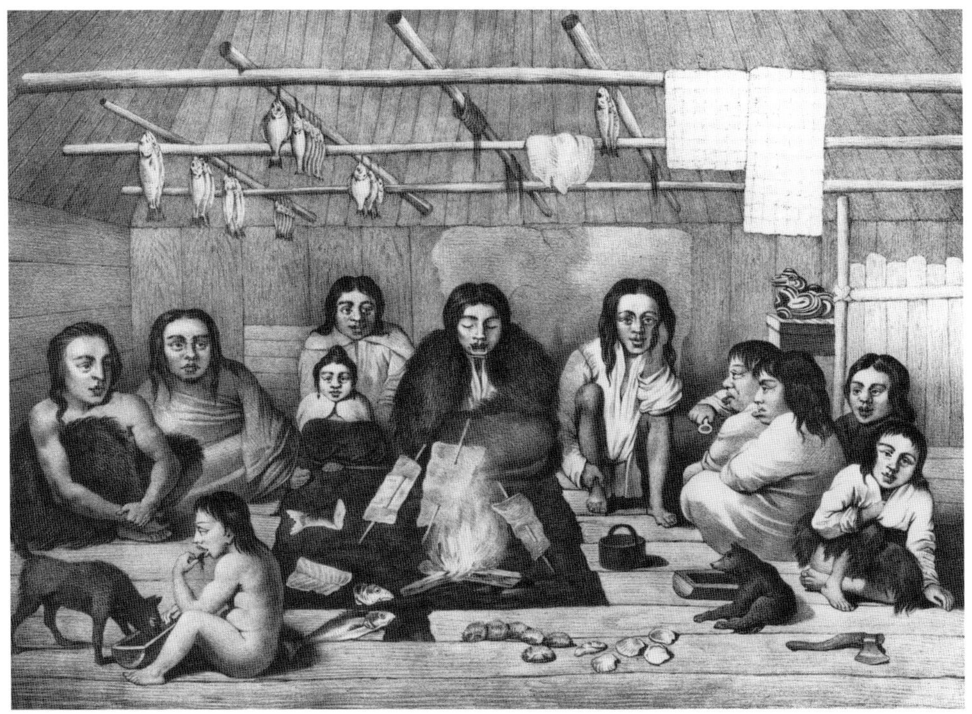

Figure 1
Engraving from drawing of Tlingit house interior, Sitka, 1827. Drawing by Aleksandr A. Postels, a scientist attached to the Staniukovich-Litke expedition of the north Pacific, in Litke (1835, 1987). By permission of the University of Washington Libraries, Seattle, WA. Special Collections. (NA 3950)

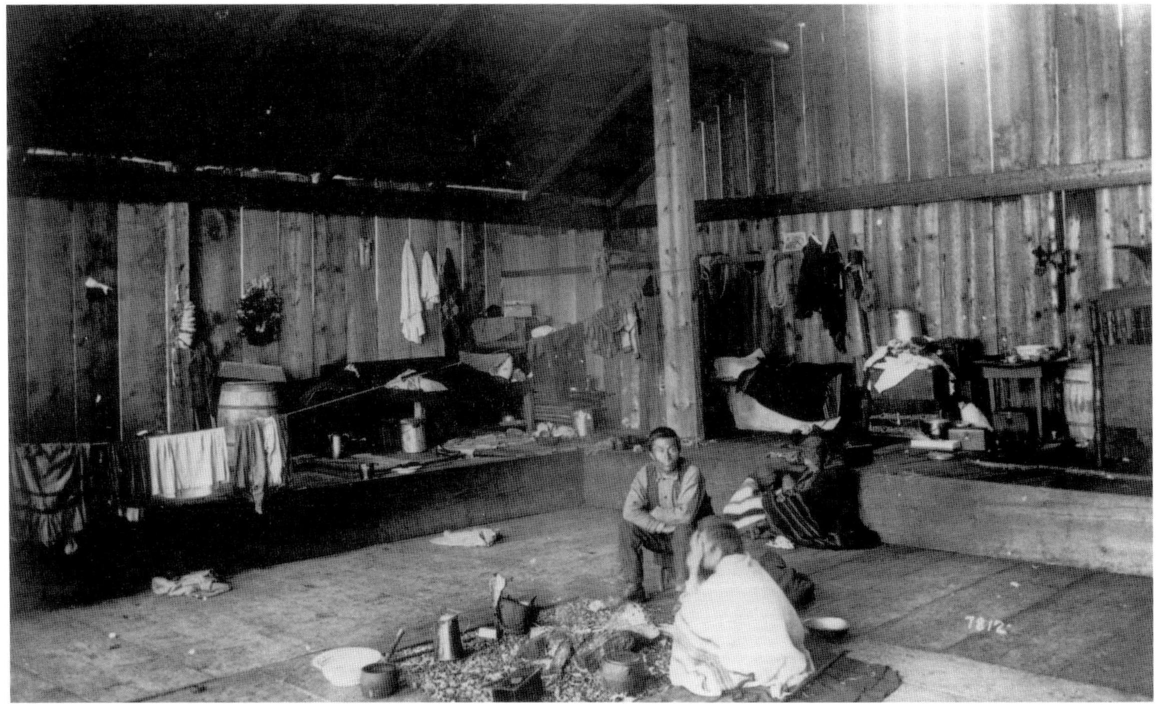

Figure 2
Tlingit house interior, Sitka, 1887. Photograph by E. J. Partridge. By permission of the University of Washington Libraries, Seattle, WA. Special Collections. (NA 2547)

Photography and the Tlingit

By itself, photography is a technology—a mere aid to seeing and recording. But how "mere" is any technology that shapes what we see and, with each passing year, more of what we understand about the past and its people? This book examines the encounter between Tlingit Indians, the indigenous inhabitants of southeastern Alaska, and the predominantly outsiders who photographed them from the mid-19th century through the early 20th century. How did the Tlingit respond to early photography and how were they portrayed? Why were they being photographed and how were their images used? To what extent did the Tlingit control their representation and use photography themselves? Or, was it simply another form of colonization over which they had little control?

I once read an essay by art historian Barbara Maria Stafford on the need for greater visual literacy. She argued that as a culture we have inherited a "Platonic view of the innate unreliability of images…[associating them] with ignorance, lumping them somewhere between decoration and titillation" (1997:B6). Since the beginning of photography, however, photographs have been interpreted as virtually synonymous with "truth." By the 1860s, "the term 'photographic' had en-

tered the language as a measure of accurate verisimilitude" (Thompson 2003:21). So strong was the idea that photography was an objectively true medium that until the process for using halftones was perfected and photographs replaced engravings in newspapers and magazines, publishers made it clear to their readers that their illustrations were based on photographs; drawings of news events were sometimes labeled "photographs" in order to lend them authenticity (Goldberg 1991). Today, the clichés "pictures don't lie" and "seeing is believing" still resonate, despite the emergence of digital photography and computer manipulation, our growing visual literacy, and postmodern critiques which have heightened our awareness of the politics of representation. One important reason for this is that photographs are qualitatively different from other images. In them, people, places, and events are *present* in an unparalleled degree of detail as the contrast between a drawing by Aleksandr Postels from 1827 of the interior of a Tlingit clan house and one photographed in 1887 by E. J. Partridge makes clear (Figs. 1, 2).

When photography arrived on the scene in 1839 through the work of William Henry Fox Talbot and Louis Jacques Mandé Daguerre, it was rightly regarded with awe. People were astonished by the unlimited detail the camera captured within seconds "as if by magic" (Thompson 2003). Photographs were so totally identified with their referents that even "civilized" persons utilized them in "primitive" ways: French nuns, it was reported, consumed little photographs of the heart of Jesus with their soup, in an attempt to ingest their sacredness and power (Goldberg 1991).

Photography was also the perfect positivist tool. Beginning in the 1840s, police began making identification pictures, and photography soon became one of the activities of all institutions concerned with observation and social control. Yet the diversity of photographic images produced and the many uses to which they were put by both photographers and subjects argues against any simple relationship between the camera and surveillance and power.

Photographs do not exactly reproduce their subjects or come "directly from Nature" as Edward S. Curtis once asserted. They are in fact imperfect records, mere slices of time framed from a point of view. As cultural constructs, they reflect the master narratives of the period in which they were produced and the individual biases of their creators. Photographic images are as problematic as written texts—perhaps more so since it is so much more difficult for most people to "see" them as constructed. After all, photographs record real people and things that were actually there, while words are so much more obviously selected and arranged by an author to persuade or reflect a point of view.

When looking at historical photographs, few of us think about what was happening just outside the image's frame, why a photographer chose to take one picture and not another, how the subject reacted to being photographed, or whether or not the image was later manipulated. Because photographs have no inherent meaning, they also rely on viewers for interpretation. Because the camera records everything—even objects or expressions the photographer failed to notice or meant to exclude—every photographic image is open to multiple readings and uses (Pinney and Peterson 2003).

In dissecting the multiple gazes or "lines of sight" contained in *National Geographic* photographs Catherine Lutz and Jane Collins have analyzed the creation of an image of non-Western people that has allowed American readers to maintain their comfortable "sense of self as modern and civilized" (1993:366). Their analysis is germane to this book in that both works examine photographs taken primarily by Western photographers of indigenous or "tribal" people and attempt to understand what these photographs reveal. Lutz and Collins identified seven distinct gazes found in *National Geographic* which open up new possibilities for interpreting historical photographs, especially with regard to issues of intimacy, scrutiny, and power. The "camera's gaze" reflects choices made by the photographer about subject matter, composition, framing, vantage point, sharpness, and depth of field. All of these shape what viewers see and how they think and feel about the subjects shown. As with most *National Geographic* photographers, early Euro-American photographers of the Tlingit confronted their subjects across the distances of class, race, and often gender. This distance, as well as the specific attitudes and beliefs they held about their subjects, influenced the images they created. The way viewers look at a photograph and think about its subjects is to a large extent shaped by how the photograph was taken and the point of view it reflects.

A second gaze, occurring in published works containing photographs, also shapes their meaning. In the case of *National Geographic*, the "magazine's gaze" reflects the mission and editorial or authorial viewpoint and is achieved largely through photograph selection, layout decisions, and captioning. When we realize that approximately 11,000 images are taken for each article or assignment, from which a dozen or so are culled to appear in the final layout, we begin to realize how narrow the *National Geographic* readers' view of "reality" is. Similarly, the 700 portfolio plates and 1,500 bound photogravures of Native Americans which appeared in Edward S. Curtis's 20-volume *The North American Indian*, published between 1907 and 1930, were selected from 40,000 images (Gidley 2003).

Viewers of photographs also add their own meanings through inference and imagination. Alfred Stieglitz's iconic photograph "The Steerage," for example, is usually interpreted as an image of hope—a moving portrayal of immigrants disembarking from the depths of steerage (in contrast to the wealthier passengers above them) to begin a new life in the New World. In fact, Stieglitz took the photograph as he was about to board the ship for Germany, and the immigrants are actually returning to their homeland in disillusionment (N. Green 2005). When images are ambiguous or when some element of composition or content—an odd angle, or obvious photo retouching—reminds us that a photographer has been at work, the viewer's gaze becomes especially important. How we interpret photographs is also culturally structured; a particular gesture or pose that indicates authority or dominance in one cultural context or time may not in another. Our gaze as viewers is also shaped by personal and political considerations.

How a photograph's subjects look back at us—a fourth gaze—also influences our reaction and interpretation. Some photographs draw us in, creating a sense of closeness and commonality with their subjects; others distance us. Does the subject confront the camera and us? What do the subject's expression and gestures tell? A smile, a glare, curiosity, confusion, indifference, all influence how we interpret what was going on at the time and how the subject felt about it.

Pose also plays a part. In Western photography, the straight frontal portrait historically has been associated with the "rougher" classes, signaling their compliance and lack of sophistication because it invites a viewer's close examination and evaluation. According to Lutz and Collins persons culturally defined by the West as weak (that is, women, children, people of color, the poor,

the tribal, those lacking modern technology) were shown in *National Geographic* facing the camera more often than not, suggesting their accessibility and social inferiority to the Western, and usually male, viewer. When an outsider appeared within the frame with a non-Western subject, the poses and expressions they adopted were indicative of the degree of mutuality between them. Poses that appeared overtly "colonial" and that clearly revealed the power differential between the two tend to distance the viewer. If we see the outsider (and ourselves as privileged viewers) being regarded with less than warmth by the non-Western subject, our unease is heightened. In a similar vein, older issues of the magazine sometimes included images of a Westerner showing a mirror or photograph to a Native subject suggesting that the latter lacked prior self-awareness. Such images played on Western perceptions of non-Western people as childlike and fed into the myth "that history and change are primarily characteristic of the West and that historical self-awareness was brought to the rest of the world with 'discovery' and colonization" (Lutz and Collins 1993:377).

Finally, there is the "academic gaze" or the analytical viewer of the images. Like Lutz and Collins, my intent is to make photographs—in this case, a collection of historical photographs limited in time, space, and subject matter—tell a more complicated story than they were originally taken to tell. Rather than read them as factual documents from the past or simply in aesthetic terms, I treat them as cultural artifacts taken for specific purposes and imbedded in the intellectual climate and power relations of their time and as visual representations that can reveal those biases.

Various aspects of gaze are evident in Figure 3, a photograph taken by Frank La Roche, a commercial photographer from Seattle, in 1903. His choice of subject reflects what he found photograph-worthy and potentially saleable on his summer field trip to Alaska. It shows a Tlingit woman paddling a canoe with the village of Hoonah in the background. To La Roche she was

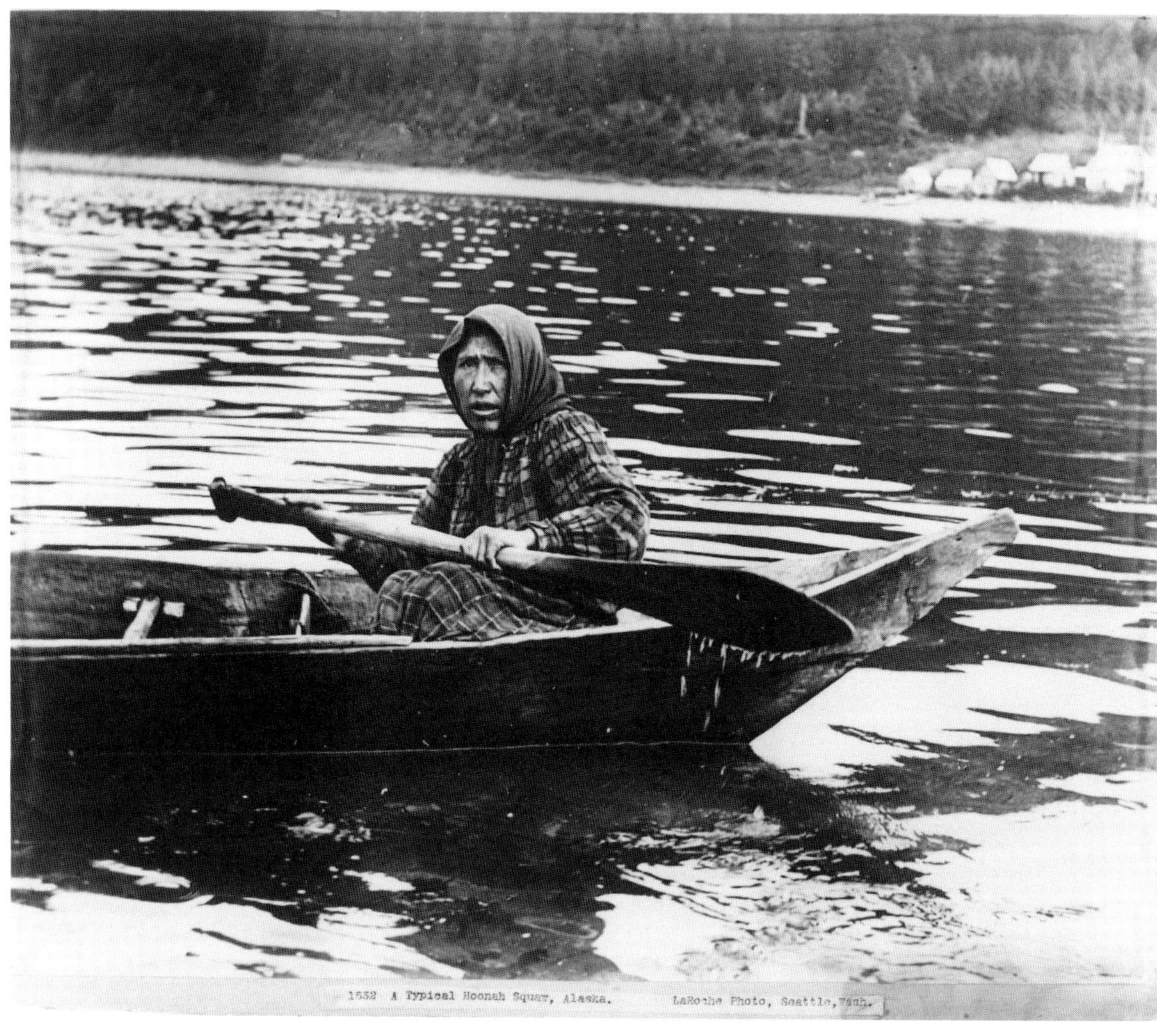

Figure 3
"A Typical Hoonah Squaw, Alaska," 1903. Photograph by Frank La Roche. Courtesy of the U.S. Library of Congress, Washington, DC. (LC–US262–12137)

an exotic subject doing something few Seattle matrons would ever have done. Her contrastive primitiveness is highlighted by her positioning in nature, surrounded as she is by water and forest, and by her use of simple technology, a muscle-powered dugout canoe hollowed out from a single log. The photographer's camera looks down at her, and although this angle undoubtedly was necessitated by La Roche's position on the deck of a summer excursion ship, the view from above and from a distance suggests detachment, not intimacy. It adds to the appropriative feeling of the image. This interpretation is reinforced by La Roche's choice of caption: "A Typical Hoonah Squaw, Alaska." She is treated as a specimen—a racial or cultural type—captured by the photographer to be viewed, sold, and collected by whites. Although the term "squaw" was widely used at the time—its racial overtones and political implications were seldom questioned—La Roche's decision to use it rather than a more neutral term like "woman" suggests that he regarded her as different and lesser—as a type. She was a "squaw."

Our interpretations as later viewers of this image are also shaped by other factors, including her gaze and our personal reactions to it. I find it somewhat disturbing; the photograph looks and *feels* to me like trespass. This reaction may be influenced by my training as an anthropologist, by courses I teach on tourism and gender, or by my past experiences as a young woman of being looked at in appropriative and uninvited ways. The subject's expression is one of surprise, tinged with distress; her gaze is wary and distancing. Nothing about the image suggests her consent; she is certainly not posing. It is difficult to look at the photograph and not be aware of the camera's intrusive presence and of the caught moment—water drips from her paddle—a moment captured by an outsider with whom she has no relationship.

Historical images are embedded in a matrix of cultural meanings. To begin to understand them, at the very least we need to know who controlled the shaping of the images and what story they wanted told. By the end of the 19th century, the notion of photographic "truth," meaning accurate verisimilitude of the object seen, began in some quarters to mean something else. As artistic expression became an accepted goal of photography, "truth" came to mean in some quarters an accurate representation of the photographer's response to the object seen, that is, as fidelity to the subjective experience of the photographer (Thompson 2003). We now know, for example, that many of photographer Edward Curtis's iconic images of Native Americans taken between 1900 and 1930 were carefully constructed by him to conform to *his* idea of "the Indian" as untouched and living in a natural, primitive state (Lyman 1982; Faris 1996). Although the romantic notion of the noble savage—dignified but doomed to disappear—was already fully developed in the

American popular imagination, it was Curtis who brought it to its fullest photographic expression. With partial financial support from J. Pierpont Morgan, Curtis spent 30 years trying to capture "the Indian." He worked in the then-dominant pictorialist tradition in photography which attempted to promote photography to the status of art. Its earliest proponents, following the ideas of English photographer Peter Henry Emerson, photographed their subjects within their natural environment and relied on their "selection of subject, lighting, framing, and selective focusing to make an artistic camera image" (Hirsch 2000:186). Later practitioners added post-camera techniques such as hand-manipulating the print to enhance its aesthetic subject matter and create painterly, soft-focused imitations of Impressionism.

To capture Indians as they were "long ago," Curtis concealed most evidence of acculturation and their contemporary lives. He selected serene natural settings that suggested a distant, pre-modern past, used large apertures and shallow depth of field to blur unwanted backgrounds, and often chose sculptural lighting and silhouettes. He also retouched his negatives and cropped, burned, and dodged during printing to remove modern elements. He even made some of the clothing and ceremonial masks his sitters wore. These were the only terms under which a group of Navajo dancers agreed to perform their sacred Yebechai ceremony for his camera; they then performed it backwards to further secularize it. Curtis recruited at least one non-Native, a trader's son, to impersonate a masked Navajo God Impersonator (Faris 2003). To create a pristine view of the Kwakwaka'wakw (Kwakiutl) for his documentary film *In the Land of the Head-Hunters*, Curtis supplied them with skin and fur tunics and gave the men wigs to cover their modern close-cropped hair. He also made some of the ceremonial masks and totem poles that appear in the film, had false house-fronts erected to conceal the milled lumber and glass-paned windows of their houses, and painted out the designs on the few dug-out canoes that remained so they could be refilmed multiple times to make the fleet seem larger.

Curtis's motivation in these manipulations was to *add* "truthfulness" to a medium—photography—which he saw as inherently "accurate" and by doing so to present the "real" Indian to the American public. His purpose was to fuse science and art (Lyman 1982; Alison 1998). By removing signs of acculturation and modernity, his photographs conformed to the contemporary Euro-American mental images of Indians. They reflected the idea that change depleted "Indianness," and that Indians were only real when they looked "traditional," that is, when they looked as non-Natives imagined them to have looked before and at contact. Such thinking remains a part of Euro-American consciousness today. I have listened, for example, to tourists visiting the Sitka National Historic Park in Alaska question the Tlingit craftspeople working there about the "authenticity" of such materials as mass-produced beads and tools such as machine-ground carving knives they were using, implying, if not explicitly asserting, that they could not be producing "real" Tlingit art because they were not using the same materials and tools their ancestors had used at some unspecified—but pre-contact—point in time.

Other early photographers also manipulated their images to conform to popular stereotypes of the Indian. Most people regarded Indians as a single category, as generic exotics, rather than as individual peoples with diverse histories and cultures. John K. Hillers's photographs from the Colorado River, for example, include images of Great Basin Indians like the Ute and Southern Paiute dressed in Plains Indian attire—the buckskins and feather headdresses that White America associated with Indians. Some photographers employed by the Bureau of American Ethnology like DeLancey Gill also provided clothing to their Native American sitters with little regard for matching their tribal affiliations. Anthropologist Joanna Scherer (1975) has uncovered photographs of different Native Americans wearing the same studio-owned clothing; others pose

with artifacts from which museum tags dangle; still others wear body paint added in the darkroom. Examining photographs from the Northwest Coast, Margaret Blackman found that early commercial photographers Hannah and Richard Maynard of Victoria, British Columbia, often combined studio portraits of Native Americans from various tribes with separate background photographs they had taken in Haida villages in order to create what they considered "good images of native people in properly 'native' settings," regardless of the individual sitter's true tribal affiliation (Blackman 1982:88).

Such manipulations reflected both the aesthetic sensibilities of individual photographers and commercial concerns: the public's nostalgia for the "vanishing race" having emerged as early as the late 1800s. "Native Americans were essentially the New World equivalent of the ancient Greeks, whose more noble civilization inevitably fell before the crass but more powerful imperial order of the Romans," explains Lee Philip Brumbaugh. "The emotional piquancy of Pictorialist imagery was based on the assumption that their idealized native subjects would soon be extinct" (1996:46). Writing in *Cameracraft* in the late 1800s, British Columbia photographer B. W. Leeson described the motivation behind his own work: "I have always appreciated the difference between a record photograph and a photographic picture and have made many attempts at the latter; the picture, 'The Passing of the Indian' being one of my latest and most successful efforts. The figure is that of the last remaining member of the Klaskeno tribe who lives with his wife here at Quatsino. I explained to him just what I wished to do, show him as the last of his tribe, asking him to look 'sick tum tum' and he responded quite well" (Blackman 1980:72).

Photographic images of the Western landscape were likewise shaped by "artistic aspirations and cultural myths," claims John Cawelti (Synder and Munson 1976:26). Although the public believed it was seeing the true majesty of nature, early photographs "documenting" the West were selectively constructed through composition, lighting, and the frequent elimination of human figures to portray nature as sublime and noble. Panoramic and dramatic views of massive peaks and canyons with a river or lake in the foreground certainly exist, but so do alkaline flats, high deserts, and plains which were seldom photographed. Unlike landscape paintings which the public realized often combined motifs and objects from different places in order to create the artist's vision of the place, photographic images were regarded as real. In fact there was continual collaboration between painters and photographers in Western explorations. Thomas Moran, the painter, and William Henry Jackson, the photographer, were together on the Yellowstone survey of 1871 and each must have used the other's work for inspiration. In Sitka, Alaska, photographer Elbridge W. Merrill and watercolorist Theodore Richardson knew and may have influenced each other.

Of course, photography from the beginning was an "important adjunct of imperialism, for it returned to the Western spectator images of native peoples which frequently confirmed prevailing views of them as primitive, bizarre, barbaric or simply picturesque" (Wells 1997:35). Individuals recorded in photographs were often seen by the public as representative of racial or social groups, as "types," and the images themselves as neutral or objective documents that confirmed their ideas about human evolution and the value of progress. From the 1850s to late 1870s, Indians were a popular subject for stereographs—photographic cards with two adjacent, almost identical images that visually merged to create a three-dimensional effect when viewed through a stereoscope. With the stereograph, photography combined public entertainment with education and filled much the same role as television does today: "it was a spectator activity, nourishing passive familiarity rather than informed understanding" (Rosenblum 1997:35). From the 1850s to 1900s, small photographic portrait cards (*cartes de visite*) and then larger cabinet cards were traded among friends; those of famous people and Indi-

ans were collected and placed in special albums.

Once the photographic halftone process was perfected in the early 1880s, photographs began to appear in popular magazines and newspapers creating more demand. Franz Boas, father of American anthropology and student of Northwest Coast Indian cultures, understood the commercial possibilities of documentary photographs of Native Americans. He hired O. C. Hastings, a photographer from Victoria, British Columbia, to accompany him to Fort Rupert in 1895 to record Kwakwaka'wakw material culture and customs. They returned with many photographs which Boas hoped to sell to *Scribner's* or another popular magazine and perhaps in this way also interest a publisher in a popular book (Rohner and Rohner 1969). The images were not sold, however, and some were used instead to illustrate Boas's monograph, *The Social Organization and Secret Societies of the Kwakiutl Indians* (1897); they eventually ended up in museum archives. Were his ethnographic images at all shaped by commercial considerations? It is hard to say. Other photographers such as John K. Hillers profited from the sale of images they made for non-commercial reasons; Hillers kept 30 percent of the proceeds from the stereographs he sold of Native Americans made while on John Wesley Powell's Colorado River Expedition (Darrah 1951). Powell kept 40 percent. Their subjects made nothing.

Commercial concerns are evident in the early use of photography in philanthropy. Thomas John Barnardo, the social reformer and self-appointed British missionary who opened a home for destitute boys in London in 1871, established a photographic department that produced more than 50,000 portraits of the children he helped between 1874 and 1905. The best known were before-and-after portraits with captions like "Once a Little Vagrant" and "Now a Little Workman." Some were given away, but most were sold as pairs of cards in packs of twenty to help fund the institution (L. Smith 1998). Barnardo manipulated many of these images (e.g., tearing the children's clothing, placing them with occupational props like shoe-shine kits) to enhance the contrast and "truthfulness" of the images. His intent was to prompt the wealthy to make generous donations and to encourage in the poor "a desire for moral and physical elevation" (Koven 1997:27; Rosenblum 1997).

During the 1880s and 1890s, reformers in the United States increasingly recognized the potential photography had for illustrating the work of social institutions and societies. The Carlisle Indian Industrial School in Carlisle, Pennsylvania, demonstrated the school's success in transforming Indian children from wild savages to civilized Americans through paired contrast photographs similar to those used by Barnardo (Malmsheimer 1987). "Wildness" was depicted by darkened skin tones, native dress, long or unkempt hair, and the students' serious, if not sullen, expressions. The contrast image showed the same individual or grouping with lighter skin, Western clothes, close-cut or well-groomed hair, smiling or earnest faces, and a more confident pose. The school offered the photographs to new subscribers of its *Morning Star* newsletter: "For TWO new subscribers we give photographs, one showing a group of Pueblos as they arrived in wild dress, and another of the same pupils three years after" (Malmsheimer 1985).

Such visual evidence was used widely in the school's reports and promotional literature, and it contributed in a significant way to the financial support received. Of course, the reality underlying these surface transformations was completely hidden. Some children died soon after arriving at the school. Those who stayed suffered acute loneliness and isolation due to their separation from their families and the prohibition against speaking their native languages, which limited their ability to communicate even with each other. "Successful" alumni of the school, especially the first generation of graduates, often became social marginals, neither fully tribal nor white. "The reformist faith in the American Dream was so deep, however, that it never seemed wrong to impose it

on others" (Hirsch 2000:276). The tableau-like images of Native and African-American students at the Hampton Institute in Virginia taken by photographer Frances Benjamin Johnston also visually demonstrated the dramatic success of education to convert warriors and former slaves into civilized members of white culture (Dykstra 2002).

We cannot interpret historical photographs or judge their impact in their time without adopting an ethnohistorical approach which recognizes that they are "constructed compositions," records of the "appearances" of past events, and artifacts of a dual encounter, an interaction between a photographer and subjects (Malmsheimer 1987:33). According to Joanna Scherer (1975) at the minimum we need some understanding of the photographers' biases and goals, some knowledge of the inclinations of the subject being photographed and, for the earlier periods, an awareness of the limitations imposed by the photographic equipment used.

It is equally important to know how photographs were used and by whom. As Martha Sandweiss points out, as long as a portrait remains in the possession of its subject or that person's family and retains its concrete identification, it can "commemorate a specific person, evoke memories or family stories, and serve as an historical memento of a particular life. When it becomes a public photograph, it can be used to tell or illustrate many stories including metaphorical ones" (2002:215). Over time the meaning and uses of photographs also evolve as competing narratives and layers of interpretation are added. There is a constant exchange between photographs and other forms of representation. Deborah Poole has referred to these "relationships of referral and exchange among images themselves, and the social and discursive relations connecting image-makers and consumers" as forming an "image world" (1997:7).

Photographs can be classified in many ways, and it is useful to think about some of these for help in interpreting their possible meanings.

One basis for classification is the photographer's purpose. From the emergence of photography in 1839 to the end of century, most photographs were considered "documentation" largely because cameras were regarded as a means of enhanced observation. Only after the magic of photography's hyper-realism—compared to paintings and drawings—had worn off, did the public begin to question at all the accuracy of photographs and whether they always depicted objective reality: Thomas J. Barnardo, the British social reformer and founder of the Dr. Barnardo Homes, defended in a highly publicized court case the fundamental truth and benevolent purpose of his manipulated photographs of "typical" or "representative" London street urchins by asserting that they "should be judged by the prevailing standards of truthfulness expected of works of art, including social realist paintings and literature" (Koven 1997:29). The camera had become one of modernity's unique ways of defining reality.

The debate soon emerged over whether photography should be used as a means of personal expression rather than a recording device. As mentioned earlier, the goal of the American "pictorialists," who flourished between 1889 and World War I, was to promote photographs to the status of art objects. Photographers began expressing their individual visions by using soft focus and radically manipulating the original image. Used this way, photography was no longer a "faithful witness but an interpreter. The subject would now tend to become not the reason for the picture, but its pretext; the picture's first function was to reveal the *photographer*" (Szarkowski 1963:4). Once this development occurred, a tripartite categorization into documentary, art, and commercial photography became possible.

Art photography, according to Alan M. Fern, the former director of the National Portrait Gallery, is that which stirs the emotions through the effect of the arrangement of forms and tones on a surface; commercial photography is that purchased by a client (such as a portrait sitter) or that which portrays an object for advertising or publication; while documentation records social conditions, events, and places (Synder and Munson 1976:11). In practice these categories often overlap. A dramatic landscape of mountain, cloud, and water—a pleasing contrast of forms and light that was taken only because it stirred the subjective emotions of the photographer—would be classified as art. If sold for use in an environmental or tourism publication, it could also be classified as both documentation and commercial photography. A portrait taken at the request of a paying sitter might, through the technical skill and imagination of the photographer, transcend its commercial categorization to become art and, with the passage of time, especially if the subject was a historically significant person or member of a minority culture, would likely transmute into documentation. Indeed, most historical photographs, almost by definition, are documentation. According to Elizabeth Edwards, "The ambiguities of the photograph, enabled images of Native American peoples produced as delegation photographs, as survey photographs, as exotica and in science to be absorbed into anthropology" (1998:190). Regardless of why the photograph was taken or for whom, its subject matter rendered it of automatic "anthropological interest." Similarly, studio portraits of Native American delegates to Washington, DC, in the 1850s, taken for "official" or documentary purposes, often ended up being sold.

Other categorizations, also based on purpose or the photographer's intent, are also possible: examples include revelation, proof, persuasion, and social reform. So are classifications based on genre such as portrait and landscape. In his examination of photographs of the Navajo, anthropologist James C. Faris (1996) uses a four-part classification: surveillance, humanist, commercial, and alternative. Each is further subdivided. Under surveillance, for example, he includes "documentary" photographs (used for official or advocacy purposes), "anthropological" photographs (used to communicate an anthropological perspective or destined for an archive or museum), and "casual" photographs (such as those taken by early tourists, travelers, and workers in an area). His commercial category includes "aestheticist" images which focus on art works or fashion details, "landscapes," and "studio" photographs (including postcards and images for personal use).

As Christopher Lyman points out with reference to Edward S. Curtis's photographs of Native Americans, "If we say that his pictures are art, we imply that they are Curtis's subjective expression of his reactions to his subjects. But when we say that his pictures are documents, we imply that they are objective representations of what his subjects were" (1982:18). Such a distinction implies that a personal attitude like racial prejudice can be conveyed by art but not by documents. And we know this is not true.

Photographs can also be analyzed in terms of how they are made to function or be used. Terry Barrett, for example, developed the following typology: descriptive, explanatory, interpretive, ethically evaluative, aesthetically evaluative, and theoretical (2006). These categories too can overlap depending upon the image, but they help with interpretation by making us think about what a particular image does most or how it most clearly was meant to be used.

Descriptive photographs are made to record subject matter accurately and are meant to be evaluatively neutral (for example, an item of material culture).

Explanatory photographs, like press photographs, are meant to visually explain their subject matter. They are specific to a particular time and place and can be dated by internal visual evidence. They usually place their subject in a social context and are in principle verifiable or refutable.

Interpretive photographs are personal or subjective images that exist only because the photographer caused something to take place: the difference between "taking" and "making" a photograph.

Ethically evaluative photographs describe but also make an ethical judgment, either praising or condemning some aspect of society.

Aesthetically evaluative photographs usually focus on the "beauty" of the visual form and how it can be rendered photographically through such skills as composition and lighting. Common subjects include landscapes, still lifes, and nudes but also much "street" photography of the beauty of everyday life. Thinking about how a photograph most clearly could be used or was meant to be used helps us interpret its meaning and speculate about its impact.

The chapters that follow examine the introduction of photography into the Northwest Coast and southeastern Alaska and Tlingit territory in the later half of the 19th century and early 20th century. Who was using this new technology and under what circumstances were the Tlingit exposed to it? Chapter 2 focuses on early studio, survey, and scientific uses of photography in the region. What subjects did these photographers capture? How were the Tlingit, and other Natives in the region, portrayed and how were their images disseminated? Chapter 3 looks at the work of visiting commercial photographers and tourists to southeast Alaska. What images of the Tlingit did they seek and why? What photographs did they carry away and help disseminate? Chapters 4 and 5 discuss the work of the professional and amateur photographers who lived in Tlingit territory. To what extent do their photographs differ from those made by visitors? Chapter 5 focuses on the life and work of one of these photographers, Elbridge W. Merrill, who lived in Sitka and photographed its large Tlingit population for 30 years between 1899 and 1929. Who was this little-known photographer and what was his relationship to the Tlingit? For what purposes were his photographs made and how does this shape our understanding of his images? The bulk of the Tlingit photographs found in archives today were taken by Euro-Americans. Given this, is it accurate to view the Tlingit as victims of yet another form of colonization, that of photography? Chapter 6 pulls together what we know about the

Tlingit's reactions to and their use of photography based on written records, oral history, and the images themselves. To what extent did the Tlingit participate in early image making? What uses, if any, did they have for the products of this new technology? Before examining these issues, however, a brief introduction to the Tlingit is in order.

* * *

The Tlingit, who call themselves *lingít*, meaning "human," occupied Alaska's southeastern coast from the Copper River, in the north, to the Dixon Entrance, in the south. Tlingit elder and historian Mark Jacobs, Jr. (Gusht'eihéen), during an interview in 1986, explained the meaning of the name "Tlingit" as follows: "The name of our tribe comes from its very activity of subsistence economy. *Tlane* means 'low tide'; *git* means 'human activity'...The name Tlingit actually means 'low tide activity people.'" Most lived on the coast, but some Tlingit occupied inland communities along the Chilkat and Stikine rivers in Alaska and in the southwest Yukon and northwest British Columbia. They were sophisticated foragers—hunters, fishers, and gatherers—who fully utilized southeast Alaska's abundant marine and temperate rainforest resources.

At the time of European contact in the 1700s, the Tlingit numbered about 15,000 people (Dauenhauer and Dauenhauer 1994). In winter they lived in permanent villages which faced the sea and backed onto the dark curtain of hemlock, spruce, and cedar forest. Their cedar-plank houses were windowless and large, enclosing as much as 2,400 square feet. An elevated wooden platform on which four to six individual families slept encircled the interior walls; a large central open space and fire pit served as a communal living and work area. Light and ventilation filtered in through an ovoid entryway, a large smoke hole in the roof, and gaps between the planks.

In summer, families left their villages to camp at the mouths of freshwater streams where they caught five species of spawning salmon and preserved them for winter use. From coastal camps they hunted for seals, preserving their skins and rendering their fat into oil. The Tlingit also hunted sea otters, porpoise, deer, mountain goats, sheep, and bear; trapped fur-bearing animals; harvested and preserved berries, roots, shellfish, herring egg spawn, and seaweed; fished for halibut and cod; and rendered oil from eulachon or candlefish. They were skilled boat builders, carvers, weavers, and traders who acted as middlemen between and among other coastal groups, visiting Europeans, and Athabaskan Indians in the interior.

The Tlingit lived in named territories called *Kwáan*; a territory's occupants were known by the same term. The people of Sitka, for example, were the Sheey At'iká Kwáan or Sheet'ká Kwáan (Dauenhauer and Dauenhauer 1994). Tlingit society was divided into two socially equal "opposites" or moieties, the Eagles (sometimes known as Wolves) and Ravens, who performed reciprocal services for each other. When Theodore Haas and Walter Goldschmidt conducted their study of Native possessory rights in southeast Alaska in the 1940s, Sitka's Eagle moiety was made up of the Kaagwaantaan and Wooshkeetaan clans, while Ravens included the Kiks.ádi, L'uknax̱.ádi, X'at'ka.aayí, K̲oosk'eidí, and T'ak̲deintaan clans (Goldschmidt, Haas, and Thornton 1998). Every Tlingit was born into one moiety and married into the opposite. Both were further subdivided into ranked clans known by their crests, often animals associated with the clan due to an historical encounter. These crests were carved on the load-bearing pillars of their clan houses and around their entryways. A large clan might have named communal houses in several villages, a small clan in only one. In Sitka, houses belonging to the founding Kiks.ádi clan once included Clay House, Strong House, Herring House, Steel House, House Inside the Fort, House on the Point, Sun House, Outside the Fort House, and Copper Shield House. A Tlingit's most important relatives were the clan members living in his or her house and village (as well as those who had been born there). The village-based

11   PHOTOGRAPHY AND THE TLINGIT

clan determined a person's rights to use both ceremonial crests and traditional hunting, gathering, and fishing areas (Klein 1995). The Tlingit traced descent and inherited through their mother's line; from birth a Tlingit belonged to his or her mother's moiety, clan, and house.

The society was hierarchical, with nobles, commoners, and slaves. Social rank based on wealth and the status of a person's clan was extremely important to the Tlingit, as were the concepts of respect and balance. Unlike the elderly in industrial and post-industrial societies who are often seen as less competent due to the pace of technological change, Tlingit elders were respected for their accumulated wisdom and knowledge.

Nature was also respected. The Tlingit viewed themselves as custodians of the land and did not "own" territories in a Western sense. Instead, territories belonging to a particular group were conceptualized as unbounded "constellations of points or locales, typically the sites of productive activities such as fishing and gathering, or historical and navigational landmarks" and others were given permission to use them if they asked (Thornton 1998a:1). Asking permission to enter or use another's territory demonstrated respect, acknowledged their custodianship, and also ensured that resources were managed properly. Wealth was obtained primarily through trade: furs and copper from sub-arctic peoples, slaves and handicrafts from the southern coast. When such luxury items were displayed and distributed at public ceremonies (*Koo.éex'* or "potlatches"), they affirmed and raised their owner's status. Often referred to as "payback parties" today, potlatches were held by members of one clan to celebrate, thank, and repay members of a clan or clans in the opposite moiety who had performed certain duties for them. These duties included handling burial preparations for a deceased chief, carving and raising a memorial or commemorative totem pole, formally presenting a presumptive heir to a chieftainship, and erecting a clan house.

Although the Tlingit traced descent through the maternal line, men occupied most leadership roles. The senior maternal uncle within a clan house was the "master of the house," and he and his immediate family occupied the status position at the back, farthest from the entry. The male leader of the most important clan house became the clan chief or "great man" (de Laguna 1988). Senior men instructed younger people in clan history, ceremonies, and general behavior and the specific skills and knowledge needed by men. Women trained young women. They also acquired wealth, and most were astute traders. To a large extent, they controlled house and family incomes; their management skills were critical to the success of potlatches, even though men were usually the formal sponsors (Klein 1995). The important role women played in Tlingit society caused considerable confusion among early European and Euro-American traders, missionaries, and authorities.

The earliest Tlingit encounter with Europeans apparently occurred in 1741 when two Tlingit canoes approached and signaled Russian navigator Alexei Chirikov's ship, the *St. Pavel* (Grinev 2005). Several days earlier Chirikov had sent two small boats ashore on Baranof Island near Sitka but his men had not returned and since he had no more small craft he could launch, he sailed away (Kan 1999). Contact did not occur again until 1775, when the schooner *Sonora*, a ship from Spaniard Juan de la Bodega y Quadra's fleet, landed on Baranof Island while exploring the Northwest Coast, inadvertently infecting the Tlingit with smallpox (de Laguna 1972; Grinev 2005).

During the closing years of the 1700s, several more expeditions—Spanish, French, Russian—as well as British and American fur traders made further contact. As early as 1799, American fur traders in the East India Marine Society of Salem began to bring back "everything from a hairball from the stomach of a cow in Madagascar to the oldest known Chilkat blanket" for the Mariners' Museum of Salem, later the Peabody Museum of Harvard University (Miller and Miller 1967:235). In 1788, the Russians gave

Tlingit chiefs at Yakutat and Lituya Bay copper coats of arms which the Tlingit accepted as valuable objects, possibly considering them Russian clan crests, but which the Russians interpreted as a sign the Tlingit had submitted to the Russian Empire. It was not until the end of the century, however, that Europeans actually settled in Tlingit territory. In 1796, the Russian American Company (RAC) established a small settlement and fort at Yakutat; three years later it established a second fort and colony at Sitka.

In 1799 Alexsandr Baranov, on behalf of the Russian American Company, obtained permission from a Kiks.ádi chief, probably Skautlelt (whom the Russians called Mikhail), to occupy land at the mouth of Starrigavan Creek, about four miles northwest of the Sitka Tlingits' permanent village Sheey At'iká ("people on the outside edge" of today's Baranof Island). A Kiks.ádi fish camp, Gaja Heen ("water coming from way up"), was located there. Baranov believed he was purchasing the land from the Tlingit in exchange for a "notable sum of goods" (Grinev 2005). The Russians quickly proceeded to build a fort, St. Arkhistratig Mikhail or Fort Mikhailovskii.

Initially the Tlingit incorporated the Russians into their trading networks as they had British, American, and French traders, but the Russians regarded other traders as intruders. They considered Alaska and its resources, especially the highly valued sea otter, to be theirs. Needless to say not all Tlingit were happy with the Russians' presence. They resented their Aleut hunters who were depleting local sea otter stock—the primary commodity in their own trade with the Americans and English—and raiding their stores of dried salmon. When Tlingit from other Kwáans arrived in Sitka to visit, they mocked the Sitkans for having enslaved themselves. "They laughed at them, boasted about their freedom, and watched for chances to instigate quarrels and insolently offend the Russians and Aleuts" (Khlebnikov 1976:54).

Mark Jacobs, Jr., also claimed that trouble began when Indian women were taken as wives without the customary payment (1990). Sitka's Tlingit raided the Russian fort several times, and, in June 1802, launched a full-scale attack and burned it down. The Kiks.ádi clan, led by K'alyáan wearing a raven war helmet, his moiety crest, were aided by other Tlingit clans from Angoon, Kake, Hoonah, Auke Bay, and Klukwan, and indirectly by American and English traders who had been trading guns (including light cannons) and ammunition for furs. The Tlingit also attacked and destroyed a large Aleut hunting party near Frederick Strait.

Two years later the RAC and its director Alexander Baranov returned to Sitka with four ships to re-establish a trading fort and colony. Baranov was aided by the well-armed sloop *Neva* which was then on a world tour. Stoonookw, a Kiks.ádi shaman, had predicted the Russian's return and advised the Tlingit to prepare a fort from which they could resist. They built Sh'is'gi Noow or Shiksi Noow ("sapling fort") on the mouth of Kaasdaheen (today's Indian River), and it is from here they fought the Russians for several days (Jacobs 1990; Kan 1999). The location was chosen because it provided fresh water and an escape route as well as gravel shoals that prevented a close approach from the sea. Tlingit and non-Native accounts differ as to how well fortified the fort was; many Tlingit accounts say it was lightly fortified, while non-Natives describe it as heavily fortified. Specifics of the battle also conflict as do interpretations as to whether or not the Tlingit ultimately retreated in defeat or embarked on a "survival march" to a planned destination.

In the end, the Tlingit could not overcome Russian firepower and sought peace by sending hostages. Then they abandoned their fort at night, withdrawing over the rugged mountains of Baranof Island to Kootznahoo Strait. Some began returning a year later and gradually established a permanent settlement along the shore of Sitka Sound next to the new Russian fort and settlement of Novo-Arkhangel'sk (New Archangel) which was established on the ruins of the former Tlingit village Noow Tlein (Grinev

2005:136–39). According to Russian accounts, the Tlingit sent envoys to the Russians that fall and then a peace delegation to Novo-Arkhangel'sk.

Sitka then developed into "a cosmopolitan community, the center of Russian-Tlingit interaction, and a magnet for other Tlingit clans whose members came to stay or at least to visit in order to trade with the Anooshi [Russians]" (Kan 1999:74–75). During the 1820s and 1830s members of other Tlingit Kwáans migrated to Sitka and acquired what became their own traditional territories in the region. It was during this period that Fedor Petrovich Litke's expeditionary voyage visited Sitka, and Aleksandr Postels made many drawings of the Tlingit. Some of these images were widely disseminated. One of Postels's drawings became the pattern on a French porcelain dinner service a few years later (Fig. 4) The Russians made an effort through trade and by holding occasional festivals and fairs (*igrushka*) for the Tlingit to maintain good relations, but they also kept up their defenses. In 1831–32 the new governor, F. P. Wrangell, built a new stockade to separate the Russian settlement from the Tlingit village and dictated that all trade with the Tlingit be handled by a single Russian clerk (Grinev 2005:166) (see Fig. 5).

It was during this period that the first missionary work among the Tlingit got under way, aided by the smallpox epidemic that swept Sitka in 1835. At first the Aleuts and Creoles (persons of mixed Russian and Native descent) living inside the Russian fort fell ill, then the Tlingit. In a matter of months, 300 Tlingit in Sitka and, conservatively, another 100 in the surrounding area had

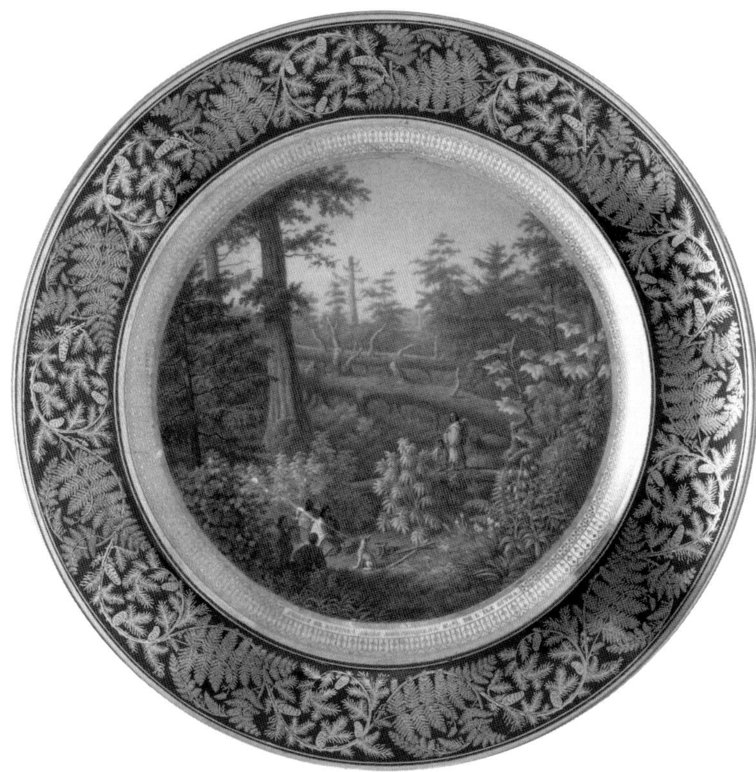

Figure 4
Porcelain plate painted with "Indians in forest of fir trees, Sitka, Alaska," 1834. Drawing by Aleksandr Postels. Porcelain produced by Sapin & Fougère, Paris. By permission of the Bancroft Library, University of California, Berkeley, CA. Robert B. Honeyman, Jr., Collection. (BANC PIC 1963.002:1876–OBJ)

died (Tikmenev 1979; Fortuine 1989). According to Grinev, the epidemic "destroyed the majority of Tlingit in the Gulf of Alaska region" (2005:173). The Russian Orthodox priest offered vaccine to the Tlingit but they initially rejected it, believing that any illness that did not respond to herbal remedies or amulets was caused by sorcery and therefore required the services of an *ixt* (shaman).

The ixt was a central figure in Tlingit life: a powerful prophet, spiritual specialist, and healer who traveled through time and space to mediate with the supernatural. In addition to healing, shamans predicted the movement of game and the arrival of salmon, found missing persons and articles, and controlled the weather. They also accompanied Tlingit war parties in order to spy on the enemy and divine details of battle. Shamans had predicted the first arrival of Europeans, the "people from under the clouds," as well as the return of the Russians (Kan 1991).

To cure their patients, they used massage, sucked foreign objects out of their bodies, and blew away evil spirits with swan's down. If such treatments failed, they donned masks, entered a trance, and transformed themselves into their *yeik* or spirit helpers in order to travel to the underworld or look into the land of the spirits, which was located just beyond the borders of the flat earth, in order to retrieve their patients' lost souls or identify the witch who had cursed them. Seminaked, with long matted coils of hair and uncut nails, the shaman inspired awe as he danced around the central fire pit to the percussive beat of drums, sticks, and rattles, his shadow flickering convulsively on the walls of a cavernous clan house. In the end, however, the ixt were powerless to prevent the deaths of smallpox victims, including influential Tlingit elders. This, combined with the obvious immunity of the Russians, eroded the shamans' prestige and paved the way for Russian Orthodox conversions. According to Veniaminov, the Tlingit—even those from outside Sitka—began to ask the Russians for vaccine. Hundreds are said to have attended a service he performed outside the fort: watching "the proceedings of the entire service with curiosity, interest, and reverence" (quoted in Afonsky 1977:55).

According to Russian sources their priest waited for the Tlingit to request baptism and also asked permission from the convert's chief and relatives before baptizing him or her into the Orthodox faith (Tikhmenev 1979). The earliest converts were Tlingit women married to Russian men and "a few native clan leaders courted by the Russian American Company and attracted by the splendor of the Orthodox ritual and the possibility of establishing ties with the high-ranking company officials who acted as their godfathers" (Kan 1991:366). In the early 1840s more Tlingit began to convert. By Easter 1843, 102 Tlingit,

including two shamans, had converted; 10 years later, there were 350 baptized Orthodox Tlingit in Sitka (Tikhmenev 1979:383).

Baptized Tlingit, especially chiefs, did receive preferential treatment from the Russian American Company. Mikhail Kukkan, for example, was appointed "head toion [chief]" by the Russians at an impressive ceremony in Sitka's cathedral and given valuable gifts and a personal seal showing a raven sitting on a branch (Grinev 2005:175). In the 1860s, Sergei Sergeev, a baptized chief of the Sitka Kaagwaantaan clan received annual Russian subsidies of 240 rubles (Grinev 2005:242).

Unfortunately for the Russians, he had little influence among the Tlingit. In addition to St. Michael's Cathedral, the subject of many later photographs, the Russians built a separate church for the Tlingit between the fort and the village. Russian clergy entered from inside the fort, while the Tlingit entered from the village; services were translated from Russian into Tlingit. Many chiefs and high-status Tlingit, however, refused to attend it since this would require them to mix with commoners and slaves. Instead, they attended services at St. Michael's Cathedral when allowed to do so by the Russians.

In Sergei Kan's opinion (1999), the Tlingit aristocracy was interested in Orthodoxy primarily to create better trade relations with the Russians. By the end of the Russian period, an estimated 560 Tlingit had converted to Orthodoxy. Although Russian American Company historian Tikhmenev claims that the Tlingits' motives for converting were not "mercenary" since most "received nothing except for crosses and icons," he also goes on to speculate that "their conversion was a temporary fascination, because their subsequent actions, during their fight with the Russians in 1855, made their faith rather suspect. When the Kolosh [Tlingit], many of them Christians, occupied the Orthodox Church they showed no reverence for holy things and demonstrated how little they could be relied upon" (Tikhmenev 1979:384). As in most contact situations, a blend-

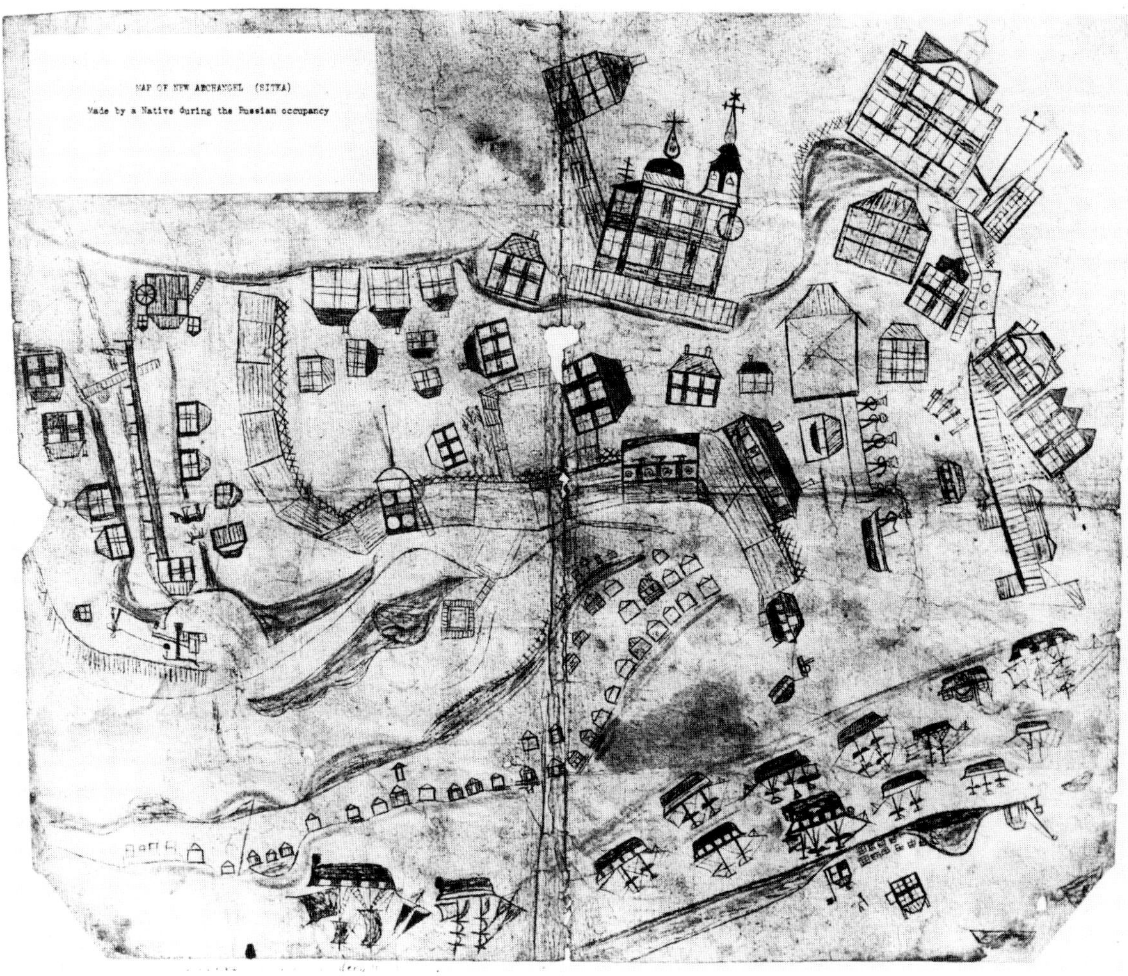

Figure 5
Tlingit map of New Archangel, 1850. The map shows Sitka harbor on the bottom and just above it, the Tlingit village. Winding through the middle of the map is the Russian stockade which separated the Tlingit from the Russian settlement. St. Michael's Cathedral, built in 1848, is at the top of the image. By permission of the Sheldon Jackson Museum, Sitka, AK...

ing of Tlingit religious ideas and Russian Orthodoxy took place. The Tlingit viewed Orthodoxy as a new source of power and fused its beliefs and rituals with their own (Kan 1985).

The Tlingit retained their economic and political autonomy during the Russian era. They bartered mink, beaver, river otter pelts, venison, fish, dentalia shells from the Queen Charlotte Islands, and potatoes—which they learned to cultivate from the Russians—for utilitarian and prestige items such as calico, woolen blankets, iron utensils and axes, copper, tobacco, flour, molasses, rice, and vodka. Whenever possible, however, they traded their furs with the Americans and with Hudson Bay Company traders from whom they obtained guns and ammunition and who usually had more attractive goods than the Russians. The Tlingit traded much of what they received from the Russians to Natives living in the interior at a considerable profit. According to the Russians, "[they] contend that we have taken the areas where their ancestors lived, and that we have deprived them of all the advantages of hunting, and use the best fishing places. On the other hand we maintain that we have provided them with the opportunity to trade and make a profit, that we supply them with items they need, and that we show them how to plant and use potatoes and the like" (Khlebnikov 1976:101).

The fur trade during the Russian era did expand the Tlingit economy. This new trade created social mobility among some Tlingit commoners who became as wealthy as aristocrats, which somewhat weakened the authority of Tlingit chiefs, despite attempts by the Russian American Company to bolster those they favored (Grinev 2005). In an effort to establish better relations with the Tlingit during the 1840s, the Russian American Company hired between 20 and 50 men each summer to work as fishermen, sailors, stevedores, and woodcutters (all were paid half the rate of Russian laborers). In the 1850s, relations between the two groups deteriorated after the company stopped hiring Tlingit workers and also curtailed trade.

Inter-Kwáan rivalry among the Tlingit also erupted at this time, including the so-called Sitka Massacre of 1852 which pitted the Kaagwaantaan clan of Sitka against outside Tlingit. They reportedly fought Chilkat Kwáans and the Naanya.aanyi clan of the Stikine Kwáan who burned down the tiny Russian settlement at Hot Springs about 13 miles from Sitka, killing one Russian. In 1855 after some Sitka Tlingit attacked the Russian sentry who was guarding the fort's wood supply, a major revolt by the Tlingit occurred. They attacked the fort but were finally forced by superior fire power to fall back and offer hostages. The Tlingit shot at the Russians from inside their church which straddled the stockade. After losing dozens of men, however, the Tlingit offered hostages to the Russians in order to stop the fighting (Tikhmenev 1979; Gibson 1987). The uneasy peace that followed—a peace that was aided by a typhoid epidemic, which sapped Tlingit resistance, and the arrival of a new Russian military contingent—lasted until Alaska's transfer to the United States in 1867 (Grinev 2005). Linguistic evidence vividly demonstrates the Tlingit resistance to Russian influence; their language contains only nine Russian loan words, compared to the nearly 400 found in Aleut (Krauss 1980). Once Tlingit territory passed into American hands, an era of dramatic change began, all of which took place under the camera's eye.

2

First Exposure: Studio, Survey, and Scientific Views

Native Americans became the subjects of photography soon after its development—the daguerreotype in 1839, the calotype in 1840. As early as 1843 the Hawaiian chief Timoteo Ha'aliliowas was photographed in Paris (Sandweiss 2002). Two years later Scottish photographers David Octavius Hill and Robert Adamson made calotypes of Kahkewaquonaby, or the Reverend Peter Jones, a Canadian Mississauga who had become a Methodist missionary and was visiting Great Britain. In America that same year an unknown daguerreotypist photographed Native delegates at a conference in Tahlequah—in present-day Oklahoma—organized by Cherokee leader John Ross; he also photographed members of Ross's family. This was followed in 1847 by Thomas M. Easterly's daguerreotypes, made in his St. Louis studio, of the Sauk and Fox chief Keokuk, his wife, and grandson.

Beginning in the late 1850s photography studios seemed to sprout spontaneously in the fertile soil of the frontier towns of Washington Territory and the Crown Colonies of British Columbia and Vancouver Island. As they did, studio portraits of Northwest Coast Natives appeared. One of the earliest is a ferrotype or "tintype" of the Snoqualmie chief Patkanim taken in Seattle around 1855, and rephotographed by George N. Moore after 1870 (MOHAI 2008). Such images were likely made for their sitters' use since daguerreotypes and tintypes could not be reproduced easily. Once glass plate negative processes were developed in the 1850s and multiple copies of an image could be made, new commercial opportunities opened up for photographers. At least five studios were operating in Victoria, British Columbia, by the mid-1860s; the first two were opened by Stephen Allen Spencer in 1859 and George Robinson Fardon in 1860, soon followed by those of Charles Gentile, Frederick Dally, and Hannah Maynard (Mattison 1999-2007). All photographed Victoria's Native population, then estimated at 2,000; most were Haida, Salish, and Nuu-chah-nult (Nootka). In Victoria Native women worked as street peddlers and domestics, the men as interpreters, packers, and guides (Blackman 1986).

With reproducible images, photographers no longer had to consider only what their sitters might want but had great incentive to think about what images they could market to other customers (Sandweiss 2002). The "vanishing race" dominated thinking about Native Americans at the time. Photographs which showed their poverty, disheveled or backward appearance, and traditional or menial urban occupations appealed to the public because they made their presumed fate seem imminent and, consequently, settlement in the West less threatening to whites (Williams 2003). The images also had curiosity value. Some people who purchased them may even have recognized their future historical value.

G. R. Fardon's portraits of Natives living in Victoria sold well and in 1862 were selected for display at the London International Exhibition; others appeared as engravings in R. C. Mayne's *Four Years in British Columbia and Vancouver Island* published that year (Mattison and Savard 1992). Although none of Fardon's photographs were of the Tlingit, we know that Yakutat traders then traveled the 870 nautical miles to Victoria in open canoes to exchange their furs for English goods (de Laguna 1972:1:35). It is thus quite possible that some Tlingit were exposed to studio portraiture at this time. The word for photograph in Chinook, the trade jargon used along the coast, is *tzum seeowist,* meaning "face picture," which suggests to Margaret Blackman (1982) that studio portraiture was the earliest exposure Northwest Coast Natives had to photography.

Public demand for photographs in the 1860s was great, especially for cartes de visite: stiff photographic cards, about 4½ x 2½ inches in size. These were carefully posed studio portraits commissioned most frequently by non-Native clients for use as calling cards. Commercial photographers also made cartes of scenery and tourist attractions, famous art works and celebrities, and "curiosities" like Native Americans to sell as collectibles. These became so fashionable that "cartomania" became a catchword in the popular press. Cartes de visite were inexpensive to produce; eight exposures of a sitter could be taken on a single glass plate using an ingenious camera with four lenses. The processed images—most were albumen prints made from wet-collodion-on-glass negatives (Rosenblum 1997)—were then cut apart and mounted on card stock carrying the studio's logo. Photographers often displayed albums or posters of sample prints in their studios so customers could select the images they wanted. Those of Natives were usually captioned with the sitter's tribal affiliation and occupation or social rank—since consumers wanted to know something about the subjects they bought—but seldom were personal names indicated and little effort was made to reveal their sitter's character in these portraits. When names were provided, they tended to be those of well-known chiefs and their close relatives. The caption on one Frederick Dally image read, "Songish [*sic*] Chiefs sister with fish for sale, Victoria." On other occasions the subject may have been someone known personally to the photographer like Mary, the Haida woman who worked for photographer Hannah Maynard as a laundress (Blackman 1986; Williams 2003).

How were these early Native sitters portrayed? Were the contemporary conventions for studio portraiture followed? Most people at the time posed in front of painted scenes with props such as upholstered chairs, drapery, and columns. Most Natives, in contrast, were posed in front of plain backgrounds and without the standard studio props. According to Margaret Blackman—who examined 143 cartes de visite of Northwest Coast Indians (1986)—Natives typically held items that linked them with their lowly occupations such as fish, firewood, or baskets filled with potatoes or crabs. The blank backgrounds had the effect of isolating and objectifying the sitter, making it easier for viewers to project their own meanings or fantasies on to the image.

Most Natives were also barefoot, and although they usually wore some item of Western clothing, it was not anyone's idea of "Sunday best." Many Natives were photographed wrapped in blankets, and some (about 20 percent of the images Blackman examined) sat or squatted on the floor. Victoria photographer Hannah Maynard sometimes posed her Native subjects sitting "cross-legged on their haunches" staring directly at the camera, in contrast to her Euro-American subjects who sat in elegant horsehair chairs or stood with their "heads slightly tilted, their eyes dreamily cast beyond the frame as if indifferent to modern miracles of technology" (Williams 1999:12). Maynard at times hung Hudson Bay blankets as makeshift backdrops or created a landscape of grass and rocks in the studio for Natives, linking them to nature and signaling their uncivilized state.

All this had the effect of heightening the images' exotic appeal to white customers. At times text was added to cartes de visite to further shape their meaning. In St. Paul, photographer J. E. Whitney's card of the well-known Indian "Cut Nose" read "who in the Massacre of 1862, in Minnesota, murdered 18 Women and Children and 5 Men" (Hirsch 2000:81). Since such images were frequently copied and reissued, they reinforced stereotypes of Native peoples as poor and primitive—if not savage, in the case of Whitney's card—and catered to Americans' belief in Manifest Destiny. Because they were photographs, white viewers could also use them as "proof" of their prejudices.

But not all photographers at the time negatively contextualized their images in these ways. Charles Gentile was something of an exception. After opening his Victoria studio in 1863, he specialized in Native portraits which he marketed to both whites and Natives. Those he sold or gave to his Native sitters "show confident-looking Indians, in non-Indian dress, posed before the camera so as to register personal qualities" (A. Thomas 1982:65). Gentile also left his studio to travel and was able to photograph some Native activities, but because he was friendly with the colonial authorities his field photographs—in the opinion of photography historians David Mattison and Daniel Savard (1992)—were propagandistic, aimed at allaying public fears of an Indian uprising.

Photographer Frederick Dally's studio images show Northwest Coast Indians seated and standing, wearing both Native and Western dress. Most pose in front of a blank backdrop, but some pose with the standard studio props of chair, drapery, and pedestal. Edward M. Sammis likewise photographed the Duwamish and Suquamish leader Chief Sealth (or Seattle) in his Seattle studio in 1864 seated in a chair in a conventional studio setting, flanked by drapery and a large urn on an elaborate pedestal. Sealth does have a blanket draped over his legs, and his folded hands rest on his woven hat and cane, but he also wears shoes (just visible) and a Western-style shirt and looks off to the side of the camera in a self-contained manner.

Cartes de visite were gradually replaced by larger, sturdier cabinet cards (in three sizes, all mounted on a 6½ x 4¼ inch card) of the same subjects. This development changed the viewing experience and created a demand for larger images which could be displayed. The larger size also gave photographers the opportunity to experiment; Hannah Maynard became well known for her portrait montages. The popularity of cabinet cards did not wane until the turn of the century when folding cameras, which allowed people to make their own postcard-size images, became popular.

Photographic equipment also accompanied early expeditions and survey teams. Sir John Franklin's last ill-fated Arctic expedition to search for the Northwest Passage in 1845 had a daguerreotype apparatus on board; Sir John Richardson's rescue ship brought the competing calotype technology (Wamsley and Barr 1998). Both technologies (made available in 1839 and 1840, respectively) and the newer wet-collodion-on-glass process developed in 1851 were taken on Arctic expeditions during the 1850s, including Leopold McClintock's final successful search for Franklin in 1857–59. On this voyage physician and naturalist David Walker acted as photographer. Most early expedition photographers were officers or men of letters, rather than common sailors, since they had access to the new technology and the leisure to pursue it (Stern 1998:48). The earliest existing photographs of Natives in the region were taken in British Columbia by Lieutenant Richard Roche of H.M.S. *Satellite* in the late 1850s (see Mattison and Savard 1992). Early survey teams also used photography to document and promote the continent's little-known terrain, coastal water-ways, and resources and, occasionally, its people.

The earliest survey photographs of Natives on the Northwest Coast and in southeastern Alaska appear in the 1860s. The 49th Parallel Survey, commissioned to demarcate the boundary between the United States and Canada, was begun by an American survey team in 1857 and completed between 1858 and 1862 with a team of British Royal Engineers. Some of the latter had been trained in photography in London and instructed "to send home periodic photographs of all works in progress, and to photograph and transmit to the War Department all drawings of all objects, either valuable in a professional point of view, or interesting as illustrative of history, ethnology, natural history, antiquities, etc." (Marien 2002:120). They were accompanied by Arthur Vipond, a civilian photographer. They photographed some of the Natives they encountered, including Salish Indians at Fort Victoria, and others in the field (Marr 1989; Monroe 1982). In the 51 years between 1869 and 1920 about 150 field parties worked in surveying the Alaska-Canada boundary (L. Green 1981).

Between 1866 and 1881, the British government commissioned five inspection tours of the coastal villages of British Columbia and Vancouver Island. Each took a photographer: Federick Dally, Richard Maynard, Oregon Columbus Hastings, or Edward Dossetter. Photography was becoming the standard tool used to document the Native population, replacing drawings and paintings as visual evidence in British reports. After British Columbia and Vancouver Island united to become the province of British Columbia in 1871 and a special office of Indian Affairs was created, these inspection tours were made aboard naval gunboats. From then on, according to Carol Williams, Natives in the region were subject to "sustained administrative inspection. The camera was part of this scrutiny" (1999:8).

Field photography reached Alaska in 1866 during the final years of its Russian occupation, when Lieutenant Charles H. Ryder served as ex-

pedition photographer for the Western Union Telegraph Survey which was surveying a cable route between North America and Siberia to link the United States with Europe (Sexton 1982). Fifteen images survive; most are shipboard shots of landscapes, and unfortunately "none provides significant information on native cultures" (Fitzhugh 1998:129).

With Alaska's impending acquisition, the government outfitted survey parties to collect information and create better charts of the territory's coastline and waters. Astronomer and geographer George R. Davidson left Victoria on the revenue cutter *Lincoln* in July 1867. His party, led by Captain W. A. Howard, had been given an impossibly broad mission. The Smithsonian Institution, for example, wanted them to collect not only meteorological information but also details of Alaska's natural history and ethnology, the later including Native vocabularies from the "Koloshians" (Tlingit) and other groups. According to historian Morgan B. Sherwood the expedition's focus was on the "acquisition of favorable evidence, evidence that could be used to convince the American public in general, and congressmen in particular, that Alaska was worth the purchase price" (1959:144). Davidson's staff included two draftsmen but no photographer, and although his party visited the Tlingit communities of Chilkat, Kake, and Sitka, the former capital of Russian America where they spent two months, no photographs of the Tlingit were apparently taken (Peirce 1869:241). They found the Tlingit at Chilkat and Kake to be uncooperative and hostile when they were not given whiskey and presents (Sherwood 1959). Davidson returned to Alaska two years later, in August 1869, with William Henry Seward and Seward's son to witness the solar eclipse. On this trip he went to Klukwan and there was helped by the Chilkat chief "Kuhklux" to draw a detailed map of the area (Maher 2006). But no photographs of the Tlingit appear in his published reports.

Photography *had* reached Tlingit villages, however. In 1868 Eadweard J. Muybridge ac-

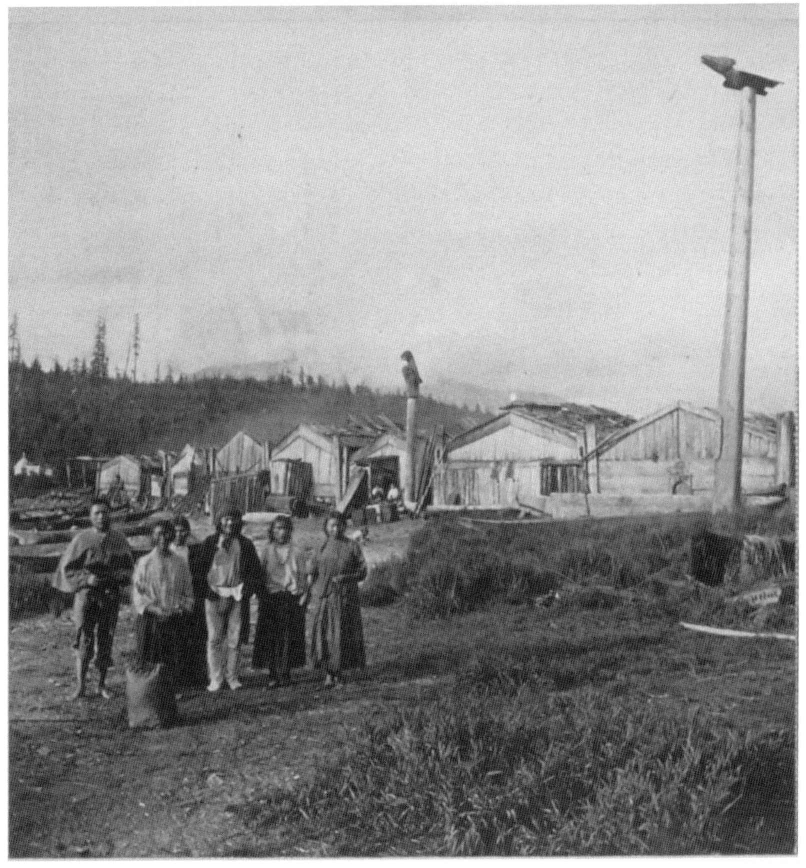

companied Army General Henry W. Halleck on his inspection tour of the newly created Military Department of Alaska (Pierce 1977; Fitzhugh 1998; Solnit 2003). Muybridge, a landscape photographer from San Francisco, was then known for his large-format photographs of Yosemite Valley and later became famous for his cloud studies and perception-altering, stop-action photographs of a horse's galloping gait. He visited Forts Wrangle (Wrangell) (Fig. 6) and Tongass and spent five days in Sitka in August 1868, less than a year after the territory's transfer to the United States. There he photographed the Russian American Company's former buildings which the U.S. Army now occupied, street scenes, "Russo Greek" priests, and members of the town's Tlingit and Creole populations. Sitka's village at this time had "forty large Indian houses, facing the western harbor, occupied by not less than one thousand Koloshes [Tlingit] during the winter" (Peirce 1869:241). General Halleck was highly satisfied with Muybridge's results and clearly recognized photography's communicative power: "These views besides being beautiful works of art, give a more correct idea of Alaska and its scenery and vegetation than can be obtained from any [written] description of that country" (Pierce 1977:209). But did they provide much insight into the conditions facing the Tlingit?

Alaska's purchase by the United States began an era of dramatic change. Alaska's first military governor was Army Major General Jefferson Davis, who arrived in Sitka in October 1867 with several hundred soldiers fresh from the Indian Wars. He adopted a firm stance "owing to the large number and treacherous character of the Indians [Tlingit]" who he allowed in the fort during daylight hours only (Dean 1994:13). He likewise prohibited soldiers from entering the Tlingit village without a pass. Despite such controls, the Army created as much disorder as it was designed to prevent, with soldiers robbing and raping the citizenry and burgling St. Michael's Cathedral, local businesses, and private homes. The year Muybridge was in Sitka, 33 soldiers were court marshaled. A German visitor described the situation:

> The conduct of the officers was bad enough, but language fails to describe that of the rank and file. Released convicts would not have been more dangerous to the public security than were these men whose task it was to enforce the law. Scarcely a day passed without a robbery, or a case of arson or a violent assault which must be ascribed to the soldiers, and the few respectable people in town were more on their guard against the soldiers than against the Russians, who were at least good-natured, or even the treacherous Indians. (Teichman 1963:188)

The presence of so many troops in Sitka, where the largest population of Tlingit lived, and the ready availability of liquor had a profoundly negative effect on the Tlingit, as noted by the Board of Indian Commissioners in 1870: "The free use of this [whiskey] by both soldiers and Indians, together with the other debaucheries between them, rapidly demoralized both, though the whites, having the larger resources, and being better cared for by the government in houses, clothing, and food, endure it the longest" (U.S. Dept. of the Interior 1870:104).

One of the earliest illustrated descriptions of Tlingit culture was written by Army Lieutenant Charles Erskine Scott Wood—a young judge advocate and aspiring writer and artist. He was sent to Alaska in April 1877 to accompany Charles Tay-

lor on his mountain climbing expedition up Mt. St. Elias. When Wood returned to Sitka in June he set off on a month's personal exploration of Alaska and Tlingit culture (Venn 2006). In 1882 he published an article about the Tlingit in *The Century*, a popular monthly magazine. It was the lead article; on the whole, the text portrayed the Tlingit favorably, although it discussed customs like shamanism, cremation, and women's wearing of lip ornaments and used terms like "savage" and "scoundrel" to describe particular individuals. Thirteen of its 20 engravings (65 percent) illustrated the Tlingit's remarkable material culture; 5 showed people or activities (2 were dark moody images which made the Tlingit appear "wild" and "savage"); the final 2 were town and village views. The most exotic image to readers may have been that of Chief Shakes lying in state surrounded by clan regalia and a bear head (Fig. 7). Yet another engraving made from a photographic portrait of a Tlingit woman (Fig. 8) contains no cultural indicators such as exotic dress or ritual paraphernalia or other signs of difference, and her return gaze is inviting (if not flirtatious).

The overall impression these images and text made on contemporary readers is hard to gauge. The Tlingit are presented as exotic and superstitious, but also as highly skilled and perhaps desirable. William S. Libbey, the Princeton geographer who in 1886 accompanied the *New York Times* expedition to climb Mt. St. Elias led by Lieutenant Frederick Schwatka, took over 200 photographs including some of the Tlingit in Yakutat (see de Laguna 1972:pls. 62, 63). Libbey also published a popular article sensationally entitled "Superstitious Neglect, Killed by the Treatment of the Medicine Man," which appeared in the *New York Times* that year. Schwatka likewise published articles in the *New York Times* and *The Century*. In 1890 U.S. Navy Ensign Albert Parker Niblack, an amateur ethnographer and collector, authored *The Coast Indians of Southern Alaska and Northern British Columbia* in the U.S. National Museum Report for 1888. Niblack photographed the Haida and Tlingit but focused on their material culture.

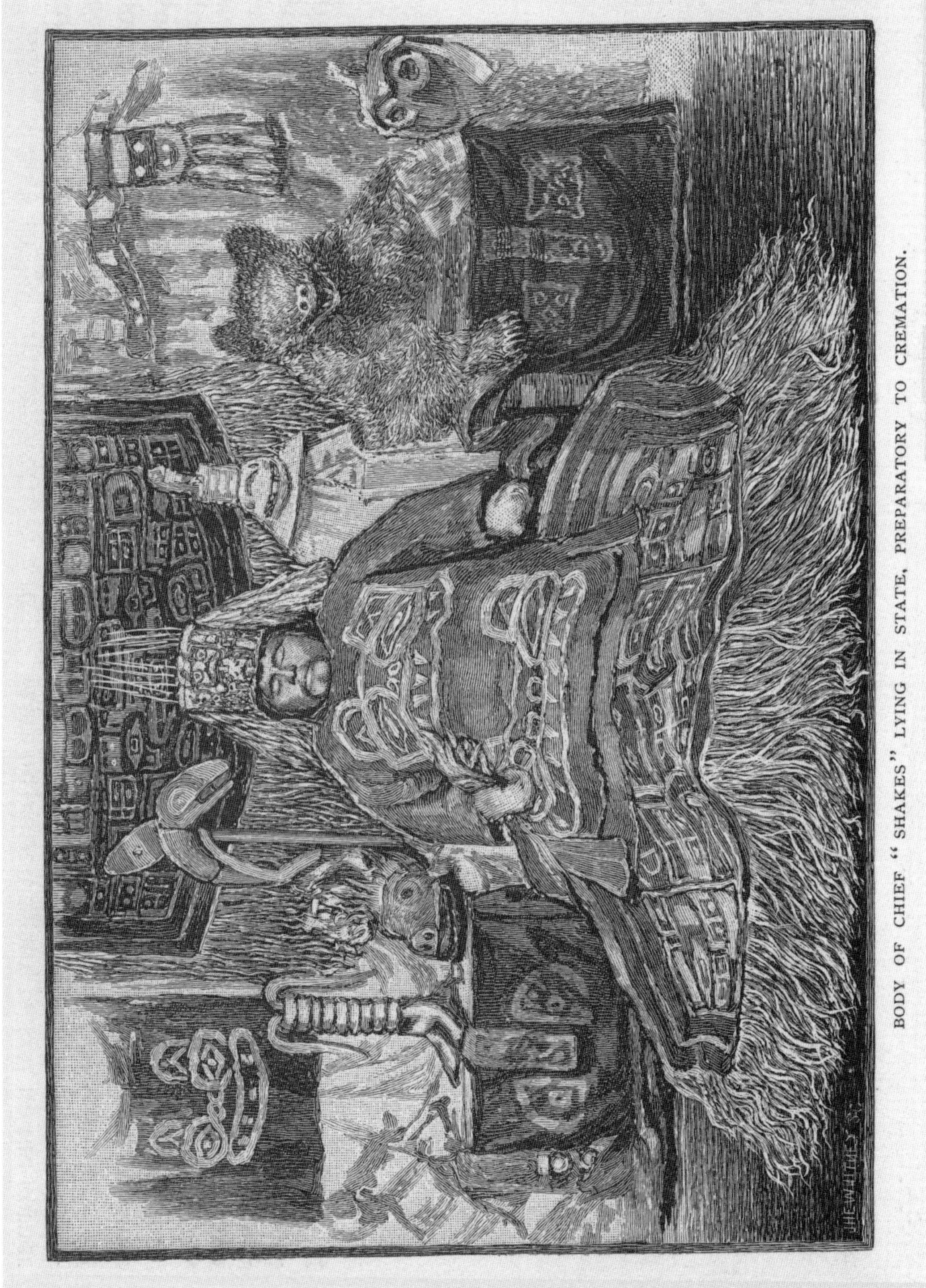

Figure 7
"Body of Chief 'Shakes' lying in state, preparatory to cremation." Engraving from Wood 1882.

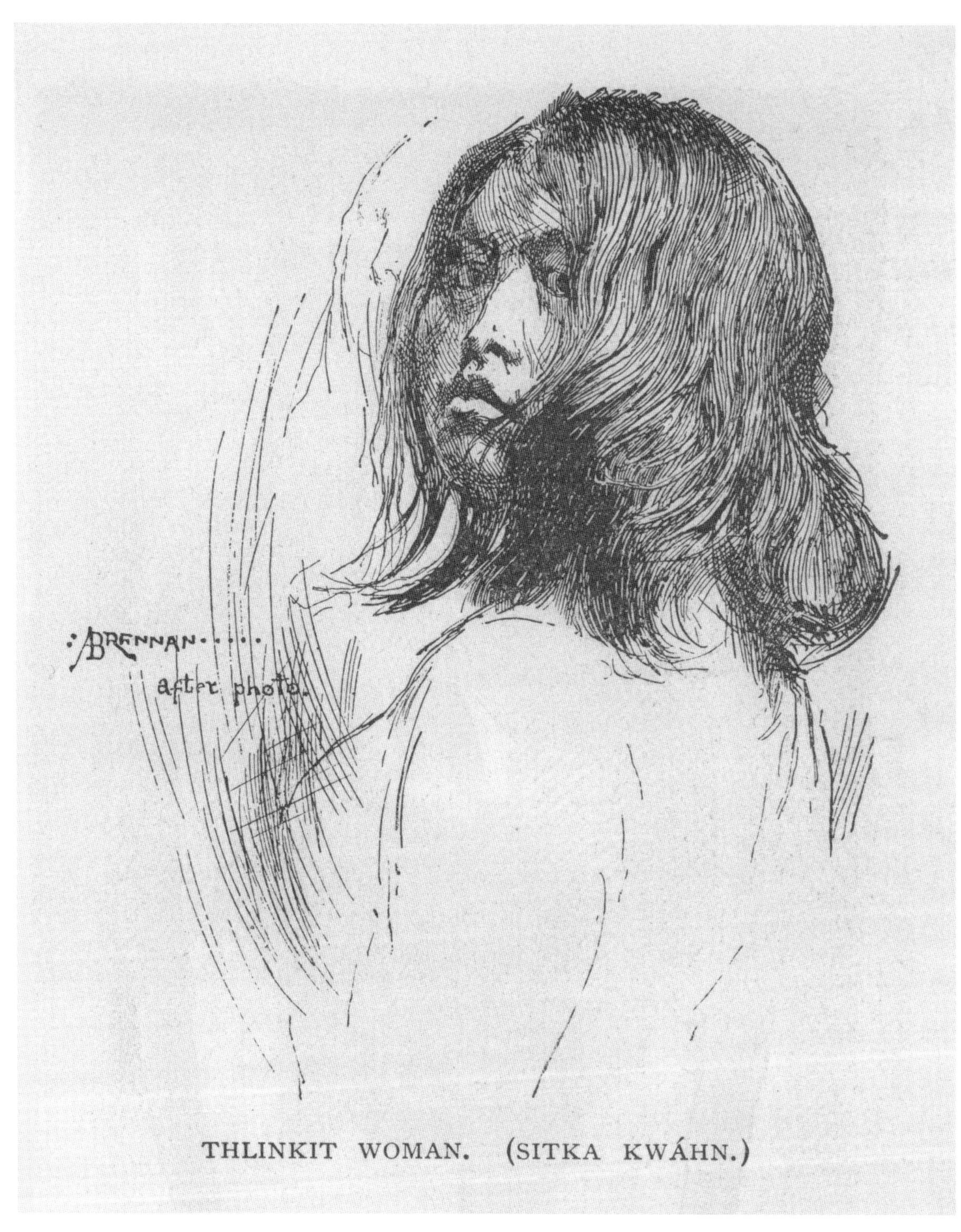

Figure 8
Engraving of a Tlingit woman (based on a photograph). From Wood 1882.

By the 1880s, both written and visual information was being widely disseminated about the Tlingit.

* * *

When the Army left Sitka in 1877, the town's customs collector became the only government official remaining in all of Alaska. Sitka's Tlingit and Creole populations took advantage of the situation by raiding government buildings and tearing down the Russian-built stockade that had separated the Tlingit village from the fort and white town. According to anthropologist Sergei Kan the Tlingit were "inspired by persistent anger against the wall...interpreting it as a continuing symbol of the Dleit Kaa [Euro-American] disrespect toward them" (1999:195). With the Army gone, Tlingit from surrounding communities also arrived to visit and engage in ceremonies which heightened fear among the Euro-American community. When some became drunk and "riotous" on liquor sold to them by whites, some white residents became fearful and called for help. As the mail steamer *California* headed south carrying their pleas to Washington, DC, and the British Royal Navy stationed on Vancouver Island, the Tlingit leaders K'alyáan and Annaxóots kept the situation under control.

Three weeks later the H.M.S. *Osprey* arrived, followed a day later by the U.S. Revenue Cutter *Wolcott* from Port Townsend and some time later by the U.S.S *Alaska*. The commander of the *Alaska*, after careful inquity, concluded that the demand for protection had been selfishly motivated by those who hoped an armed vessel permanently stationed at Sitka would encourage outside investment (Anonymous 1879). The perceived indignity of having a British ship respond to a call for help from American citizens was played up in the press as the "Osprey Incident," placing pressure on Washington to reestablish federal authority in Alaska. It did so by inaugurating a naval administration. Commander Lester A. Beardslee initially sought good relations with the Tlingit, allowing them to settle their own disputes as much as possible. Three prominent Kaagwaantaan leaders enlisted in the Navy, were given uniforms, and took up the duties of policemen (Fig. 9). They were later joined by K'alyáan, Sitka's Kiks.ádi clan leader. Other Tlingit worked for the Navy as laborers during the day and as part-time policemen at night. One of their main functions was to arrest drunk and disorderly Tlingit and confine them to the guardhouse until they sobered up.

A more serious consequence of the Navy's administration for the Tlingit was the threat it posed to their traditional trade arrangements and land use. The Chilkat Tlingit monopoly over the fur trade with interior Indians was compromised when Beardslee "negotiated" directly with the latter in 1880 to allow white prospectors to cross the Upper Yukon River region to get to the Chilkoot Pass which the Chilkats controlled. He sent the U.S.S. *Jamestown* from Sitka armed with a Gatling gun to encourage compliance (Carlson 1947). The Navy also confined the Auk Tlingit to a small part of their traditional lands which were rapidly evolving into the mining town of Juneau, even denying them access to their own waterfront.

Although the Tlingit still owned southeast Alaska under aboriginal title, they had no way to gain legal title. When they attempted to file mining claims, they were denied because they were not U.S. citizens. Euro-American settlers, in contrast, could obtain immediate title to any land they claimed, including "mining claims that had been recorded by the customs office without any legal basis" (Worl 1990:152). According to Dauenhauer and Dauenhauer, "In the absence of native title, newcomers could claim land right up to the smokehouse or outhouse of a Native dwelling, leaving little to the residents" (1984:38). Photographs from the period exposed none of these wrongs. In an attempt to seek redress, Tlingit clans organized and hired a lawyer to present their case to the President. They sought the right to govern themselves and legal recognition of their hereditary ownership of land and fishing streams. Although the Organic Act of 1884, which finally established a civil government in Alaska, recognized Native peoples' possessory rights, it did not solve the land ownership issue.

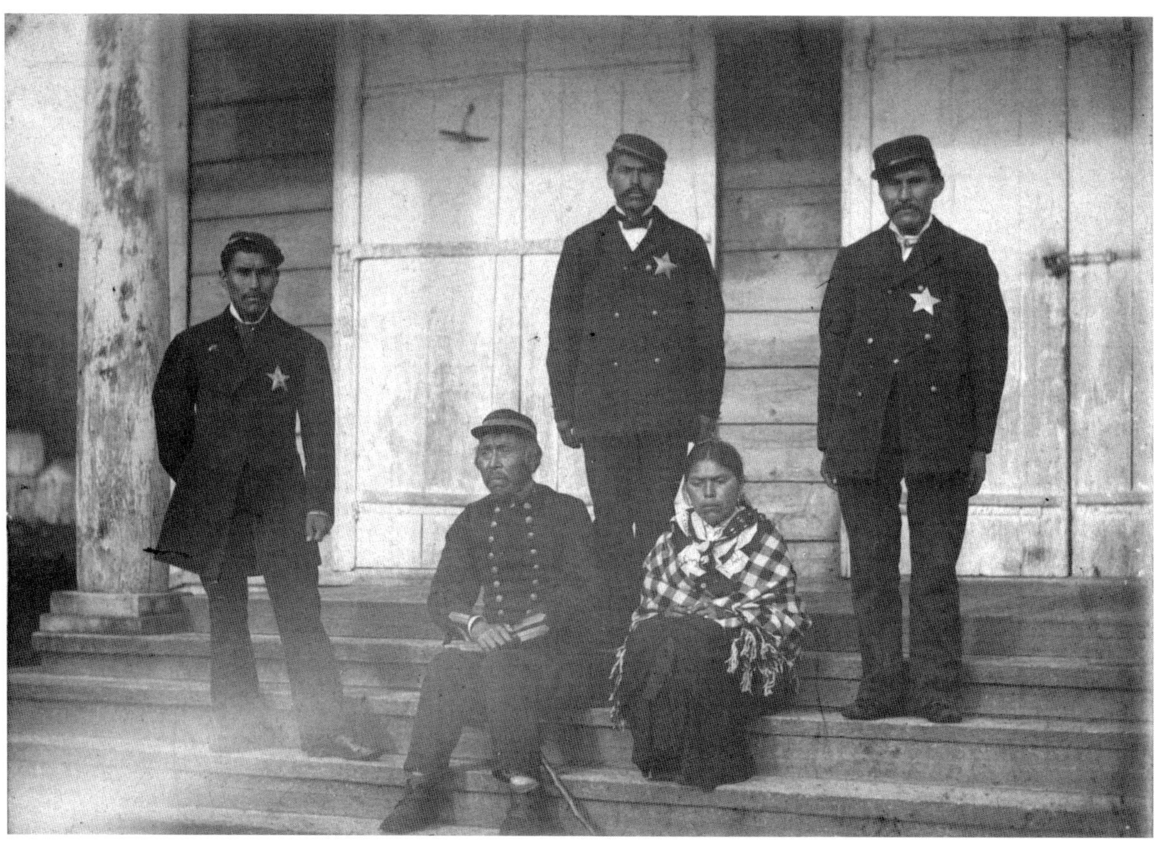

Figure 9

Indian Police Force, Sitka, 1881. Annaxóots is in the foreground and beside him is Mary, the daughter of another member of the Kaagwaantaan clan, who he reportedly sent to warn the white population of Sitka of a possible attack on the night of February 6. The other policemen cannot be positively identified. They were enrolled on the U.S.S. *Jamestown's* roster so they could receive salaries as first-class seamen. They were also given naval uniforms, which Annaxóots wears in this photograph. Photographer unknown. By permission of the Alaska State Library, Juneau, AK. (P297–098)

The establishment of U.S. forest reserves in the early 1900s also took land from the Tlingit. The Tongass National Forest adjacent to Sitka, established in 1902, withdrew 16 million acres from use including "all lands not previously homesteaded or claimed by miners and canneries. Not only had the Tlingit lost all legal access to their streams and waterways, but their land base, too, was now confiscated" (Dauenhauer and Dauenhauer 1994:39–40). The Native Allotment Act of 1906 technically allowed Indians to obtain title to 160 acres of land but no surveys were done until 1914, and the Bureau of Land Management did not acknowledge subsistence use as proof of "use and occupancy" (Kan 1999:455).

Tlingit land claims began in 1929. In 1968 the Tlingit and Haida land suit was settled awarding Natives $7.5 million (less than 10 percent of the $80 million they had sought). In 1971, with the passage of the Alaska Native Claims Settlement Act, Alaska's 50,000 Indians, Aleuts, and Eskimos received 4.4 million acres and nearly $1 billion. Twelve regional for-profit corporations were created; the Tlingit became shareholders in the Sealaska Corporation. Each person received 100 shares of their corporation's stock. Anyone born after 1971 (called an "after born") received none. Villages also formed corporations and were given title to a portion of their regional corporation's land based on the number of eligible shareholders. The for-profit corporate structure valued development, expansion, and the extensive extraction of natural resources.

The adoption of patrilineally inherited English surnames in place of Tlingit names also confused property ownership. According to Thomas Thornton (1998a), the Tlingit began combining the name of the place a person was tied to by Tlingit traditional property law with his or her first name in English (for example, Situk Jim, Sheep Creek Mary, Dry Bay George) in order to lessen the confusion.

American education was also threatening Tlingit culture. According to historian Andrei Val 'Terovich Grinev, during the Russian era "no more than 20 Tlingit received primary education" (2005:259). With the arrival of the Presbyterians in Sitka in 1878 and the assistance of the Navy, this changed. Missionaries John G. Brady and Fanny Kellogg opened a school in Sitka for several months in 1878. In 1880 it was reopened by Alonzo Austin. That same year Commander Henry Glass, who replaced Beardslee, made education compulsory for all Tlingit children between the ages of 5 and 15. As a military man, he approached the task methodically; every Tlingit home in the village was numbered and so were its children. A sailor cut circular tin badges and stamped them with each child's house number, gender (B or G), and number within the household. Tlingit children wore these badges on cords around their necks. Muster was called each morning at school and all absentees carefully noted. The following day, the oldest male resident in each truant's home was brought before Commander Glass. If he could not offer an excuse that Glass accepted, he was fined a blanket or kept in the guardhouse for a day. The money collected from the sale of these blankets, as well as fines from other "petty misdemeanors" (such as not keeping a village house properly whitewashed), was used to pay for school improvements and supplies (Glass 1890:9–10). Faced with such penalties, Tlingit parents in Sitka began delivering their children to school.

In 1882 the dynamic Reverend Sheldon Jackson arrived in Sitka to build a permanent boarding school for Native boys. (It carried many names over the years: the Sheldon Jackson Institute, the Industrial Home for Boys, the Sitka Industrial and Training School, and the Sheldon Jackson School.) Its motto was "Competent Christian Citizens." Students came from Sitka but also from outlying villages including Kake, Angoon, and Hoonah. After the Presbyterian-run boarding school for Tlingit girls in Wrangell burned down, the Sitka school became co-educational (although carefully gender segregated). Sheldon Jackson also established the First Presbyterian Church of Sitka; most of its Tlingit congregation was made up of older pupils from the mission school and some of their parents (Brann 1952, Jackson 1903). This introduced a new division into Tlingit society between Natives who were Russian Orthodox and those who had become Presbyterians, whether initially motivated by sincere belief or simply the desire to benefit in a general way from an institution so closely identified with American power (Kan 1999).

Despite conversions, many Tlingit resented the missionaries' attacks on their culture. The Presbyterians objected to fundamental Tlingit social practices such as communal living, matrilineal descent and inheritance, polygyny, and potlatching, as well as pernicious customs like witchcraft, slavery, and blood revenge. Many were also suspended from membership for "adultery," theft, and drinking (Sitka Presbyterian Church 1885–1929).

The combined force of missionary teachings and American laws produced dramatic change among the Tlingit during the 1880s. The Tlingit's matrilineal rules of inheritance and suc-

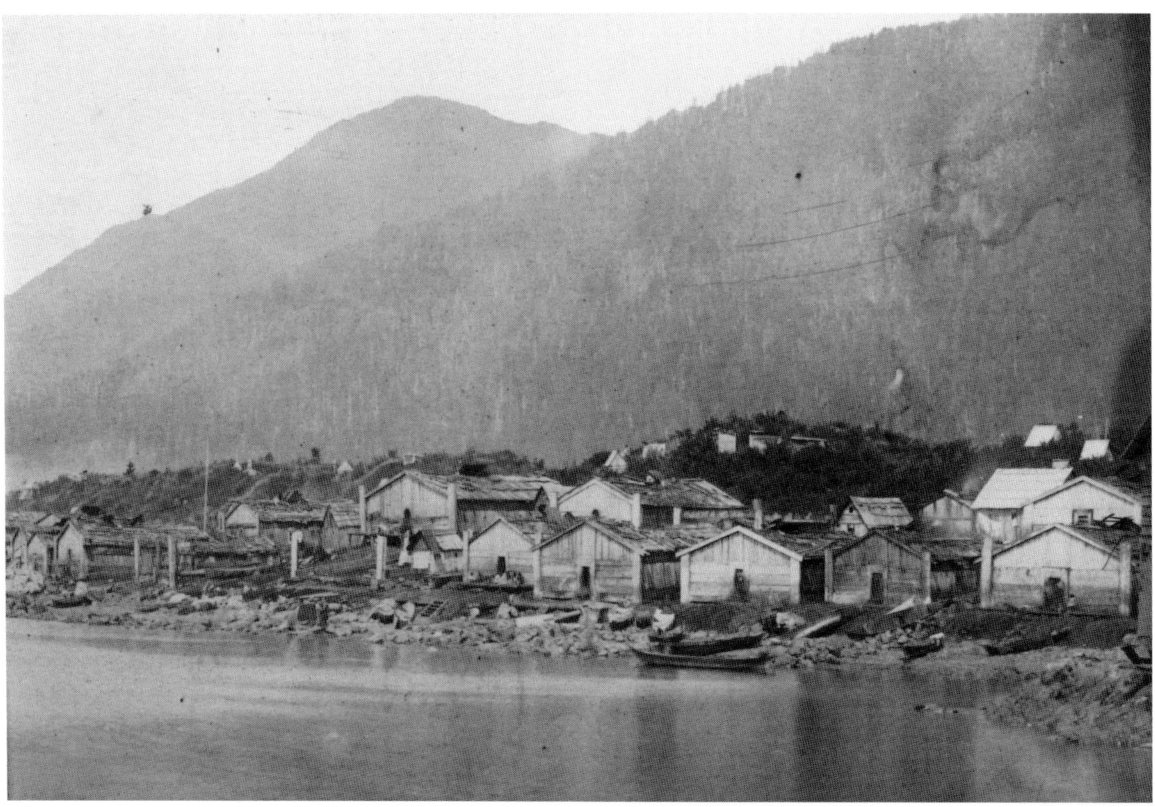

Figure 10
"Thlingit Village, Sitka, Alaska 1880." This view shows the village before change accelerated under the naval administration. Note the large size of the clan houses, the corner house posts and roof openings, and lack of windows. Photograph by the Seattle Photograph Gallery, Peterson and Brother Proprietors. By permission of the Presbyterian Historical Society, Philadelphia, PA. (RG 239–13, no. 533)

cession conflicted with the American practice of a widow and her children inheriting her husband's property. Tlingit men held clan property and regalia in trust as members of their mother's clan and did not pass them on to their wife or sons when they died since the latter belonged to a clan in the opposite moiety. Tlingit custom dictated that a widow should marry another man in her husband's clan—usually a younger nephew—whether or not he already had a wife. This allowed her to remain in the household and to be supported, but both the missionaries and American law opposed the resulting polygyny as well as the "communal living" of extended families.

The Navy supported change. When any of Sitka's Tlingit, "usually the younger members of a family...showed a disposition to abandon" communal living, they were encouraged by Commander Glass: "their [new] houses were planned for them, and they were often assisted by some of the men from the U.S.S. *Jamestown* [the Naval ship stationed at Sitka] in putting them up" (Glass 1890:8). In 1877 C. E. S. Wood described Sitka's traditional clan houses as large square handhewn plank buildings with circular openings covered with bark, bear, or seal skins for doors. This was soon to change. In 1884 alone, the Navy built ten new houses in Sitka's village. Every native house

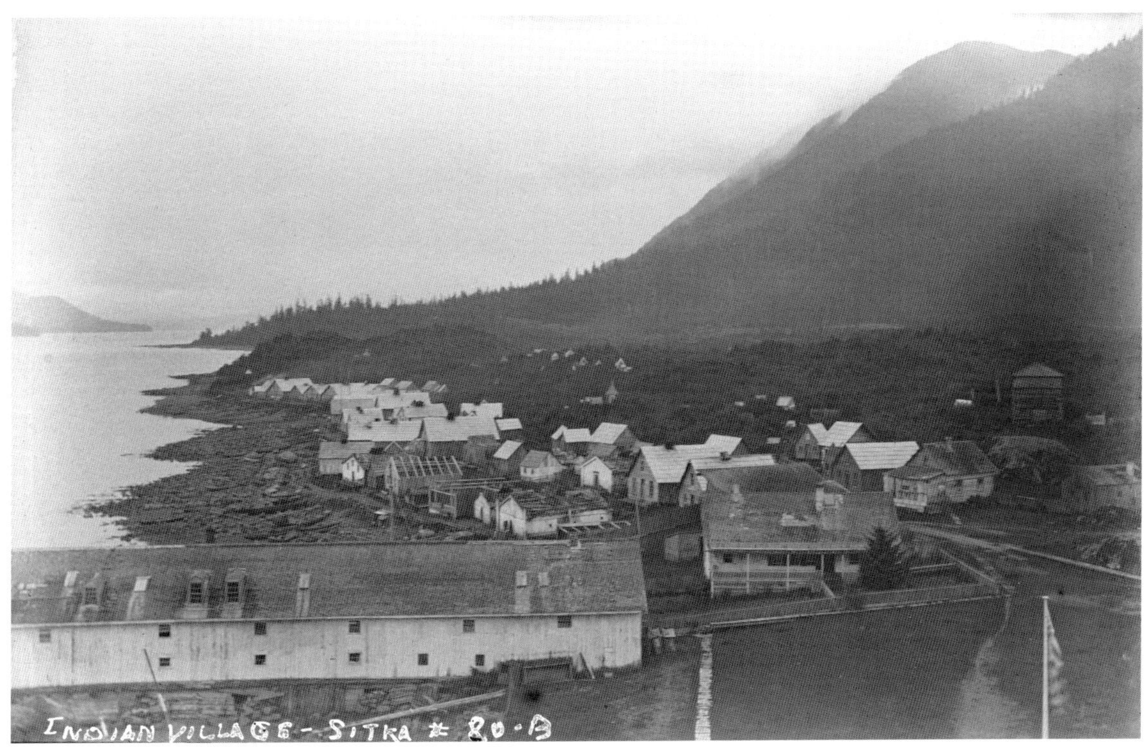

Figure 11
"Indian Village, Sitka," 1890s. Photograph by William Letts Oliver. By permission of the Bancroft Library, University of California, Berkeley, CA. Oliver Family Collection. (1960.010, series 2:0460)

was "rebuilt or clapboarded, until," it was said, "the Indian portion [of Sitka] no longer has any individuality or character of its own, and is as much a Yankee fishing village as a Tlingit village. Only the canoes and an occasional salmon rack on the beach give it any picturesqueness or color of its own" (U.S. Census Office 1893:52). These changes show clearly in period photographs and the printed engravings made from them (Figs. 10, 11).

In an attempt to end Tlingit slavery, Glass assembled Sitka's leading elders on the parade ground and read out a formal declaration abolishing it. Slaves were usually war captives acquired from other Tlingit groups whose status was then passed on to their descendants. Glass presented each slave with a written document carrying the seal of the U.S.S. *Jamestown* and his signature, giving them "the protection of all officers of the government." Many freed Tlingit slaves left Sitka at this time and returned to their home villages. Glass also called together the chiefs of the six leading clans at Wrangell and Sitka for a conference aboard the U.S.S. *Jamestown* to negotiate a peace and end the warfare that had existed between them for decades. These "grave deliberations" lasted several days during which "as accurate a computation as possible of the losses on both sides were [*sic*] made" (Glass 1890:11–12, 14). A formal treaty was then drawn up and accepted by the chiefs.

Unfortunately, the Navy was also involved in far less peaceful endeavors. Commander E. C. Merriman sent a combined force of Navy and Revenue Marines to the village of Angoon, about 90 miles from Sitka, in October 1882. Its residents had stopped work while mourning the death of a shaman who had been killed in a mishap aboard a Northwest Trading Company whaling boat and were demanding 200 blankets from the company as compensation. According to naval accounts, they had also seized two white employees, a steam launch, and other company property. When Merriman arrived, he countered with a demand of 400 blankets from the Tlingit, and when they were not forthcoming bombarded the village, destroying its homes, canoes, and winter food supply (see Strobridge and Noble 1999:153–54). (Nearly a century later, Angoon received $90,000 from the federal government in restitution.) The Army had also resorted to gunboat diplomacy, destroying four Kake Tlingit villages in 1869 in retaliation for the Tlingit murder of two white traders which, in turn, had been their redress for the deaths of two clansmen shot by an Army sentry in Sitka. Photographs of these events seldom reached the public.

The Navy and Presbyterians both attacked shamanism and witchcraft, often confusing the two. Witches were a negative force, while the shaman who identified them was predominantly a healer, although his (or her) powers were "ambivalent" and dangerous which was why he had to "be treated with utmost caution and care, and according to ceremonial protocol" (Dauenhaurer and Dauenhauer 1994:109).

After some white residents of Sitka rescued an accused witch from death in 1882, the Navy confined the responsible shaman to the guardhouse. Commander Glass then gathered "all the Indians" and through an interpreter denounced the shaman's pretensions to power, challenging him to prove his power then and there by "bringing any plagues he chose on the commander and his officers and men" (Glass 1890:13). When nothing happened, Glass had the shaman publicly shorn, removing his long uncut hair which was a major symbol of his power. The shaman was then scrubbed and placed in the guardhouse to

begin a month's labor. When his imprisonment was up, he reportedly left town. Sitka's Russian Orthodox priest complained to his superiors in Russia that "hunting shamans" was Glass's "favorite pastime and sport" (Kan 1991:370).

Sheldon Jackson also sensationalized Tlingit witchcraft cases in his speeches and publications in order to draw support for the Presbyterians' work in Alaska (Jackson 1886:11). He characterized the Sitka Industrial Training School to outsiders as "the 'City of Refuge' for those fleeing death—the 'House of Hope' to those sitting in the habitations of cruelty—the 'House of Help' to the starving, homeless, friendless waif—an asylum to the escaped slave—the protector of helpless girlhood" (Jackson 1903:15).

The school even constructed "model cottages" on its grounds—the first ones around 1890—to house newly married Tlingit graduates and keep them away from the evil influences of the Native village. Built on mission-owned land that had been part of the traditional territory of the Kiks.ádi, this residential community had its own "Cottage Hall" where members held meetings and performed plays and musicals. As noted in *The North Star/The Northern Light* 1,5 (August 1898), they agreed to keep the Sabbath, provide a Christian education to their children, abstain from alcohol and gambling, avoid "heathen" (that is, Tlingit) festivities and customs, and pass on their property only to those who would keep these rules. Despite such direct attacks on Tlingit culture, cottage residents maintained some traditions, including subsistence activities like fishing for salmon, digging clams, hunting deer, and collecting berries and medicinal plants.

The belief in shamanism and witchcraft also persisted among the Tlingit for decades. In 1902, Governor and former Presbyterian missionary and merchant John G. Brady was disturbed enough at the continued reliance on shamans and belief in witchcraft to invite several prominent Tlingit to his office: "I displayed the vital organs of the body, telling them the causes of consumption [tuberculosis], from which the white people suffer as well as they. I talked all forenoon, and in the afternoon we had another session. They listened all day, but as I ended my talk an Indian chief cried aloud, 'Well, that is what the white man say. We are Indians, and we know that there are witches' " (Hinckley 1982:254).

Both Euro-Americans and the Tlingit lobbied hard for civil government in Alaska. Several white deputations from Sitka traveled to Washington, DC, and Tlingit representatives from Sitka, Klawock, Juneau, Angoon, and Wrangell drafted a resolution to be presented to the U.S. Congress and the president. When the District of Alaska was established in 1884 with passage of the Organic Act, Sitka became its capital and acquired a governor, district judge, clerk of the court, attorney general, marshal, and deputy marshal. Federal mining laws and the state laws of Oregon were applied to the territory and Congress appropriated federal funds for education and appointed missionary Sheldon Jackson as Alaska's first General Agent of Education. But only U.S. citizens—not the Tlingit—could own property or vote.

One of the most serious threats to any culture is education. At Sitka's Industrial Training School parents were made to sign agreements "indenturing" their children to the school for five years, promising "at no time [to] bias or influence [them]...against the treatment, influence, management or control of [the school and]... not allow any other person so to do" (Wilbur 1979:257). Bertrand Wilbur, the school's medical missionary in the 1880s, described the system:

> Maternal uncles and aunts have more to say about them than their own parents for such was the Tlingit [matrilineal] custom. The students were all indentured to the school for a term of years, the school having absolute control of them for the free board, lodging and clothes they received. When we remember that in their own homes they were entirely without restraint or discipline by their parents it is a marvel we had so little trouble to get them to conform to the rules and regular life and really hard work of the school. They were all ages from six or seven to sixteen or more and because of the bad influences of most of the native homes they were seldom allowed to visit their relatives. Had it not been for the indenture their relatives would have had them in school one week and out a month and nothing could have been accomplished. Once in a while some of the big boys would run away, get a canoe and it would cause a lot of trouble to find them and bring them back. They were put in a barred room, with limited food and in a little while they were ready to be good again. (Wilbur 1979:257–58)

Tlingit children were not, in fact, "without restraint or discipline" at home. According to the late Tlingit elder Bill Brady (Guunaanasti') in an interview in Sitka in August 1986, "From an early age I was taught that number one, you listen very closely. Number two, you're always courteous and respectful to your elders, and number three, you had to learn how to take care of your family." Beginning in the summer of 1905, a few pupils from the school were allowed to go home on vacation; later, the school introduced a summer recess from June until September. By then, school officials felt that "the influence of the old customs, while yet great, is not so potent as in former years and the children returning to their home carry with them a breath of civilization and Christianity which may help to complete the destruction of the heathenish rites that yet exist" (Beattie 1907:120).

Despite this loosening of restrictions indenture agreements were enforced by the superintendent of the school and backed up by Sitka's civil authorities. "Went down to the Wharf to intercept Nora Keene whose mother had not returned her to school according to promise," Superintendent James Condit wrote in his diary on December 19, 1922. "Promised to make trouble for them if the girl was not returned" (Condit 1922). Two weeks later, he brought Judge DeArmond to the family's fish camp on Squashauski Bay to "interview" them and see that Nora was returned. As late as 1932, 17 children were still indentured to the school; most at this late date were from broken families or the offspring of Tlingit mothers and non-Native fathers (Yaw 1932).

Tlingit children were also rounded up to attend public school. As a boy, the late Tlingit elder Albert Davis (Aankadaxtseen) was trapping for mink and otter in the 1920s when authorities came to get him: "That's where our major income came from. That [trapping] let us survive over the winter and that is where I was when the U.S. Deputy Marshall came out intending to arrest my father and uncle if they didn't bring me into Sitka in five days to go to school...and I couldn't speak the English...so they gave me an interpreter. You talk about cry all day—huh, huh, huh. And they never knew what they were doing to me" (Davis 1990).

After passage of the Nelson Act in 1905 separate public schools were established for Natives and whites in Alaska. Children of "mixed blood," however, could attend "white" schools if they and their parents lived a "civilized life." As Raibmon (2005:135) points out this created problems and pointed out the "fictitious nature of colonial dichotomies" that assumed binary racial and cultural authenticity classifications: Native or white, traditional or modern, authentic or inauthentic. When the daughters of Mary Davis, who was considered by the wider society to be a "half-breed," were denied permission in 1906 to continue attending Sitka's white public school while living in the "Indian Ranche," the case (Davis v. Sitka School Board) was taken to court. Mary, a widow from Hoonah, had remarried Sitka widower Rudolph Walton, a prominent jeweler and business owner, a graduate of the Sitka Industrial Training School, and leading elder of the Presbyterian Church. Yet when the court ruled against her in 1908, it argued that "each generation must decide for itself what constitutes a civilized life."

The standards imposed by the court and by the Presbyterian Church were strict. In August 1905 Walton had been called before the church's elders to explain why he "had taken to his house as his wife according to heathen custom and without legal marriage Mary Davis and had so lived with her for two or three days before they were legally married" (Sitka Presbyterian Church 1905). Davis and Walton also remarried according to Tlingit custom in the sense that they had come from clans in opposite moieties. Apparently such factors and their residence in the Tlingit village overrode their Christianity, education, and Western life style in both the court's and the church's view. They were not "civilized" enough.

With the expansion of southeast Alaska's economy in the late 1870s and 1880s and the threat to their own subsistence, many Tlingit took up wage labor in the fishing industry, mining, and related pursuits. The first salmon canneries opened at Klawock and at Starrigavan Bay near Sitka in 1878. Klawock operated for the next 51 years using Tlingit and Haida crews, while Sitka's cannery closed after two seasons. In 1880 the Northwest Trading Company opened a trading post and whaling station at Killisnoo, hiring Tlingit from the nearby village of Angoon to hunt whales. Other canneries and salmon salteries opened during the decade at Naha Bay, Loring, Ketchikan, Wrangell, and Haines. Most were owned by non-residents and used Chinese labor which was perceived as more docile, hiring the Tlingit only when supplementary labor was needed.

Discoveries of gold at Telegraph Creek near Wrangell in 1861 and on Gold Creek near Juneau in 1880 led to mining in Tlingit territory. Further gold fields and mines were discovered in the southeast, British Columbia, the Yukon, and the interior of Alaska in the 1880s and 1890s. Until the White Pass and Yukon Railway was completed in 1900, Chilkat, Chilkoot, and Sitka Tlingit packed mining supplies over the mountains using the Tlingit's historic Chilkoot trail. These enterprises were joined in the early 1900s by a cold storage facility for halibut at Sitka, another cannery at Hoonah in 1912 (today used by the Hoonah (Xunaa) Tlingit as a tourist attraction), and a flourishing commercial herring fishery in the 1910s and 1920s. Tourism also began creating income-producing opportunities in the 1880s.

As more outsiders arrived, the Tlingit were forced to become politically active. Individually and collectively, they wrote letters to state and federal officials, including the President, protesting the loss of traditional salmon streams and the over-exploitation of salmon stock by commercial fishers and canneries. The Alaska Native Brotherhood (ANB) and the Alaska Native Sisterhood (ANS) were formed in 1912 and 1914 by the Tlingit to fight for citizenship, an end to discrimination, and legal protection of their resources and rights. Three years later, Alaska's territorial legislature granted citizenship to Alaska Natives, but only if five whites would legally testify that the individual in question had given up Native culture. In 1924, the U.S. federal government granted citizenship to all Native Americans, but Alaska's legislature instituted a literacy test which prevented most Tlingit and other Natives from taking advantage of this new right.

* * *

With the completion of the transcontinental railroad in 1869 the Northwest became the site of economic expansion and settlement. Photographers, artists, and writers were hired by the government and by the railroads to produced images and narratives that would stimulate interest in the area's potential. Artist Vincent Colyer, a Quaker humanitarian and ardent assimilationist, visited southeast Alaska in 1869 on behalf of the newly created Board of Indian Commissioners. He recommended federally funded schools and medical care for Alaskan Natives which Congress rejected, although it did provide some money for education through the Interior Department. Colyer described the Tlingit as having superior intelligence, praised their rapid acquisition of American ways, and distinguished them from "Indians" living outside Alaska. Although Colyer did not photograph the Tlingit, he made numerous watercolor sketches on his trip. His watercolor of the Tlingit village at Wrangell—viewed from the water with its houses, canoes, and two totem poles—was published in *Harper's Weekly* in February 1870. It showed a tranquil scene and is likely to have helped ameliorate any negative stereotypes of the Tlingit or other Alaskan Natives that resulted from the earlier adverse publicity generated by the conflict between the Tlingit and Army troops based at Sitka.

Congress and the Secretary of the Interior accepted Colyer's opinion that Alaskan Natives were different from "Indians," and decided to make them subject to the same statutes and laws as non-Natives. Not enough whites were moving to Alaska to settle to warrant a policy of Native removal and reservations.

Naval and U.S. Revenue Cutter Service (later, Coast Guard) ships cruising the waters of the Northwest Coast and southeastern Alaska in the late 1800s usually carried photographers on board, either crew members who were amateurs or "official" ship photographers. The latter were frequently the chief engineer or surgeon who was given the work as a second assignment. In 1875, a crew member on the Revenue Cutter *Walcott* photographed the Haida (Blackman 1982). In 1891, A. L. Broadbent, assistant engineer and photographer on the Revenue Cutter *Bear*, photographed the Tlingit in Sitka. A decade later, H. W. Spear, another Revenue Cutter Service engineer, photographed the Tlingit residents of Klinquan (Fig. 12).

Various members of U.S. Coast and Geodetic Survey teams, such as Herbert G. Ogden and astronomer John F. Pratt, also photographed coastal Alaska villages and their residents. The Geological Survey of Canada (GSC) photographically documented its work along the Northwest Coast and far north; some of its employees photographed Natives and their communities in addition to the region's land and rock formations. Geologist George Mercer Dawson, one-time director of the GSC, seems to have been the first person to photograph the Haida Gwaii in their villages on the Queen Charlotte Islands of British Co-

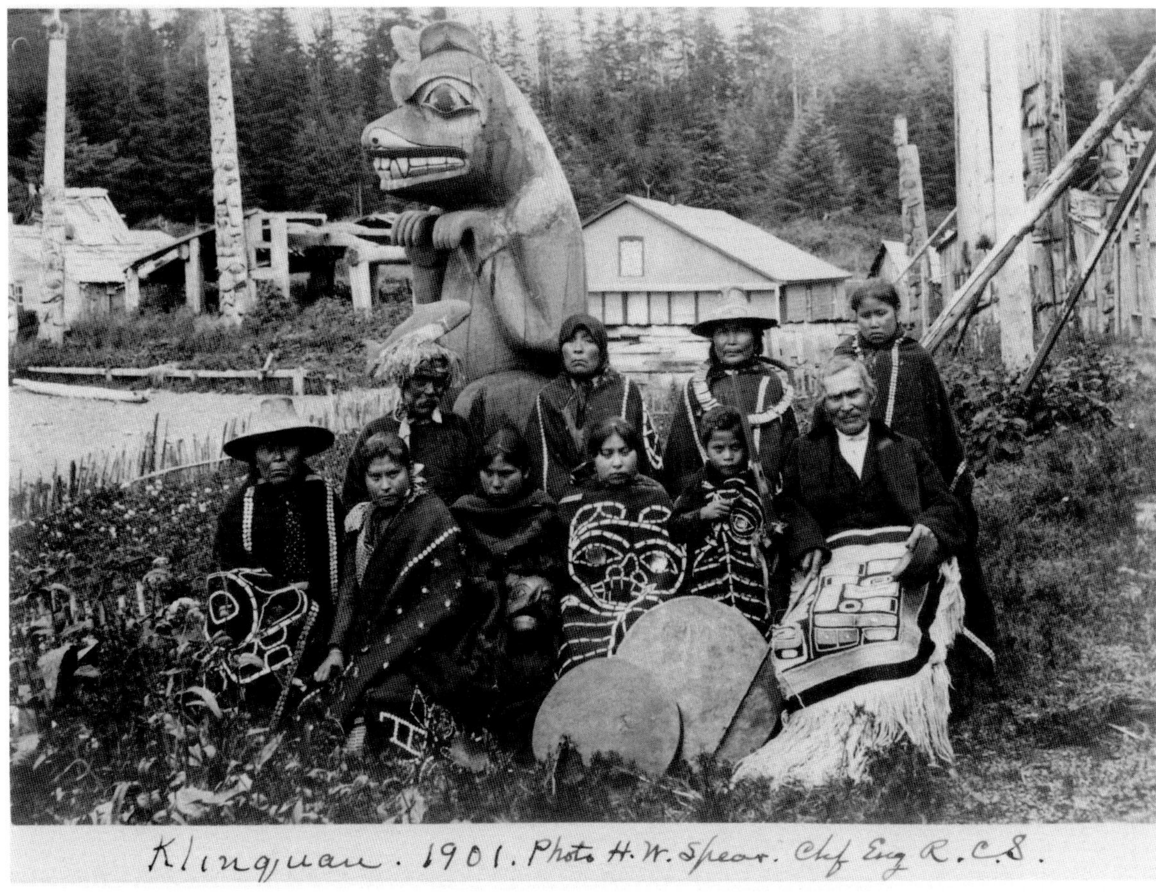

Figure 12
Klinquan, 1901. Photograph by H. W. Spear. By permission of the Presbyterian Historical Society, Philadelphia, PA. (RG 239–16, no. 2070)

lumbia in 1878—ten years after Muybridge's work in Sitka (Blackman 1982). Most Tlingit by this time regularly wore Western ready-made clothing. One of Pratt's photographs, taken in 1894, shows three Tlingit at Klukwan posed outside dressed in Western suits and dresses. In 1903, the Miles Brothers studio of San Francisco was hired by the Valdez, Copper River, and Yukon Railroad Company to photograph a proposed route to Nome. In the course of doing so, they photographed the Tlingit and other Natives living along the Copper and Kotsina Rivers (Fig. 13).

The value of photography for both descrip-tive and explanatory purposes in published re-ports was increasingly recognized. Between 1871 and 1881 commercial photographers were com-missioned by the regional superintendent of the Office (later, Bureau) of Indian Affairs to supply photographs to supplement regular government reports about Northwest Coast Indians (Williams 2003:208 n.6). In 1879 and 1881 photographer Oregon Columbus Hastings accompanied U.S. Indian Commissioner Israel W. Powell on his inspection tours of Native villages. Photographs now began replacing drawings and paintings, be-coming a new tool of Western expansion. The

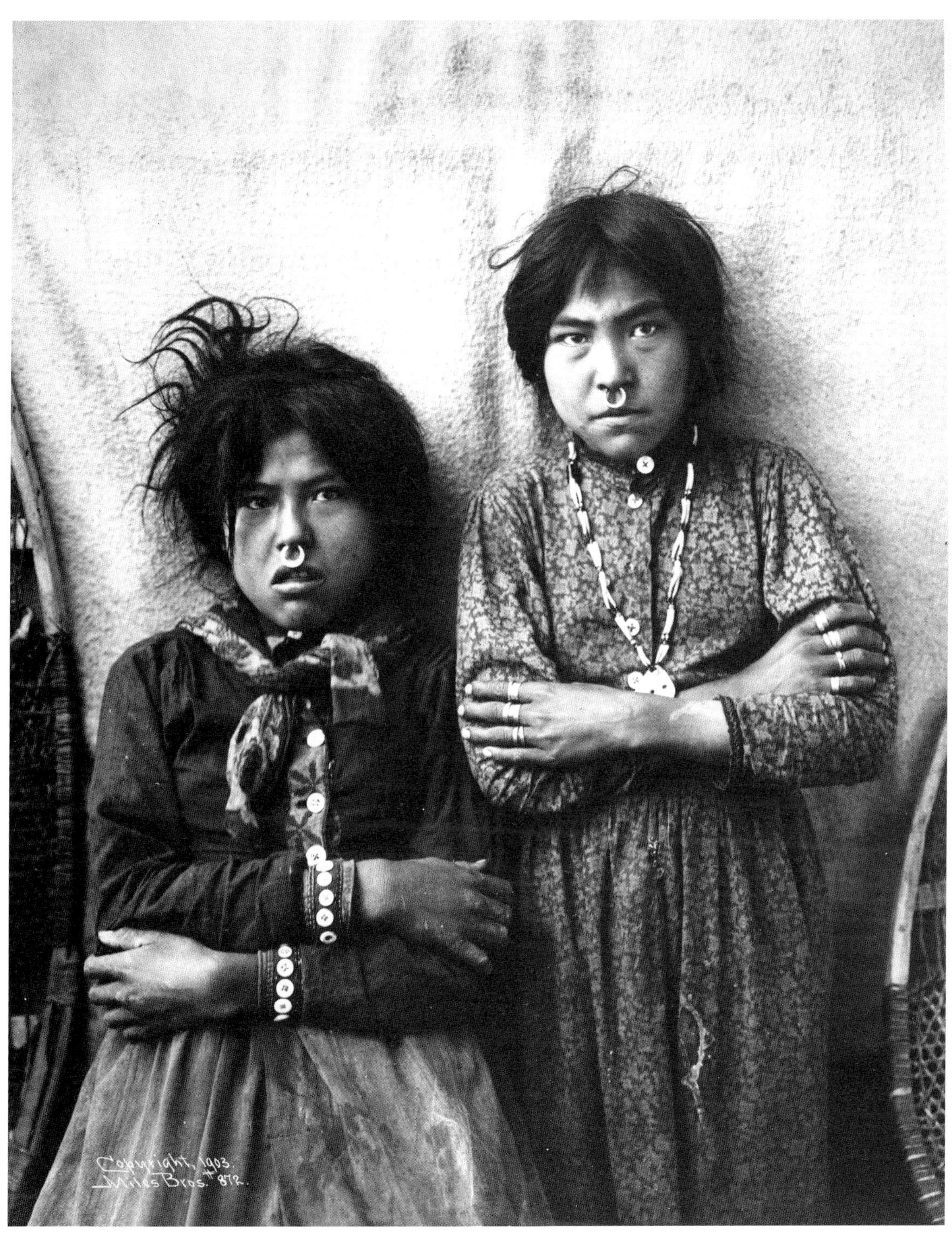

Figure 13

"Two Tlingit girls, Tsacotna and Natsanitna, wearing nose rings, near Copper River, Alaska, 1903." Photograph by Miles Brothers. Courtesy of the U.S. National Archives and Records Administration, Washington, DC. (ARC 524404)

technology for reproducing photographs from metal plates—photolithography and photoglyphic engraving—emerged in the 1850s, but the images still had to be tipped into the printed text by hand. It was not until the late 1870s that the technology to produce a halftone plate that could be used in a printing press to print photographs along with the texts emerged (Rosenblum 1997:453). This inexpensive process, generally known as relief or letterpress printing, was not eclipsed until the 1960s. The U.S. government's tenth census (1880) report on Alaska, published in 1884, contained no photographs and only eight drawings and color reproductions of paintings. These were somewhat informative supplements to the text, but they lacked realism. Ten years later the *Report on Population and Resources of Alaska at the Eleventh Census: 1890* contained 71 photogravures including 8 of the Tlingit. These provided much more visual information but they also reflected the government's gaze, reiterating and reinforcing the messages contained in the text. According to the Report:

> Of the 4,737 Thlingits of Alaska few live beyond Yakutat or below Prince Frederick sound. While living in permanent villages and enjoying trade with the whites ever since the beginning of this century the most astonishing changes have come over these people within [the last] 10 years…Wars and uprisings are wholly a thing of the past; witchcraft and slavery have about disappeared; cremation had given way to earth burial; the one lodge with a central fireplace where several branches of one family lived under a patriarchal rule, has given way to log cabins or clapboarded and bay-windowed cottages; the blanket is cut and sewed into a fitted garment, and ready-made clothing is the men's usual garb. Government schools and mission schools have taught the young generations, and the mines, canneries, and sawmills have been so many industrial schools for the elders. These intelligent and industrious Thlingits were never to be confounded with the plains Indians, and

are far from being a savage or uncivilized people. It is the Thlingit's aim to dress and live as the white man, and he fills his home with beds, tables, chairs, clocks, lamps, stoves, and kitchen utensils, and buys silk gowns for his wife. He is no longer picturesque, distinctive, or aboriginal. (U.S. Census Office 1893:44)

The Report's eight images of the "Thlingit" included "Funeral ceremonies of Thlingit chief—lying in state" (re-using the image published by Wood in 1882) and "Dead Thlingit chief about to be cremated." These descriptive titles are factual enough, but when combined with the above text, they reinforced the idea that the Tlingit's traditional funerary customs were strange and rightfully being replaced with "earth burial." A third photograph, "Thlingit house, interior," illustrated to the Euro-American viewer the primitiveness of Tlingit clan houses, with disorganized clutter and people crouched on a dirt floor around an open fire pit and, as the text pointed out, "several branches of one family living under a patriarchal rule." A fourth photograph, "Thlingit house (modern)," provided a positive contrast by showing the Western-style architecture that was extolled in the text. Two further photographs, "Thlingit girls gaffing a salmon" and "Thlingit canoe," demonstrated the simplicity of traditional Tlingit subsistence strategies. The remaining two photographs signaled progress. "Thlingit girls—effect of civilization" showed two girls standing in nice ready-made clothing ready to face the future. "Thlingit school children" suggested the positive changes to come through the power of education.

It was toward the end of this period of very rapid change among the Tlingit that Edward H. Harriman, the country's most powerful railroad magnate, initiated a scientific expedition and family vacation to Alaska and British Columbia. The expedition included 14 members of the Harriman family and their servants, 25 scientists, a chaplain, 11 hunters, packers and camp hands,

3 medical staff, 65 officers and crew, and 2 photographers. Harriman and C. Hart Merriam, chief of the U.S. Biological Survey and principal organizer of the trip, knew the importance that illustrations would have to the appeal and accessibility of their published reports. To that end they included two landscape painters and a wildlife artist in addition to the two photographers on the trip. On May 31, 1899, the expedition left Seattle aboard the luxuriously outfitted *George W. Elder* with Seattle photographer Edward S. Curtis and his assistant, D. G. Inverarity. Over the next two months the *Elder* covered 9,000 miles and made more than 50 short stops so its scientists and passengers could collect plant and animal specimens, study glaciers, hunt, hike, and explore. A small steam launch allowed small parties to remain in one place for several days.

Curtis and Inverarity took 5,000 photographs on the trip, mainly of icebergs and geological formations. At least eight other members of the party also used cameras, including Harriman and Merriam, who took most of the group's images of Native people (B. Davis 1985).

The first volumes of the *Harriman Alaska Series* were published in 1902. The importance of photography to the expedition is evident: volume 1 alone contained 85 photographic reproductions and 236 engravings (more than three-quarters of which were translated from photographs onto a metal block using a code of lines or dots). Thirteen volumes were eventually published; the first two directed at the general public, the last eleven for professionals.

The group encountered the Tlingit at Wrangell, Sitka, Yakutat, and at sealing camps above Pt. Latouche. To John Burroughs, the most famous nature writer of his day and a member of the expedition, the Tlingit were of secondary interest. In his "narrative of the expedition" in the *Harriman Alaska Series* he merely mentions the "line of [Native] houses close to the beach" at Sitka and the fact that some members of the group visited "the Indian village" there. He had somewhat more to say about the seal camp they visited at the head of Yakutat Bay.

The Indians had come up from their village below, and some of them, we were told, from as far away as Sitka. They were living here in tents and bark huts and hunting the hair seal amid the drifting icebergs that the Turner and Hubbard [glaciers] cast off. This was their summer camp; they were laying in a supply of skins and oil against their winter needs. In July they go to the salmon streams and secure their stores of salmon. During these excursions their village at Yakutat is nearly deserted. The encampment we visited was upon the beach of a broad gravelly delta flanked by high mountains. It was redolent of seal oil. The dead carcasses of the seals lay in rows upon the pebbles in front of the tents and huts. The woman and girls were skinning them and cutting out the blubber and trying it out in pots over smoldering fires, while the crack of the Winchesters of the men could be heard out amid the ice. Apparently their only food at such times is seal meal, with parts of the leaf or stalk of a kind of cow parsnip, a coarse rank plant that grows all about. (Burroughs and Grinnell 1910:61)

When they returned to Yakutat in late June on the homeward leg of the voyage, Burroughs noted only that the Tlingit gave them strawberries that "grew in abundance" in the sandy soil. A few days after this, however, the party reached a "deserted" village near Cape Fox which he describes as follows:

There was a row of a dozen houses on the beach of a little bay, with nineteen totem poles standing along their fronts. These totem poles were the attraction. There was a rumor that the Indians had nearly all died of small pox a few years before and that the few survivors had left under a superstitious fear, never to return. It was evident that the village had not been occupied in seven or eight years. Why not, therefore secure some of these totem poles for the museums

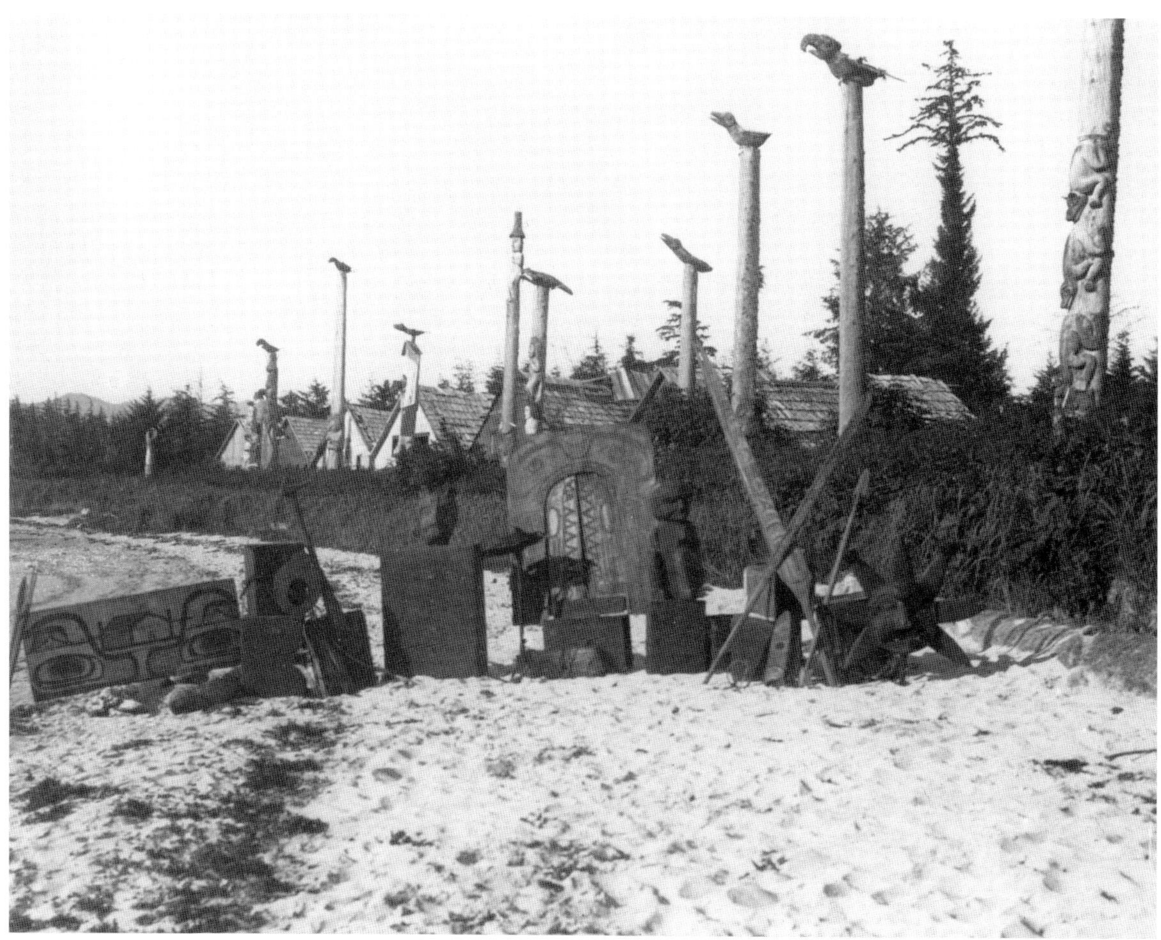

Figure 14
"Relics." Artifacts from the "deserted village" visited by the Harriman Expedition on its return voyage wait to be carried on board, 1899. Photograph by W. B. Devereux. By permission of the University of Washington Libraries, Seattle, WA. Special Collections. (NA 2138)

of the various colleges represented by members of the expedition? This was finally agreed upon, and all hands, including the ship's crew fell to digging up and floating to the ship the five or six of the more striking poles. This occupied us till the night of the 27. (Burroughs and Grinnell 1910:116–17)

The ethical violation of removing totem poles and ceremonial objects from this Cape Fox village seems clear from today's perspective, but it was not then. The village looked abandoned; photographs taken by expedition members show plants growing through the walls and floors of the houses and debris scattered about.

Manifest Destiny, Americans' divine mandate to expand Christian influence and education across the continent while exploiting its resources, also ruled the day. Assimilation was the desired and presumably inevitable future for the Tlingit and other Natives, and the apparently abandoned village seemed legitimately ripe for plunder. Mass communications, including the photography contained in publications like the 1890 Census Report, helped spread these ideas and convince the public that the "possession of territories, resources, bodies, and property of natives-turned-enemies is justified" (Fine-Dare 2002:14).

A photograph of the Tlingit artifacts collected by the Harriman Expedition taken by mining engineer W. B. Devereux is captioned "Relics," suggesting that the objects belonged to a vanished race (Fig. 14). Expedition members must also have reasoned that their goal was admirable; the totem poles would be saved for posterity and would serve an educational purpose once displayed in their home museums. Yet we cannot escape the imperialist mentality that informed such enterprises. Expedition members traveled in luxury aboard a specially outfitted ship, they named glaciers after themselves and the schools they represented (Harriman and Wellesley, for example), and generally felt free to take what they found, with one notable dissenting voice.

Naturalist John Muir objected to taking the Cape Fox poles; he considered it pillaging and refused to pose for the group's celebratory photograph. The caption on one group photograph taken by Edward S. Curtis seems ironically apt. "Who are we?" In 2001, more than 100 years after their removal in 1899, four totem poles and a dozen other artifacts taken by the Harriman Expedition were repatriated to their owners' descendants under the Native American Graves Protection and Repatriation Act (NAGPRA) passed in 1990.

Before going to Alaska, Curtis had photographed Tulalip Indians and other Natives around Puget Sound for several years and had begun increasingly to idealize them, that is, to picture them as they might have looked in the past rather than in their current impoverished state. He often paid individuals a dollar in order to photograph them, either in his Seattle studio or while they were fishing, trapping, and hunting. Curtis's Indian photographs were popular

and sold well in Seattle; two had won the grand prize at the National Photography Exhibition and become part of a world tour. Their romantic nostalgia captured not the Indians so much as "the *fin de siècle* spurt of an America that had sadly, but finally solved its Indian problem. The Indians were now history" (Goetzmann and Goetzmann 1986:230).

After the Harriman Expedition and the exposure it gave Curtis to prominent men of science and their research techniques, Curtis developed more of an ethnographic interest in Native people and went on to produce his 20-volume survey of the customs and cultures of the Indians of North America. His images gave no hint of the effect of government agents, soldiers, reservation life, poverty, Western education, or missionaries on Native life. His concern was to document their "traditional" life before it completely disappeared and to have his work stand as a memorial to these once proud and autonomous peoples. "Working at a time before standards for ethnological photography had been formulated, Curtis treated his subject matter aesthetically, softening forms and obscuring detail to emphasize his overall concept of the mythic nature of American Indian life" (Rosenblum 1997:178). His photographs of the Tlingit and Eskimo while on the Harriman Expedition, however, are not so obviously "interpretive" or "made."

George Bird Grinnell's article on "The Natives of the Alaska Coast Region," published in the first volume of the Harriman report (1911), contained 47 captioned illustrations. Only 4 of these were tipped-in photogravures (which faithfully reproduced the original photographs); the others were less expensive line engravings based on the photographs, plus 1 colored reproduction of a watercolor. Engravings removed the texture, detail, and tonality found in photographic images that provided the visual foundation for belief in the reality of what the images depicted. This is evident when comparing the engraving of seal hunters (Fig. 15) with the original Curtis photograph from which it was copied (Fig. 16).

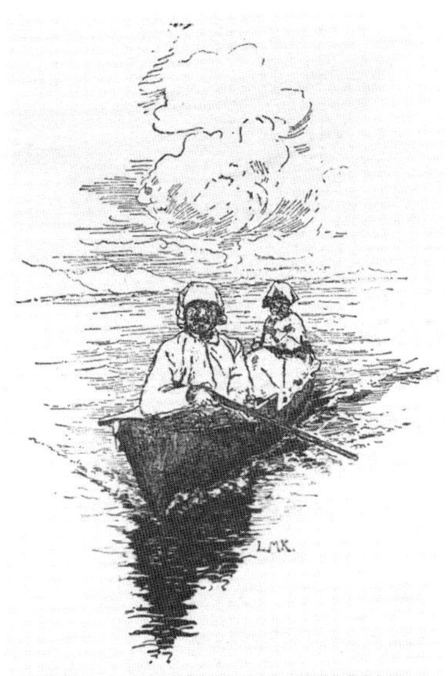

Figure 15
Tlingit sealers in tow near Yakutat, 1899. Lineblock engraving based on photograph by Edward S. Curtis. From Burroughs and Grinnell 1910.

Figure 16 (below)
"Sealers in tow, Glacier Bay" (caption on mount), 1899. Photograph by Edward S. Curtis. By permission of the University of Washington Libraries, Seattle, WA. Special Collections. (NA 2096)

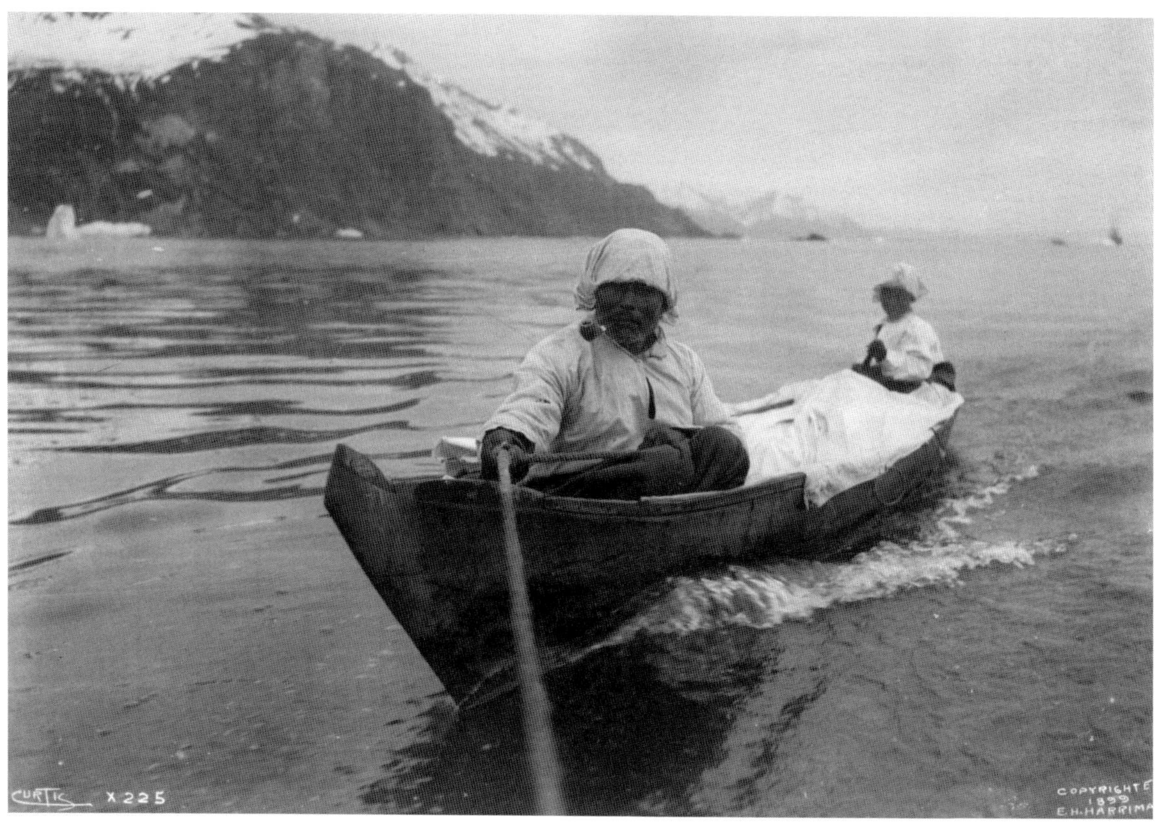

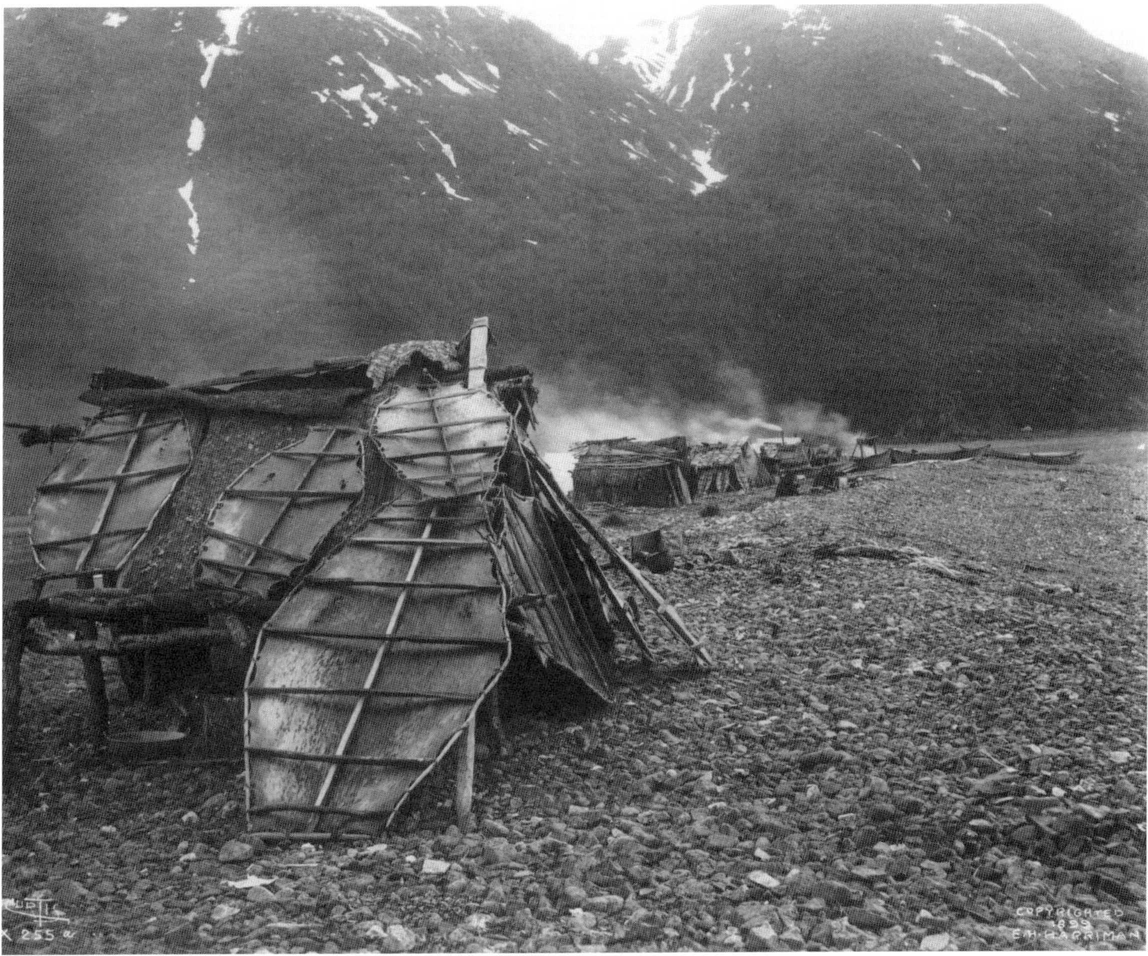

Figure 17

Sealers' huts on beach, Yakutat Bay, 1899. Photograph by Edward S. Curtis. By permission of the University of Washington Libraries, Seattle, WA. Special Collections. (NA 2103)

Although the engravings used in the Harriman reports introduced some distortion, they still carried the authority of the photograph. The photographic source of each engraving was clearly indicated in each entry in the "List of Illustrations."

It is instructive to try to read these images for the collective impression they might have given contemporary viewers. Three of the four photogravures in Grinnell's article are of the "deserted" Cape Fox village and its totem poles; the fourth shows the temporary and crudely made sealers' huts on the beach near Yakutat (Fig. 17). None of these photographic reproductions include people. The vast majority of the engravings (86 percent) likewise lack people, showing material culture instead. The remainder (14 percent) show men or boys in canoes or women standing or cleaning seal skins. The impression given is one of an outdated culture. It may be ingenious and have had impressive artistic skills once, but it can hardly compete today. The choice of sub-

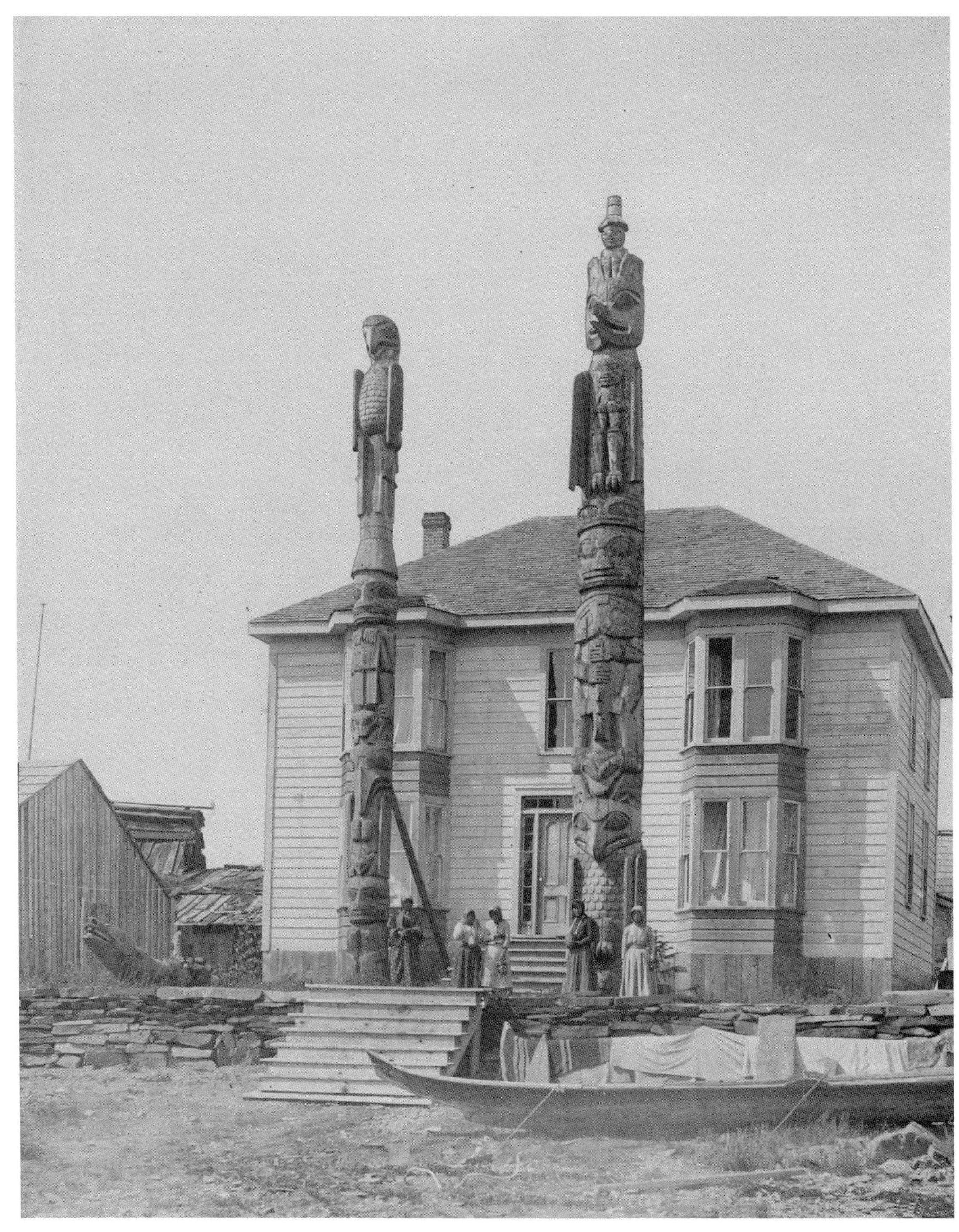

Figure 18
Chief Kadishan's home, Wrangell, 1893. Photograph by H. G. Ogden. By permission of the Alaska State Library, Juneau, AK. (P87–0009)

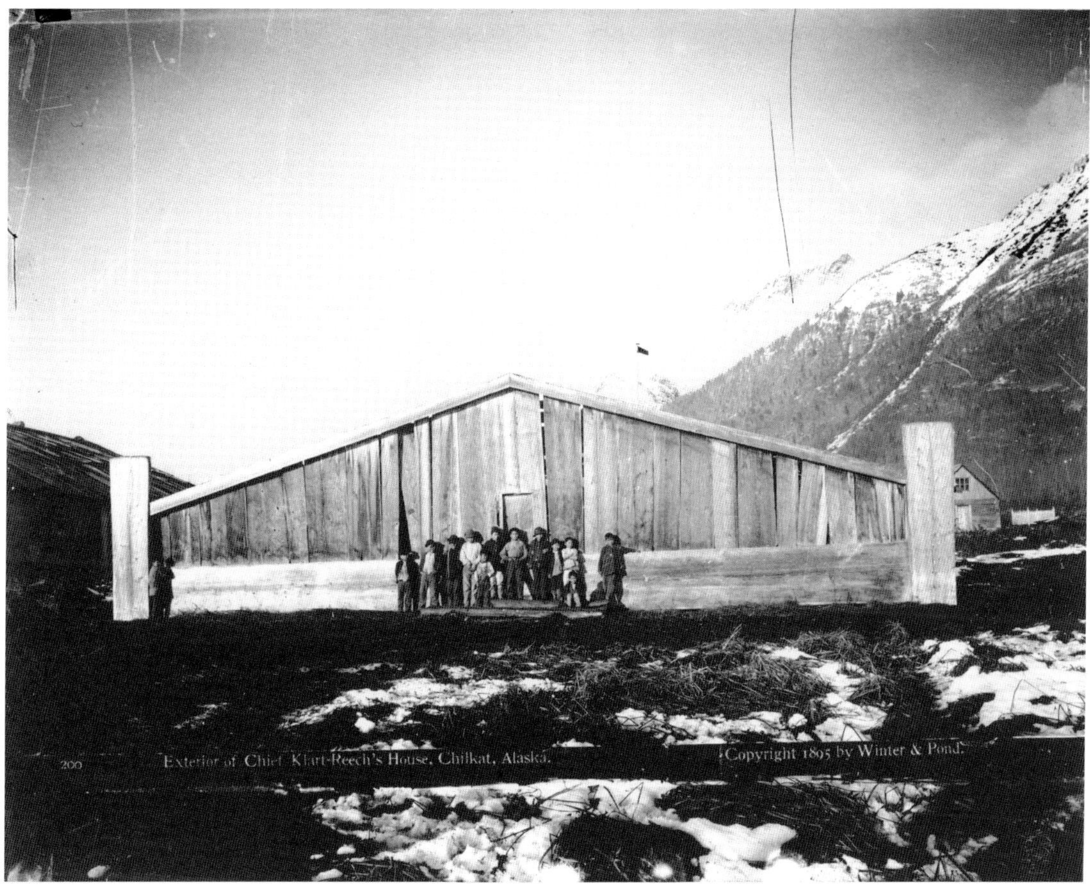

Figure 19
"Exterior of Chief Klart-Reech's [Shaadax'icht] House, Chilkat, Alaska," 1895. Photograph by Winter & Pond. By permission of the National Anthropological Archives, Washington, DC. (00122900)

ject matter, captions, and heavy use of engravings rather than more "modern" and detailed photogravures all suggest the past.

The dramatic contrast between an image taken by H. G. Ogden, of the U.S. Coast and Geodetic Survey, in 1893 and two others—one taken by photographers Winter & Pond in 1895 and another taken by Curtis while on the Harriman Expedition in 1899—illustrates the difficulty of using single photographs as data. Ogden's image (Fig. 18) shows Chief Kadishan's home in Wrangell which was built in 1887 and described by then Alaskan Governor Alfred Swineford as

"the finest and most pretentious residence I have seen anywhere in the territory" (Wyatt 1989:31). This large two-story dwelling with bay windows, glass-framed front door, and milled lumber displayed Kadishan's individual wealth as well as the general movement among the Tlingit, then well under way, of replacing traditional clan houses with American-style homes. Yet other Tlingit chiefs, such as Shaadax'icht at Chilkat, even eight years later still lived in traditional clan houses (Fig. 19). Curtis's photograph (Fig. 16), taken in 1899, shows simple huts on the beach, the temporary shelters the Tlingit built at their summer fish and sealing camps. None of these images by themselves accurately depicts how most Tlingit lived most of the time in the late 1880s and 1890s.

Survey and scientific expedition photographs were seen by a large public. Many were presented in albums to members of Congress to create support for funding more scientific expeditions and national parks. They were also shown as lantern slides at public lectures and sold as popular stereographs. They appeared in published reports, some of which, such as the Harriman reports, reached a broad public. They were copied as woodcut illustrations and chromolithographs and appeared as line engravings in popular publications like *Harper's Weekly: The Magazine of Civilization*, *The Century*, and *Frank Leslie's Illustrated Weekly*. According to photography historian Naomi Rosenblum, they helped establish a social documentary style which had as its goal the presentation of clear information that often, but not always, depicted "Native peoples with a sober directness unleavened by the least sense of the picturesque" (1997:346).

Photography also became a valuable research tool of early anthropologists. In 1874, before the professionalization of the discipline, the field manual *Notes and Queries on Anthropology* (subtitled *For the Use of Travellers and Residents in Uncivilized Lands*) was published by the British Association for the Advancement of Science and the Royal Anthropological Institute, laying out guidelines for collecting photographic evidence which could then be used by armchair anthropologists. Its third edition contained the following advice: "A snap-shot camera of some sort is quite indispensable as many incidents must be seized as they occur, and some people will not consent to be photographed so these must be taken instantaneously, and without their knowledge" (Royal Anthropological Institute 1899).

In 1879 the U.S. government's newly established Bureau of Ethnology (later the Bureau of American Ethnology or BAE) hired James Gilchrist Swan to obtain photographs of Northwest Coast peoples. He approached the task by first searching for images in local photography studios around his home in Port Townsend, Washington. As Elizabeth Edwards has pointed out, the ambiguities of photographs and the analogical nature of photographic inscription enabled images of Native Americans produced with entirely different purposes in mind (survey photographs, exotic cartes de visite) to become "anthropological" simply by virtue of their subject matter. Swan later began taking his own photographs: Figure 20 shows Tlingit (possibly Haida) women in the 1880s wearing labrets (lip ornaments worn by all non-slave women to signify their maturity and marriageability). The BAE's photographs, as many others, may be seen today as objectifying and appropriating, but they were motivated "by the belief it was necessary to understand Native American cultures in all their diversity in order to ameliorate the plight of indigenous peoples" (Edwards 1998:190). Since it was also widely believed that Native peoples were destined to disappear, considerable photographic effort was put into salvage ethnography.

Franz Boas, the father of American anthropology, studied photography in Berlin before leaving to undertake his first field research among the Cowichan of Vancouver Island in 1883. Most of the surviving photographs from this early research are landscapes, reflecting his cultural geography orientation (Fleming and Luskey 1986). Five years later, however, on a return field trip sponsored primarily by the British Association for the Advancement of Science, Boas concentrated on collecting linguistic and physical data and hired E. C. Brooks, a commercial photographer from Victoria, to take his photographs. In keeping with prevailing ideas about race and the fledgling field of anthropology's interest in scientifically documenting population differences and physical types, Brooks photographed several Haida prisoners in specimen-like frontal and side poses, while Boas wrote down their body measurements and made plaster casts (Rohner and Rohner 1969:146).

Photographs were viewed as a portable and

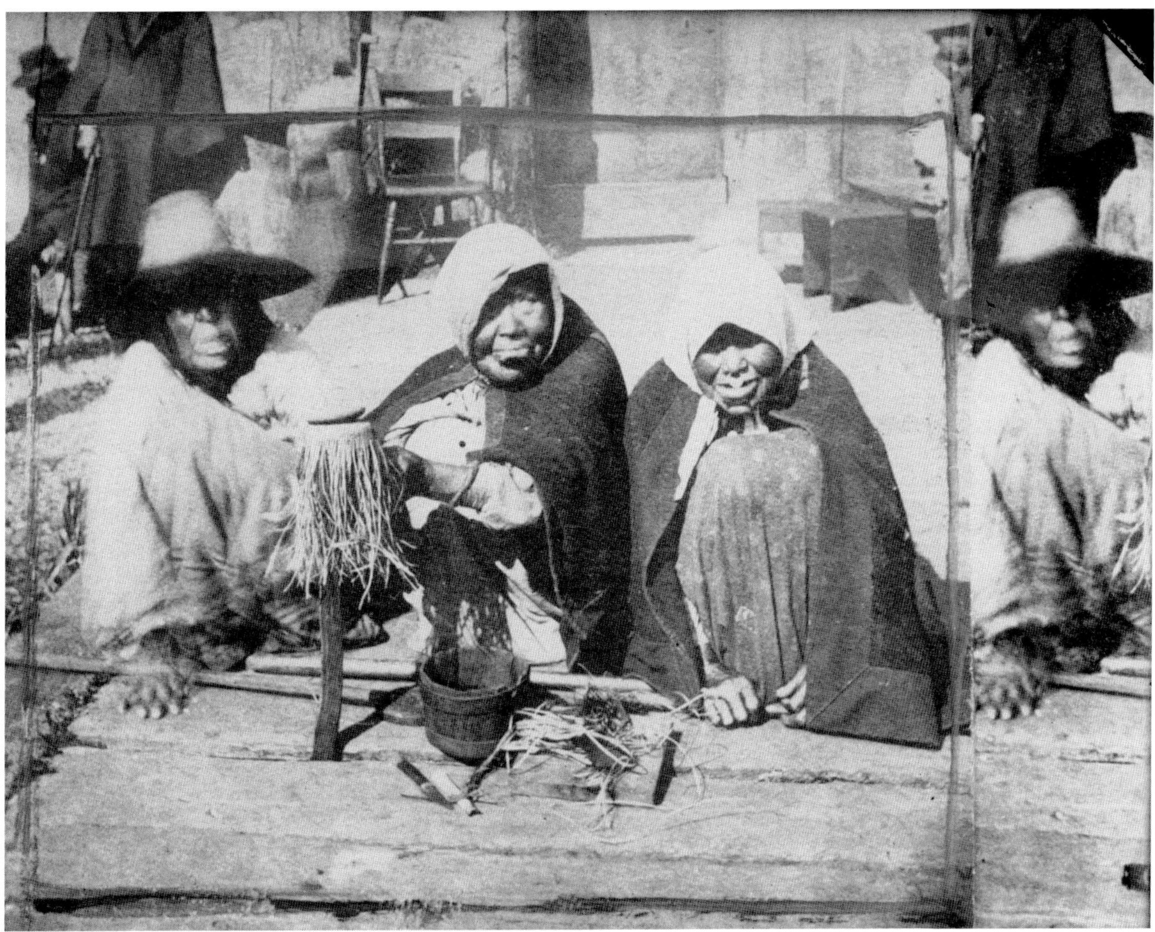

Figure 20
Tlingit (or Haida) basket makers wearing labrets. Photograph by James G. Swan, 1880. By permission of the National Anthropological Archives, Washington, DC. (GN 13639)

objective representation of racial morphology that could be examined as information by scientists everywhere. The "type" was one of the most important concepts in 19th century anthropological analysis and was applied to populations all over the world. Photography considerably strengthened the reality and fixity of the concept, helping establish the parameters of race (Edwards 1998). Boas's statistical training also encouraged him to take type photographs, according to Ira Jacknis (1984), in order to amass as many data points as possible. In 1897 Boas organized the Jessup North Pacific Expedition to investigate the origin of American Indians with teams of scientists working on both sides of the Bering Strait (but not including Alaska). An estimated 3,000 photographs were taken; most were "type" portraits.

Boas later worked with photographers O. C. Hastings from Victoria and George Hunt, whose mother was a high-ranking Tlingit woman who had grown up among the Kwakwaka'wakw and whose father was an English Hudson Bay Company trader. Boas used sequences of photographs in an attempt to make complete records and "to build a narrative and infuse the images with ethnographic honesty" (Edwards 1998:202). Still photographs were regarded as representative of the larger sequence of activity. He also used photographs to document artifacts, to record monumental architecture and sculpture in detail, and to elicit information from informants about their family and clan history and their use of material culture. His 1897 monograph on the Kwakwaka'wakw was one of the first anthropological works to be illustrated with field photographs (Jacknis 1984). Boas's 1909 *The Kwakiutl of Vancouver Island* used 27 photographs as well as 11 drawings and 4 color drawings as plates: all of material culture. Although he used photography, Boas valued the written text over the visual. To him anthropology was a psychological science best expressed through language. Indeed, most of his publications are editions of native texts with English translations; photographs were supplemental. Similarly, linguist John R. Swanton spent four months in Sitka and Wrangell in 1904 collecting oral literature, later published without photographs as *Tlingit Myths and Texts* (1909).

Boas objected to photographs that romanticized Indians. While a professor at Columbia University in 1907, he wrote to President Theodore Roosevelt to complain about the inaccuracies and theatricality of Curtis's images in the first two volumes of his American Indian work. Roosevelt appointed a scientific committee to investigate, but it ruled in favor of Curtis. Curtis's work also received a positive review in the *American Anthropologist*. These favorable views reflected the romantic intellectual tradition that had governed 19th century scientific inquiry and had shaped Curtis's thinking about the American Indian and resulted in his interpretive photographs. Boas was the prophet of the new, empirically based anthropology that espoused complete accuracy and cultural relativism, even though Boas believed in the inevitability of assimilation. This intellectual shift, combined with such technological developments as hand-held cameras, favored a less mediated and more spontaneous approach

to field photography which Curtis's work clearly did not represent.

The 1880s and 1890s also witnessed an explosion in museum collecting in the Northwest Coast and southeast Alaska, prompted largely by Philadelphia's Centennial Exposition of 1876 which featured Haida, Makah, and Tlingit artifacts and excited public interest in these cultures (Cole 1985). World fairs and international expositions became extremely popular and remained so into the early 20th century. Ethnological displays at these fairs often included indigenous peoples in recreated "villages" or living cultural tableaux which were "built with the consultation of well-known anthropologists, some of whom brought students to the exhibits to offer them 'an adventure in social Darwinism'" (Fine-Dare 2002:22–23). As the chief assistant to Frederic Ward Putnam, Director of Harvard's Peabody Museum and the head of anthropology at the 1893 Chicago's World Columbian Exposition, Franz Boas brought 14 Kwakwaka'wakw from British Columbia to live in a mock village at the fair where they could perform their daily tasks "in context." They were displayed with groups as diverse as Alaskan Eskimo, Philippine Igorot, and Japanese Ainu in a way which suggested a continuum from savagery to enlightened civilization, the latter made possible by American expansionism and economic "progress" (Drinnon 1980, Rydell 1985, Willinsky 1998, Fine-Dare 2002). Boas and Putnam hired Chicago photographer John H. Grabill to record Kwakwaka'wakw dances so photographs could be sold to visitors as well as given to the dancers and singers. Native students from the Carlisle Indian Industrial School were also displayed at the fair as proof of Indian adaptability and progress (Moses 1996). Alaska Natives participated in several of these "imperial theme parks," to use Robert Rydell's description, in addition to Chicago's World Columbia Exposition in 1893: St. Louis's Louisiana Purchase Exposition in 1904, Portland's Louis and Clark Exposition in 1905, and Seattle's Alaska-Yukon-Pacific Exposition in 1909. More than four million fairgoers were exposed to ethnographic displays at the Portland and Seattle fairs alone (Rydell 1984:185). Thousands of souvenir photographs of Native peoples, including the Tlingit, were purchased, fueling the desire for more images and for touristic travel.

Museums borrowed the idea of living cultural tableaux from these expositions and developed life-group displays in an attempt to modernize and popularize their exhibits. The American Museum of Natural History, for example, saw its mission as providing New York City residents, especially its new industrial and immigrant working class, with entertainment that was both educational and elevating. It had to compete for their attention with moving pictures, saloons, vaudeville houses, waxworks, and amusement parks as well as fairs and expositions. Some practitioners, however, were concerned about presenting "Otherness as visual spectacle" in this way (Griffiths 2002:22).

Boas, who was an assistant curator at the museum between 1896 and 1905, feared that museum-goers would not pay sufficient attention to other artifacts in the museum or to explanatory labels because they would be too fascinated with these semi-clad models of indigenous people and in learning about the technical means that had been used to replicate real human beings. Boas also objected to the evolutionary approach the museum adopted and wanted collections arranged by tribe and context instead.

This was an era of avid museum collecting. When Chicago's Field Columbian Museum (later the Field Museum of Natural History) sent George A. Dorsey on a lengthy collecting trip in 1897–98, he took freelance photographer Edward P. Allen with him. In the Haida and Tlingit villages they visited Allen photographed shaman burials, village housing, totem poles, and Natives at work, while Dorsey purchased—and sometimes absconded with—artifacts to enhance the museum's collections. This was not unusual behavior for collectors at the time, and it was justified by the intellectual climate as indicated by the behavior of the Harriman Expedition the following year. Many Tlingit sold their ceremonial regalia (*at.óow*) to museums and collectors because elders were not sure whether their descendants would be interested or know enough to carry out the proper ceremonies. In some communities, "progressive" Tlingit were very influential; in Kake they cut down and burned all mortuary and memorial poles in 1912 (Kan 1999:459).

World fairs, with their ethnological tableaux and souvenir images—combined with museum displays, Wild West shows, early cartes de visite, stereographs, and popular publications—were transforming contemporary Native communities into market commodities. A London newspaper, describing Buffalo Bill's Wild West Show in 1887, for example, noted the popularity of "Indian curiosity stores and photograph stands, the latter sometimes selling 1,000 [images] a day" (Bol 1999:218). Native American images were commercialized in other ways. As early as the 1870s, the Allen and Winter Tobacco Company of Richmond, Virginia, included a picture card of a "celebrated Indian Chief" with each pack of its straight-cut cigarettes. This fed into a perception of Native Americans not as human beings but as "curiosities to be collected and sold and as quaint, and sometimes gruesome, souvenirs to be displayed" (Fine-Dare 2002:30). What did visitors actually photograph and how were the Tlingit portrayed once transportation opened the region?

3

Captured Views: Visiting Photographers and Tourists

To maximize profits from the shipping boom that followed the discovery of gold and the spread of salmon canneries along Alaska's southeastern coast, ship owners began to seek paying passengers in the 1870s. Commercial photographers were among the first to take advantage of this opportunity. Some had come earlier to help document survey, expedition, or ethnographic work, but now they came on their own. Most were guided in their selection and treatment of photographic subjects by the desire to produce saleable images and by their sense of being emissaries of a "higher civilization" (Rosenblum 1997:168). They produced thousands of descriptive, explanatory, and ethically evaluative images to sell back home as stereographs, prints, and postcards. These played an important role in shaping the American public's view of Alaskan Natives.

Canadian photographer Richard Maynard left Victoria, BC, for Alaska in the summer of 1879. He found Sitka to be "a pretty looking place but all homes are rotten" (Maynard 1879). Since the Russian departure many of the town's buildings had physically deteriorated. According to German ethnographer Aurel Krause, who stayed in Sitka for several weeks in 1881 and 1882, even architectural jewels like "Baranof's Castle," the

Russian American Company's Chief Manager's former residence, and St. Michael's Cathedral were in "urgent need of repairs," and most of the log stockade had been removed (Krause and Krause 1993).

Maynard brought both 5x8" and 8x10" cameras and used ready-made dry plates, invented in 1871, which had light-sensitive silver salts suspended in a gelatin emulsion on a glass plate (Baldwin 1991). These were quite easy to develop and could be processed any time after exposure. Nevertheless, photography was still cumbersome since it required using a tripod, and the glass plates were both fragile and heavy. Maynard made at least four additional photography field trips to southeast Alaska over the next 13 years. His journal entries from 1882 reveal some of the challenges facing both visiting photographers and tourists in these early years.

Sunday, August 20. 9:30 a.m. going into Sitka. Thousands of Black fish following the ship—passengers firing at them. At wharf in pouring rain. Got passengers ashore. Crazy after Indian curios. All I have bought is a map of the coast. 50 ¢ (1.75 in Victoria)—Walked to Indian River very wet & no views—but looked round for good places.

Monday, 21. Raining, but could see Mts. to-day—cleared by 9 & I took two views, but rained again with wind & had to stop. After lunch took two views from castle with large camera. Church and Customs House with stereo (same views as with large)—Indian Rustic Bridge—Main St. in Sitka—& Indian village from the wharf—Leave at 6:30. Was very disappointed not to see Mt. Edgecombe and on not going to Glacier Bay—An old lady on board has fallen out with nearly everyone & today just before the ship left she took her things & went ashore—everyone pleased to see her go. She struck the Capt. & Major Wetmore both with her cane. Boat overcrowded. Beds in cabin on floor & expect more passengers at Wrangel.

August, 22. Went to change my plates last night before going to bed. It was rather rough & I got sick. I thought I would never get through. Had to stop several times then I settled my accounts & felt better & finished my plates. Sick all night. Up at 5 a.m. had a walk and went back & lay down. Had breakfast and felt better. They are now going round making a collection to give the Capt. a testimonial (I gave 2.50). Arrived at Wrangel at noon & the men in lowering my canoe let her fall & split her so I could not use it but got ashore in the ship boat...Underweigh [*sic*] at 7 pm still raining. (Maynard 1882)

Stereographs of unfamiliar landscapes and of native peoples in their villages had been popular with the public since the mid-1850s. By the mid-1870s most photographs were being taken in stereo format. Stereographs functioned as a visual encyclopedia—as well as entertainment—making it possible for people to travel without leaving home. According to Hirsch (2000:94), "The concept that one could be educated through the use of photographs and that history could be recorded and learned by means of photography got a lift from the stereo card" (Figs. 21, 22). Their depth of field, achieved by two slightly dissimilar images which merged when viewed through the stereoscope, were especially appropriate for scenes, groups, and architecture. They were "an unprecedented leap forward in realistic representation which opened up great expectations" and stimulated public demand for even more images of far-off places and exotic peoples (Marien 2002:82).

It is estimated that 2,000–2,500 stereographs of Indian subjects had been published by 1885. Scenic views, especially of the West, were also in high demand (Russell 1998, Darrah 1964). The popularity of stereo cards revealed "what most people considered the primary function of the typical 19th century photographer: to find and record people and scenes from the flow of real-world time for future contemplation" (Hirsch 2000:94).

Lantern slide lectures, which became popular in the 1860s, also fueled this desire for visual information and spurred commercial photographers on to seek out little-known places. Other commercial photographers who traveled to Alaska included Isaac West Taber from San Francisco, Bertram C. Towne, and the brothers E. J. and W. H. Partridge from Portland, and Frank La Roche from Seattle. La Roche made over 100 trips to Alaska between 1890 and 1902, focusing mainly on the Klondike but also photographing the Tlingit and other Natives in the ports and villages of southeast Alaska on his return trips to Seattle (Coleman 1995).

As photographer Richard Maynard, from Victoria, approached Taku Inlet in 1882 he anticipated "lots of orders from passengers for views." Photographers also discovered a demand for their services among the residents of the communities they visited. When Maynard arrived in Departure Bay on board the S.S. *Dakota*, he discovered that residents were "glad to see me as they wanted photos taken" (Maynard 1882). Posters announcing the date of a photographer's scheduled arrival were often posted so locals could arrange to have their portraits taken. Some photographers, like Arthur C. Pilsbury who first went to Alaska in 1898 to photograph the Gold

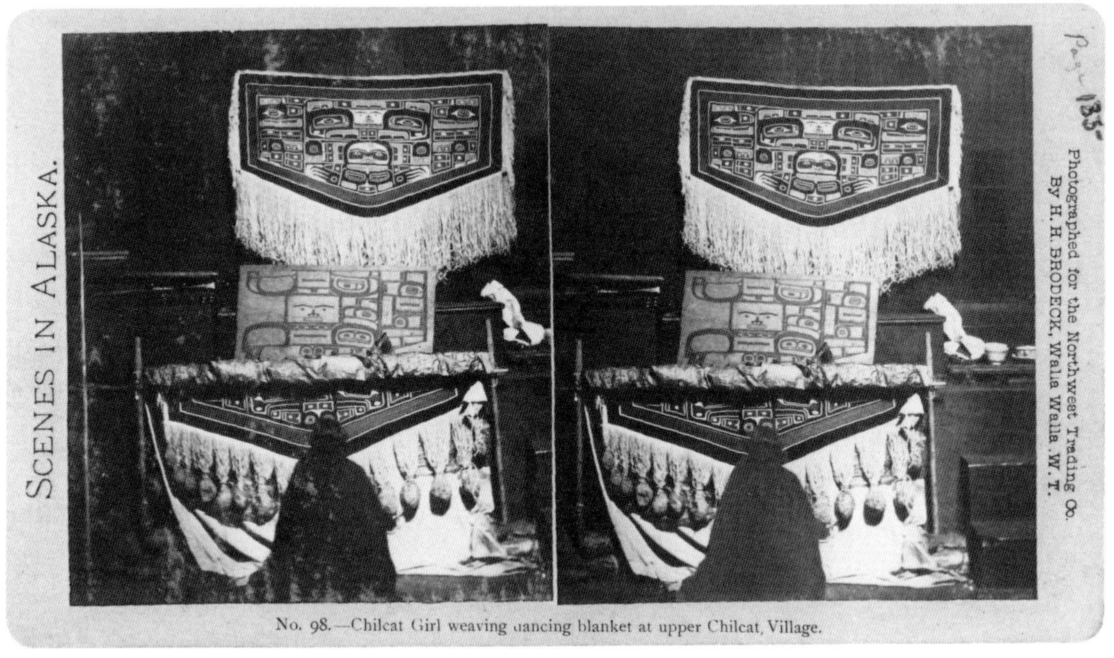

Figure 21
"Chilcat girl weaving dancing blanket at upper Chilcat Village," 1880s. Stereograph photographed by H. H. Brodeck for the Northwest Trading Co. By permission of the Presbyterian Historical Society, Philadelphia, PA.

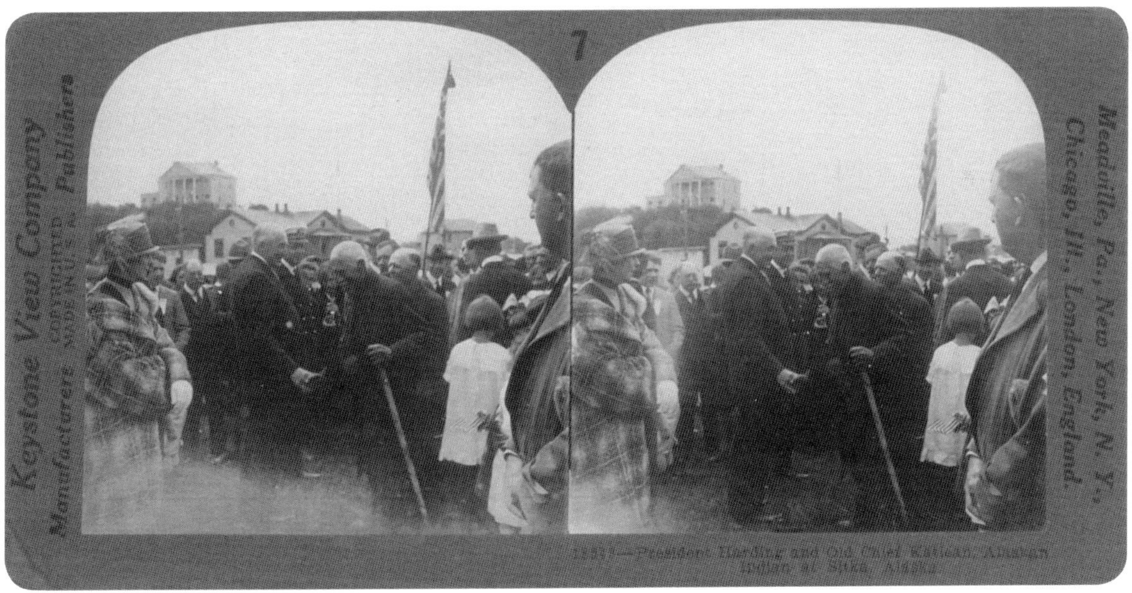

Figure 22
"President Harding and Old Chief Katlean [Ḵ'alyáan], Alaskan Indian at Sitka, Alaska," 1923. Harding died soon after this photograph was taken; Ḵ'alyáan died the following year at age 101. Keystone View Company. By permission of the Bancroft Library, University of California, Berkeley, CA. Stereographs of the West. (1980.034:7)

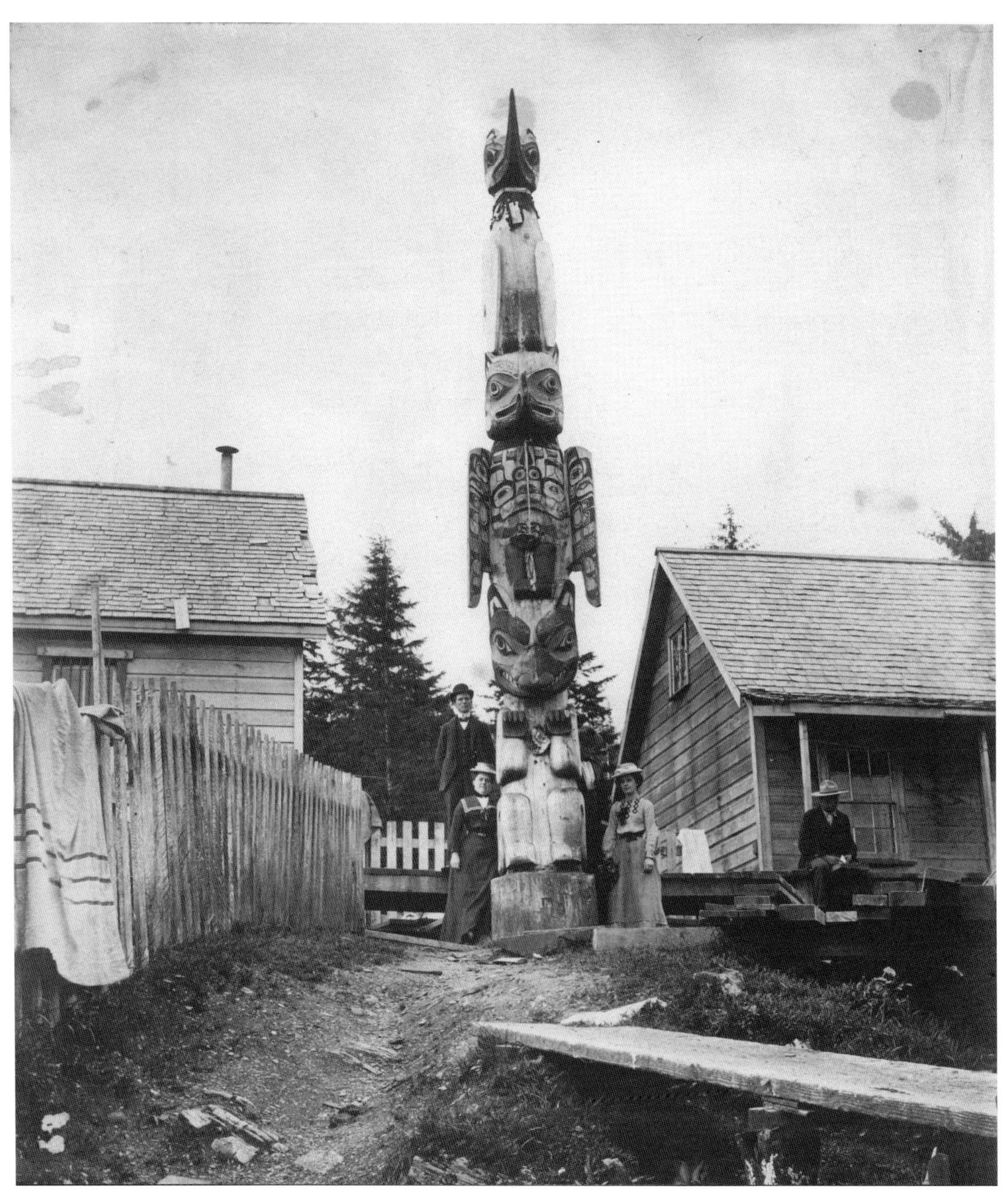

Figure 23
Tourists pose with totem pole in Ketchikan. Photograph for the Alaska Steamship Company. By permission of the Alaska State Library, Juneau, AK. (P44–03–079)

Rush, convinced local shopkeepers in the towns they visited to take consignments of their work (Harrison 1980).

In 1884, the same year a civil administration was inaugurated in Alaska, the Pacific Coast Steamship Company began well-advertised cruises up the Inside Passage designed just for tourists; 1,650 "excursionists" traveled to Alaska that year (U.S. Dept. of Interior 1893:250). For $130 from San Francisco or $98 from Seattle (the equivalent of $2,834 and $2,136 in 2007), a passenger could travel for a month with all transportation, meals, and accommodation expenses covered. The company ran five steamers—the *Queen, G. W. Elder, Idaho, Ancon,* and *Corona*—which typically stopped at Victoria and Nanaimo in British Columbia and then Tongass, Loring or Metlakatla (after 1887), Wrangell, Juneau, Douglas, and Sitka. Some included stops at an additional cannery. The trips ran between May and September. By 1890, over 25,000 people had taken the Pacific Coast Steamship Company excursion (U.S. Dept. of Interior 1893:250).

Although Alaska's scenery, especially its glaciers, was the primary attraction, the opportunity to see Native life was also a powerful inducement. In its advertising brochures, the company identified totem poles as a special feature which made Tlingit villages interesting and described the "curiosities to be seen in their houses and surroundings...They are the artistic savages of the world" (Jonaitis 1999:104). Totem poles appealed to tourists because they combined exoticism and familiarity: "the foreignness of a Native sensibility" with the Western artistic category of sculpture (Fig. 23). The word *totem* also suggested "a primitive belief system" and endowed the poles with a "mysterious aura" (Jonaitis 1999:116).

In 1884, when tourist excursions began, economic assimilation among the Tlingit was well under way. Most families combined their traditional subsistence activities with some form of wage labor including "fishing for or working in canneries, mining, logging, sealing, and even hop picking in Washington" (Raibmon 2005:139;

Wyatt 1987). Even before mining and the commercial fishing industry had arrived in the southeast, some Tlingit had worked for wages—for the Russians as early as the 1840s and later for the U.S. Army and Navy administrations. As the military presence in southeastern Alaska diminished in the 1880s, which most heavily impacted the economy of Sitka, tourism became especially important to the region. It was said that more than half the tourists visiting spent from $50 to $100 on Tlingit "curios" alone (U.S. Dept. of Interior 1893:251).

What photographer, tourist, or artist could fail to be entranced by the beautiful sheltered seaway that lay between Alaska's mainland coast and the island fretwork of the Alexander Archipelago, with its mercury-colored waters, deep fjords, mist-shrouded mountains and glaciers, surfacing whales, and glimpses of Indian villages and canoes? Watercolorist Theodore J. Richardson made several trips to southeastern Alaska, spending time in Sitka and Wrangell to paint scenery and Tlingit subjects. Canadian watercolorist Emily Carr visited Sitka in 1907 and was so inspired by the Haida and Tlingit totem poles she saw in the Indian River Park that she undertook a series of paintings of all the region's totem poles and Indian villages. Professional and amateur photographers alike sought beauty, wilderness, and authentically "primitive" people. Henry Herman Brodeck's photograph of a blanket-wearing Tlingit couple in an apparently wild setting, but actually at Indian River on the edge of Sitka, fulfilled this desire (Fig. 24).

By 1890, two steamship companies, the Pacific Steamship Company and the Alaska Steamship Company, were operating in the southeast. Five thousand people made the trip that summer, most wanting souvenir photographs as well as curios to impress family and friends at home. Purchasing photographic scenes which could be viewed later on as an act of remembrance "evolved into an *aesthetic of finding*," according to photography historian Robert Hirsch, and created in ordinary people "an appetite for collect-

　　VISITING PHOTOGRAPHERS AND TOURISTS

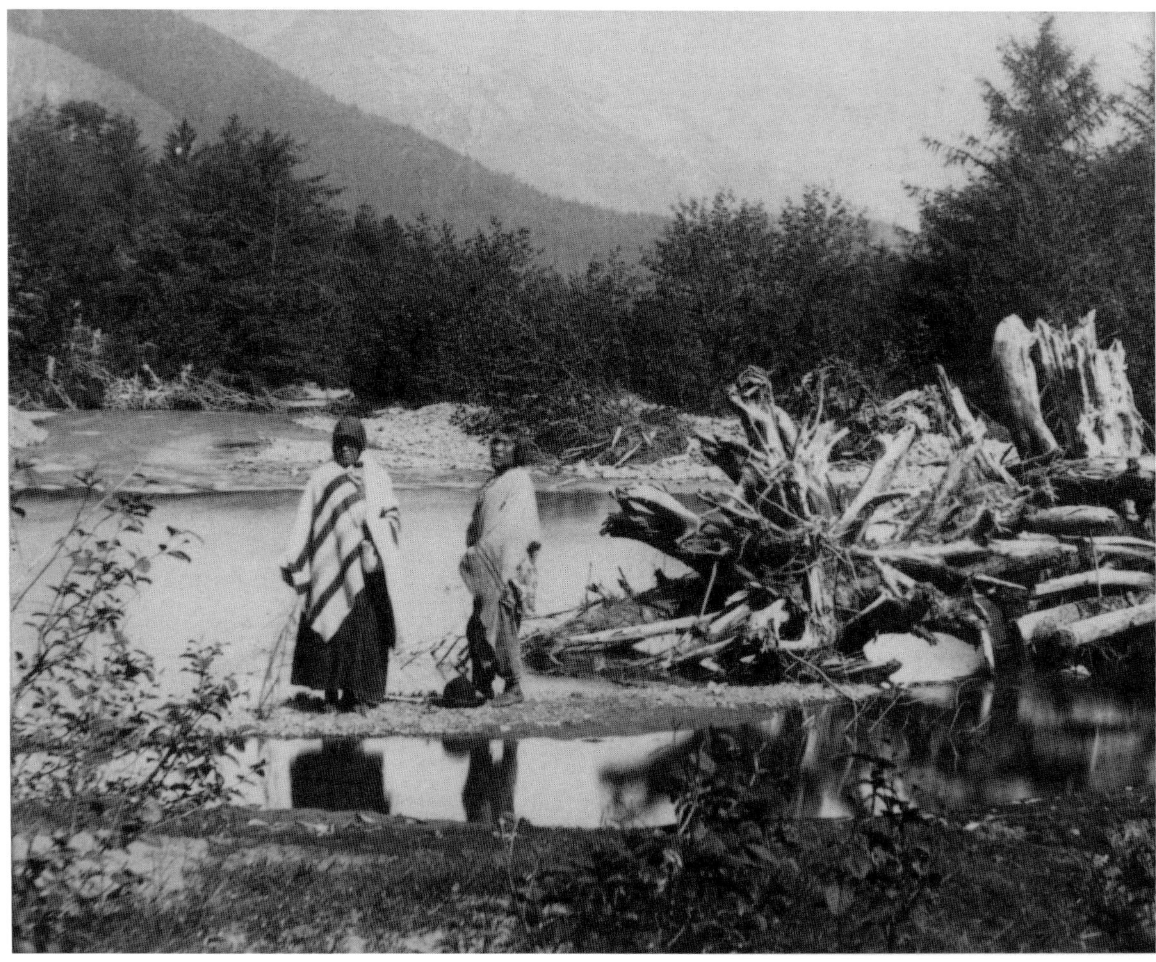

Figure 24
Tlingit couple on Indian River, Sitka, 1882. Half of stereograph by H. H. Brodeck for the Northwest Trading Company.
By permission of the Presbyterian Historical Society, Philadelphia, PA. (RG239–17, no. 2115)

ing items from the material world" (2000:94).

How much visiting photographers and tourists knew of the Tlingit's complex history or culture is unclear. One of the earliest travel books about Alaska, published in 1868 by the English engraver and artist Frederick Whymper, described the "Kaloshes" [Tlingit] as having a "bad reputation": "Their dress is commonly a blanket, at least in summer time; they frequently black their faces all over, and sometimes paint themselves in red, black and blue stripes and patches. They wear a pin of bone or metal stuck in their lower lip; this is said to denote maturity; it is at least never worn by the young. They appear to be more than usually lazy natives, probably from the fact that Nature has been so kind to them; salmon is abundant, deer and bear meat are to be had for the hunting, and the berries are innumerable" (1868:78). The book contained only two illustrations, both drawings of grave boxes which Whymper described in an embellished fashion. "These people invariably burn the deceased. On one of the boxes I saw a number of faces painted, long tresses of human hair depending therefrom. Each had represented a victim of the (happily) deceased one's ferocity. In his day he was doubtless more esteemed than if he had never harmed a fly. All their graves are much ornamented with carved and painted faces and other devices" (1868:79).

Eliza R. Scidmore visited Alaska in 1884 and published *Alaska: Its Southern Coast and the Sitka Archipelego* (1885), which became the standard guide for the next 20 years. She did not think that much of Sitka or of the Tlingit, but for virtually the opposite reasons articulated by Whymper. In her opinion *too* much progress had taken place: "There are no totem poles...to lend outward interest to the village and the Indians themselves are too much given to ready-made clothes and civilized ways to be really picturesque"(1885:54). Much had changed in the 15 years between their two visits. Yet despite the many changes that had occurred by the mid-1880s, the Tlingit were still sufficiently different to satisfy most visitors' authenticity requirements. The towns that passengers visited also had significant Native populations. Over 70 percent of Sitka's population in 1880 was Tlingit. The Native village (or "ranche") was home to 721 people; another 182 Tlingit lived in the general vicinity, compared to only 157 Euro-American and 219 Creole residents.

One of the visiting photographers to market an extensive collection of photographs to Alaskan tourists was W. H. Partridge of Boston. A souvenir packet of his images labeled "Alaska, U.S., 1887" in the George Eastman House, Rochester, NY, lists on the back inside flap 96 views that tourists could buy in various sizes and formats. A dozen mounted "boudoir" views (8 x 5") could be purchased for $4.50 (equivalent to $101 in 2007 using the consumer price index) and an unmounted set for 50 cents less. A dozen lantern slides cost $6.50 ($146 in 2007), and 8 x 10" prints could be purchased for 75 cents each ($17 in 2007).

Of the 96 images listed, 21 (22 percent) were of Sitka revealing the town's importance as a destination for Inside Passage tourists. Sitka photographs included: "Indian Ranch," "Squaws on Wharf," "Indian Mission Children," "Sitka Mission Home," and "Brady's Indian Curios." Partridge offered 9 additional views of Sitka in an 8 x 10" format only; 7 were images of Tlingit artifacts from the collection of George T. Emmons. The 2 remaining photographs from Sitka were views of the harbor. The descriptive language used with Partridge's images reinforced the exotic, frontier appeal of southeastern Alaska and the Tlingit: "squaws," "mission children," "curios."

In 1891 the Puget Sound & Alaska Steamship Company commissioned photographer Frank Jay Haynes from Tacoma, Washington, to photograph the sea journey to Glacier Bay, Alaska. (Glacier Bay remained a featured destination until 1899, when an earthquake filled the bay with icebergs from Muir Glacier; Taku Glacier near Juneau then became more important.) Seventy percent of the 24 images Haynes sold in a packet of "Alaska Views" were of scenery and glaciers; 4 (16 percent) were of Tlingit subjects. These included "Indian Avenue, Sitka" and "Trading Street and Greek Church, Sitka"; the remaining 2 showed the pier and Chief Kadasan's totem poles and impressive house in "Fort Wrangle [Wrangell]."

An additional idea of what subjects tourists found intriguing comes from the photographs contained in two family albums now in the archives of George Eastman House. Both were assembled by summer cruise ship passengers and are made up entirely of commercially produced photographs. The first album was kept by an unknown tourist while on an Inside Passage cruise aboard the *Corona*, which visited Sitka and the communities of Wrangell, Chilkat, Juneau, and Yakutat in the summer of 1880. This album contains 47 photographs: a third show nature scenes (primarily glaciers and floating ice), almost the same number show Tlingit subjects, a quarter are town and harbor views, and the rest (13 percent) depict miscellaneous subjects.

The content of the second album from the summer of 1890, ten years later, reveals much

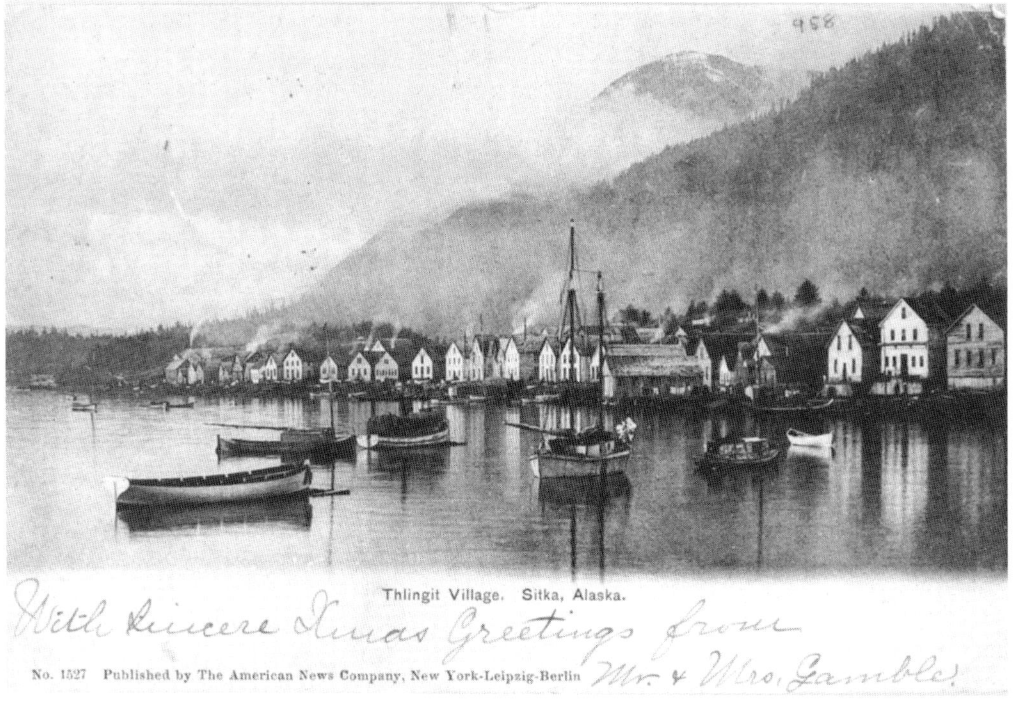

Figure 25
"Thlingit Village. Sitka, Alaska." Postcard sent to Henry Solomon Welcome, "With Sincere Xmas Greetings from Mr. & Mrs. Gamble." Courtesy of the National Archives and Records Administration, Washington, DC. (958)

the same. Its 29 photographs, all taken by photographers working for I. W. Taber of San Francisco, include mainly nature scenes and Tlingit subjects (38 percent each); the remaining quarter depict town and harbor views. Taber's photographers often went to considerable lengths to obtain images. One, identified only as "Mr. H," made it safely back to Sitka from Yakutat aboard the U.S.S. *Rush* after the schooner he had been traveling on was declared unseaworthy (de Laguna 1972:199).

As these collections show, the Tlingit—despite the changes that had occurred which some visitors like Eliza Scidmore regarded as diminishing their exotic appeal—were of equal interest to many visiting tourists as Alaska's spectacular scenery. An Alaskan Steamship Company pamphlet entitled "A Trip to Wonderful Alaska" used the Tlingit in its marketing; it described one of Juneau's special sights as "the big house of Chief Johnson or Yosh-Nash, head of the Raven branch of the Taku tribe," much of whose status was derived from a "great pot latch" he had given which cost over $20,000 in blankets, furs, and other commodities. Had visiting photographers and early tourists not had to rely on summer steamers to reach southeast Alaska, a wider range of Tlingit subjects could have been photographed. During the summer and early fall many families were away from their permanent communities at sealing or fish camps or else working in canneries.

Professional photographers produced stereograph cards, mounted prints, and, by the 1890s, inexpensive photographic postcards (Silversides

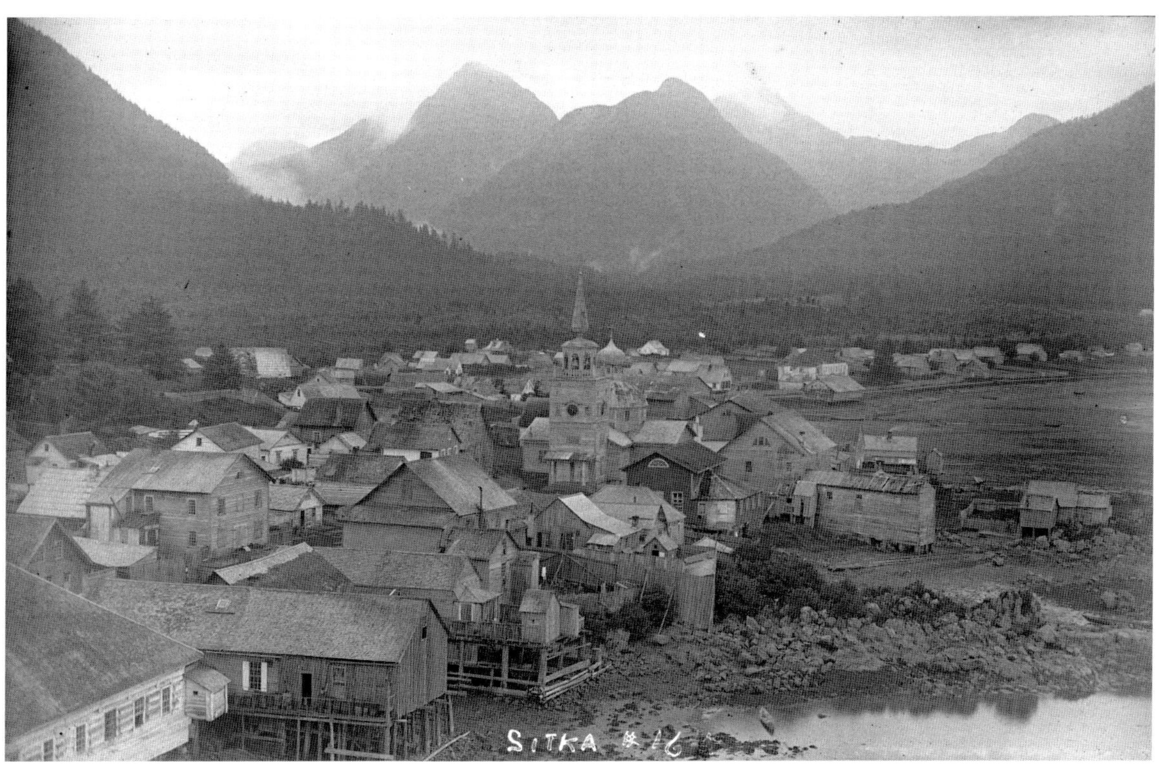

Figure 26
"Sitka," 1897. Photograph by William Letts Oliver. By permission of the Bancroft Library, University of California, Berkeley, CA. (1960.010 ser.2:0452)

1994) (Fig. 25). The earliest recorded Alaska post-cards were issued by the American Souvenir Card Company in 1897. Steamship companies and even missionary organizations, including the Presbyterian Women's Board of Home Missions, also produced postcards (Griffin 2000). When tourist and writer Septima Collis browsed through several stores in Sitka in 1889, she found "photographic views of Alaska from the cameras of Tabor [sic], of San Francisco, and Partridge, of Portland; they were quite cheap, and much better than I saw any-where else" (Collis 1890:10).

Some photographers also published books. The selection of photographs used in Frank La Roche's *En Route to the Klondike: A Series of Photographic Views of the Picturesque Land of Gold and Glaciers* (1898), according to Marnie Coleman,

suggested "a deliberate attempt to undermine the prevailing image of the native Alaskan" (1995:146). Although La Roche's racial stereotypes were typical of the late 19th century, his choice of images and accompanying text seemed designed to "quell fears that natives were unresponsive to 'civilizing' efforts by whites" (p. 147).

The photographs tourists purchased from commercial photographers—and those they later took for themselves—repeated the same views. Once stereograph and postcard dealers and distributors collected enough images to satisfy their customers, they reproduced them again and again and did not seek new ones (Marien 2002:24). Consequently, the same images crop up repeatedly in archives today. For Sitka these included the view from Castle Hill (Fig. 26), the

   VISITING PHOTOGRAPHERS AND TOURISTS

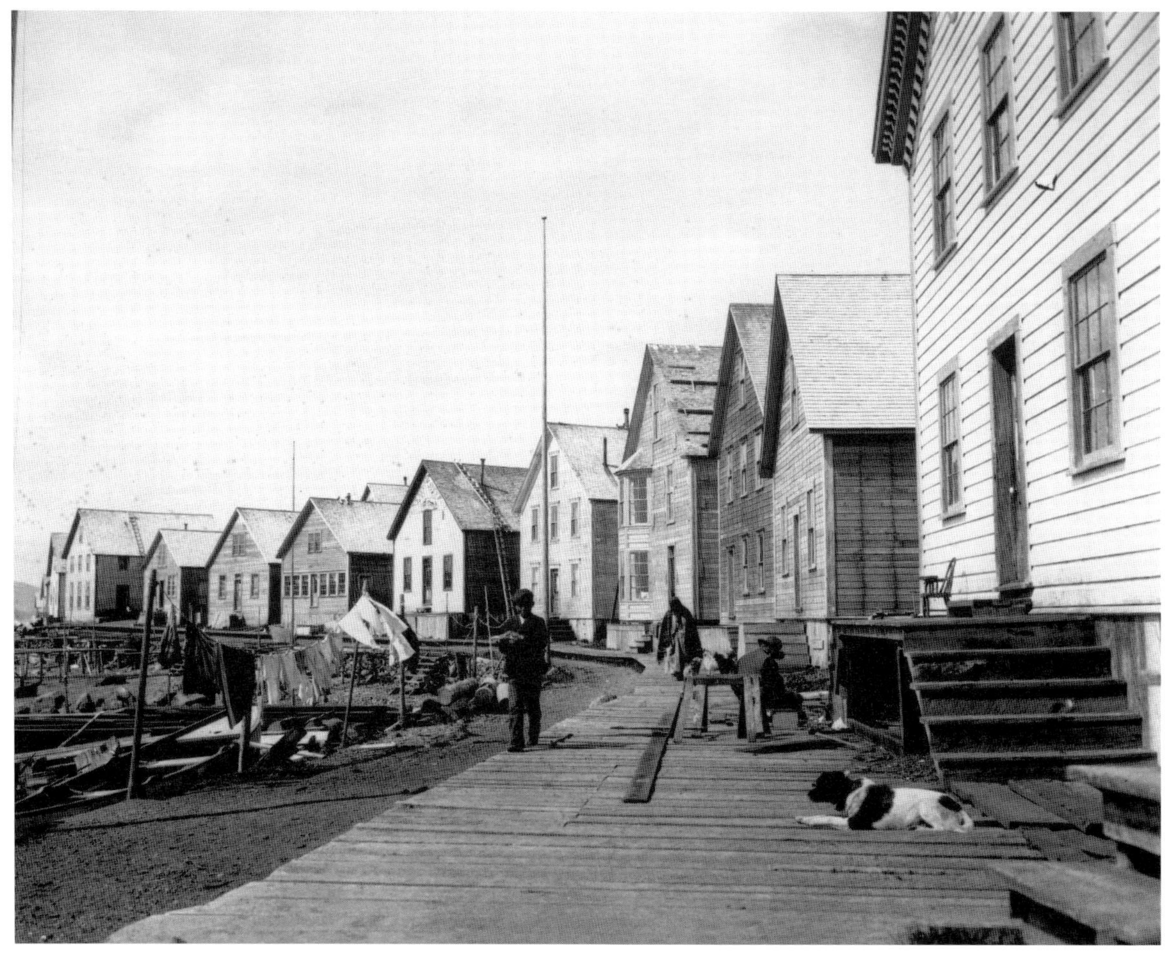

Figure 27
"Indian 'Ranch,' Sitka, Alaska," 1906. Photograph by John N. Cobb. By permission of the University of Washington Libraries, Seattle, WA. Special Collections. (NA 2716)

Tlingit village from the water, Front Street in the village with its beached canoes, St. Michael's Cathedral, the old Russian trading post and its line of Tlingit vendors, Native children from the mission school, and, after 1906, the totem poles in the newly established Indian River Park.

Fisheries biologist and amateur photographer John N. Cobb captured the nearly identical scene of Sitka's "Indian Ranch" in 1906 (Fig. 27) as that taken by commercial photographer Isaac W. Taber almost 20 years earlier (Fig. 28). An album of snapshots in the U.S. Library of Congress, Lot 4540E, taken by the Child family to document their summer vacation to Alaska in 1910, includes ten photographs from Sitka: the town from the water, the "Greek Church," the Haida war canoe (brought to Sitka after being displayed at the Louisiana Purchase Exposition in 1904 and the Louis and Clark Exposition in 1905), and the 13 totem poles (9 Haida and 4 Tlingit) returned to Sitka at the same time.

When a steamer docked, locals flocked to the pier to retrieve their mail, send packages out, and see who had arrived. The ships also

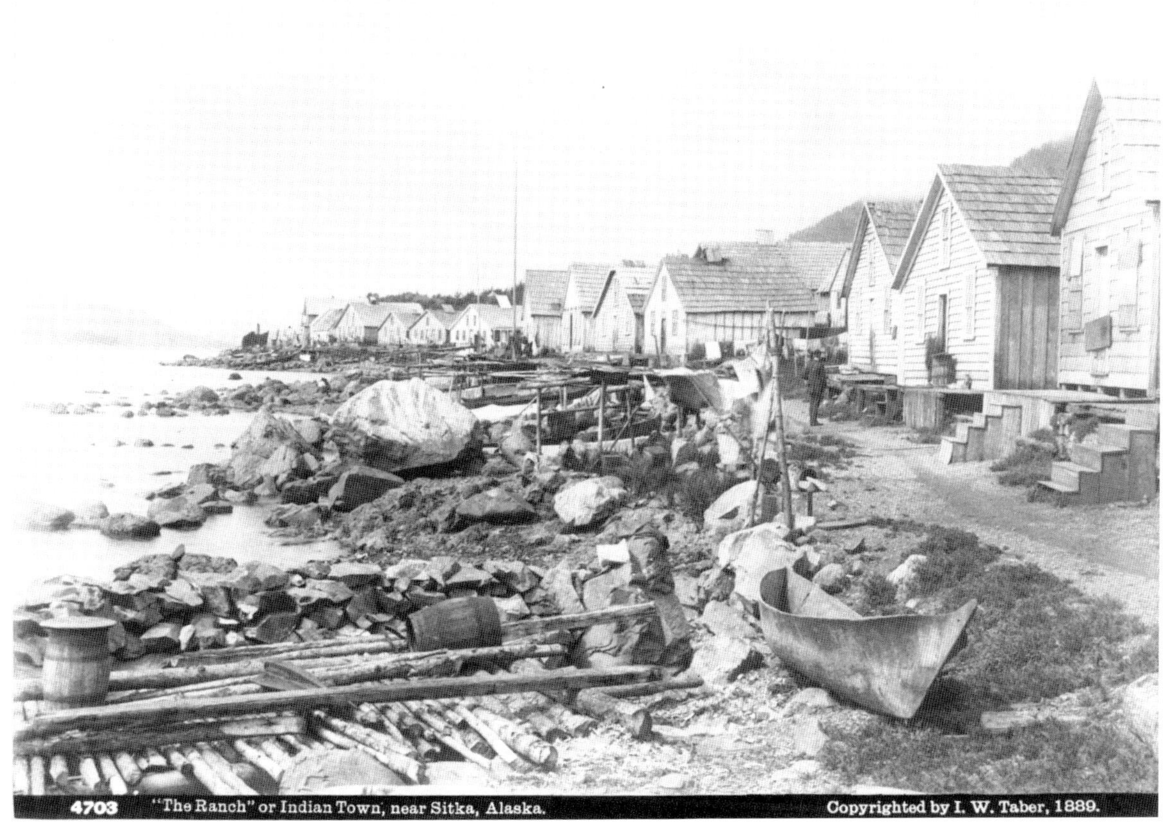

Figure 28
"Indian Town," 1889. Photograph by Isaac W. Taber. By permission of the Alaska State Library, Juneau, AK. (P01–3460)

brought eagerly awaited supplies. Many Tlingit went to the pier to sell their crafts to arriving tourists (Fig. 29). The blankets and head kerchiefs these women wore—a style those in Sitka had adopted from Russian and Creole women before 1867—were old fashioned and visually set the Tlingit apart despite their adoption of ready-to-wear Western clothing. For several years, the Sitka Industrial Training School's brass band also marched to Sitka's pier playing tunes like "Three Cheers for the Red, White and Blue." It "seemed like a gala day," commented a visitor in 1890, "with its inhabitants all out of doors" (Sessions 1890:88).

Many tourists visited the mission school and photographed its grounds and uniformed children. Most also visited the campus's museum, opened in 1889, which housed Sheldon Jackson's extensive collection of native artifacts from throughout Alaska (Carlton 1999). The museum appealed to tourists but was also intended to be an educational repository for the mission's students and future generations of Natives. Tourists could also visit the nearby "cottages" where school alumni living "a civilized life" resided. Most tourists were impressed with the missionaries' work

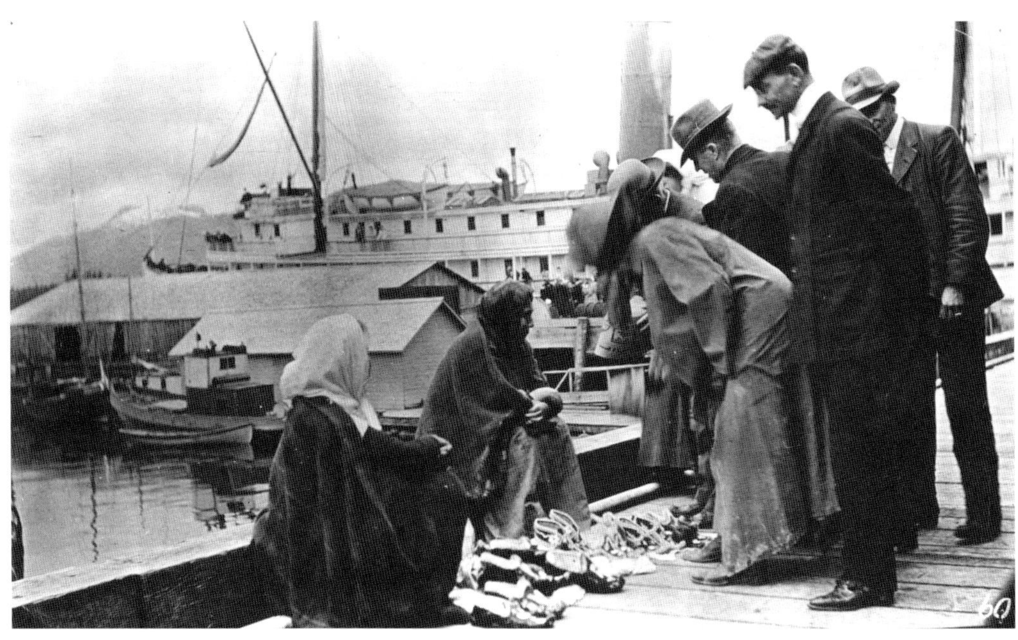

Figure 29
"Buying moccasins from the squaws," 1920. Tourists examine the beaded footwear available for sale on
the steamship dock at Douglas; a passenger ship is in the background. Photograph by Einar J. Evans. By
permission of the Alaska State Library, Juneau, AK. (PSL-Petersburg-People-01)

and gave donations. Passengers from the *Ancon* (Fig. 30) and the *Corona*, two ships that called at Sitka in August 1889, gave $395 ($9,182 in 2007) so the school could buy a team of horses to haul firewood and other heavy materials. The students dutifully named them Ancon and Corona. Passengers from the *Queen* (Fig. 31) once donated $30 ($697 in 2007) to the school band.

Sheldon Jackson, the Presbyterian minister who founded Sitka's school and became Alaska's General Agent of Education, was a promoter at heart and organized his own tourist excursion to Alaska in 1884 for 150 delegates and friends of the National Education Association. It included a visit to the Sitka Industrial Training School and to other Presbyterian missions in Wrangell and Juneau and proved very popular with the delegates. To further benefit from tourism, the school initiated a local tour service in 1892, a

horse-drawn carriage with seats for ten. Some visitors viewed this aspect of the school's work with a jaundiced eye: "Everyone in town is on exhibition, even to the Mission boys and girls, who, brushed and combed and scrubbed, in uniforms alike to a hair-ribbon, marshal themselves in prim order, and deliver the little set speeches drilled into them by their teachers between steamers" (Knapp and Childe 1896:11). Father Nikolai Mitropol'skii Kashevarov (Kashevaroff), priest of St. Michael's Cathedral, also instituted tourist tours to earn money.

Since Indians and their material culture were nearly as important an inducement to come to Alaska as the territory's remarkable scenery, most visitors upon reaching Sitka considered it obligatory to walk through the Tlingit village. After Alaska's civil government was established in 1884 and tourism really got under way, Governor

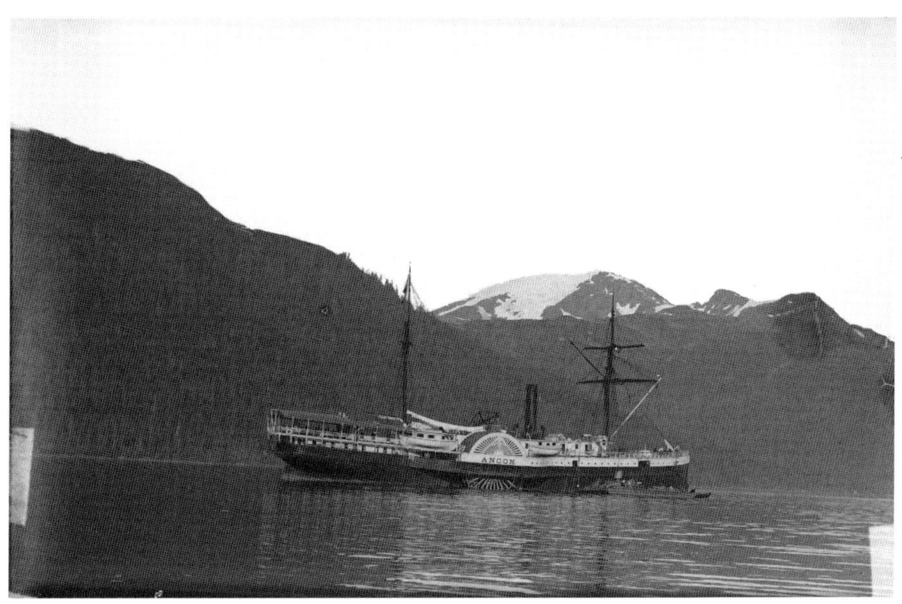

Figure 30
"S.S. Ancon—Douglas Island," 1890s. The steamship was later wrecked at Loring, AK.
Photograph by William Letts Oliver. By permission of the Bancroft Library, University of
California, Berkeley, CA. Oliver Family Photograph Collections. (1960.010 ser. 2:0418)

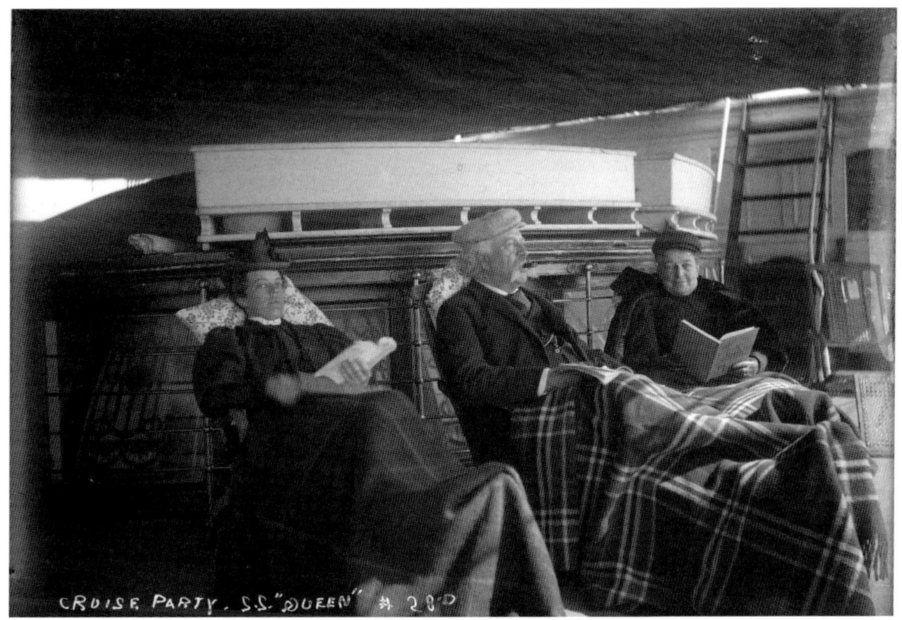

Figure 31
"Cruise party, S.S. 'Queen,'" 1890s. Photograph by William Letts Oliver. By permission of the
Bancroft Library, University of California, Berkeley, CA. Oliver Family Photograph Collections.
(1960.010 ser. 2:0477)

Alfred P. Swineford offered a "weekly prize for the cleanest [Tlingit] household" (Hinckley 1965:72). At Sitka, early tourists often visited number 67, the home of Emeline Baker or "Princess Tom" (or Thom), a prosperous Tlingit merchant. In her "orderly and well kept" village home she entertained visitors by bringing out the baskets, bracelets, earrings, and carvings she had purchased from Tlingit craftsmen in Sitka and villages along the coast (Collis 1890). She at first traded by canoe but later bought the schooner *Active* which she ran between Sitka and Yakutat, sending manufactured household goods north and returning with Tlingit baskets, other crafts, and furs traded from the interior. Yakutat baskets were especially valued by collectors. A guidebook published in 1913 noted, "while many stores in various parts of the United States carry Indian baskets for sale, few of these carry genuine Yakutats" (Underwood 2003:76). According to Israel C. Russell, a member of the 1890 expedition to Mt. St. Elias sponsored by the National Geographic Society and the U.S. Geological Survey, the sale of baskets "brings a comparatively large revenue to the village [Yakutat] and enables the natives to live in comfort" (Russell 1890:873).

A substantial segment of the American public was enamored with Indian crafts. Mail-order catalogs marketed Native baskets throughout the United States; the Frohman Trading Company of Portland offered hundreds of Indian baskets for sale, with Yakutats selling for between $4 and $20 dollars a piece in 1902 ($99 and $497 in 2007). Some enthusiasts devoted entire rooms of their homes to their collections. Others were content to create bric-a-brac displays or to fill curio cabinets in their parlors with Indian crafts (Lee 1991). Early histories and guidebooks supported tourism and the curio-buying craze. "To those travelers in Alaska who become addicted to the curio or basket-buying craze, the advice is offered that more satisfaction will be found in the article that is purchased in its native environment than can be derived from the same thing if it be obtained in a commonplace store" (Underwood 2003:78).

In some circles Native-made handicrafts were beginning to be viewed as "art." Most museums, however, continued to display Indian artifacts—including carved Tlingit masks, elaborately woven Chilkat blankets, and finely made and decorated spruce-root baskets and hats—in a natural history context, simply as part of the life ways of people in a particular part of the world (Jonaitis 1986).

According to Douglas Cole (1985:285), the first museum to exhibit Northwest Coast pieces as "art" was the Denver Art Museum in the mid-1920s. Both collecting and exhibiting are forms of appropriation. True hobbyists and tourists sometimes carried appropriation a step further, even dressing up as Indians. A Muybridge stereograph from Sitka in 1868, labeled "Sitka, Group of Distinguished Chiefs," on closer examination reveals five whites dressed in Tlingit ceremonial garb. Playing Indian had become normative behavior in some circles, serving whites as a form of cultural validation, according to Rayna Green, by connecting them to "the very beginnings of the mythological structure called America" (1988:48).

The tourists' almost insatiable demand for curios was primarily met by the Tlingit vendors who sat on the piers and along the main streets of the towns they visited. Sitka's Princess Tom went to the pier on at least one occasion dressed in "yellow kerchief, pink waist, magenta shawl, white stockings, and purple parasol" (Knapp and Childe 1896:11). Indeed, she became one of the sights tourists to Sitka came to see, especially after 1896 when her photograph (Fig. 106) appeared in *The Thlinkets of Southeastern Alaska*, by Francis Knapp and Rheta Childe. Tourists were fascinated by her clothes and silver jewelry, her reputed wealth, her two husbands, and her tidy home, which helpfully displayed both her names on a signboard over the door (Lukens 1889, Raibmon 2005).

In the early years of tourism the Tlingit sold the objects they made for everyday use (such as, knives, baskets, halibut hooks, wood bowls) and occasionally, those made for ceremonial use. Even

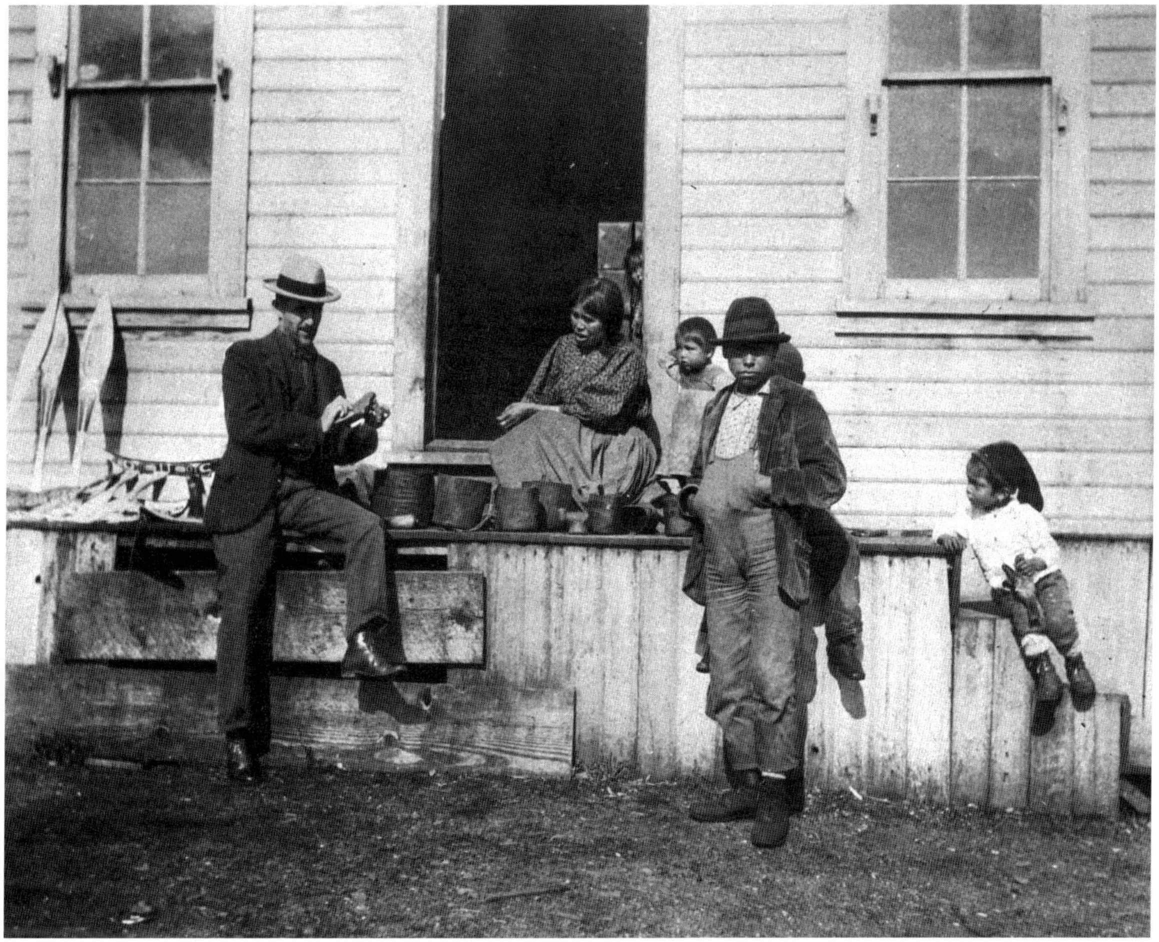

Figure 32
"George T. Emmons examining a stone adze, baskets, canoe model, and other materials he was collecting from the Tlingit, photographed in Sitka, Alaska," 1890s. By permission of the Royal British Columbia Museum, BC Archives, Victoria, BC. (PN01551)

everyday items often had other significance. Halibut hooks combined technology with magic: each hook was decorated with an image such as land otter or raven that acted as a charm (Jonaitis 1981).

As the supply of old objects dwindled, it has been claimed that some Tlingit "commenced to despoil the graves of their own relatives" to obtain more (Cole 1985:101). Museum collectors often blamed the higher prices they had to pay for hats, masks, staffs, shamans' figures, Chilkat blankets, and other old objects on the pressure created by tourists and local collectors, while ignoring their own role. Many collectors were based in Sitka over the years, including John J. McLean, Edward G. Fast, L. A. Beardslee, John G. Brady, George T. Emmons (Fig. 32), Sheldon Jackson, Aurel Krause, Louis Shotridge, and Elbridge W. Merrill (for a detailed discussion of the collecting of Northwest Coast and Alaskan artifacts see Cole 1985 and Miller and Miller 1967).

Most tourists were satisfied with the new items which the Tlingit almost immediately began to make—animal-form bowls, mountain goat horn spoons, wooden spoons with animal figures on the handles, baskets with lids. Silversmiths like Jim Jacobs, known as Sitka Jim, and Rudolph Walton converted silver coins into carved silver bracelets, rings, teaspoons, and even pickle forks and tongs (Cole 1985). The first silver bracelets the Tlingit produced were wide and made for their own use, but as tourist demand increased silversmiths changed to narrow bracelets that could be manufactured more quickly and used less metal (Emmons 1991).

They also made new items specifically for the tourist trade. Tlingit women likewise wove spruce-root baskets with simplified designs, in smaller sizes, and with novelty shapes such as bottles and teapots, and also beaded leather moccasins. Few visitors probably appreciated the time and skill that went into making baskets. Although Tlingit weavers sometimes worked in their presence, most of their production took place during the late fall and winter when tourists were not around. "Spruce roots had to be dug, roasted, peeling, and split; grasses had to be gathered and trimmed; and dyes had to be prepared" (Raibmon 2005:152; Emmons 1904a). Only then could the baskets be woven. By the turn of the century, the Tlingit were "copying designs from dress goods, carpets, and curtains" to add to their repertoire of Tlingit designs and they also began using commercially made aniline dyes (Stromstadt-Brown 1906:6).

The Tlingit took full advantage of the new commercial opportunities tourists created. As Ruth Phillips notes, tourist art "is the product of a careful, anthropological study of the material culture and aesthetics of the Western other by Native artists and craftspeople" (1995:116).

Students at the Sitka Industrial School also carved miniature wooden totem poles, paddles, and canoes for sale. Ever since it had opened, the school had been sending student-made crafts to Presbyterian mission societies throughout the Midwest and eastern United States. Proceeds from the sale of "mats of braided grass, toy Indian hats, odd little carved boxes, and even Alaska dolls dressed in fur" were used to purchase books and clothes (J. Wright 1883:177).

Few tourists were likely to have been interested in the intricacies of Tlingit culture or in knowing the details of their daily lives, but they did expect and want to have some direct experience of it. The Alaska Steamship Company advertised the opportunity to visit an Indian village "with its totem poles and dried fish; its smoky huts and dirty children; its stolid 'citizens' and numerous dogs" (Raibmon 2005). Most visitors to Sitka felt it obligatory to visit the Tlingit "ranche." Some penetrated backstage to look at the deteriorating grave houses on the hill behind the village or by entering Tlingit homes. This practice predated tourism to the region; Lady Franklin and her niece Sophia Cracroft had toured homes on a visit to Sitka in 1870 (DeArmond 1981). Most tourists also visited the grounds of the mission school where they received an opposing image of Tlingit life—one of civilization and change. Collis (1890) characterized visiting Sitka's two Tlingit communities as a movement from "savagery to civilization" (see Kan 2004), but she also revealed contradictory views of the village Tlingit who she disparaged in her writing. While ridiculing the "gaudy" colors some women wore and their "profusion" of silver and gold jewelry, she also acknowledged that the latter was "very well made." While ridiculing the women's wearing of blankets, she accurately described their functionality; they performed "the service of hood, jacket, skirt, cushion, or lap-rug, just as the occasion required" (Collis 1890:99).

Since cruise ships made short stops, most visitors to Sitka only had time to walk through part of the village, look at St. Michael's Cathedral, visit the mission school and museum, and browse through a couple of stores before having to re-board. Virtually all tourists, however, found the time to examine Tlingit "curios" and haggle with women vendors over their price. The Alaska

Steamship Company promoted in its brochures the opportunity tourists would have to use sign language or some Chinook trade jargon during their dealings with Natives and the extra meaning their purchases would have if they bought them directly from an "old Indian woman, in the far-off wilds of Alaska" rather than from a store in Seattle (Raibmon 2005). Tourist photography reflects this interest. One of the most common images tourists to Sitka took was of women vendors in front of the massive log building on Lincoln Street known as the trading post "as they squat or lie face downward, like so many seals," as visiting travel writer Eliza Scidmore (1885:99) ungraciously described them.

For most tourists, photographic images of the Tlingit were not that different from the objects they made; both were "curiosities" or exotic items which visitors wished to possess and later, to display. Sitka's general merchandise stores and curio shops recognized this and sold both Tlingit crafts and photographs. After purchasing a camera in 1886, merchant Edward DeGroff began photographing Sitka's Tlingit to add to other merchandise in his Northwest Trading Company store. He also commissioned stereograph images from professional photographers, including H. H. Brodeck of Washington Territory and Sitka's Elbridge E. Merrill. The reverse was also true. Merrill, whose photographic work is discussed in detail in Chapter 5, sold spruce-root baskets, beaded moccasins, miniature paddles, canoes, and totem poles as well as older Tlingit artifacts along with his photographs.

Tourism has been likened to pilgrimage; both involve journeys in which travelers are freed from the constraints of their ordinary lives and exposed to new, and possibly life-changing, experiences (Turner and Turner 1978, Graburn 2001). Postcards and photographs, as Elizabeth Edwards has pointed out, are "relics" of this sacred journey. They also provide visual proof of the tourist's presence in the places visited, validating his or her daring and privilege. Tourists usually select photographic subjects that encapsulate their ex-

perience of the destination or, at least, the image of it they wish to portray back home. These images then become vehicles for sharing their trip with others, helping them construct a narrative of their experience (Edwards 1996, Stewart 1984, Lofgren 2004). The Tlingit, as living curios, were one of the main objects of the early tourist gaze in southeast Alaska. They represented wildness and the edge of the civilized world.

What is regarded as "picturesque" and, therefore, photograph-worthy is often linked to ideas of authenticity. To be authentic, people and places should appear as tourists imagine they did in the past. Traditional societies are generally assumed to be rooted in a timeless past and to undergo very little change from within (Dominguez 1986). Native peoples, many outsiders feel, should look and act as their forebears did; at most, they can be on the cusp of change.

The physical environment should also appear unspoiled by modern encroachments. Tourists also seek signifiers, that is, subjects and scenes which typify their preconceptions about the place they are visiting—chateaux in France, Shinto tori in Japan, thatched cottages or Tudor buildings in England. As John Urry (1990) has pointed out, we all become semioticians when we travel, searching for signs of "Frenchness," the "Orient," and so forth. Particular scenes come to symbolize or stand for a place largely through the power of previous images including stereographs and the photographs reproduced in newspapers and books. Dazie Stromstadt-Brown's guidebook, *Sitka, the Beautiful*, published in 1906, was fairly typical. It included four photographs—the Tlingit village with picturesque sailboats in the foreground, blanket-draped Tlingit women selling handicrafts on Lincoln Street's plank sidewalk, Sitka Sound with Fuji-like Mt. Edgecombe rising in the distance, and the hemlock and spruce-lined forest path ("Lover's Lane") to Indian River. These were the signifiers sought by early tourists to Sitka.

Photographs signify a place and its people both through what they explicitly show and through what they merely suggest—"denotation"

      VISITING PHOTOGRAPHERS AND TOURISTS

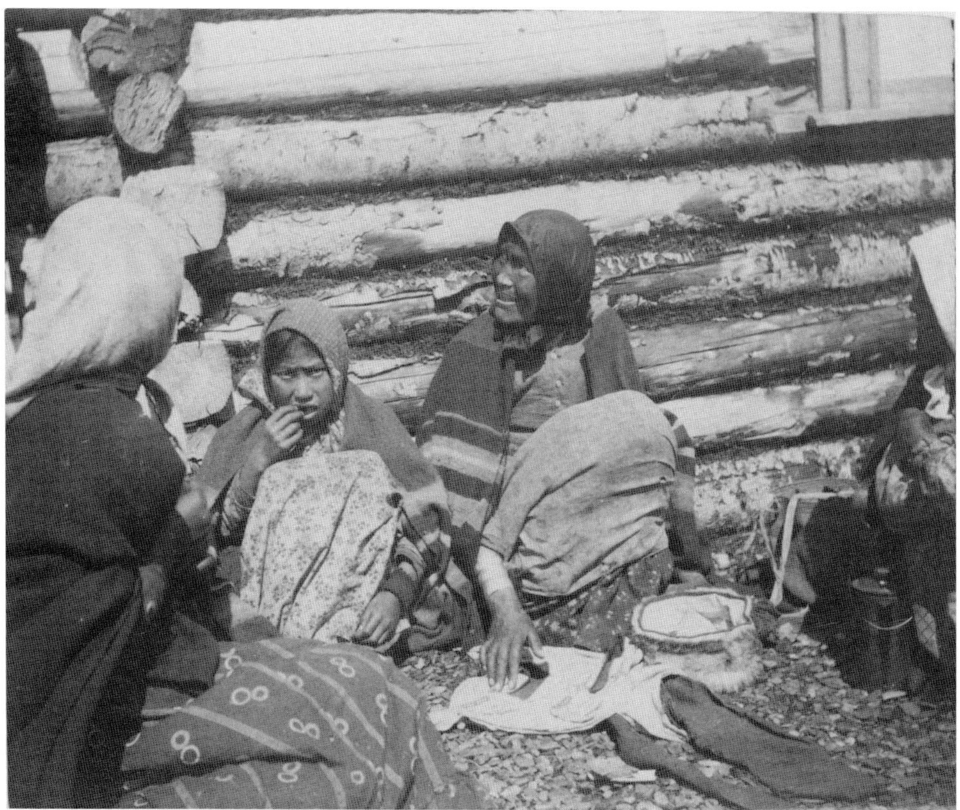

Figure 33
Tlingit women at Sitka, 1884. Photograph by Eliza R. Scidmore. By permission of the National Anthropological Archives, Smithsonian Institution, Washington, DC. (SPC NWC Tlingit NM No # Scidmore 00143700)

and "connotation" to use Barthes' (1964) terms. Early tourists and photographers visiting southeast Alaska sought images of obviously Native things (such as blanket-draped Tlingit vendors, village scenes, carved canoes, totem poles), the wilderness setting (glaciers, a dramatic ocean foreground with mountain backdrop), and, in Sitka, the town's wood-plank sidewalk and Russian-built log buildings and onion-domed cathedral. What these images represented was the "frontier," the edge of the tamed and known world.

Photographs of the Tlingit's unique (some characterized it as "weird") material culture as well as Sitka's tumble down appearance and remnants of its Russian past would have elicited feelings of mild shock in most of the untraveled outsiders who viewed them. Despite the progress being made by Alaska's coastal Natives and their impressive communication skills which may have made them *less* exotic and picturesque to tourists than Indians in the Lower 48 as Sergei Kan (2004) maintains, they were still curiosities. Photographs of Tlingit vendors or of everyday village scenes also suggested the intimacy of the touristic encounter, that is, the ability of tourists to be in proximity to the subjects in their photographs.

Tourist photography often has a candidness and spontaneity about it that contrasts with the images produced by professional photographers. A photograph of two Tlingit children taken in

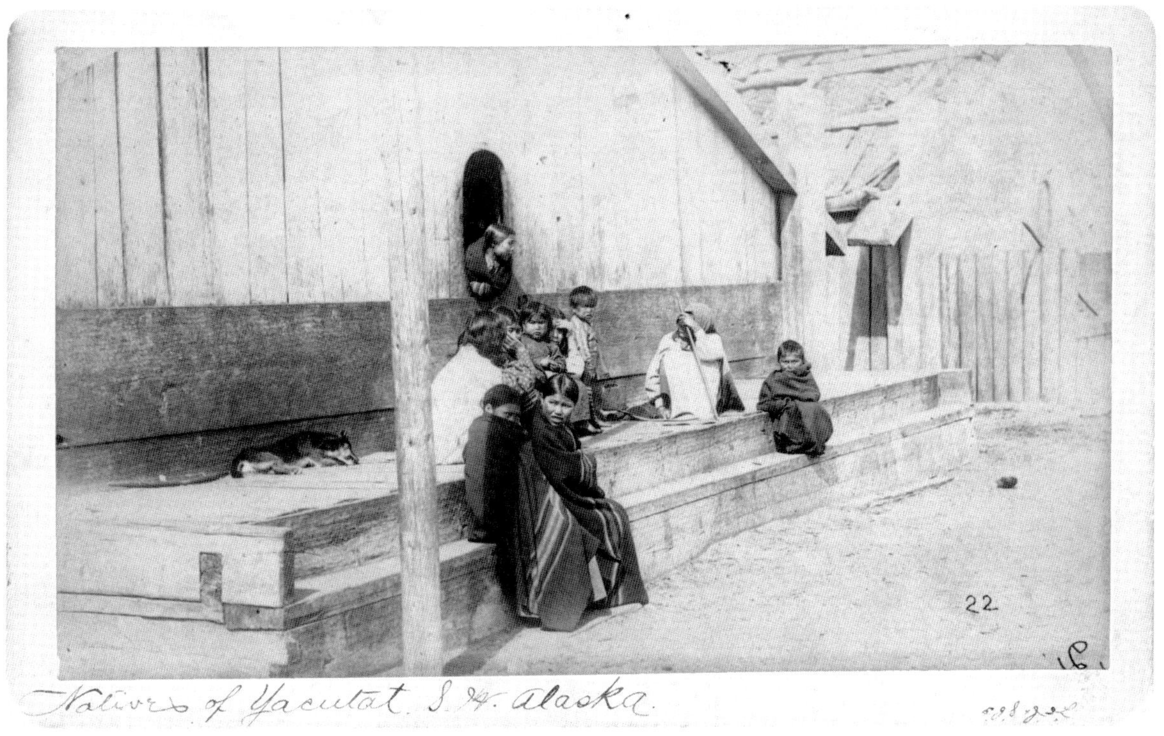

Figure 34
Cabinet card of "Natives of Yacutat [Yakutat], S.W. Alaska." Photograph by Mrs. Wilhelmina Swineford while on a summer excursion in 1887 aboard the U.S.S. *Thetis.* By permission of the Alaska State Library, Juneau, AK. (P27–056)

early 1883 by Eliza R. Scidmore shows them eating while seated on the ground in front of their village home. Their mouths are open and they look surprised—caught unaware in the midst of their everyday activities. Composition and background are secondary to Scidmore's subjects. The children have door frames protruding from their heads and their limbs are cropped. In Figure 33, also by Scidmore, the main subject is off center and looks away from the camera and the object on the ground in front of her is difficult to decipher.

On this visit to Alaska Scidmore was just beginning her career. She later published a number of magazine articles and in 1885 collected them into her first guidebook, *Alaska, Its Southern Coast and the Sitkan Archipelago.* She returned to Sitka in 1891 and then published *Appleton's Guide-Book to Alaska and the Northwest Coast* (1893). She became a well-known travel writer and photographer, visiting Japan and other parts of Asia and publishing six more books and numerous magazine articles on travel, customs, and politics. In 1890 she joined the National Geographic Society, served in various positions, and is credited with being one of the first women to have a photograph published in the magazine—a 1914 hand-tinted photograph of a Japanese child. She was also responsible for having Japanese cherry trees planted in Washington, DC, and following her death in 1928, her ashes were interred in Yokohama at the request of the Japanese government.

Amateur photography was still a comparative novelty when 19-year-old M. Seward McClure from San Francisco proudly wrote on the back of a photograph he had taken of Wrangell's Tlingit in August 1887 (now in the U.S. Library of Congress, Lot 11156–6): "Developed by self; printed and mounted by others. Exposure by self." He, as Scidmore had, was undoubtedly using a dry-plate hand camera which had become available in the early 1880s. Such cameras were used by serious hobbyists only since they required that the photographer do his or her own darkroom work. Commonly referred to as detective cameras, even though they were too large to be concealed, they were relatively inconspicuous to operate (Rosenblum 1997).

Figure 34 was taken in Yakutat in 1887, the same year McClure photographed the Tlingit in Wrangell. It was apparently taken by Mrs. Wilhelmina Swineford, the wife of Alfred P. Swineford, the District of Alaska's governor, while on a summer tour of southeastern villages aboard the U.S.S. *Thetis*. Unlike the images taken by most professionals, the horizons in amateur photographs were often crooked. In Figure 34 a shadow falls across the principal subject in the foreground, and only some people seem aware of the camera. A second image taken in Sitka, which includes a shaman with long coiled hair, shows people looking in different directions and crops off some of their bodies (Fig. 35). Yet both images draw the viewer in because of their informality and immediacy. Like McClure and Scidmore, Swineford must have been using a hand camera since the simplified Eastman Kodak box camera was not introduced until the following year.

With the introduction of the Eastman Kodak box camera in 1888, which had a fixed-focus lens and required no darkroom work, tourists could much more easily make their own photographic records of their trips. Photography was now opened up to a new category of user; the Kodak slogan "You press the button and we do the rest" said it all. The loaded camera, which cost $25 ($562 in 2007), allowed users to take 100 exposures before returning it to the lab, where for an additional $10 ($225 in 2007), the film was processed and the camera reloaded and returned to its owner (Wells 1997). Its f/9 lens allowed pictures to be taken in good light, and its short focal length of 2½ inches resulted in good depth of field. These simple cameras became so synonymous with amateur photography that to take a picture of someone was to "kodak" him or her.

In 1890 12- and 24-exposure pre-rolled film was introduced. This was loaded by the user and removed from the camera for laboratory processing; after 1895 it could be loaded and unloaded in daylight. These developments gave members of the public more control over photography and disassociated it from travel alone, encouraging more home and family photography. By the end of 1898, the *British Journal of Photography* estimated that there were over 1,500,000 roll-film cameras in use throughout the world (Coe and Gates 1977). Two years later, in 1900, the inexpensive Kodak Brownie was introduced. It cost only $1 ($25 in 2007) and a roll of 6-shot film 15 cents (less than $4 in 2007); 100,000 sold the first year. Now almost everyone could become a photographer or "snapshot artist."

What kind of pictures did tourists take? Sets of professionally produced stereo-cards, prints, and postcards were available to buy on almost any topic relating to landscape, people, or objects of anthropological interest. This left accidental encounters, street scenes, and the small events that occur during travel, as well as tourists' traveling companions and mode of transportation as subjects for amateur photographers to record (Wells 1997). Figure 36, taken with the earliest Kodak which produced 2½-inch-round images, shows dogs walking down Front Street, the waterfront lane in front of Sitka's Tlingit village.

The Kodak's 100-exposure film invited profligate shooting, just as digital photography does today. This meant that images of the Tlingit—in communities like Wrangell, Juneau, and Sitka; canneries like Loring; and mines like Douglas on

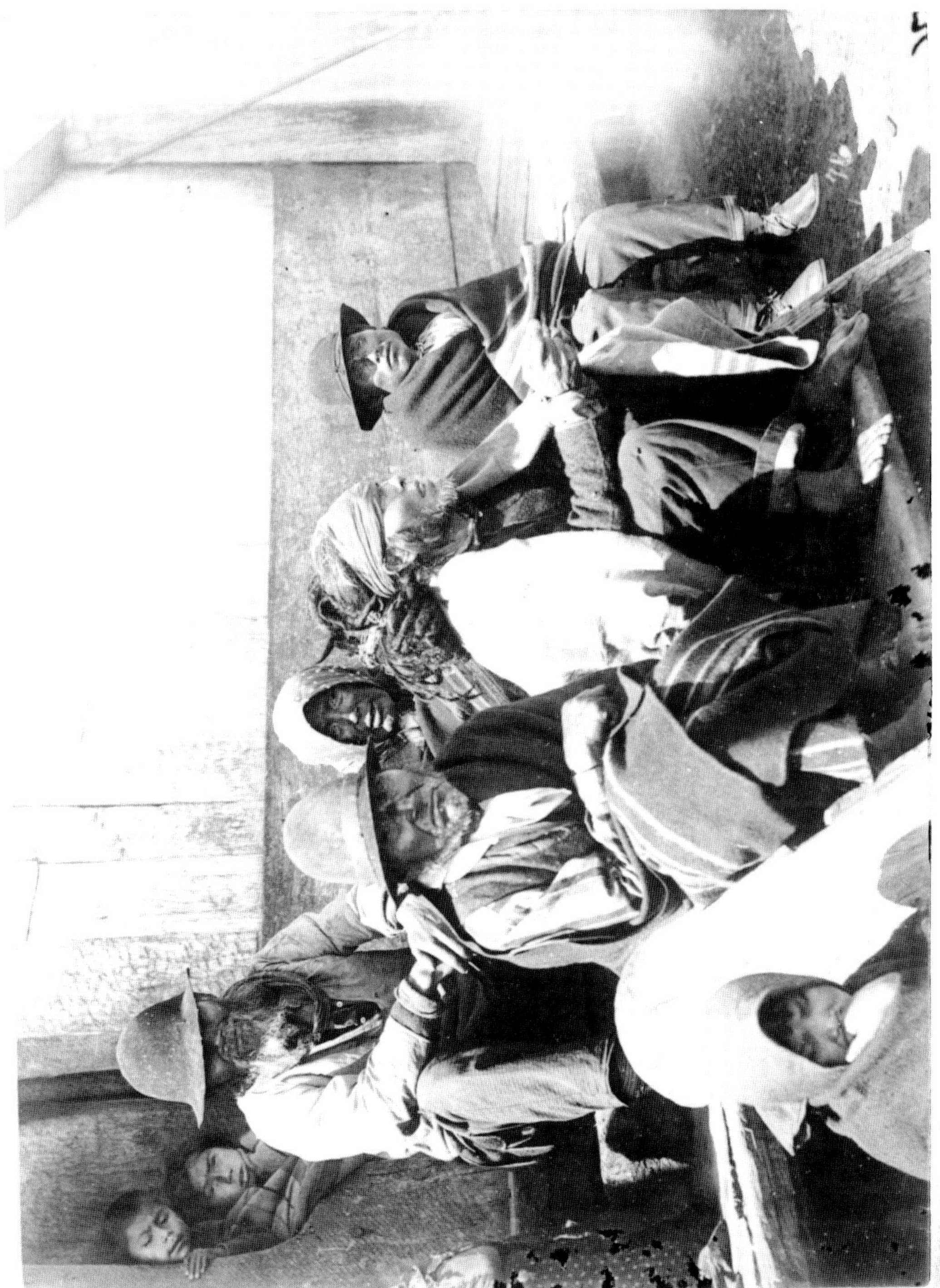

Figure 35

Tlingit in Sitka as photographed by Mrs. Wilhelmina Swineford while on a summer excursion in 1887 aboard the U.S.S. *Thetis*. The man second from the right has the uncut coiled hair of a shaman. By permission of the Alaska State Library, Juneau, AK. (P27–004)

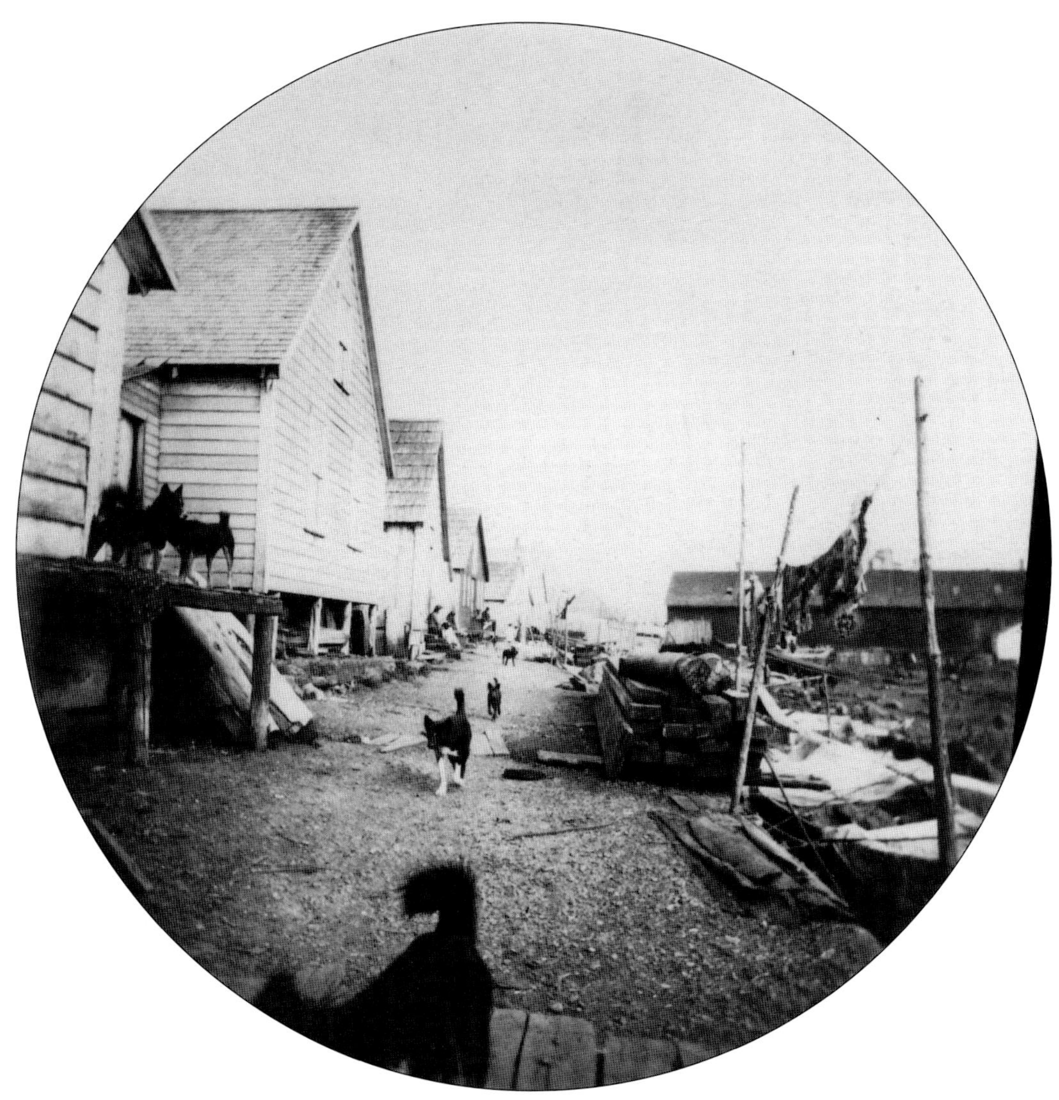

Figure 36
Kodak tourist photo of "Indian Street Sitka," c. 1888–90.
By permission of the Presbyterian Historical Society,
Philadelphia, PA. (RG 239–13, no. 529)

the steamship lines—became increasingly common and widely dispersed. The portability and simplicity of Kodak cameras also allowed tourists to take images from unusual vantage points and without their subjects' knowledge.

Figure 37 is an early Kodak image of about 20 Tlingit men gambling on the beach at Sitka. One man is caught in the act of putting his jacket on; none seem aware of the camera. The invasion of people's privacy that this type of photography allowed soon became a topic of public discussion, aired in editorials and cartoons, although this concern was seldom applied to tourist photography of Native people.

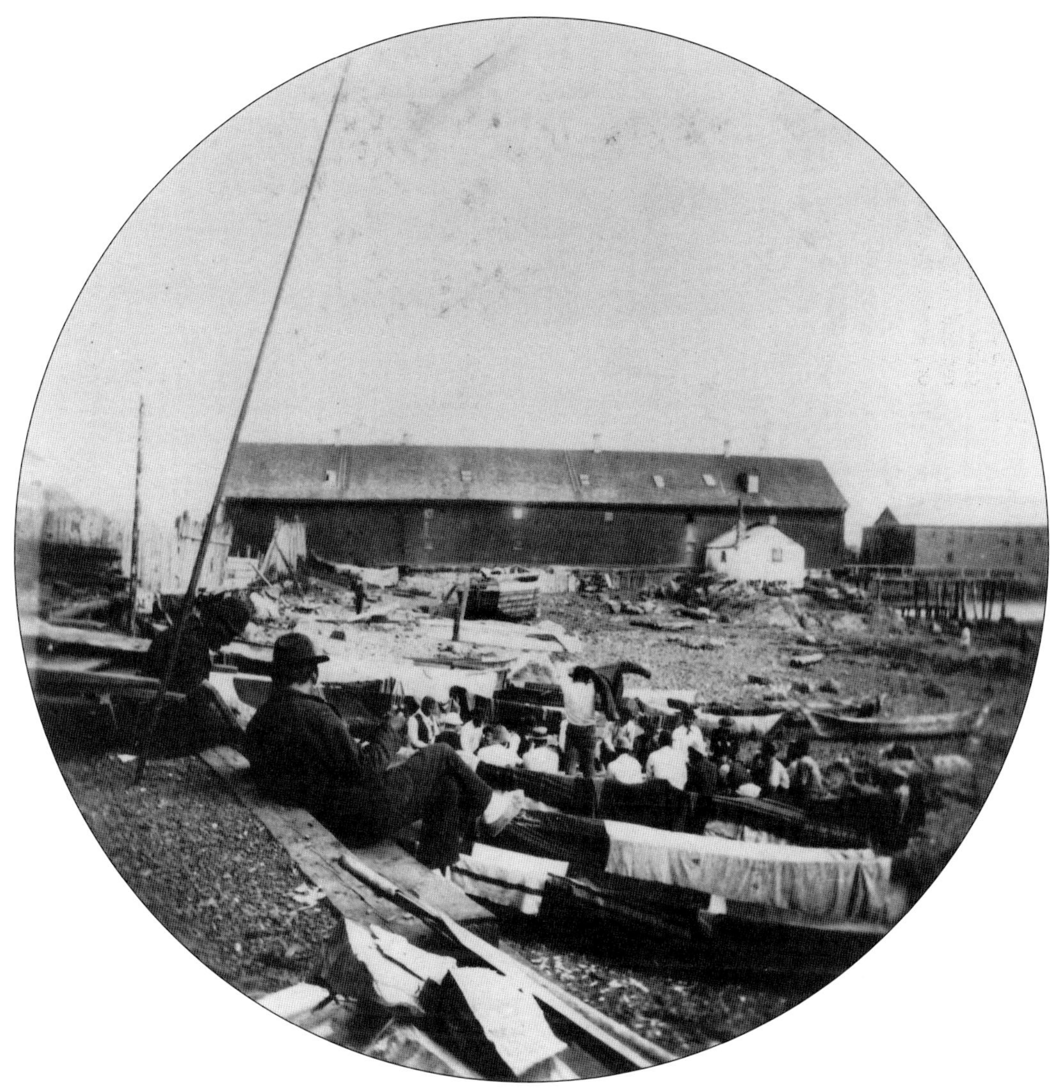

Figure 37
"Gamblers at Sitka," c. 1890. By permission of the
Presbyterian Historical Society, Philadelphia, PA. (RG
239–13, no. 546)

The aesthetic quality of much early tourist photography was poor. According to photography historian Naomi Rosenblum,

Untutored in either art or science, they [tourists] tended to regard the image in terms of its subject rather than as a visual statement that required decisions about where to stand, what to include, how best to use the light. Further, since they were untroubled by questions of print size or quality, they mostly ignored the craft elements of photographic expression. This attitude, coupled with the fact that "every Tom, Dick and Harry could get something or

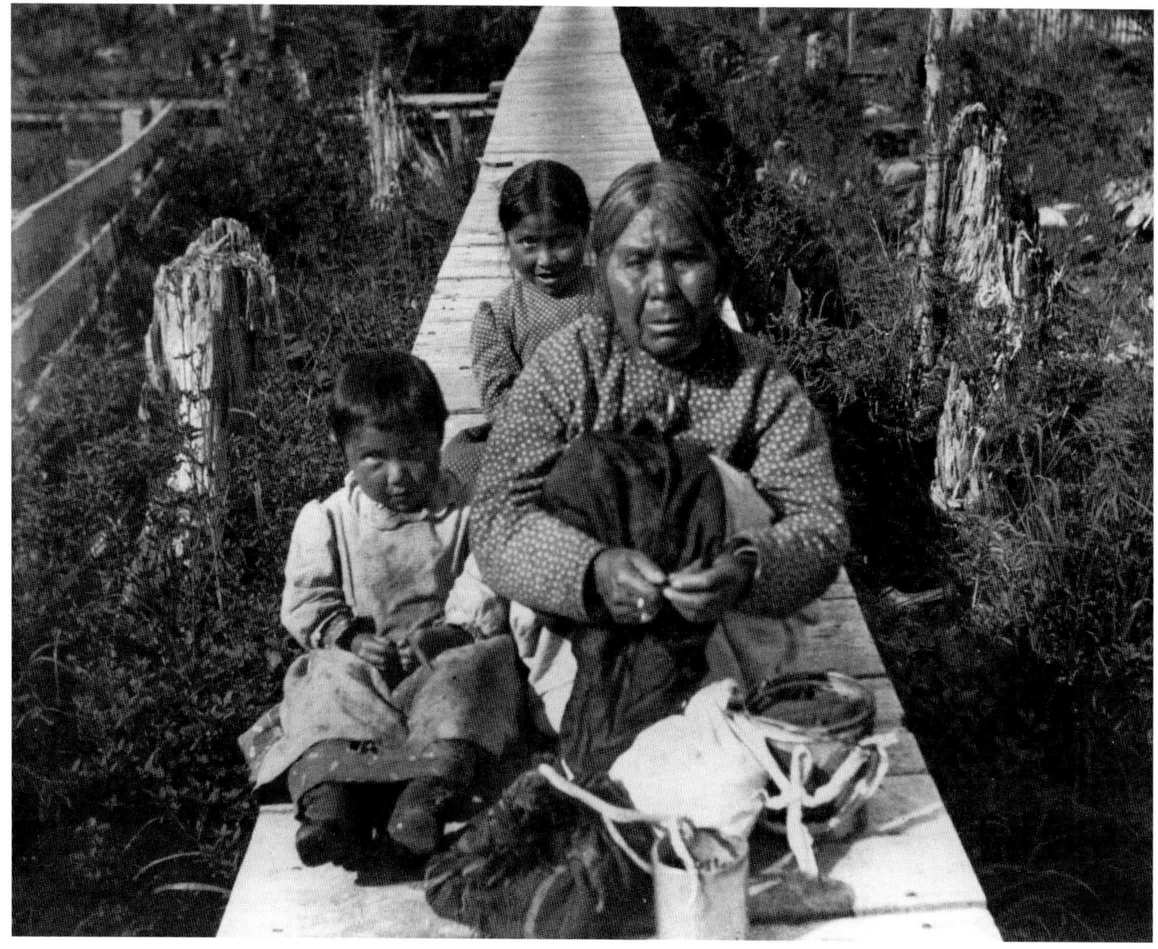

other onto a sensitive plate," contributed to the emerging polarity between documentary images—assumed to be entirely artless—and artistic photographs conceived by their makers (and others) to embody aesthetic ideas and feelings. (1997:260)

Figure 38 shows a Tlingit woman and two children sitting on a plank sidewalk with a tin of berries they have just gathered. It is a typical tourist image, although more compositionally skilled

than most. It and others like it which showed "traditional" aspects of production further authenticated the tourist's experience (Edwards 1996).

In Figure 39 a group of Tlingit women and a boy clean salmon on the beach. Written below the photograph in the family album in which it was placed is this caption: "The women appear to be doing the work and attending to business. The men are at the saloon, maybe, the sign of which shows." The caption suggests a common stereotype of drunken Indians, but in this case

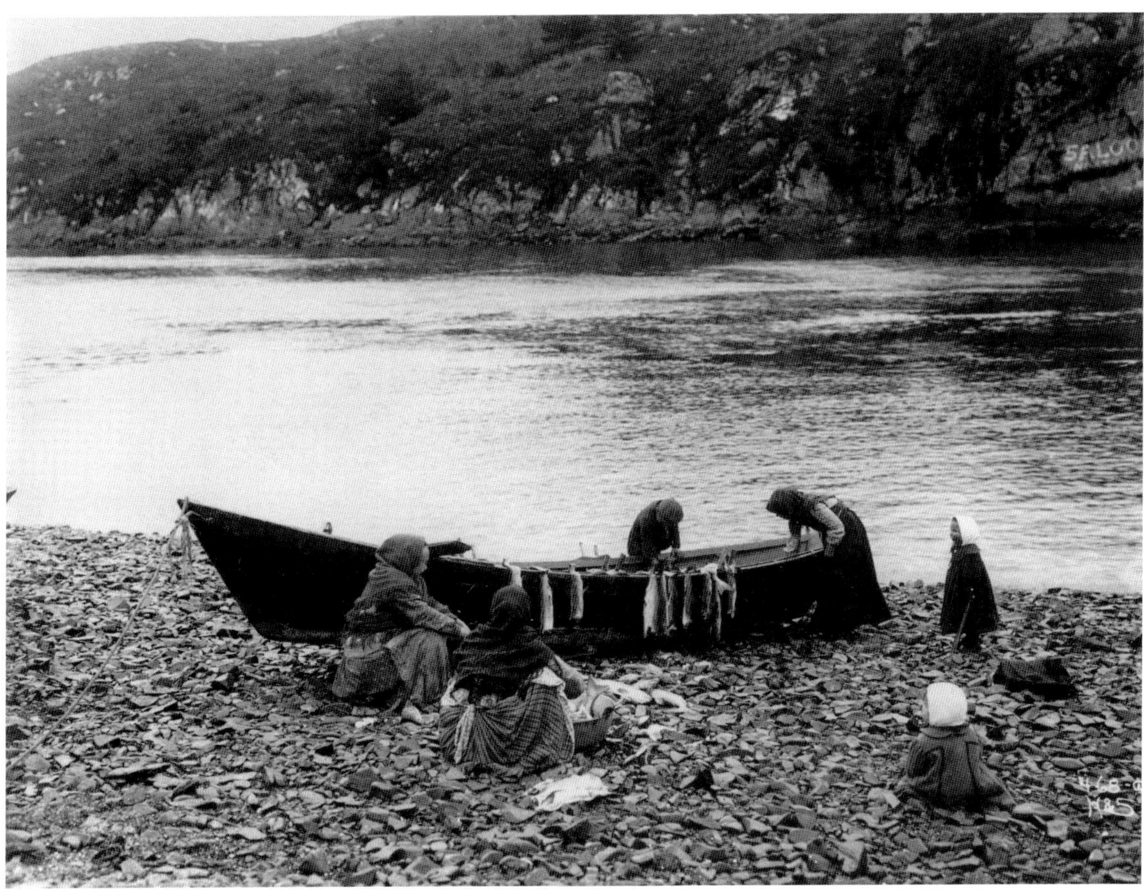

Figure 39
Women cleaning fish, 1907. Photograph by Webster & Stevens. By permission of the University of Washington Libraries, Seattle, WA. Special Collections. (NA468A)

the word "saloon" painted on the rocks on the opposite shore helped prompt the thought.

Not long after easier transportation began bringing visiting photographers and tourists to southeastern Alaska, commercial photographers began to open studios in the region's larger communities. Resident amateur photographers also became active. To what extent did the photographs they took of the Tlingit differ from those taken by visitors? What advantages did year-round residence bring? It surely created greater access, the opportunity to photograph a greater range of Tlingit subjects, and the possibility for a different relationship with the Tlingit. No longer were interactions of necessity short-lived and impersonal. Familiarity, if not friendships, could develop. The Tlingit also would have been exposed to a new type of photography. One in which they were not just the objects of an impersonal, and arguably exploitative, gaze. As a result they are likely to have developed more interest in photography themselves.

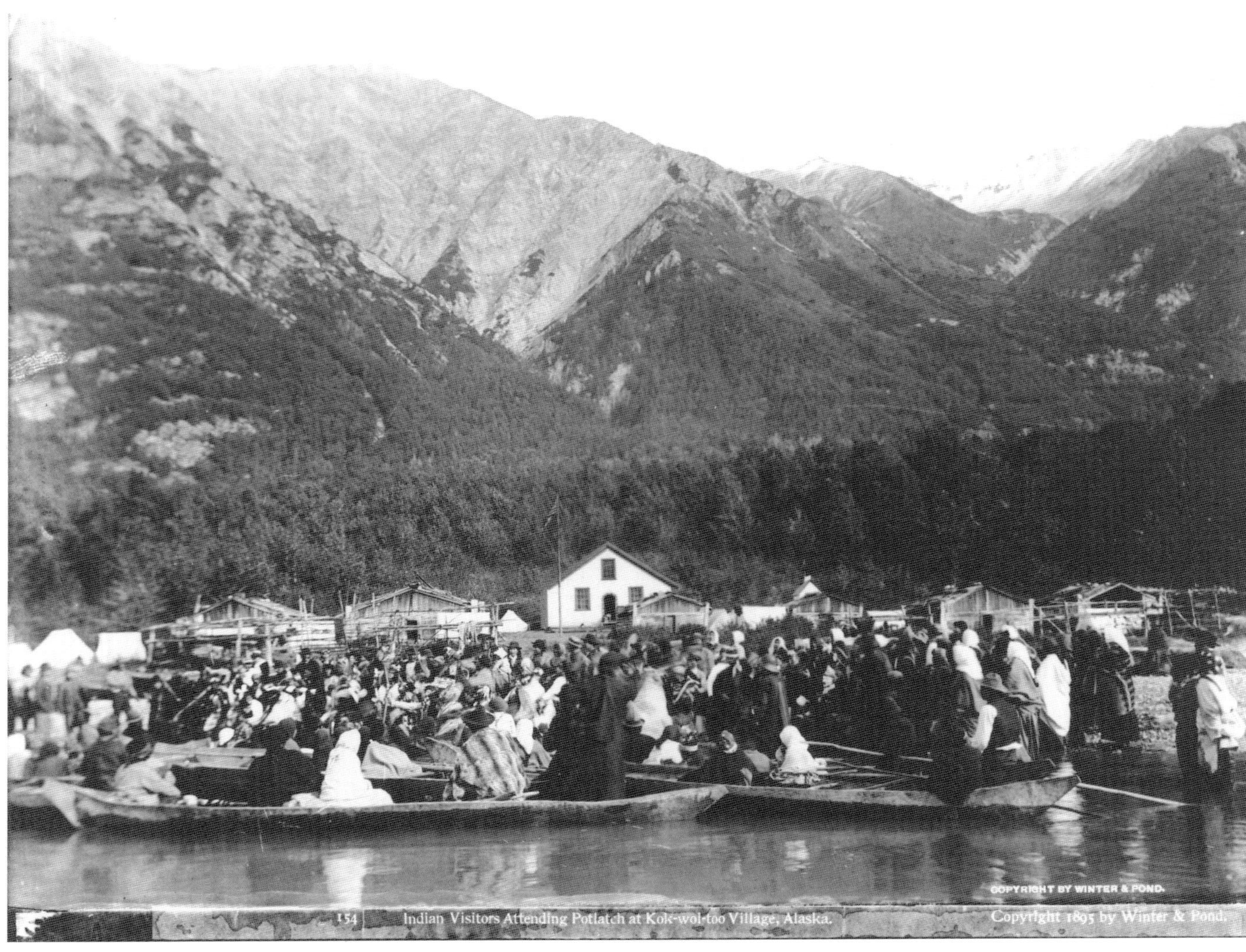

Figure 40
"Indian Visitors Attendng Potlatch at Kok-wol-too [Kaatx'awultu] Village, Alaska," before 1895, when the village was destroyed by a mudslide. Photograph by Winter & Pond. By permission of the Alaska State Library, Juneau, AK. (P87–0048)

4

Privileged Portrayals: Resident Photographers

In the late 1880s commercial photographers began to open studios in southeast Alaska's larger communities of Juneau, Ketchikan, Sitka, Wrangell, Skagway, Haines, and Douglas. An examination of Polk's *Alaska-Yukon Gazetteer and Business Directories* from the turn of the century until 1915 reveals that there were never more than half a dozen commercial photographers working in the southeast at any one time. Fewer than two dozen operated in all of Alaska and the Yukon Territory during the period.

One of the most significant studios was opened by Lloyd V. Winter and Percy E. Pond in Juneau in 1893 (Wyatt 1989). They took over George M. Landerking's two-year-old business and proceeded to produce many striking images of the Tlingit and Haida Gwaii peoples. As resident photographers they were able to develop long-term relationships with some Native people. Since they owned a small boat and traveled throughout the region when the weather permitted, they could visit Tlingit villages like Kake and Angoon which were off the steamship routes and obtain images that were unavailable to visiting commercial photographers and tourists. Figure 40 shows Tlingit canoes filled with guests arriving for a potlatch at a small village. They were

also able to photograph the year round which meant that they could take photographs in the winter and observe the ceremonial events that usually took place then. According to Jane Alison (1998), after the photographers unwittingly observed a secret dance in 1894, they had to be initiated into the Chilkat tribe since outsiders were forbidden to see it. They were given Tlingit names at this time.

Winter and Pond's photographs are notable for the range of subjects and conditions they show. They did not limit themselves to narrow stereotypes or attempt to create falsely romantic images of the Tlingit by removing traces of modernization or Western culture despite their desire to produce saleable images. One exception to this is the interpretive image they created of the former shaman "Skun-doo" (Sxandu u) re-enacting a healing ceremony in their studio. His long matted hair had been cut by white authorities in 1888 in an attempt to force him to renounce his profession, but he was still willing to re-enact ceremonies for photographers (de Laguna 1991). Yet another Winter and Pond image, described as portraying a "traditional" shaman, makes no attempt to romanticize him and shows him standing outside wearing Western ready-made

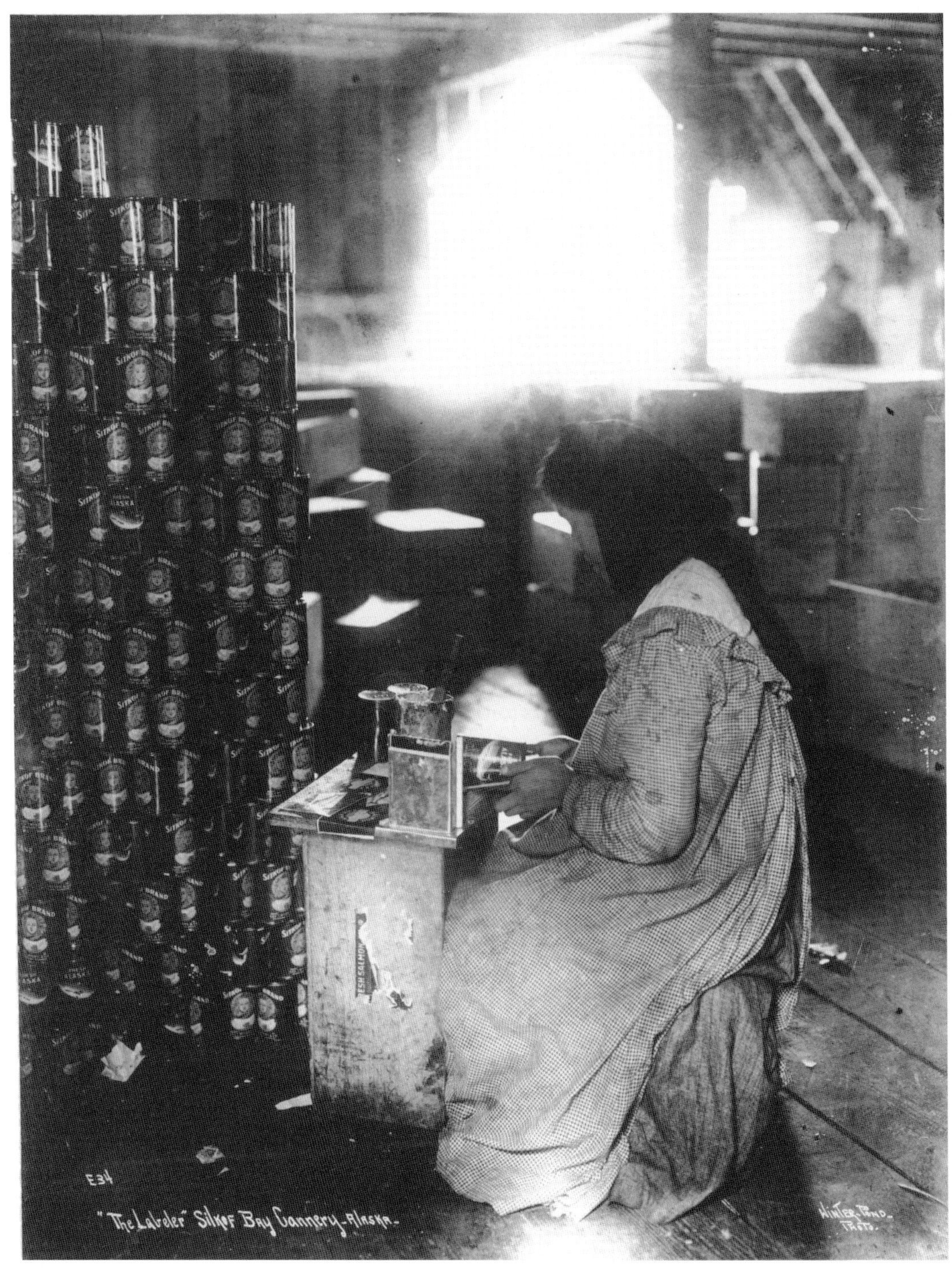

Figure 41
"'The Labeler,' Silkof [Sitkoh] Bay Cannery, Alaska," c. 1907–10. Tlingit woman attaches Sitkof brand labels to canned salmon. Photograph by Winter & Pond. By permission of the Alaska State Library, Juneau, AK. (P87–0190)

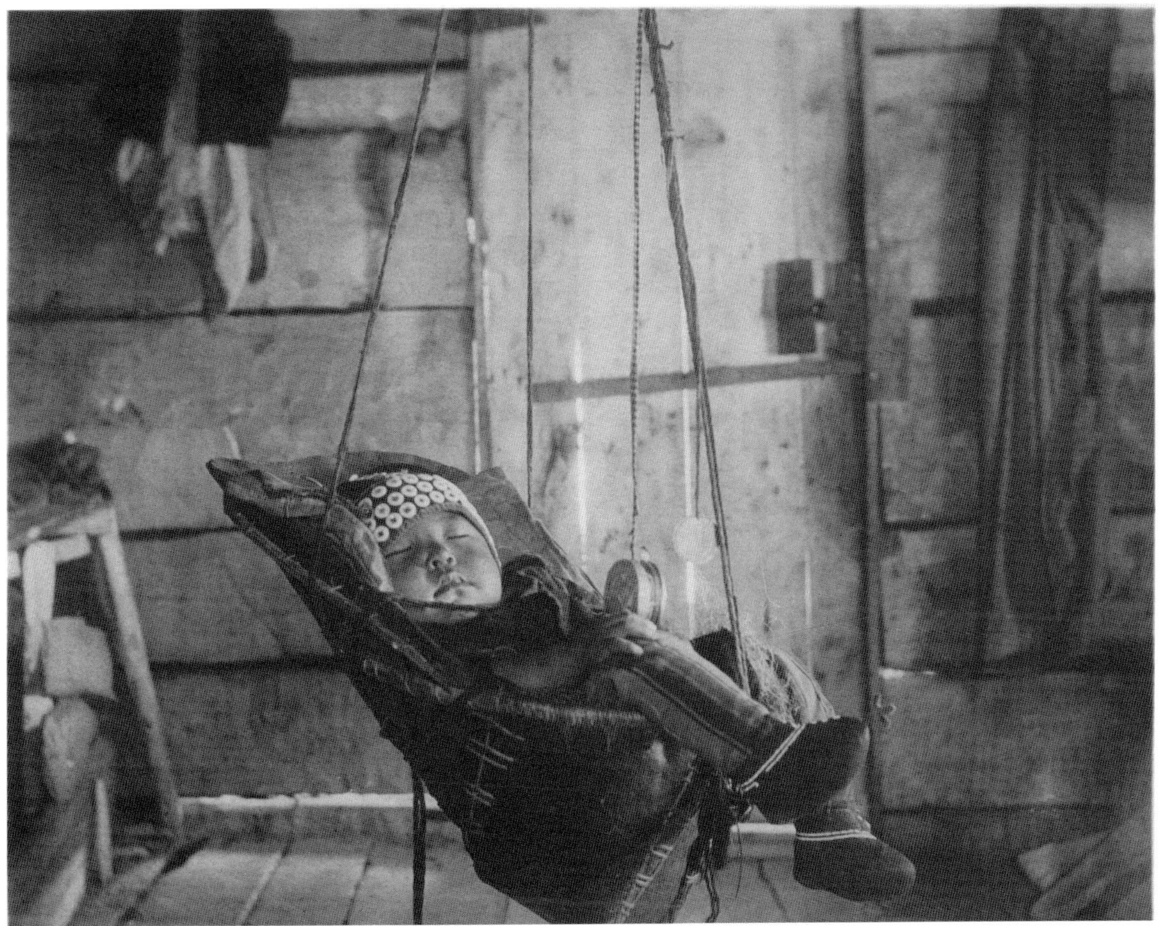

Figure 42
"Alaska Slumberland," 1905. This image was marketed as a Christmas card by the Winter & Pond Studio of Juneau. By permission of the Museum of History and Industry, Seattle, WA. (SHS 1765).

clothing. Figure 41 of a woman cannery worker likewise openly shows one of the modern developments then transforming Tlingit life.

Winter and Pond sold many Tlingit photographs over the years, including an unmanipulated but sentimental view of a Tlingit infant in a hammock cradle which they marketed as a Christmas card (Fig. 42). Their most widely distributed images, according to Victoria Wyatt, show Natives who appear economically impoverished or not "prosperous in European terms" which probably reflected the reality of the time

for most Tlingits (1992:29).

William H. Case and Herbert Draper also opened a studio in Juneau after working in Lake Bennett for several years (Fig. 43). They produced a range of images of Native people, from naturalistic scenes of outdoor activities, ceremonial events like Sitka's 1904 potlatch, and formal studio portraits, to re-enactments (Fig. 44) and soft porn. Unlike Winter and Pond, they frequently appealed to Euro-American stereotypes of Native people: stoic savage, warrior, chanting witch doctor, sexually available women. Their images

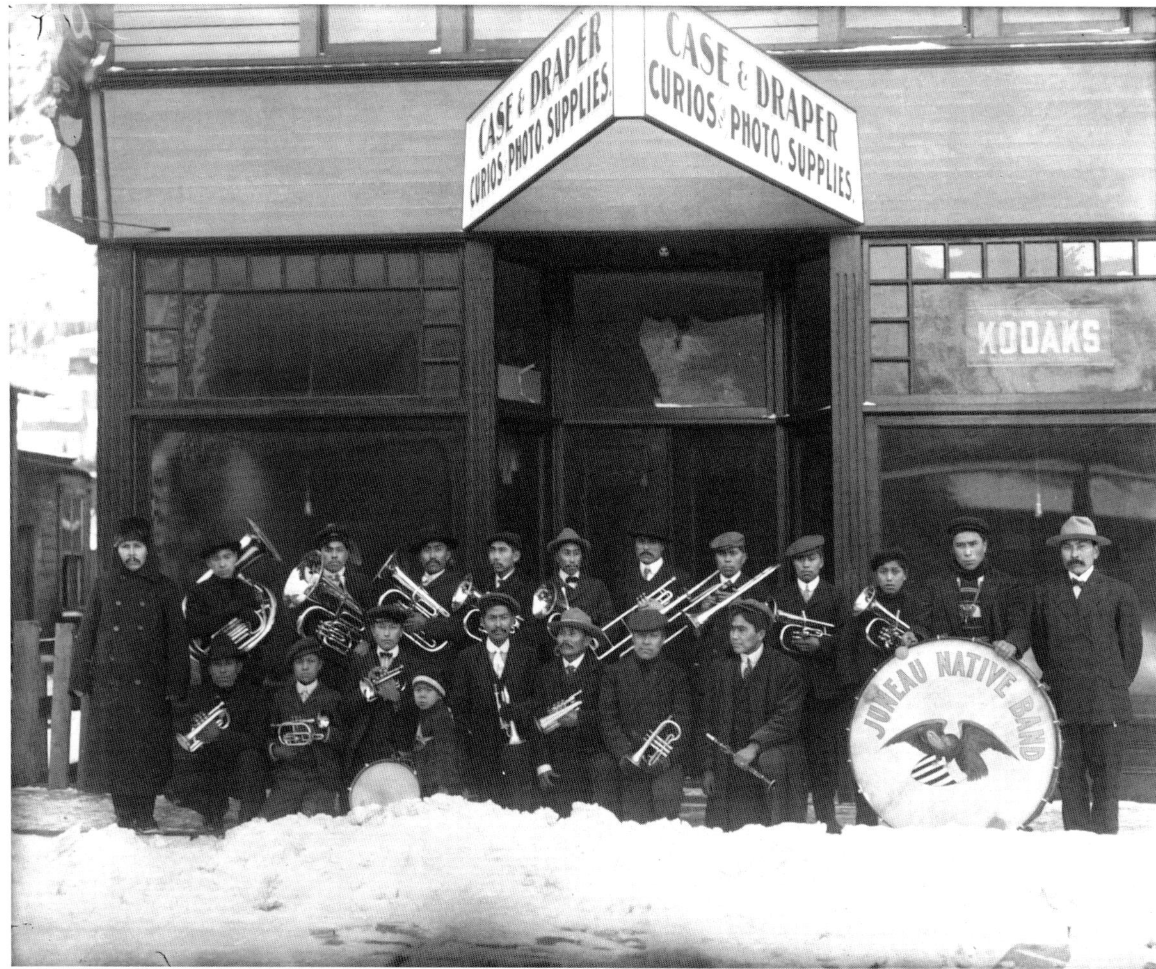

Figure 43
The Case & Draper Studio in winter with Juneau's Tlingit band, 1905. By permission of the Alaska State Library, Juneau, AK. (P226-184)

of Sxandu ú's curing ceremonies include colorful captions like "Skun-doo. A cunning, foxy, old medicine man, Kak-Yon-ton [Kaagwaantaan] clan of the Chilkats. The last of the notorious Indian shaman" and "The most notorious, crafty old medicine-man of all the Thlinget [*sic*] shaman."

Words like *crafty*, *foxy*, *cunning*, and *notorious* resonated with Euro-Americans, calling up stereotypes of Natives as elusive and untrustworthy. When such language was combined with imagery that showed Sxandu u wearing a bear claw head-dress and bone necklace and holding a rattle, the message communicated was superstitious savagery. Alan Trachtenburg has similarly shown how the meaning of Civil War photographs changed once they were captioned and placed in albums. When viewed separately without captions, the carnage and waste was all too apparent. When arranged with interpretive captions and viewed collectively, the images took on the look of a noble crusade (Thompson 2003).

The Case and Draper studio also produced

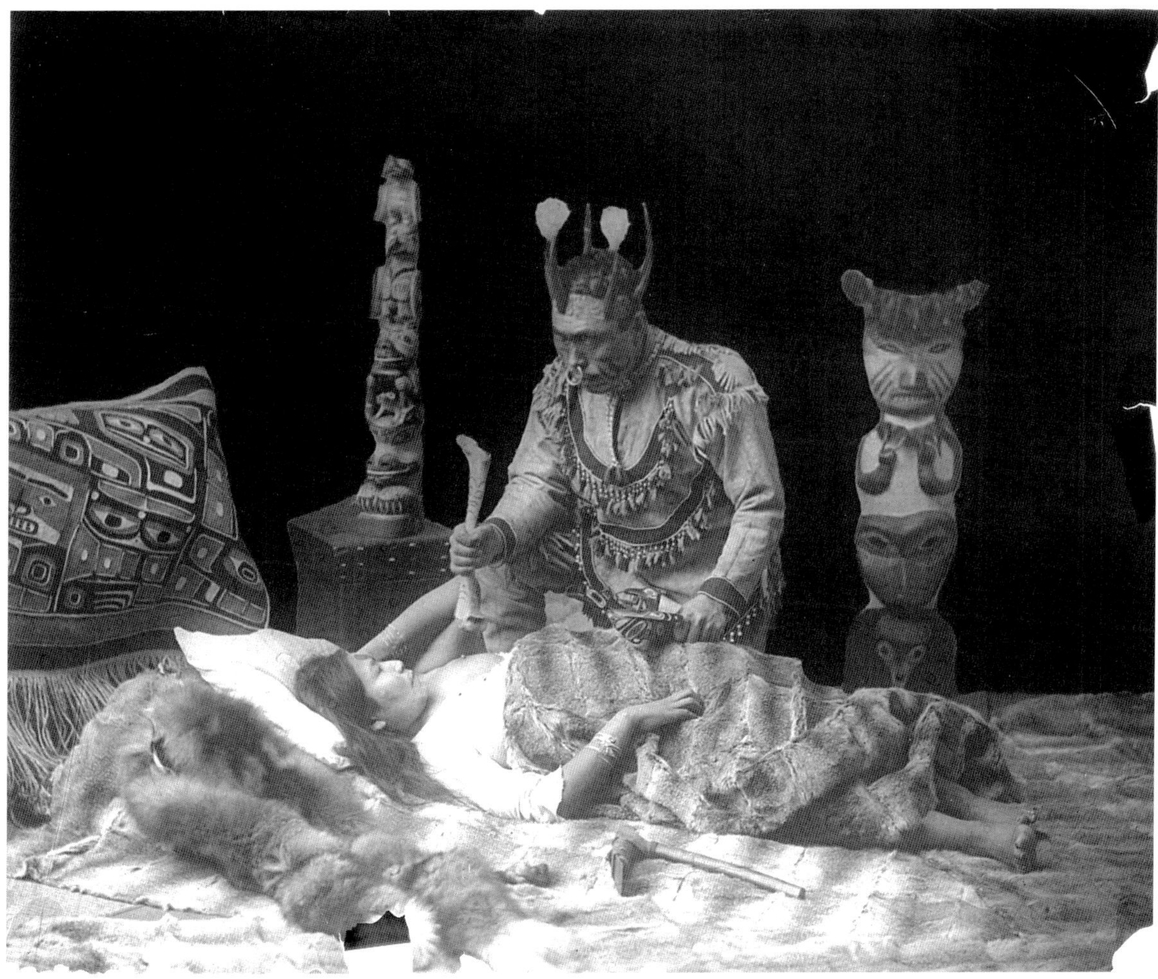

semi-nude images of Tlingit women. Two of their popular models were "Stene-Tu" and "Kaw-Claa." "Stene-tu" is variously described in captions as "Stene-Tu, the Kluk-wan princess," "Mrs. Stene-Tu, A Thlinget belle," "Chilkat maiden," and a "Type of Chilkat beauty." Those of another model named "Sha-e-dah-kla" are variously captioned "Reverie of a Stickene Maiden" (Fig. 45), "Type of Stickene Clutch," "Stickene Maiden," and "Type of North American Amazon." All images are in the U.S. Library of Congress (Lot 12930F).

Following Barthes (1964), one of the first to discuss how linguistic messages frame viewers' interpretations and feelings about photographic images, it is easy to understand how words like *maiden*, *clutch*, *Amazon*, *beauty*, *belle*, and *princess* served to further sexualize these semi-nude images. "Amazons" were a mythical race of female warriors, alleged by Herodotus to exist in Scythia.

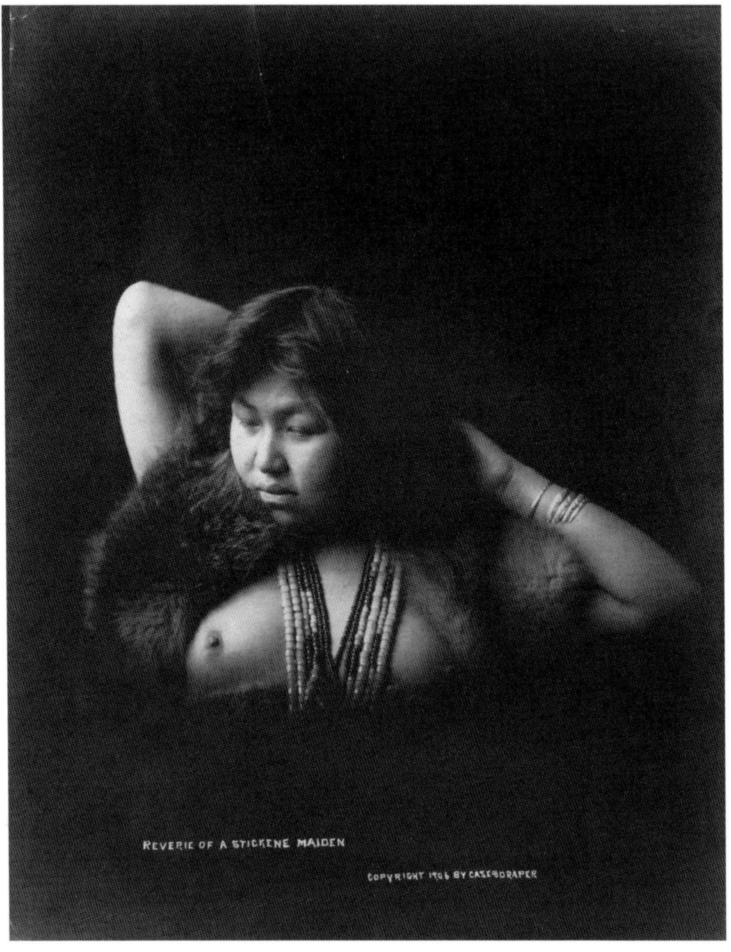

Figure 45
"Reverie of a Stickene Maiden," 1906.
The model is identified as "Sha-
e-dah-kla." Photograph by Case &
Draper. Courtesy of the U.S. Library
of Congress, Washington, DC. (LC–
USZ62–127138)

most likely combined the late 19th century reference to the physical proximity of dance partners with the meaning to hold tightly. "Girl," while a perfectly neutral term when applied to a female child, in the late 19th century carried the additional meanings of prostitute, maid-servant, and sweetheart. Likewise, "maiden," a young unmarried girl, suggested maid-servant, virgin, and something that had never been taken before. Both "girl" and "maiden" when applied to adult women denied them the maturity and respect their adult status deserved. The terms suggested instead that the women pictured were as dependent and compliant as young girls and, therefore, available to the viewer. Such captioning—especially when combined with semi-nude poses—suggested the sexual availability of Tlingit women, some of whom were then engaged in prostitution in mining areas (Crosby 1914:174).

The poses also clearly presented the women as objects of sexual scrutiny and desire. The subject in Figure 45 has downcast eyes, and her arms are held behind her head in a provocative manner that projects the fantasy of availability. She wears

What could be more exotic? "Princess," while literally meaning a female sovereign or female relative of a male sovereign, has a long history of use as a reference to young American Indian women and was exotic in the democratic context of American society. When used to caption a semi-nude image, it also suggested that viewers were being given voyeuristic access to a high-status woman. "A beauty" in the most literal sense simply refers to a beautiful person or object; colloquially it implies an exceptionally good specimen. (In the 19th century it also carried the slang meaning of vagina.) "Belle" referred to a handsome woman who worked to enhance her personal charms, presumably with seduction in mind. "Clutch"

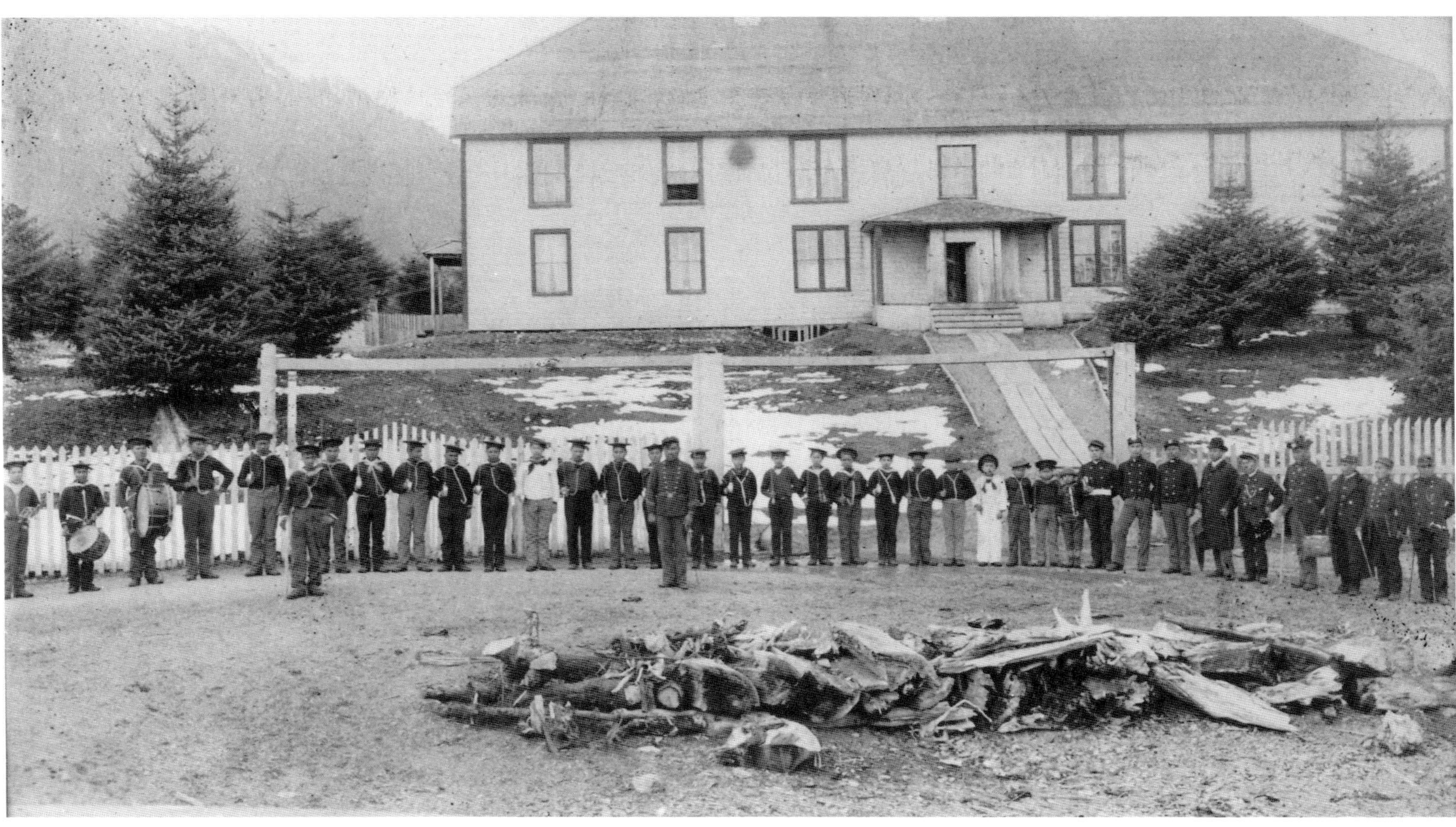

Figure 46
"Sitka Industrial Training School band," 1890. Photograph by Reuben Albertstone. By permission of the Presbyterian Historical Society, Philadelphia, PA. (RG 23–13, no. 563)

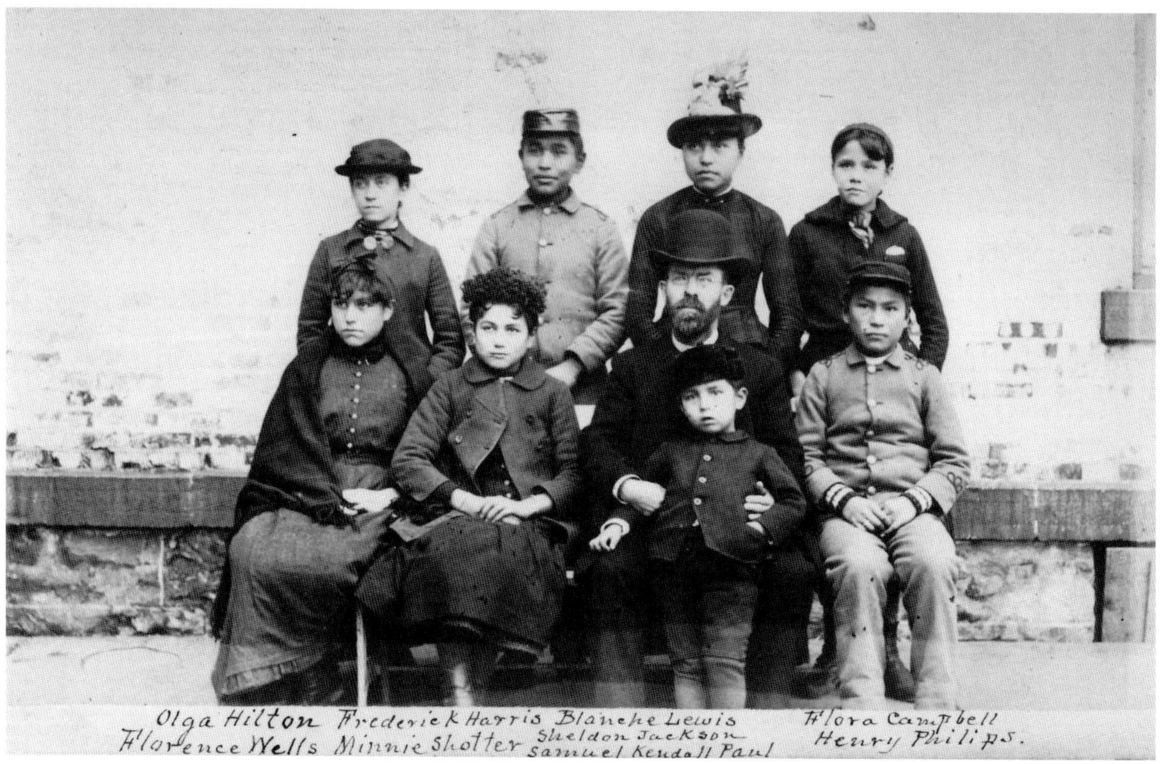

Figure 47
Sitka Industrial Training School students on their way to school in Northfield, MA, pose with Sheldon Jackson in Sitka in 1886. Back row left to right: Olga Hilton, Frederick Harris, Blanche Lewis, and Flora Campbell. Front row left to right: Florence Wells, Minnie Sholter, Sheldon Jackson holding Samuel Kendall Paul, and Henry Phillips. Photographed by Dr. C. P. Marshall. By permission of the Presbyterian Historical Society, Philadelphia, PA. (RG 239-12-30, no. 496)

fur and beads, signifying her closeness to nature (and, perhaps, animalistic desires) and her exotic "Indianness." Another subject is posed with her forefinger demurely held against her chin, suggesting girl-like innocence. She is also dressed to heighten her exotic appeal, with face paint, a shaman's crown of carved mountain goat horns which mimic bear claws, and a Chilkat blanket normally worn by high-status Tlingit as a ceremonial robe.

Although decisions made by the photographer about captioning, pose, and clothing frame how viewers react to and understand a photograph, ultimately it is the viewer who determines what an image means. Once a photograph is taken, it becomes an object that is independent of the time and circumstances under which it was made. The image—whether an original photograph, a postcard, or a reprinted illustration—is reinterpreted by its viewers in terms of their own background and personal desires. These images were probably marketed to Juneau miners.

Sitka's first resident photographer was apparently Reuben Albertstone, who opened the Sitka View and Portrait Company around 1890 (Fig. 46), working initially with L. Moosbauer. Evidence of another Sitka studio exists in a single cabinet card showing the shoreline of Sitka Sound with the buildings of the Sitka Industrial Training School behind. On the back is printed:

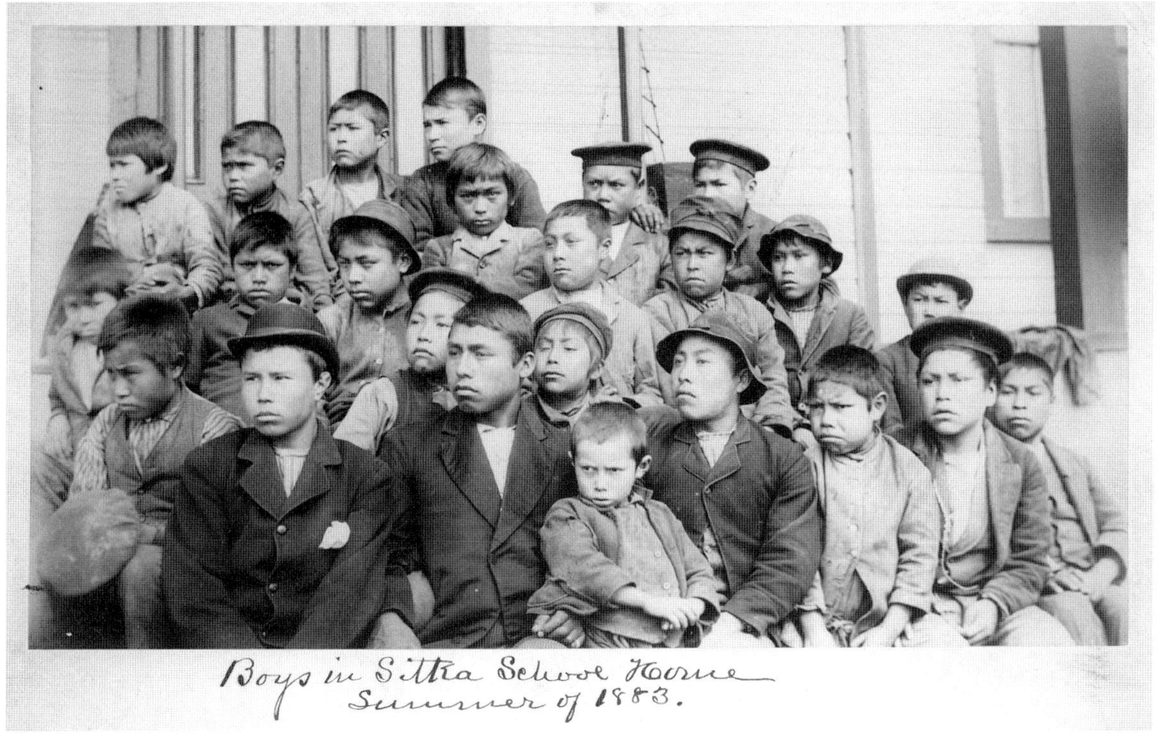

Figure 48
"Boys in Sitka School Home, summer of 1883." Photograph sent by Linnie Austin to Sheldon Jackson. Photographer unknown. By permission of the Presbyterian Historical Society, Philadelphia, PA. (RG 239–12–30, no. 494)

"E. Chamberlain, photographic studio, Sitka, Alaska. This negative is carefully preserved for future orders. Duplicates and enlargements furnished at any time." I could find nothing more about this studio, which was followed by Elbridge W. Merrill, whose work is discussed in detail in the next chapter.

Resident amateur photographers also began photographing the Tlingit in the 1880s, including missionaries and the staff at the Sitka Industrial Training School. Dr. C.P. Marshall's familiarity with his Tlingit sitters is not only evident from their poses, but also by his naming of them (Fig. 47). The students are not anonymous or specimen Natives going off to school but real people with hopes, dreams, and fears about the future. Bertrand Wilbur, a Presbyterian medi-

cal missionary, took many photographs between 1894 and 1901, once noting that "the water at Sitka was so cold that it was difficult to wash out the hypo but I did not realize it at the time I was making my prints. I did all my own developing and printing for a while, but later sent the plates to Seattle where they were eventually lost" (Wilbur 1979).

Other missionaries, such as S. Hall Young at Wrangell, also took photographs. An image in an album kept by David Waggoner, a missionary from 1901 to 1928, shows Young holding his camera, seated with a group of Tlingit elders and deacons from Angoon. Candid snapshots taken by Waggoner show Alaska Native Brotherhood delegates attending a 1927 convention in Angoon and people gathered for a church service at a sum-

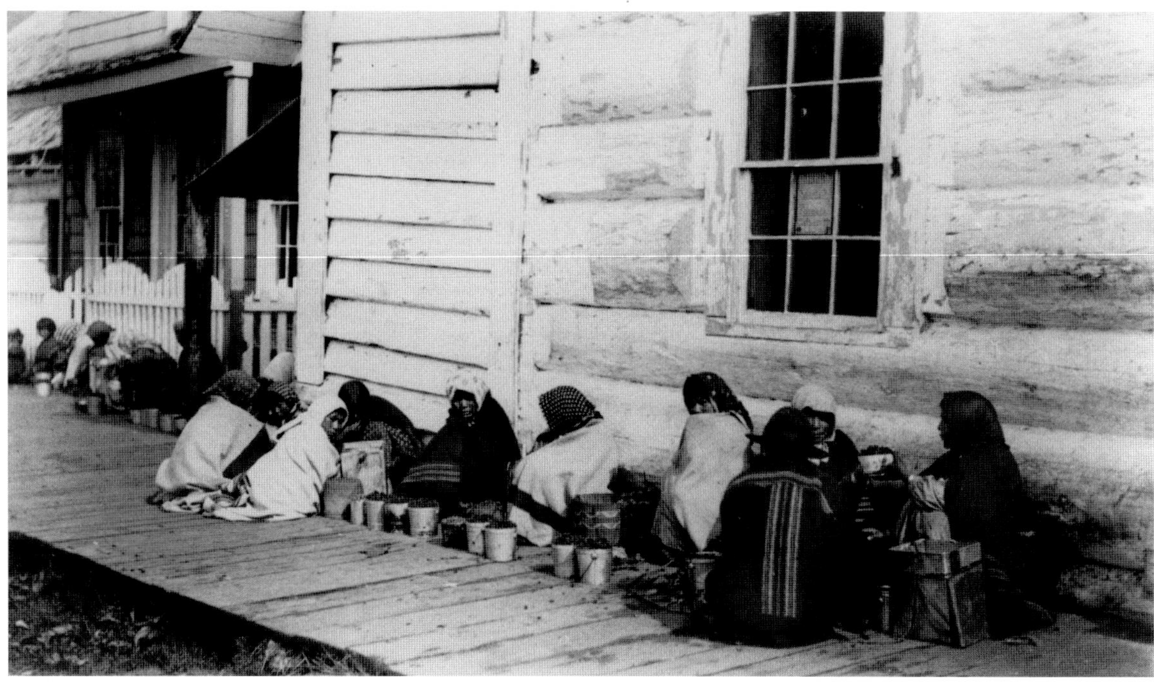

Figure 49
Tlingit vendors selling salmon berries at Sitka, 1887. Photograph by Bertram C. Towne. By permission of the University of Washington Libraries, Seattle, WA. Special Collections. (NA 1503)

mer fish camp. The Reverend Sheldon Jackson likewise took photographs, but many more were mailed to him by teachers and other school staff to help him document the Presbyterian mission's work. A group portrait of 24 Tlingit boys attending Sitka's boarding school was sent to him "compliments of [teacher] Linnie Austin" (Fig. 48).

The Sitka Industrial School also commissioned photographs of the mission's students to show the miraculous change Tlingit children were undergoing. Some were published in the school's newspaper, others were sent south and used as illustrations in church publications to garner financial support for the school's work. While some people considered such change to be a loss, missionaries extolled it and were eager to spread the good news of Christianization and assimilation through their reports, letters, lectures, and photographs.

In the October 1910 issue, *The Thlingit* published a photograph of women vendors sitting in front of the old Russian trading post on Lincoln Street selling salmon berries more than 20 years earlier (Fig. 49), describing the scene as that of "some of the older women from the native village who have never been in the school." The paper contrasted this image with one of neatly uniformed students who it described as "the younger generation—a generation reaching out for new things: a written language, practical means of working, greater pleasures, added cares, new hopes, new faith, a new life." The women vendors, on the other hand, represented a "passing people," the "old life," and "a declining age."

Missionaries and Native boarding schools in other places also used photography to support their work. Frederick Dally noted that the priests and Natives at a mission he visited in British Columbia intentionally adopted a prayer pose for his camera (Marr 1982:15). Elsewhere in the U.S. a federally funded system of Indian boarding schools was established, based largely on the Carlisle Indian School (1879–1918) started by Captain Richard Pratt, a career military officer and Christian reformer. To Pratt, Indian societies were indolent, superstitious, and communistic, in contrast to Western civilization which was industrious, enlightened, and individualistic. The schools used a curriculum centered on discipline, English-language instruction, and healthy doses of Christianity to effect change. Male students were taught trades and agriculture, while girls were taught domestic skills. Both followed a rigid regimen of discipline and timed activities. "The goal of the boarding schools...was no less than transformation of the soul" (Margolis 2004:75). Pratt sent photographs to politicians, parents, tribal leaders, and reservation officials and included them in annual reports and as illustrations in religious and popular periodicals.

Although Sitka's Industrial School was not part of this system, its curriculum and mode of operation were much the same. Military-like discipline was maintained with student life marching swiftly to the sound of bells. Edward Marsden, once a Tsimshian student at the school and later a Presbyterian minister, described the students' daily routine in the March 1890 issue of the *North Star*, the school newspaper. The wakeup bell rang at 6:00 in the morning (at 4:40 or 5:00 for those helping in the kitchen); six bells regulated the flow of breakfast, including a bell to rise when finished, a second to turn, and a third to march out; fifteen bells marked the time allotted to march to class; five bells signaled lunch, followed by the verbal commands "Fall in line. Attention. Right face. Mark time. Forward march" into the dining room. More bells regulated classes and the work schedule. The last bell of the day was the call to prayer at 7:30 at night. An hour later a bugle blew for bedtime and again at 8:40 for lights out.

Boys and girls were carefully segregated, with separate dormitories and hospitals. According to Tlingit elder Jessie Weir Price, an early graduate of the school, in an interview in Sitka on August 30, 1987:

> The boys stayed on the one side of campus, and we stayed on the opposite side. During the meals, the boys couldn't sit with us...Thanksgiving and Christmas time was the only time we had mixed tables. When they said grace in the morning, they rang the bell in the dining hall for everyone to be quiet, and then somebody said a prayer. When we were through eating, the girls had to remain seated. We couldn't get up. The woman in charge rang the bell, and the boys stood up. They were quite sure the boys were all across campus before they rang the bell for the girls. But we accepted it because that's the way things were.

The children were also monitored by the school's administration. One superintendent conducted an inquiry among the girls after several boys were caught climbing the fire escape to talk to them, and, according to concerned officials, were only "prevented from entering [the girls' dormitory] by the wire screen over the windows and the sealed window of the fire escape" (Condit 1922). Misconduct was dealt with quickly. After two boys pilfered from a Tlingit-owned store in town, the owner helped the school set a trap. When the boys came in again and one of them slipped a jar of jam into his pocket, he was arrested and taken to jail. The two boys later met with Sitka's Judge DeArmond, who gave them a stern lecture and made them apologize and make restitution to the store's owner. They also had to apologize to the student body and faculty of the school and write a full account of the affair for their fathers (not their maternal uncles which would have made more sense, given Tlingit matrilineal descent). Judge DeArmond vetted their accounts and later read the replies they received. Finally, the boys were told to make it right with God (Condit 1923).

Most of the time children at the boarding

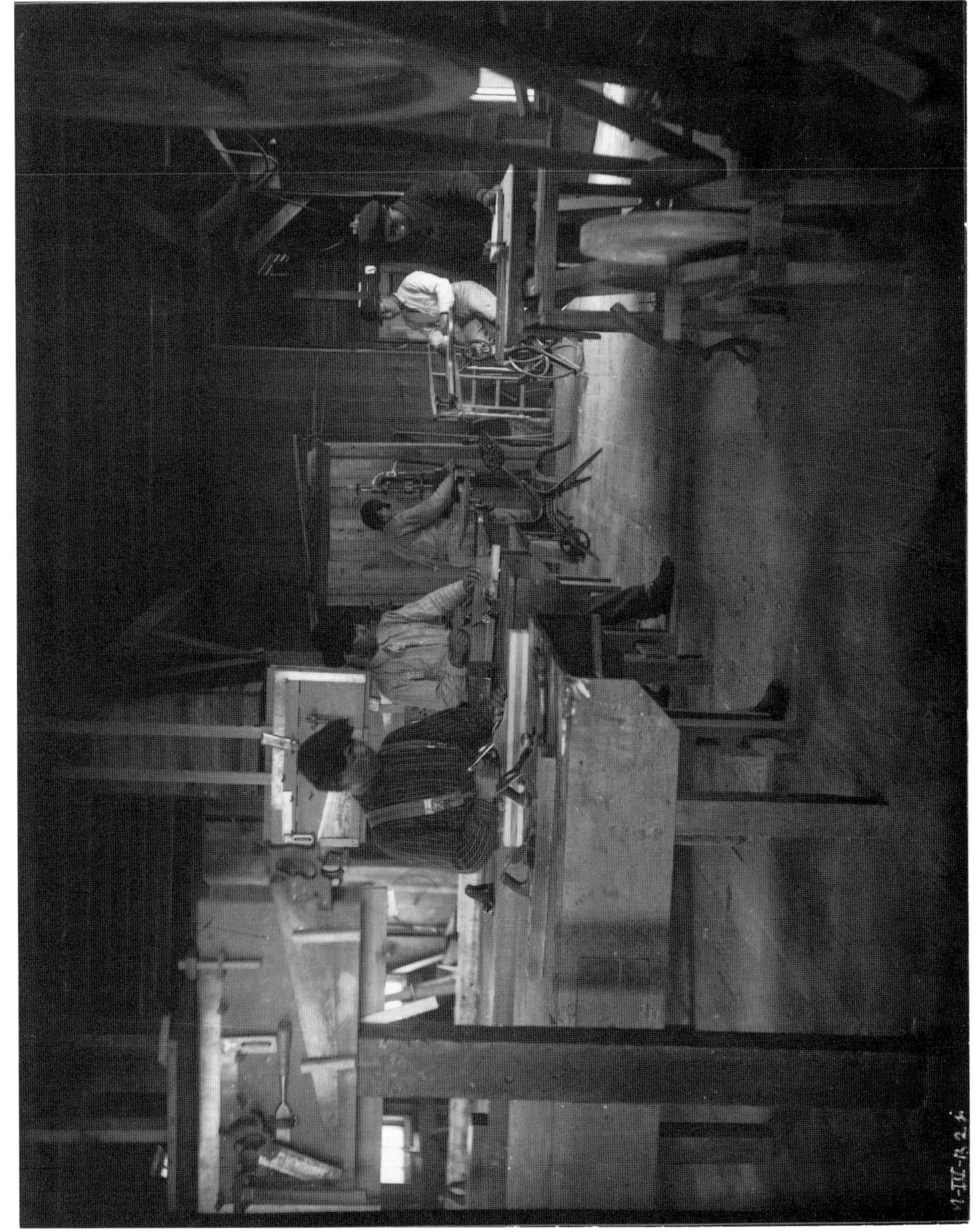

Figure 50.
Sitka Industrial Training School boys work at carpentry. Photograph by E. W. Merrill. Courtesy of Stratton Library, Sheldon Jackson College, Sitka, AK. (M IV B2j)

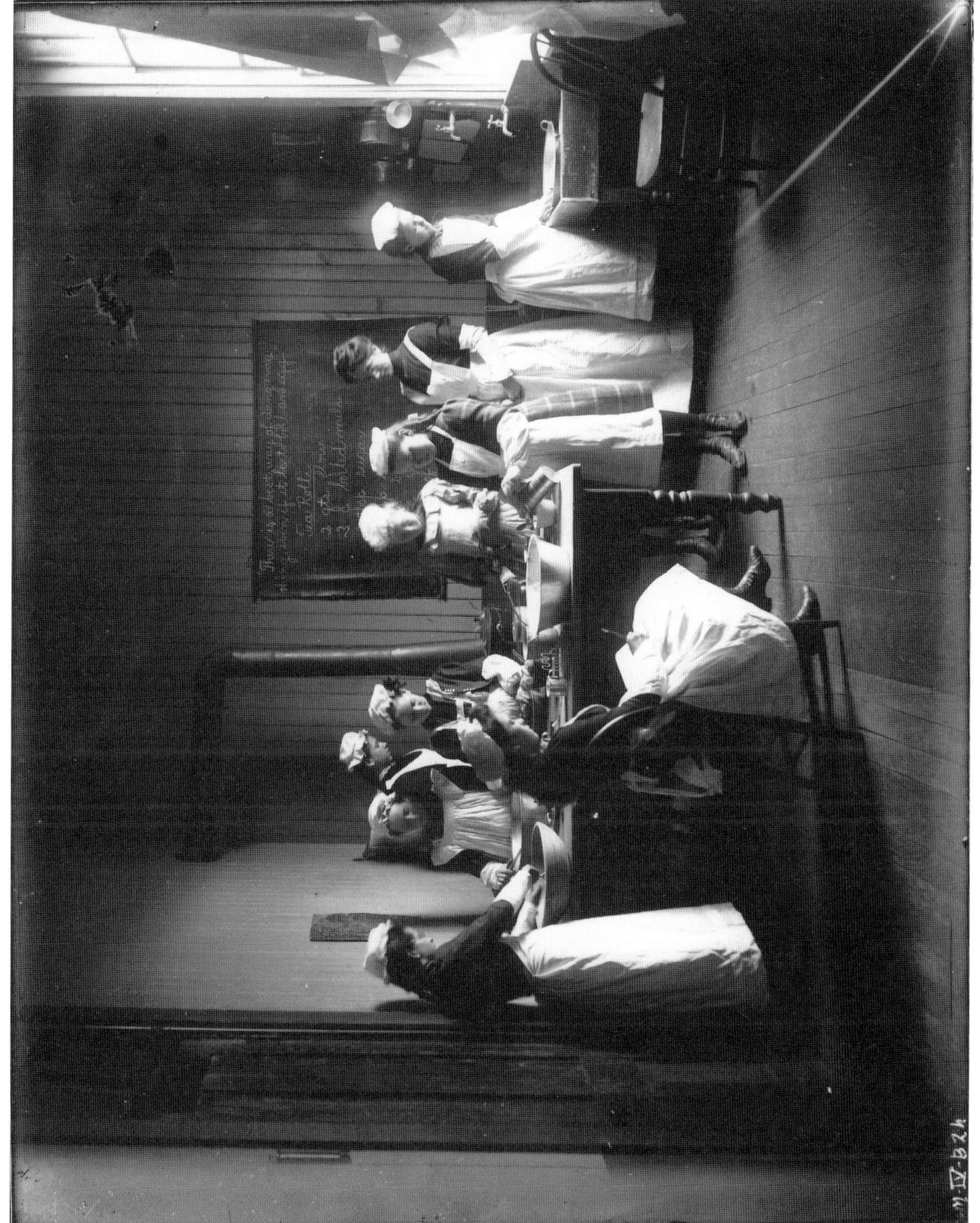

Figure 51

Cooking class at Sitka Industrial Training School. Non-Native girls sometimes joined the classes. Photograph by E. W. Merrill. Courtesy of Stratton Library, Sheldon Jackson College. Sitka, AK. (M IV B2h)

school were too busy to get into trouble. Half the student body attended school in the morning, while the other half worked. In the afternoon, they reversed. Boys typically worked in the garden, chopped wood, took care of dormitory and campus repairs, and performed errands and small jobs in the bakery, kitchen, dining room, and laundry. Boys also learned trades, including shoe making, carpentry, blacksmithing, pipe fitting, boat building, steam engineering, and machine repair (Fig. 50). Girls learned to cook, sew, and maintain a home and were kept busy working in the school's laundry, bakery, kitchen, dining room, and their own dormitory. The message on the blackboard in Figure 51 seems to underscore the school's ethnocentric and assimilationist stance: "There is a best way of doing everything even if it be to boil an egg." In 1919 the students built a "practice house" out of a run-down cottage on campus. Here they learned Euro-Amer-

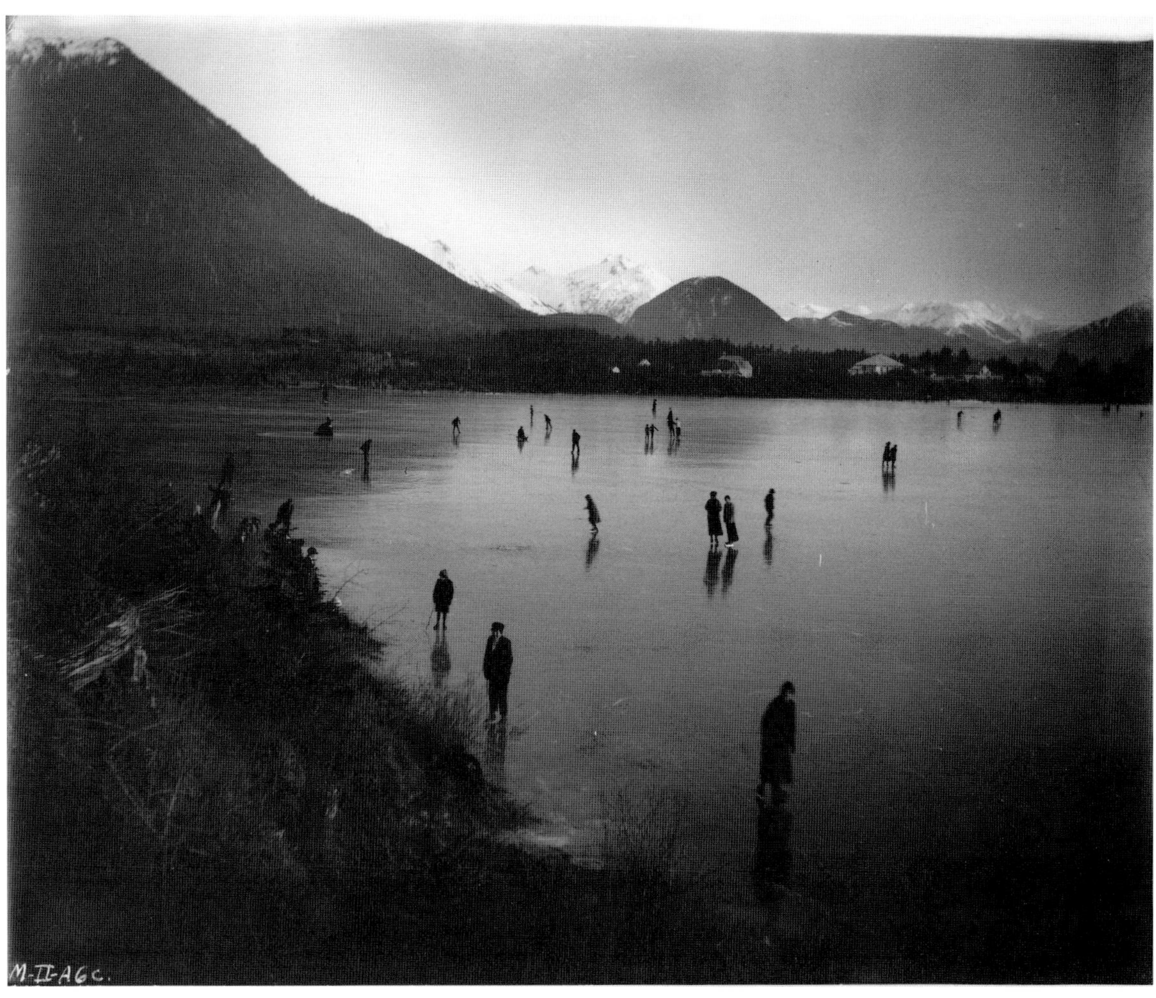

Figure 52
Skaters on Swan Lake, Sitka. Photograph by E. W. Merrill. Courtesy of Stratton Library, Sheldon Jackson College, Sitka, AK. (M II A6c)

ican living habits. Jessie Weir Price, a graduate and devout Presbyterian, recalled on August 30, 1986, that

> the boys came and did all the repairs, fixed the furnace, and fixed the windows. And we [girls] went there as students in the home economics department. We made curtains and scrubbed down the building. And they taught us how to invite people out to our homes. They even taught us how to place a napkin...a certain corner had to be someplace so you could put it up. Those things we were taught...Those days we paid only fifty dollars a year [tuition, about $500 in 2007] if we had it. If we didn't, it was okay. We just did the work for our keep, which was really wonderful because most of us couldn't afford anything.

Students at Sitka's mission school also had band, glee club, and choral practices and a student newspaper to publish, as reported in the *North Star* (1888–99), the *Thlinget* (1908–12), and the *Verstovian* (1914). Tlingit children especially enjoyed music and "seemed to be able to pick up any instrument and to read music almost by instinct" (Wilbur 1979:258). Religious instruction also took up their time, though their teachers often despaired about the depth of their devotion.

Most boys looked forward to their half-day hunting trips and to fishing from one of the school's Columbia River boats. In winter they had skating parties at Swan Lake in the middle of town (Fig. 52). After a student saved Naval Ensign Coontz from drowning after he fell through the ice, Coontz "settled a small life pension on the boy which he left in the hands of Reverend Alonzo Austin [superintendent of the school]" (Coontz 1930:133). The mission's students "were always ready for fun and loved a joke and were a healthy happy lot," in the opinion of medical missionary Bertrand Wilbur (1979:258).

While undoubtedly correct, this opinion overlooks a number of other truths. Boarding school was a difficult transition. According to

one teacher, writing in the late 1890s, during their little free time children "sat carving their favorite and odd figures of fish and crow. Miniature ships, too, they get up with ingenuity, full rigged, and little Indian canoes" (Mayberry 1853:14). Children often stole off in small gangs to speak Tlingit among themselves which the school forbade. The December 1908 issue of the *Thlinget* explained that the language was doomed to disappear and that its lack of written characters—at the time—meant that if their students retained it, they "would forever remain intellectual paupers." Teachers and administrators also believed that those who learned and spoke English abandoned their "old customs" sooner.

Some students resisted. "Selena McCullough broke out in rebellion because I had refused to let her go home for summer," Superintendent James Condit noted in his diary on March 30, 1923, "and [I] had to be backed up. Unrest among students because nine are going home with fish eggs people as we call them [visiting Tlingit] who are here for herring eggs" (Fig. 53).

When one Tlingit family took their daughter from the school to their summer fish camp and refused to send her back in 1922, Superintendent Condit went to considerable effort to find out why, as he recalled in his diary October 17. He eventually learned that "caste matters" were at the root of the problem; their daughter had been taunted at school as a "slave" by other Tlingit children. Her brother, who had been expelled earlier for misbehavior, was allowed back at the parents' insistence in order to lend his sister moral support.

The toll a boarding school education took on Tlingit children was more than emotional. Many suffered from illnesses—as did Tlingit living in the villages—although they received good care. In 1896 alone, missionary physician Bertrand Wilbur (despite his characterization of the students being a "healthy and happy lot") and nurse Ester Gibson treated 189 Tlingit patients, performed 93 operations, and dealt with a thousand outpatient visits. "Consumption" or tuber-

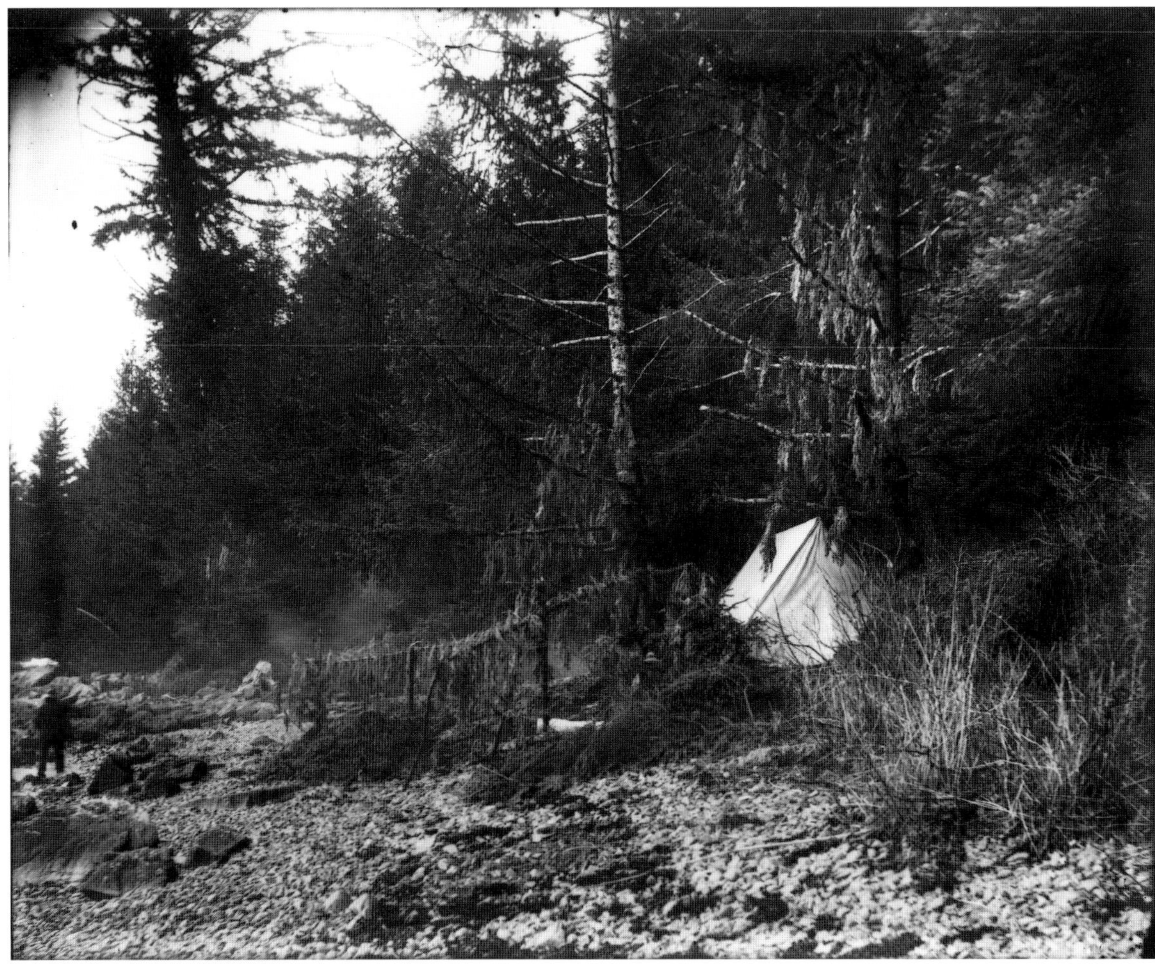

Figure 53
Herring egg camp near Sitka. Photograph by E. W. Merrill. Courtesy of Stratton Library, Sheldon Jackson College, Sitka, AK. (M II B10f)

culosis was an especially serious problem, and very ill students were sometimes forced to leave school for the safety of others. Principal Lottie Stevenson, who had been at the school since 1914, reported in the mid-1920s that the school had lost 25 percent of its students to tuberculosis (Yaw 1985:36).

This side of the students' lives was not discernible in the photographs used by the Sitka school which were characterized by a particular iconography only partially due to the require-

ments of group portraiture. Most were posed images taken in front of school buildings and sometimes in the classroom. The Western-style buildings, neat grounds and classrooms, clean uniforms, and symmetrical arrangements of the student group portraits—with teachers authoritatively positioned—emphasized order, discipline, and obedience (Fig. 54). While they were intended to demonstrate that the Tlingit were being successfully Christianized and Americanized, none could reveal the actual thoughts or beliefs

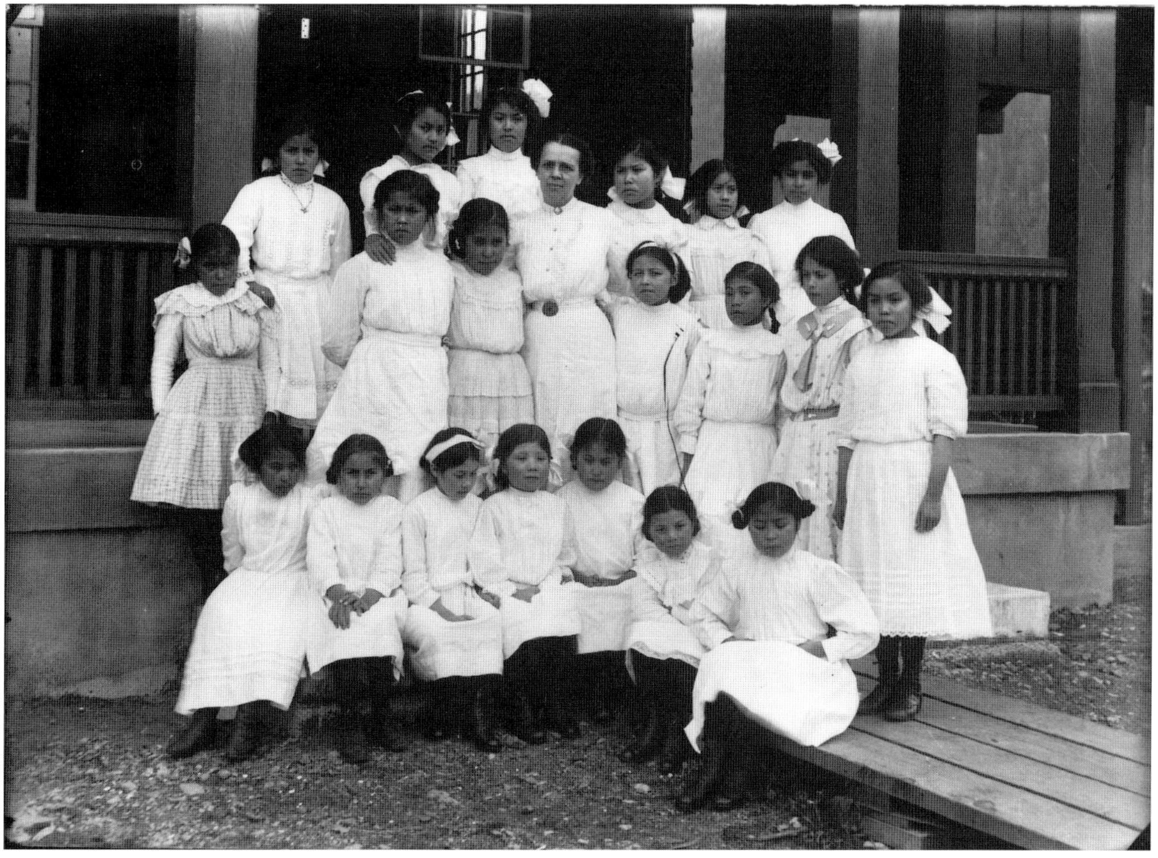

Figure 54
Sitka Industrial Training School students cooperate for the camera, 1900. Photograph by E. W. Merrill. Courtesy of the Sitka National Historical Park, Sitka, AK. (3745)

of the children in the images. Most children are expressionless or distracted, concentrating on keeping still for the camera and its non-Native photographer. The photographs do not show tears, illness, or despondency. Nor do they show children at play or left to their own devices. And oddly, none show individualism—that hallmark of American identity. As Eric Margolis found in his study of Indian boarding school photographs in the Lower 48, there are no photographs of "the winner of the spelling bee" or the single "champion athlete" (2004:77). The boarding school, including Sitka's with its indenture agreements, was a "total institution" controlling all aspects of

a child's life (Goffman 1961). The school did provide an education, however, which many Tlingit valued and which some students chose to pursue further after graduation by attending high school or college in the Lower 48.

Naval officer George T. Emmons, who was stationed in Sitka for 15 years between 1884 and 1899, was another amateur photographer who had close contact with the Tlingit. His law enforcement activities aboard the U.S.S. *Pinta* and his collecting work took him up and down the coast (Cole 1985). He soon developed an avid interest in Tlingit culture, learned the language (speaking it well enough to interpret on occasion),

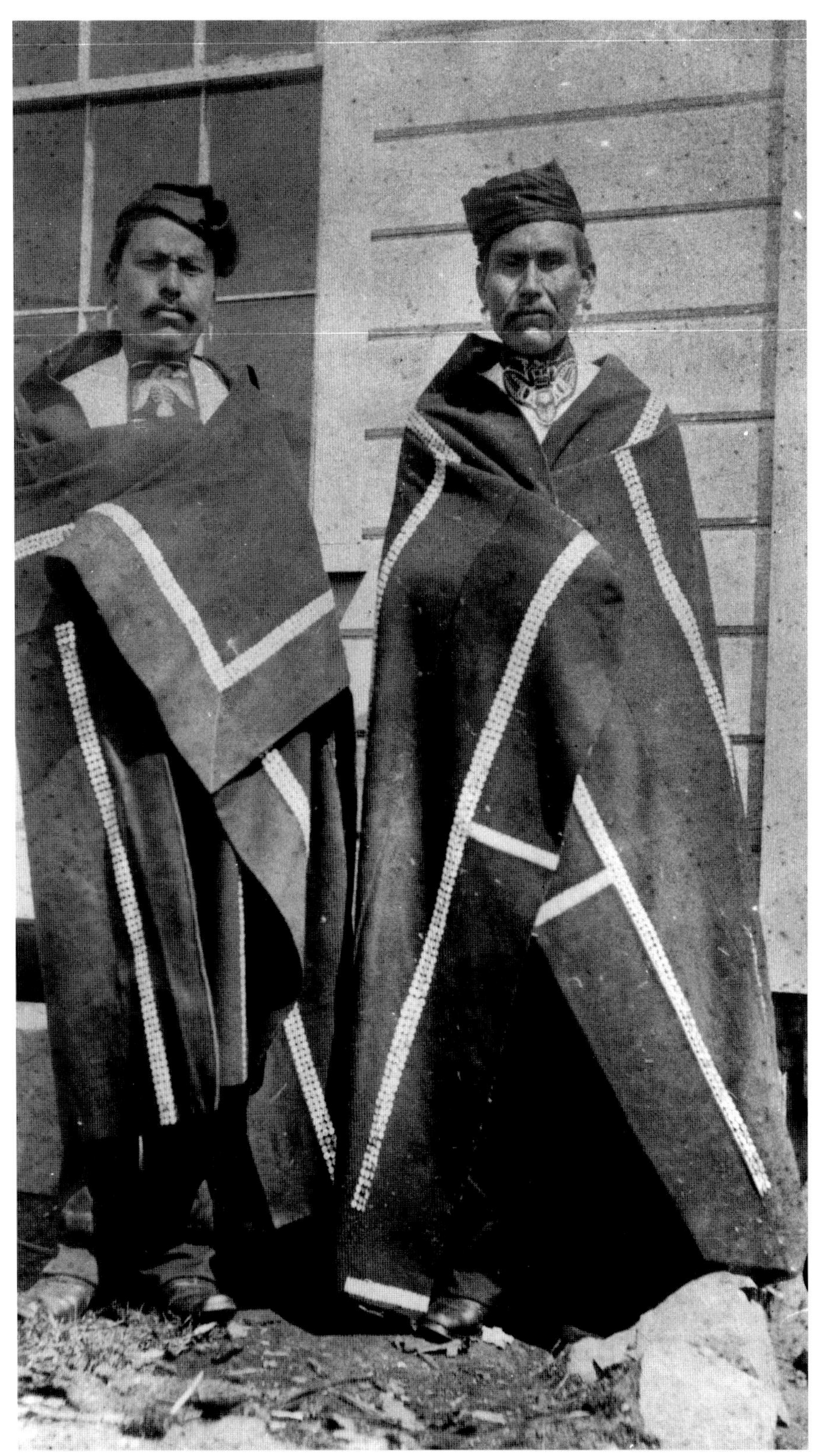

Figure 55
"Two Chiefs in dance blankets/ the left Sitka man—5 ft. 10 in., 160 lbs./ the right Chilkat man—5 ft. 10 in., 150 lbs.," 1880s. Photograph by George T. Emmons, attributed to Edward DeGroff. By permission of the University of Washington Libraries, Seattle, WA. Special Collections. (NA 2515)

and often traveled by canoe with Tlingit assistants to villages like Klukwan and Hoonah in search of old objects for his growing personal collection and to sell to museums. Emmons kept detailed provenance records on the thousands of artifacts he collected, amassed a wealth of ethnographic information for a planned book on Tlingit life (edited by de Laguna in 1991), and published several articles in anthropology journals on basketry, the Chilkat blanket, the potlatch, and other subjects. Even after he retired from the Navy and left Sitka, he returned to Alaska for many years to continue his research and collecting. During this long period, Emmons took many photographs of the Tlingit. Some images document ethnographic objects and processes, but others were taken of familiar scenes, the people he knew, and "backstage" activities like Tlingit tending a cremation fire. This contrasted sharply with the public activities that tourists and visiting commercial photographers typically caught on film. Emmons was clearly close to some Tlingit; in the opinion of his contemporary, Alaska Governor John G. Brady, the Tlingit "esteem him very much" (Cole 1985:243).

Emmons was especially close to the Shotridge family of Klukwan, and was honored by them upon the death of Chief Tschartritsch by being designated as the person who would bury his ceremonial robe (Low 1977). Nevertheless, Emmons's photographic gaze was often detached. On the back of a posed portrait of two Tlingit men wearing button blankets (Fig. 55), for example, he methodically noted "Two Chiefs in dance blankets/the left Sitka man—5 ft. 10 in., 160 lbs./the right Chilkat man—5 ft. 10 in., 150 lbs." The men are not named, although Emmons clearly knew them. The "scientific" notation shapes how we understand the image today and Emmons's relationship to the subjects. At the time, it reflected contemporary thinking about race and the scientific need to document differences as well as Emmons's own view of his "ethnographic" role. Despite his closeness to the Tlingit, he raided shamans' graves (as did other collectors, both non-

Natives and Tlingit) in his quest for artifacts, thus breaking a strong Tlingit taboo.

How he balanced his personal relationships and respect for Tlingit culture with the detachment evident in some of his photography and in his collecting activities is difficult to understand when viewed from today's perspective alone. While it is possible that Emmons simply allowed "his acquisitiveness to overcome his sensibilities," in the words of biographer Jean Low (1977:10), it seems more likely that he was committed to saving these objects for posterity (although he also profited from their sale).

It is important to note that Emmons was assisted in his collecting work by the Tlingit, most likely men who had been Christianized and were leaving their old customs behind and who undoubtedly believed that the clan regalia and sacred objects they were collecting would never again serve their original purpose. By Emmons's time some Tlingit had been involved in collecting for at least 20 years.

In 1867 Edward G. Fast, who was then stationed in Sitka, noted: "I congratulate myself upon having secured the assistance of several intelligent and courageous natives (one of them a medicine man of old), who at great personal risk scoured the country for hundreds of miles, obtaining many of the articles from ancient graves, to touch which is considered such a heinous sacrilege that their lives would have been sacrificed upon the spot had they been detected in the act" (1869:5-6). We do not know what payment they received from Fast or how dire their economic need may have been. Fast exhibited his enormous collection to the public in San Francisco and New York and then offered it for sale, asking $10,000. It was eventually sold to the Peabody Museum of Archaeology and Ethnology, now part of Harvard University, which considered the collection to be "so complete that it was thought advisable to keep all the objects belonging to it in one series" (Peabody Museum 1873:5). The Museum paid $2,500 (equivalent to nearly $45,000 in 2007) (Cole 1986:13).

As Virginia Dominguez (1986) has pointed out, artifact collecting must have conveyed mixed messages to Native people. On the one hand, collectors assigned "great value to a greater range of things [including utilitarian objects]" than the Tlingit themselves did, yet by assuming that the Tlingit should be willing to sell anything and even to raid their sacred sites, collectors ironically ended up assigning all Native things less value.

Photography was used by Alaska Governor John G. Brady during a collecting trip for the Alaska Exhibit to be held at the 1904 Louisiana Purchase Exposition in St. Louis. Brady had first come to Sitka as a Presbyterian missionary in 1878 and ended up becoming Alaska's governor. As such he had a close—if sometimes problematic—relationship with many Tlingit. As he collected totem poles and other Tlingit and Haida artifacts, he made sure that photographs were taken of them to give to their donors. "The chief engineer took photographs of all," he told his wife Elizabeth in a letter on November 24, 1903, "I hope he got good ones for I want to use them [on] the papers which I intend to give [the Tlingit]." Earlier, in 1902, Brady had made sure that photographs were taken to commemorate Haida Chief Sonihat's donation of a totem pole and war canoe from the village of Kaasan to display in the national historic park Brady was proposing to establish in Sitka. In this case, photographs were used not just for an outsider's purpose but were also given to Native people.

Other resident amateur photographers turned their cameras on the Tlingit. They include the mail clerk John E. Thwaites, customs agent Clarence Leroy Andrews of Sitka, community member and store owner Vincent Soboleff of Killisnoo and Angoon, cannery worker Fhoki (or Saiki) Kayamori of Yakutat, museum collector Louis Shotridge, himself a Tlingit, and George Johnston, an inland Tlingit from Teslin in the Canadian Yukon.

John E. Thwaites worked in southeast Alaska between 1905 and 1920 as a federal mail clerk. While living on the mail boat S.S. *Dora* for sev-eral years, he took full advantage of the mail service to photograph the Tlingit and other subjects and create photographic postcards of his Alaskan views. Figure 56 is captioned "Native couple at Shakan, Alaska. Each over *100 years* of age. They were curring [*sic*] up a seal when asked to pose." While Thwaites did not try to eliminate modern intrusions—non-Natives are clearly visible in the right of this image—he did, to some extent, emphasis the "exotic," such as curing a seal and living to great age.

C. L. Andrews was Sitka's customs officer in 1898. He took many photographs of the Tlingit, and his diaries provide important insights about how they responded to and used photography which will be discussed in Chapter 6. Andrews had learned the rudiments of photography the previous year when he accompanied a mountain-climbing expedition up Mt. St. Elias. Rather than return to Seattle at the expedition's end, he decided to stay in Alaska and secured a job with the U.S. Customs Service in Sitka. He later moved to Skagway and then Eagle, Alaska. Self-taught in Russian, he became a recognized authority on Alaskan history, and in 1909 he was appointed head of the information bureau at the Alaska Building at the Alaska Yukon Pacific Exposition in Seattle. He later served as a journalist for the *Alaska-Yukon Magazine* and the *Alaska Daily Empire* and was employed by the U.S. Bureau of Education's School and Reindeer Service and took many photographs of the Eskimo at this time.

In 1922 Andrews published *The Story of Sitka*, a short history and guidebook, reprinted in 1981. It included 14 illustrations—10 photographs and 4 drawings—but none were of Tlingit subjects with the partial exception of one image of the Tlingit village from a distance. Andrews may not have considered the Tlingit to be exotic subjects to be visually exploited. He did bemoan the replacement of their "picturesque" canoes by gas boats, but largely because he admired the technical skill and craftsmanship that had gone into making the canoes. "The loss in the picturesque is partly compensated by the gain in

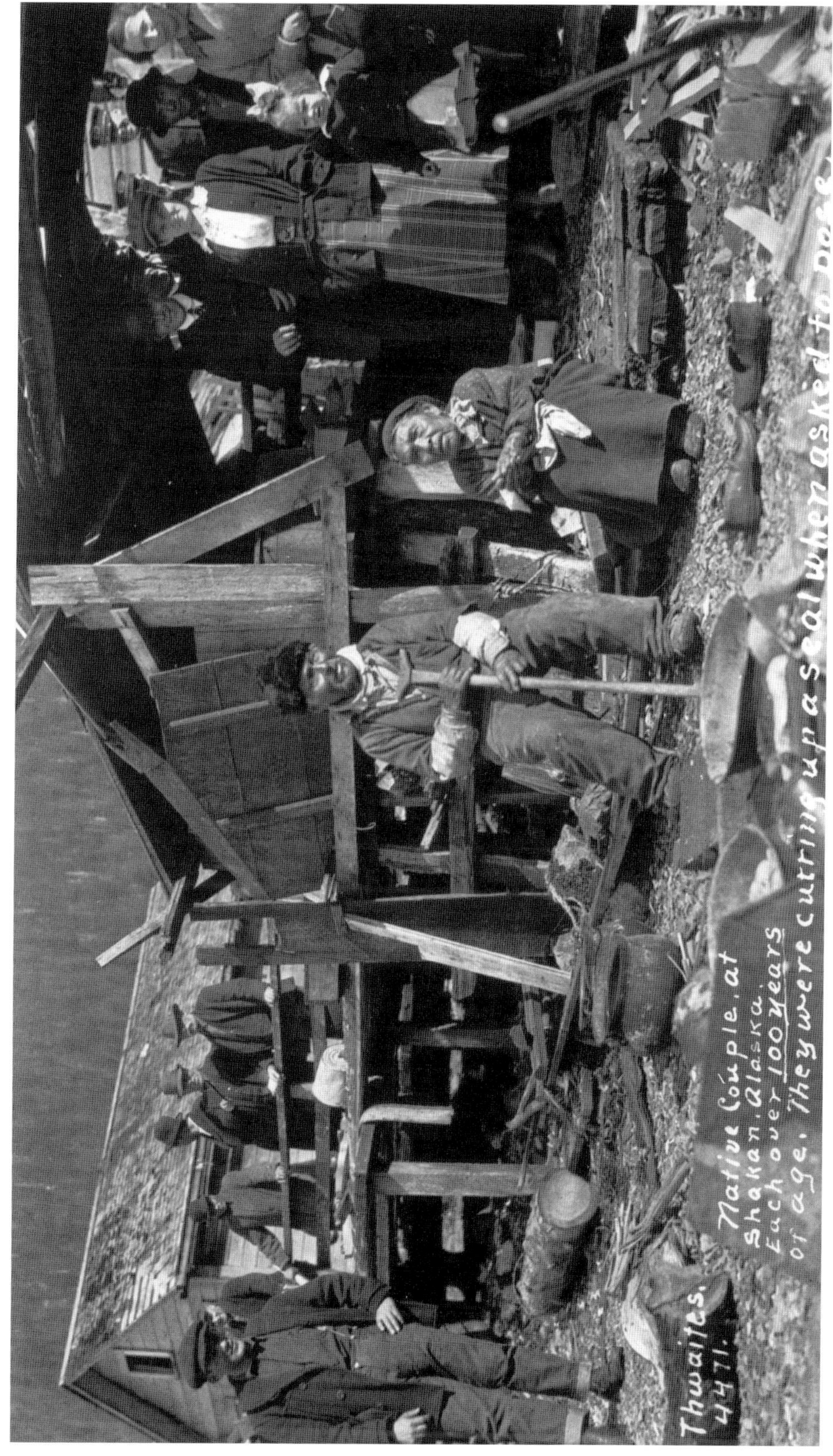

Figure 56

"Native couple at Shakan, Alaska. Each over 100 years of age. They were curring [sic] up a seal when asked to pose." 1913. Photograph by John E. Thwaites. By permission of the University of Washington Libraries, Seattle, WA. Special Collections. (NA 3158)

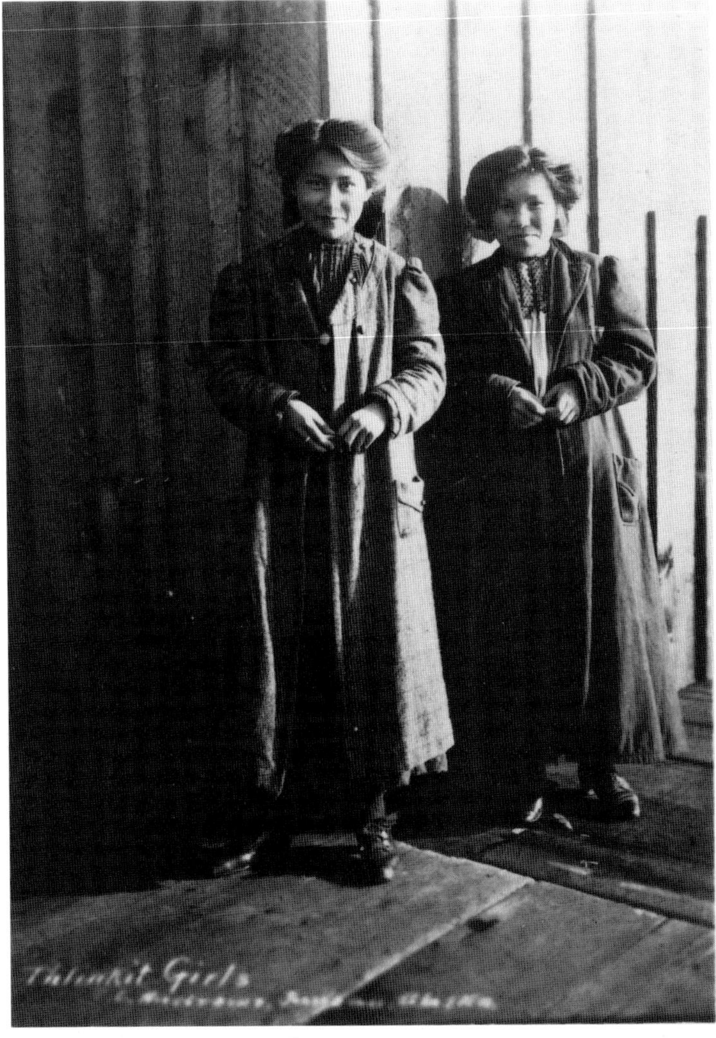

Figure 57
"Thlinkit Girls," 1897. These two cannery workers seem very comfortable in front of C. L. Andrews's camera. On the reverse is written, "To Mr. Hubbell with compliments of C. L. Andrews." By permission of the University of Washington Libraries, Seattle, WA. Special Collections. (NA 2919)

utility," he noted, "but the native canoe was a wonder of marine architecture, cut from a single log and shaped with fire and adzed into elegant lines. An occasional specimen is sometimes yet to be seen on the beach or carefully covered from the weather in some sheltered or secluded cove" (Andrews 1981:102).

In the section of his book called "What to See" Andrews does describe, in somewhat exotic terms, "The picturesque dark-skinned Thlinget women [who] sit at the doors of their little tents hour after hour, offering the strangely carved totems, the beautiful baskets of spruce roots woven in mystic designs, the beaded moccasins, etc., products of their industry during the long winter when the tourist boats do not call at the Sitka wharves" (1922:93–94). His text on the whole reveals a respectful attitude toward the Tlingit that is evident in his photographs (Fig. 57).

Vincent Soboleff grew up in the Tlingit village and company town of Killisnoo where his father, Father John (Ivan) Soboleff, was priest of the Russian Orthodox Church. In 1896, after receiving a camera from his father, he began photographing his family, Tlingit neighbors, nature, and a host of local activities. Soboleff continued

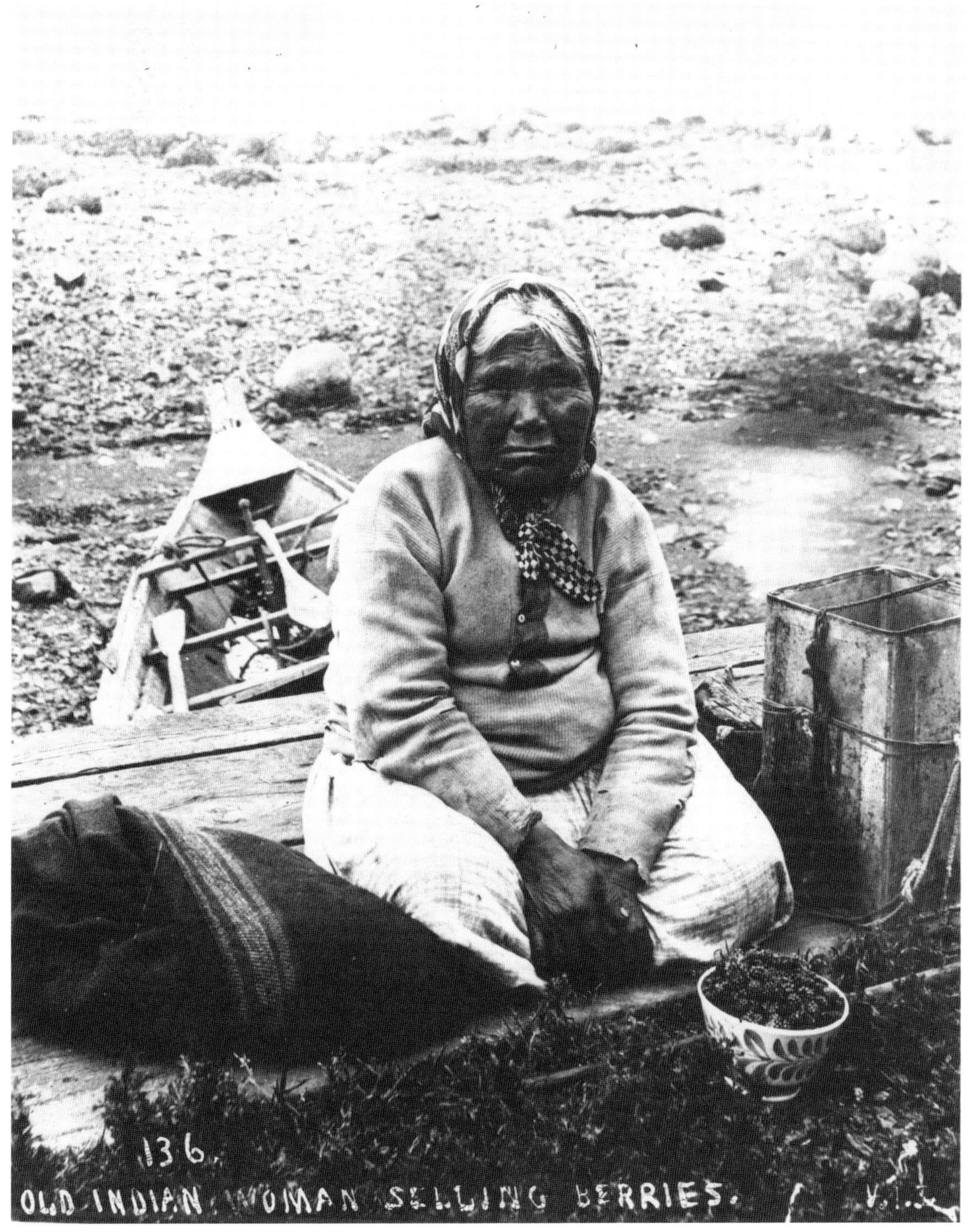

Figure 58
"Old Indian woman selling berries," 1900. Photograph by Vincent Soboleff. By permission of the Alaska State Library, Juneau, AK. (PI–045)

to take photographs into the 1920s, even after he began operating a store in the nearby Tlingit community of Angoon. Many of his photographs display the familiarity that came with community membership. His family was close to the Tlingit; his brother Alexander married a Tlingit woman from Sitka, and their children, due to matrilineal descent, were accepted as full members of the Tlingit community and their mother's clan. Despite this, some images in feeling and captioning are surprisingly impersonal. Figure 58 is titled "Old Indian woman selling berries." His writing on the reverse side of the image adds the information that she is from Killisnoo and that the berries are nagoon berries, but he does not name her. It is easy to make too much of the fact that many photographers—even those close to the Tlingit—did not name their subjects. How many people today have boxes or drawers filled with un-named photographs of family and friends? Still, this image's title treats its subject as the Other and distant from Soboleff.

Fhoki Kayamori moved to Yakutat in 1912 after leaving Japan and living for several years in Seattle, where he became a cannery worker for the Libby, McNeil & Libby Company. For nearly 30 years he photographed the town, cannery workers, community events, school classrooms, Alaska Native Brotherhood activities, Tlingit dances, and funerals. His photographs reveal a close relationship with the community; local children called him "picture man." Some of his images catch wonderfully candid moments such as Tlingit children being taught how to brush their teeth (Fig. 59); others are posed portraits (Fig. 60). During World War II, when an estimated 200 Alaskans of Japanese descent were removed and placed in internment camps, Kayamori was

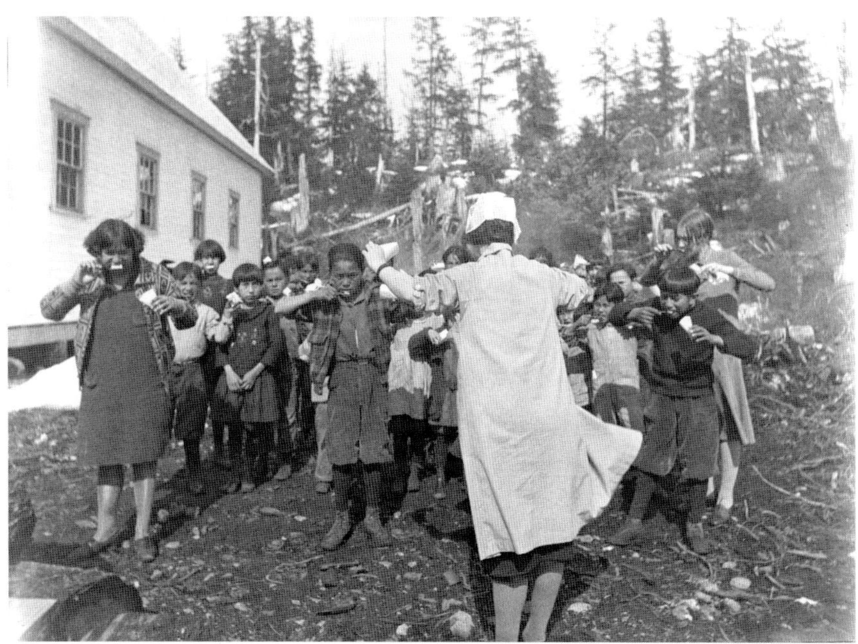

Figure 59
"Brushing teeth, Mission School, Yakutat, Alaska," 1920. The school later became the Covenant Church. Photograph by Fhoki Kayamori. By permission of the Alaska State Library, Juneau, AK. (P55-395)

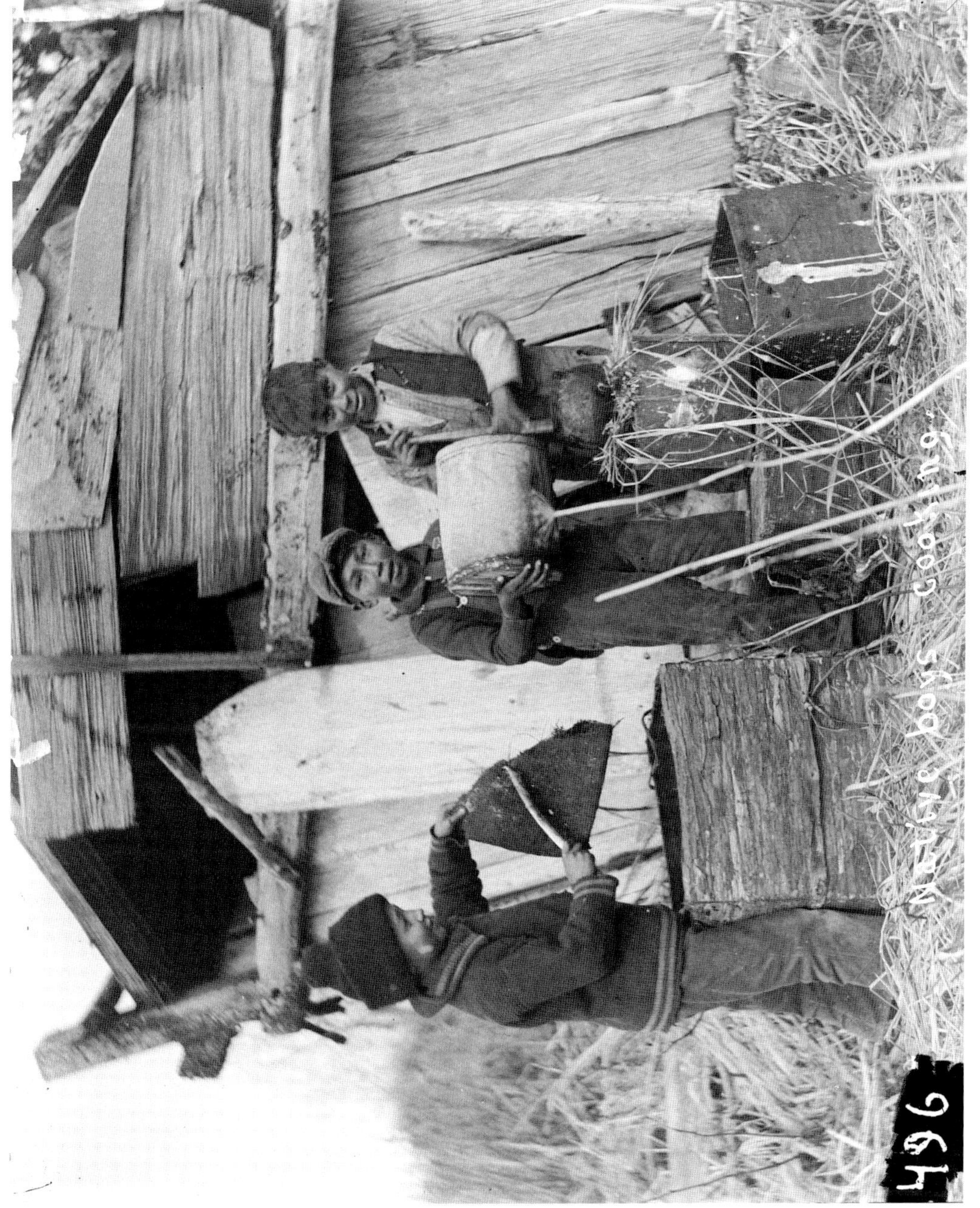

Figure 60
"Native boys cooking." 1920. Photograph by Vincent Soboleff. By permission of the Alaska State Library, Juneau, AK. (PI–609)

not as "lucky." As a photographer, his activities were perhaps suspect. Two days after Pearl Harbor was bombed, he committed suicide. Most townspeople concluded that he could not face the idea of leaving his long-time home; a few suspected him of having been a spy.

Around 1915, Stoowukáa or Louis Shotridge, a Chilkat Tlingit born in Klukwan and educated in the Presbyterian mission school at nearby Haines, began taking photographs as part of his collecting work for what is now the University of Pennsylvania Museum of Archaeology and Anthropology. Shotridge came from a high-ranking Tlingit family; he belonged to the Kaagwaantaan clan through his mother and was the grandson of the prominent chief Shaadaxícht (whose name was Germanized in writing to "Tschartritsch" and later anglicized to "Shotridge") (Milburn 1994). His father, Yeil Gooxú or George Shotridge, belonged to the Gaanax.teidi clan and was the hereditary head of Klukwan's Whale House and the custodian of its valuable clan objects. In 1905, when Louis was just 19, he met George B. Gordon, curator of American Archaeology at the University of Pennsylvania Museum, at the Lewis and Clark Exposition in Portland. Shotridge was attending with his wife Florence (Kaatkwaaxsnéi), a high-ranking member of the Lukaax.adi clan from Chilkoot, who had been recruited by Governor John G. Brady to demonstrate Tlingit weaving at the fair. Gordon eventually hired the handsome and talented couple as part-time curatorial and interpretive assistants, and after they tired of touring the United States with an Indian grand opera company and exhibiting their work at Indian craft fairs, they moved to Philadelphia in 1912 (Fig. 61).

Three years later, Louis was made a full-time Assistant Curator at the Museum. Gordon clearly recognized the advantages Shotridge's knowledge of the Tlingit language and group membership gave him for collecting and interpreting Native artifacts. Florence continued to work at the Museum as an unpaid volunteer, becoming popu-lar in her role as an "Indian princess" (Milburn 1994:557). She helped Louis, guided school children through the galleries, and wrote articles for the *Museum Journal*. Together they led a collecting trip to Alaska funded by John Wanamaker in 1915, basing themselves in Haines.

In June 1917 Florence died of tuberculosis (Fortuine 1989). After her death Shotridge continued his collecting work, making a long trip among the Tsimshian Indians on the Nass and Skeena Rivers in British Columbia and undertaking a second expedition funded by Wanamaker (Dean 1998). In 1919 he married Elizabeth Cook, a Tlingit woman from Sitka, and after 1922 spent most of his time there. After Elizabeth died in 1928, also of tuberculosis, Shotridge married Mary Kasakan of Sitka, a controversial match because she had been married when they became involved and he had paid for her divorce (Milburn 1986).

Shotridge photographed the artifacts he purchased or hoped to obtain for the Museum for descriptive and documentary purposes and for future use as illustrations in the articles he wrote for the *Museum Journal*. On October 14, 1922, he wrote Gordon:

> I enclose two photographs—one show [sic] a painted house-front, and the other a carved ceremonial baton, both offered to me at Sitka. I numbered each on the back side: Photograph No. 1 show [sic] the painted house-front of the Sitka Kaguan-ton [Kaagwaantaan] Council House, and the design on it represent [sic] the "Wolf at maternity", the characteristic crest object of the party. The piece is not very old, but the fact that it has been out in the weather for about twenty-five years made it appear so. The chief in charge set his price at one thousand dollars, but I feel that it could be purchased for half that sum. I pasted to the photograph a piece of paper on which I marked out the dimensions of it, in case this be considered for some space in the Northwest Coast Hall of the Museum. (Shotridge 1922b)

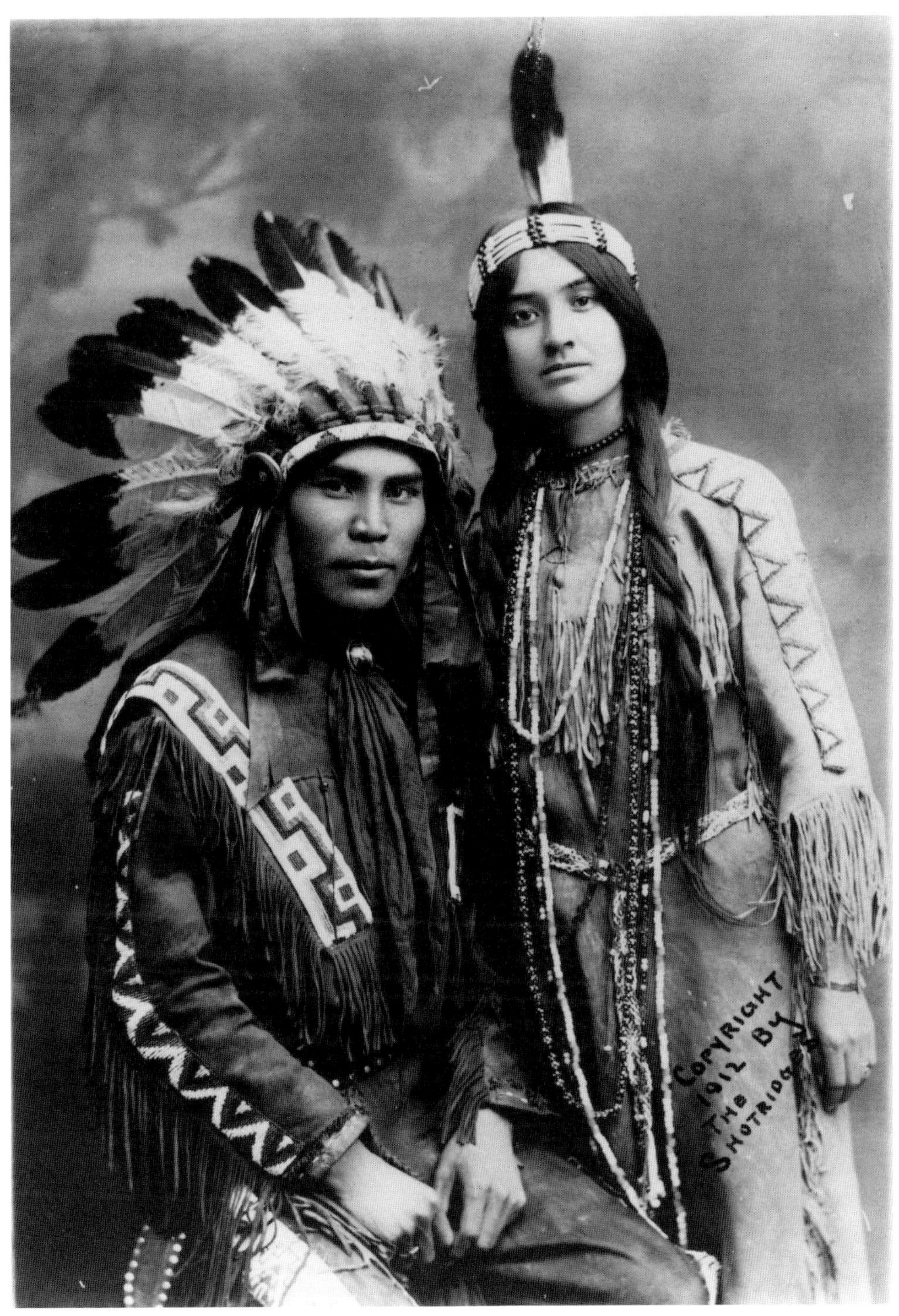

Figure 61
"Situwuka [Stoowukháa] and Katkwachsnea [Kaatkwaaxsnéi]," 1912. Louis and Florence Shotridge in Plains Indian dress while working for the University of Pennsylvania Museum. Photographer unknown. By permission of the Alaska State Library, Juneau, AK. (P01–4151)

He also took individual and group portraits and explanatory photographs of Tlingit activities he believed had ethnographic value: village buildings, canoe races, fishing, and funerals. On his collecting trip along the Nass and Skeena Rivers, he took more than a hundred still photographs and some motion picture footage, explaining in a letter to the Museum's director, Horace Jayne, on January 6, 1932, "There are many scenes in through the territory to be recorded by means of the motion pictures, but most of these are of common place, so I am saving my films for carrying out my plan on taking first all the old-time Tlingit Arts I can take. I want to take the weaving of the Chilkat Blanket." The financial needs of many Tlingit helps explain the willingness of some to be photographed and to sell clan objects. Shotridge continued, "I put before the local Camps of the Alaska Native Brotherhood and Sisterhood here, the staging of the Old-time Potlatch Dances, to be filmed in the open air. Since these two organizations are now in debt with [the building of] their great Hall [in Sitka] the members are doing everything possible in raising funds, and they are willing to perform for me for the price of One Hundred and Fifty Dollars [$2,277 in 2007], with about one hundred performers" (Shotridge 1932).

When Shotridge was laid off by the Museum in 1932, as a result of the Depression, he was asked for the immediate return of the movie camera. He complied and also sent most of his photographs back to Philadelphia. Of his 185 images now in the Museum's Archives, 27 percent are portraits of individuals and groups, 25 percent show items of Tlingit material culture, 17 percent are townscapes of street scenes and cemeteries, 17 percent show activities, 10 percent are landscapes, and a final 2 percent are personal-interest photographs, such as Shotridge's workroom and campsites. While many of his images are technically less proficient than those taken by professional photographers (the subject may be crooked, the lighting poor), their informality and unstudied nature—like tourist snapshots—

often gives them a feeling of greater immediacy than more carefully constructed images. Many of Shotridge's photographs of Tlingit activities and informal portraits of adults and children also reflect the special intimacy that came with his insider status. A photograph of a canoe race reflects a participant's point of view by including the notation "canoe race—eagles win," moiety information an outsider was unlikely to note (Fig. 62). Yet other Shotridge images are indistinguishable from those taken by many non-Native photographers.

Despite his Tlingit heritage and high rank, Shotridge's outlook was strongly influenced by mainstream American society. He had attended the Presbyterian mission school in Haines, and by the time he began taking photographs for the Museum, he had spent many years outside Alaska. In addition to his curatorial work for the Museum, he also had studied music and English, attended business courses at the Wharton School of Finance and Economics at the University of Pennsylvania, performed as an "Indian" for White society, and worked briefly with anthropologist Franz Boas to create a Tlingit grammar. When collecting, Shotridge demonstrated a determination to get what he wanted that rivaled if not surpassed that of Emmons and other Euro-American collectors. He saw collecting as a way of saving important historical objects for future generations, both Tlingit and non-Native, and of demonstrating the greatness of Tlingit culture to the outside world. Other Tlingit attitudes toward these historical and ceremonial objects were mixed. According to Shotridge, in a letter to Gordon on January 7, 1924:

> When the Tlingit realized that the method which the people had employed in building up ones [sic] social standing was overthrown by modern ideas, each man quietly placed the object, which had come to exist only through an unceasing efforts [sic] of many generations, in the bottom of the family chest with a vague hope for its recovery of the honor which it rep-

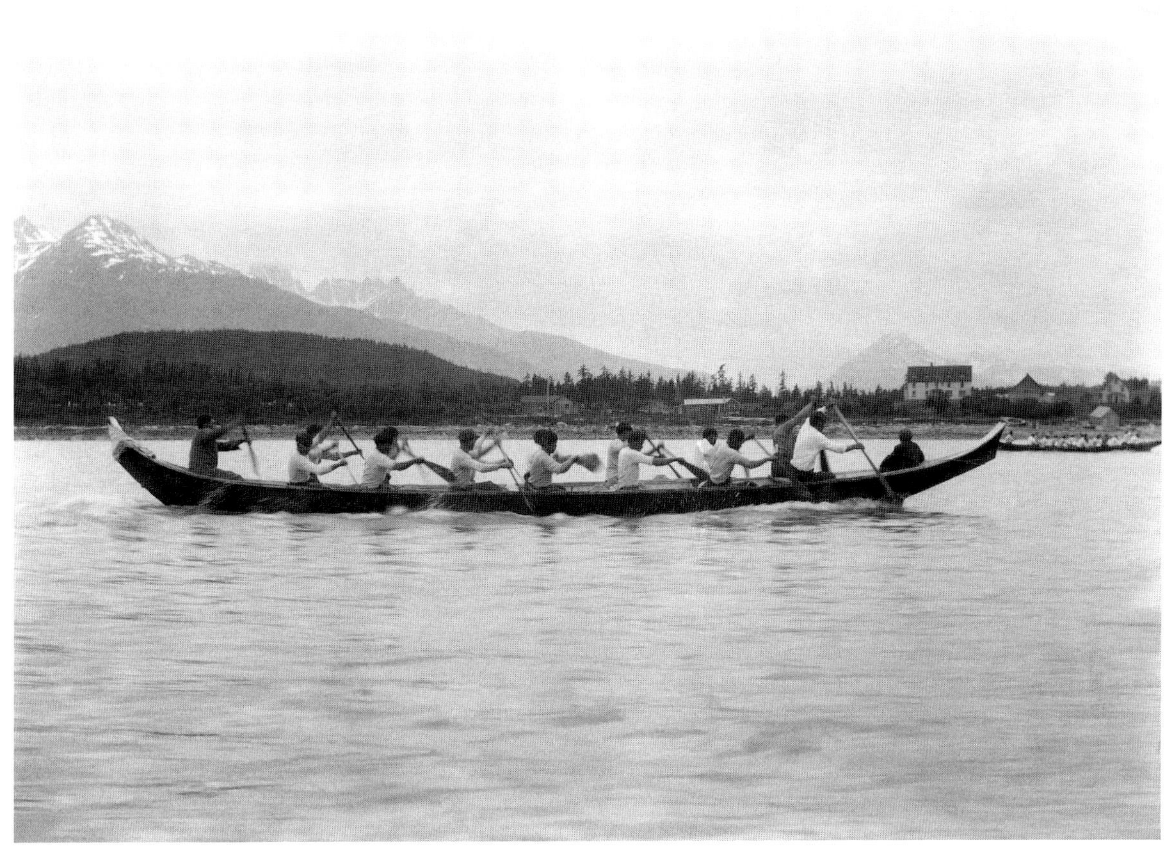

Figure 62
"*Canoe Race—Eagles Win,*" 1918. Photograph by Louis Shotridge. By permission of the University of Pennsylvania Museum of Archaeology and Anthropology, Philadelphia, PA. (773)

resents, but it is disappointing that these hopes are gradually vanishing. With a rather limited knowledge of the past the present generation hold on to the old things, each man with a fear that another man might laugh if he let go what he has in exchange for the needed cash. There are a few aged leading men, however, who have taken courage to offer that which had been almost sacred, each taking comfort in thinkin [*sic*] that since he himself have done his part in upholding what he keeps in the standard of social recognition he should be justified in ending all with his own time...The chief of the Kaguan-ton [Kaagwaantaan] clan of Sitka of-

fered one ceremonial hat, carved to represent the Ganook, a mythical being which was spoken of as the god of rain. The old piece is a unique representation of a very interesting record of condition in the Tlingit life of the past. It represents also the early art of the people. One Thousand Dollars is the price placed on this one piece. This is a specimen well worth having, but the price is in excess of my means... I enclose a small print showing the hat. You will note that it now bears clear marks of decay. When I put together my notes on this, I believe it will make an interesting article for the Museum Journal.

As a modernist Shotridge was convinced of the necessity of his pursuits and often ignored the feelings and traditions of members of his own culture. Both of his remarriages, for example, had scandalized conservative Tlingit because he did not follow the custom of marrying a woman from the same clan as his previous wife (Milburn 1986). Like Emmons, he removed artifacts from shaman graves, and even after he no longer worked for the Museum, he took a skeleton from a cave on the north shore of Peril Strait that was probably a Kaagwaantaan shaman. "When we came into town the unloading of the thing had to be all night-work, to avoid suspicion and possible trouble from the Indians," he noted in a letter to Mason on March 7, 1932. In a letter to Horace Jayne, April 5, 1932, Shotridge said,

> This is when I should be out on a hunt for more dead shamans. Two Indian friends have reported to me on their discoveries...The discoverers of the chests are two of those Indians who still entertain some vague belief in the supernatural powers of the old-time prophets, hence their fear in opening the old chests to examine their contents. I have no funds with which to obtain these finds, but I though [sic] of supplying a powered boat, and bring the old things into a storage, keep them there until such time when some museum have use for them. It is evident that these chests contain some rare and valuable material.

Shotridge was relentless in his quest to obtain one important group of Tlingit artifacts, the Klukwan Whale House collection, over which his father, George Shotridge (Yeil Gooxú), had been the *hitsaati* or hereditary custodian. In 1885, G. T. Emmons had reported that the Whale House was in the "last stages of decay," although its art works were still in good condition and the house was still being used for ceremonies. In 1899, four years after Figure 63 was taken, the house was torn down and a new house of milled timber was begun. To celebrate the erection of a new clan house Yeilgooxú sponsored a potlatch and invited a Sitka clan from the opposite moiety to attend. Unfortunately, he died not long after and the house was never completed. It was finally destroyed by a mudslide in 1913, but its art works and artifacts were saved and stored for many years outdoors protected by tarps.

Although Louis Shotridge, as a member of his mother's clan, was not an heir to these objects under Tlingit matrilineal inheritance rules, he claimed his right to the collection using American law as his justification. In a letter of April 22, 1923, to his mentor and employer Dr. Gordon, he reported:

> I have been very busy in trying to straighten the dispute of the Whale House Collection of which I spoke in my last two letters to you. This affair stirred not only the whole Chilkat, but all persons concerned in other localities as much. So I decided to let the excitement quiet down a bit before my uncle and myself [sic] disturb more peace. Some time in July next we plan to take possession of the Four Pillars and the Screen of the old Whale House of Klukwan, and if the opposition yields we shall ship these to the University Museum immediately. I will make a stop in Juneau for the purpose of given [sic] a friendly talk to the leading man of our rival party, but this is only to lay before him our intention, and I expect to acquire all possible information on his own intention in order that we may guard against some serious trouble. False rumors and gossips are our main obsticles [sic]. The native population of Haines has voted against us, but the Kluckwan [sic] majority appeared in our favor, but we have decided to ignor [sic] all community interest and proseed [sic] with our plan. I shall explain more when I have more time.

The political maneuvering that Shotridge resorted to in his quest for this collection over many years seriously destabilized the communities of Haines and Klukwan, so much so that a peace-making ceremony had to be held in

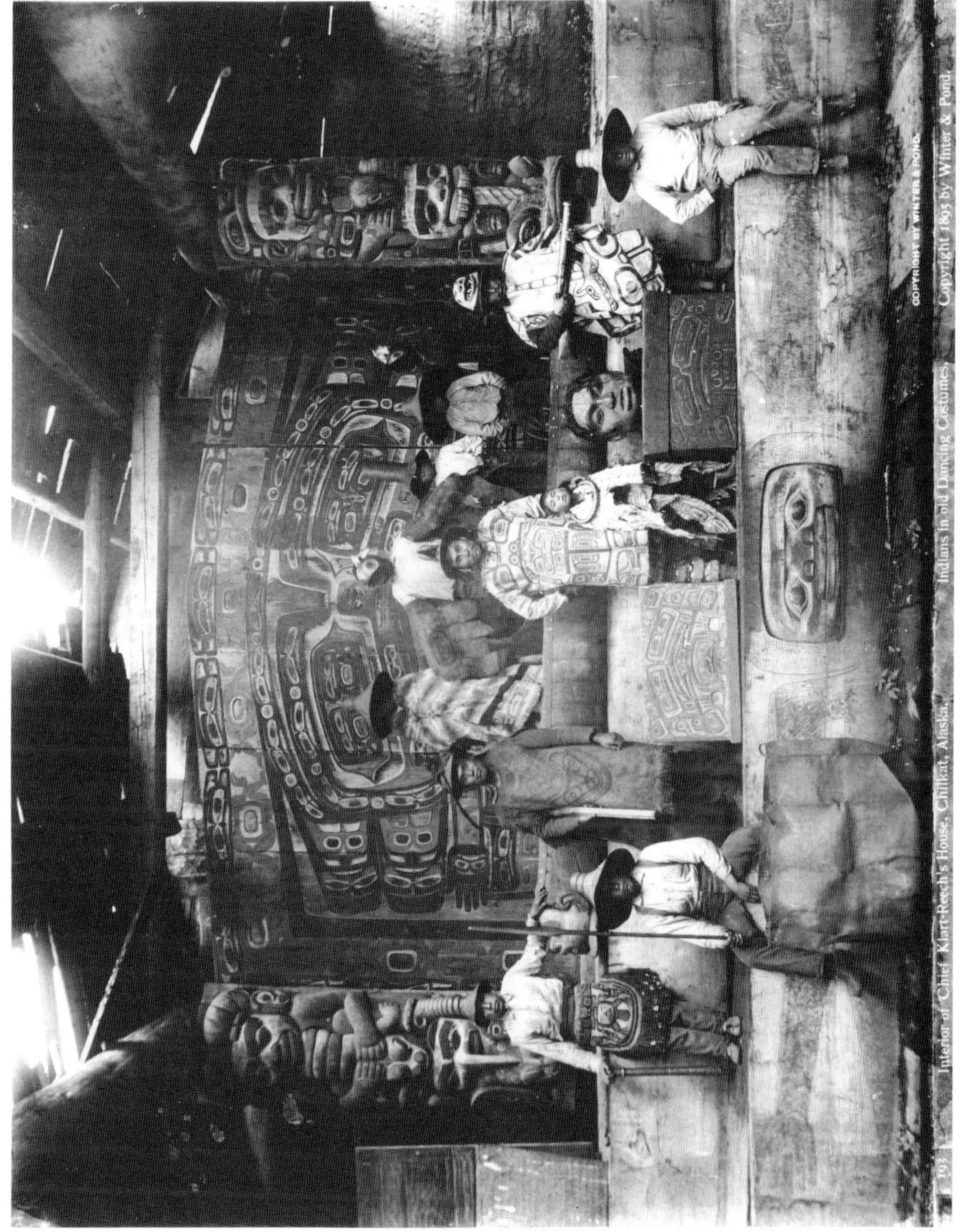

Figure 63
'Chief Klart-Reech's [Shaadaxícht] House, Chilkat, Alaska.' 1895. Interior view of the Klukwan Whale House with Yeil Gooxú (George Shotridge), its hereditary custodian and the father of Louis Shotridge, in the center. Photograph by Winter & Pond. By permission of the Alaska State Library, Juneau, AK. (P87–0010)

1925 "to restore amicable relations" (Milburn 1986:14). This ceremony finally forced Shotridge to give up, but the controversy over whose property law should apply continued. Many years later, in 1984, the Klukwan Village Council challenged in court the right of 14 people—the so-called Whale House group—to sell the artifacts. The latter had managed to spirit them out of Klukwan by truck and had transported them to a private art dealer in Seattle to find a buyer. For a detailed discussion of the whole case see the *Anchorage Daily News* series, posted at www.ankn.uaf.edu/Curriculum/Tlingit/WhaleHouse and articles in the *Sitka Daily Sentinel* ("Klukwan Artifacts Recovered in Seattle," 27 August 1984, p. 1 and "Lawyers Argue Over Klukwan's Artifacts," 6 November 1984, p. 1).

After losing his job with the Museum in 1932, Shotridge eventually found work in Sitka as a government fisheries stream guard. This was not a popular position since it involved preventing fishing in restricted areas. Shotridge died on August 6, 1937, in Sitka; he was found at Redoubt Bay with a broken neck, apparently the result of an accidental fall. Some people suspected foul play stemming from the Klukwan controversy (Millburn 1986, Cole 1985).

In recent years a number of important collected artifacts have been returned to the Tlingit under the Native American Graves Protection and Repatriation Act (NAGPRA). The brass Peace Hat commissioned by the Russian American Company in the shape of a Tlingit spruceroot hat and given to Sitka's Kiks.ádi in the early 1800s as a symbol of peace was repatriated from the American Museum of Natural History in 2003. The Raven-of-the-Roof hat, collected by Shotridge, was returned to Sitka in 2003 by the University of Pennsylvania Museum of Archaeology and Anthropology so that it could be used in a Coho clan memorial potlatch for Sarah Davis James. Several other artifacts (Eagle hat, Petrel hat, Wolf hat, and Shark helmet) were loaned to Sitka's Tlingit in 2004 for use in the Centennial Potlatch sponsored by the Kaagwaantaan clan to commemorate the so-called last potlatch of 1904.

One other photographer should be mentioned. George Johnston, an inland Tlingit from the Canadian Yukon village of Teslin, began taking photographs at the end of the period covered by this book. In the mid-to-late 1920s he purchased a mail-order pocket Kodak B folding camera (available 1925–34) and began photographing his community—sports teams, children's concerts, people fishing, craftspeople at work, funeral rites, and friends posed with his prized 1928 Chevrolet. Johnston's pictures are similar in subject matter and style to most people's personal snapshots; many of the people in his posed groups have their feet cropped off, horizons are sometimes crooked, and images are too dark. They are nevertheless important records since they help reveal life and change in this Canadian village from the late 1920s until the early 1950s (Geddes 1997, Thornton 2000).

The next chapter focuses on the work of resident photographer Elbridge Warren Merrill and his relationship with the Tlingit living in Sitka. He was an exceptionally skilled photographer whose large body of work on the Tlingit, taken between 1899 and 1929, is little known outside of southeast Alaska. Other early collections of Tlingit photographs exist, including those taken by professional photographers Lloyd Winter and Percy Pond and amateurs Louis Shotridge, Vincent Soboleff, Fhoki Kayamori, and George Johnston. Yet Merrill's work deserves special attention both for its own intrinsic quality and range and also because it has been embraced by the Tlingit community today. As Christopher Pinney (2003) has pointed out, photographs are records of "dialogic events" which record the negotiations between a photographer and his or her subjects. What do we know about this one photographer and his relationship with the Tlingit? Do Merrill's photographs reveal a bias or point of view that reflects his non-Native identity? What messages about the Tlingit do they communicate to us today?

5

Sitka's "Father of Pictures": Elbridge Warren Merrill

Elbridge Warren Merrill was a commercial photographer who worked in Sitka for 30 years between 1899 and 1929. His photographs were highly regarded at the time and frequently purchased and given as gifts and as prizes at community events. James Condit, superintendent of the Sitka Industrial School, noted in his diary in 1923 that his wife Nellie had given him a Merrill photograph for his 60th birthday which he described as "a beautiful thing—close up of an old tree, bit of trail, lichens, moss, ferns." The school's newspaper, the *Verstovian*, thought it newsworthy in January 1916 to report that Merrill had donated "a beautiful picture of the Silver Bay Range" to hang in the teachers' living room. Merrill's images of the Tlingit, town life, and the natural beauty of the surrounding mountains and sea were sold to tourists, and they illustrated contemporary newspaper and journal articles as well as books about Sitka and southeast Alaska.

His most important legacy is his Tlingit work (Fig. 64). He photographed subsistence activities, village life, ceremonial events, Native students at the boarding school, Tlingit organizations and individuals, and their ingenious and highly symbolic material culture. After his death, the *Alaska Weekly* reported on November 29, 1929, that "No truer friend of the Thlinget existed for he knew them and understood their customs and modes of thought. When the last words were spoken, no more sincere mourners were present than the old Indian men and women who stood about his grave with bowed heads—silent, as it is their wont but grieving as the stoical grieve." Merrill's images stand today as a visual affirmation of Tlingit culture and have been embraced by the Tlingit community, especially in Sitka. Who was this little-known photographer and very private person? What was his relationship with the Tlingit, especially given the racism of the times and the commercial nature of his work?

Merrill was a "Boston man," the term the Tlingit once used to refer to any American, but which accurately described him. He was born on June 23, 1870, not far from Boston on a farm on the Merrimack River, the son of Samuel F. Merrill and Mary E. Pillsbury, descendents of English settlers who had arrived in the New World in the 1600s. Despite this impressive lineage and the assumptions many of his Alaskan contemporaries made, Merrill was not from a privileged background. His early life was painful and the economic circumstances of his immediate family tenuous. When Merrill was not quite 3, his

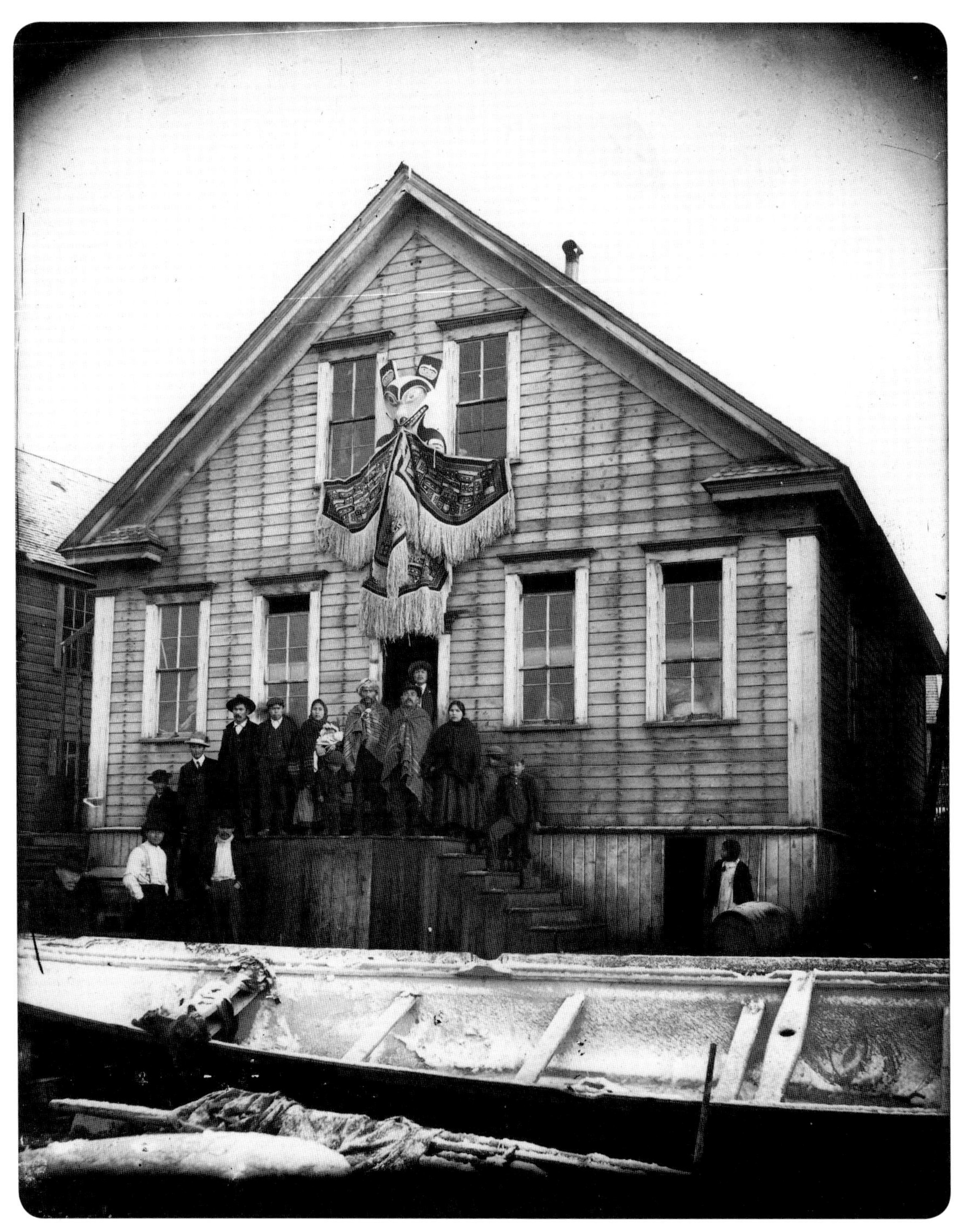

Figure 64
Members of Annaxóots family pose with the Panting Wolf house post on display above them, Sitka, 1904.
Photograph by E. W. Merrill. Courtesy of Stratton Library, Sheldon Jackson College, Sitka, AK. (M II B6d)

father died and his mother was forced to move with her children, Adelaide, Elbridge, and Samuel—a daughter, Ella, had died earlier—into her brother's home in nearby Danvers (Old Salem). A little more than year later, Mary married Leander S. Falls, a local milk collector. Mary had grown up on a farm in Newburyport known as the "city milk farm," so perhaps she already knew him (Pilsbury 1898). But this marriage also was marred by tragedy when only four days later Samuel, Merrill's younger brother, died. His death was followed six years later by the death of Leander Falls. Just 10 years old, Merrill had now lost two fathers and two siblings. Mary and her two children once again had to live with her brother. Sometime after 1885 when Adelaide married Albert Merrill, a shipping clerk who may also have been a cousin, Merrill and his mother moved into their home. Their combined household was not poor—by 1890 Albert had become a successful horse dealer and professional starting judge who officiated at the "most prominent race tracks in the East" and enjoyed "a reputation in that capacity second to no man in the country" (Meek 1890:181)—but Merrill and his mother took in piecework as "necktie cutters" to make ends meet.

By 1890, at the age of 20, Merrill had begun experimenting with photography. His earliest-known photographs include images of Danvers's Fourth of July Parade in 1891 and of his uncle's business, the Harvey H. Pillsbury Carriage Exchange, on Maple and School Streets. This prominent local business had a showroom and office on the first floor, and a factory on the second and third floors that produced harnesses, horse-drawn carriages, buggies, and wagons. In 1878 it had been chosen as the installation site for one end of a demonstration telephone line. Around his 21st birthday, Merrill changed his middle name from Samuel to Warren, perhaps because of the deaths of his father and younger brother, both of whom had been named Samuel. By 1895, at age 25, the *Danvers Directory* noted that he was employed in Boston as a "photoprinter," but his income remained modest. He owed the town of Danvers a

mere $2 in taxes the following year (see the *Valuation of the Town of Danvers* for 1896). Another early Merrill photograph shows Company K of Danvers's volunteer militia on parade down Maple Street. It was most likely taken in May 1898 on the eve of the militia's departure for Framingham to join the Eighth Regiment of the Army Corps. The United States had declared war on Spain in April, and volunteer militias had been called up. This image is the last record of Merrill's photographic activities in the East. The photographs, in the archives of the Danvers Historical Society in the Peabody Library in Danvers, are all stamped "Photographed by E. W. Merrill, Danvers, Mass."

When news of the Klondike gold strike began filtering east in early 1898, Merrill was 27 years old and still living with his mother, sister, and brother-in-law. He could not have escaped reading accounts of local men's preparations for Alaska's goldfields and their later exploits which were published in popular magazines like *Harpers*, *McCall's*, and *Scribners*. The article "Klondike Hardships," in the April 9, 1989, issue of the *Danvers Mirror*, reported that fellow resident Frank Purdy had contracted spinal meningitis while carrying his supplies over White Pass. At the time, "There were two wests in American perception: the west of such natural resources as minerals, timber, and arable land; and the west of ancient Native American peoples, vast geological wonder, and trackless wilderness" (Marien 2002:12). Merrill may have been attracted by both; he was undoubtedly ready for a change. Alaska offered adventure, independence, myriad photographic subjects, and unsullied nature, widely regarded as the source of spiritual healing.

Oral tradition in Sitka places Merrill's arrival as late 1898, when the small steamer *Gertrude* sputtered into Sitka Sound and expired on the beach, eventually rotting away (Fig. 65). Records show that a steamer christened *Gertrude* was completed in New Whatcom (Bellingham), Washington's Globe Mill in early July 1898. *The Daily Reveille* on July 3 reported that its party of a dozen men were making their final preparations

     ELBRIDGE WARREN MERRILL

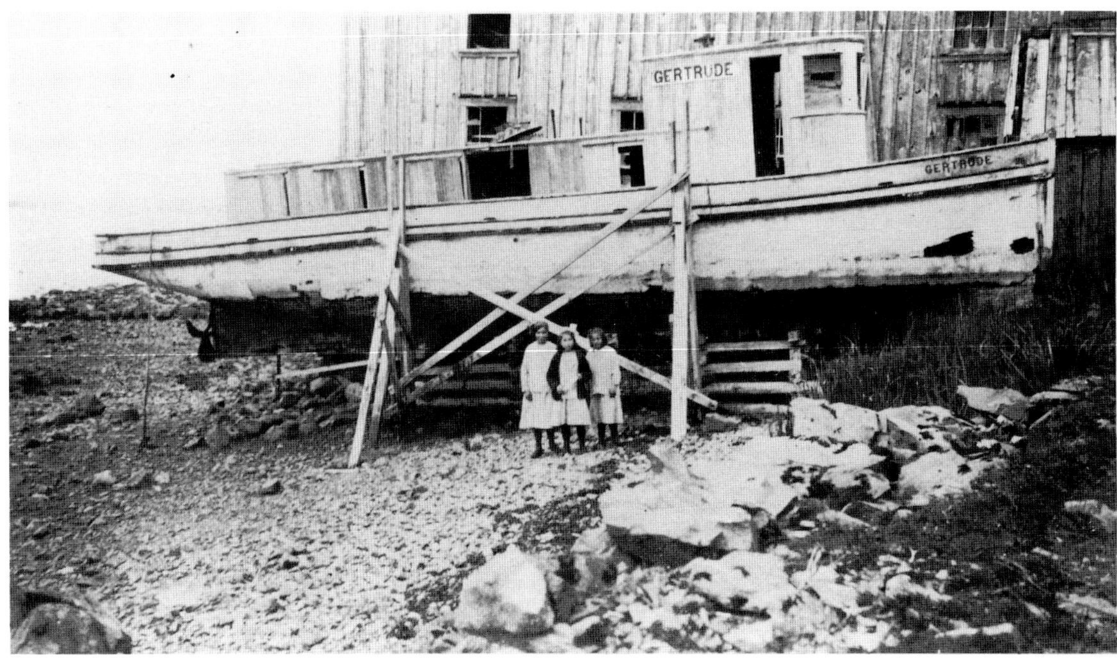
Figure 65
The remains of the *Gertrude* on the beach in front of John Brady's sawmill, 1900. Photograph by E. W. Merrill.
Private collection.

for southeastern Alaska and planned to tow a supply scow "for a two-year cruise in the waters, prospecting inlets and rivers for gold." The party finally left Bellingham on August 5; seven weeks later, on September 26, they reached Mary Island, the U.S. Customs Port of Entry for Alaska. Four days later they reached the next port north—Wrangell in southeast Alaska—and departed the same night. After that no further record of the *Gertrude* is found. What happened may never be known. Despite protected waters for most of the journey north, the Inside Passage was poorly charted and had few navigational aids. The (Seattle) *Argus*, September 2, 1899, reported that the area was also beset with thick fog and frequent storms, especially in October, when the *Gertrude* would have approached Sitka on the open Pacific side of Baranof Island.

Once in Sitka, Merrill decided to stay. His handwritten notation on a photograph of potlatch dancers in winter—"copyright 1899 by Merrill"—indicates that he began taking photographs his first year. He may have left Sitka for a while, as local oral tradition maintains, perhaps to clear up business back East or to explore more of Alaska. This appears to be supported by his signature on Sitka's Millmore Hotel guest register, January 31, 1900, where he lists his residence as Boston: a number of Merrill's early Alaska photographs also are stamped "Merrill, Boston."

But by December 1900 he was in business in Sitka with a stock of views for sale. An advertisement for his work in *The Alaskan*, December 22, reads: "E. W. Merrill, photographist, has a quantity of first class negatives from which he can supply orders for views of Sitka and vicinity" (p. 3). Merrill's first studio was located in the "Trading Post," the large Russian-built log building on Lincoln Street (Fig. 66) which appears as the backdrop in many early photographs

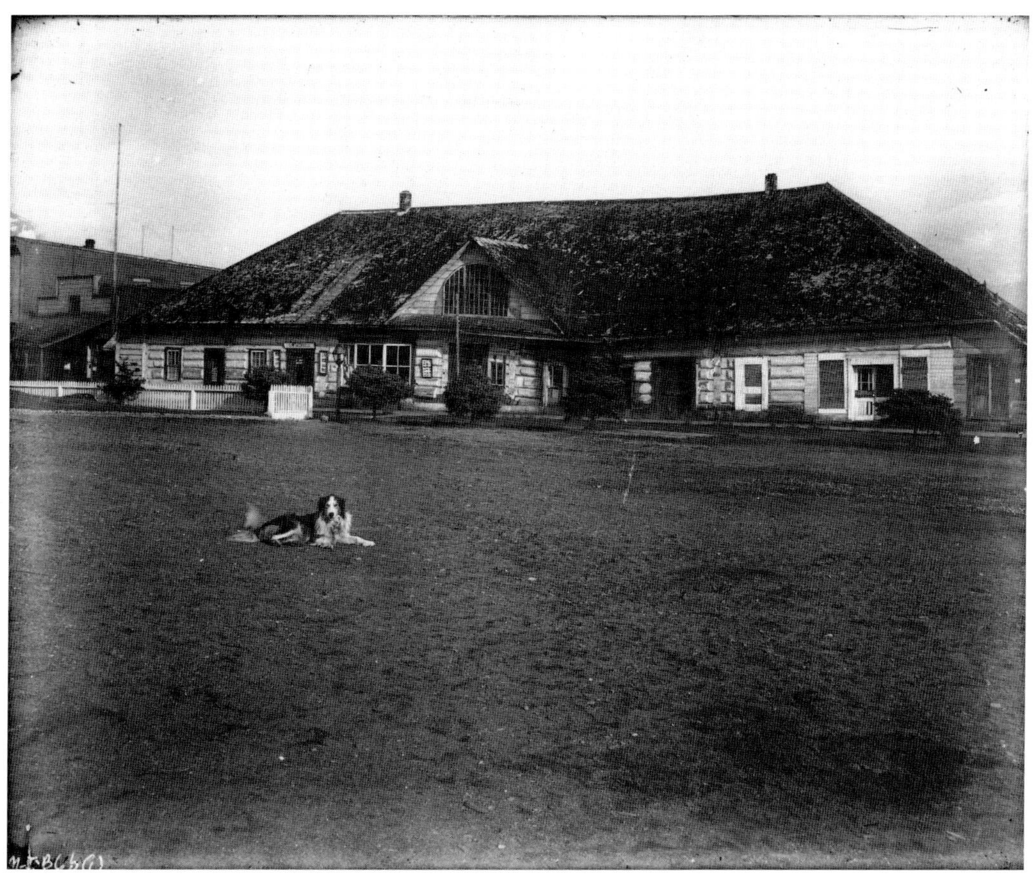

Figure 66
Old Russian "Trading Post" on Lincoln Street, 1900. Merrill's studio and shop sign is visible on the left side of the building. His dog Rover is in the foreground. Photograph by E. W. Merrill. Courtesy of Stratton Library, Sheldon Jackson College, Sitka, AK. (M I B6b)

of Tlingit vendors. In early 1905, he moved to the Callsen Building, also on Sitka's main street, where he displayed and sold his photographs as well as Tlingit artifacts and curios. From then throughout the 1920s, ads for "E. W. Merrill Photography" and E. W. Merrill "Dealer in Alaskan Curios and Photographs" appeared regularly in local newspapers and journals like *The Sitka Tribune*, *The Sitka Progress*, and *The Pathfinder*.

When Merrill landed, Sitka was a segregated community and, to a large extent, remained so until his death in 1929. On his arrival the town's population comprised 771 "Indians," 275 "Amer-

icans" (which included the 47 men on the U.S.S. *Pinta* and 44 U.S. Marines), 174 "Russians," and 28 Chinese and Japanese. The latter had come to work in the canneries but were also branching out into local businesses like Lung Sing's laundry, according to the 1897 Census. Except for commerce, Natives and non-Natives stayed in their own areas. Most Tlingit lived in the village, often referred to as the "ranche," or on the opposite side of town in the cottage settlement built on the grounds of the Sitka Industrial Training School. Non-Natives lived between the two and in outlying homesteads. The expressions "down

    ELBRIDGE WARREN MERRILL

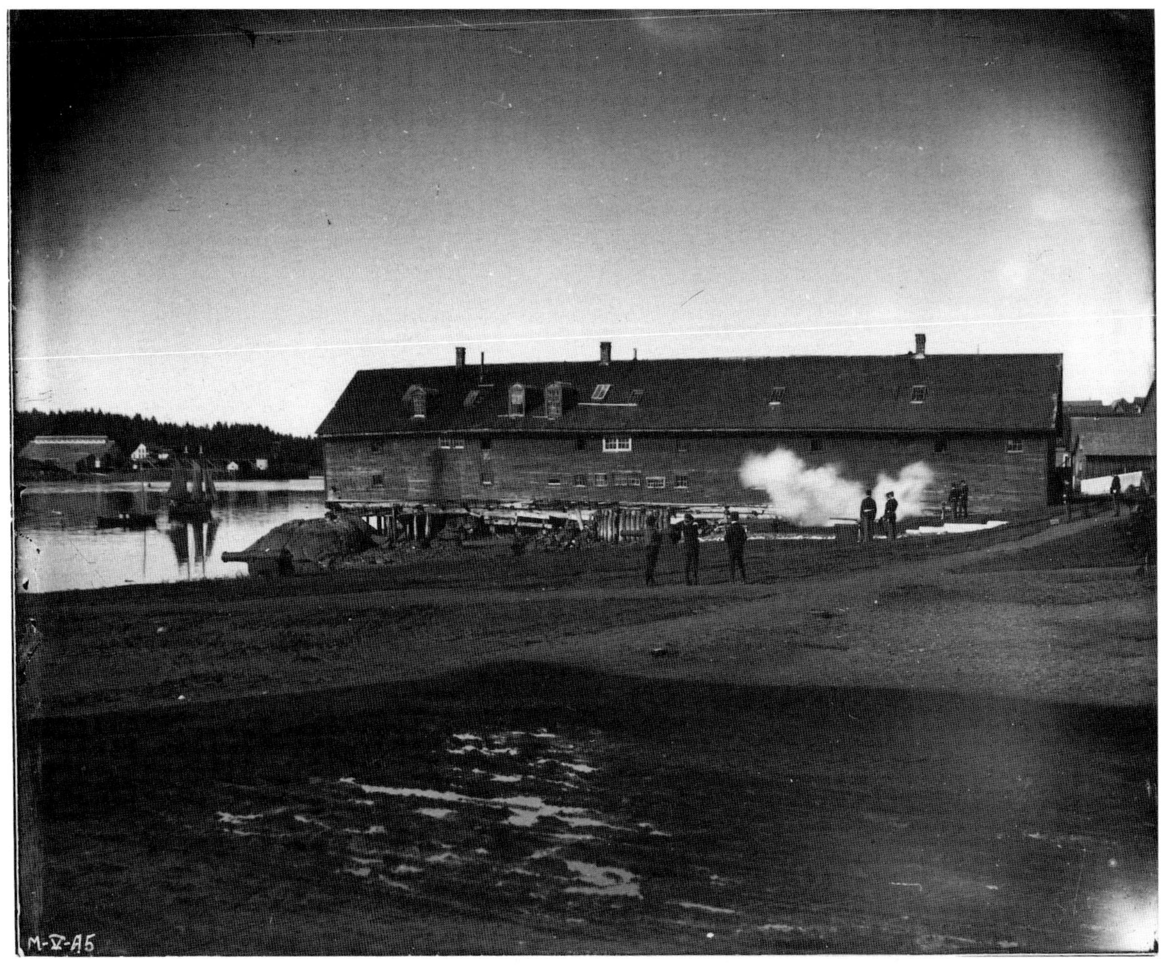

Figure 67
U.S. Revenue Service marines stationed at Sitka shooting cannon near Herring Rock on July 4, 1905. Photograph by
E. W. Merrill. Courtesy of Stratton Library, Sheldon Jackson College, Sitka, AK. (M V A5)

to the ranch" and "out to the cottages" were used as direction indicators in Sitka through the 1920s, officially replaced by the simple designations "East" and "West" ends of town (with St. Michael's Cathedral as the midpoint) when a resolution was passed by the City Council in 1927.

Although some friendships existed between the Tlingit and Sitka's Euro-American residents, especially with long-term residents like miner Tom Haley and merchant Tom Tillson, both of whom spoke some Tlingit, prejudice and discrimination were widespread. In 1901, Tlingit residents James Jackson (Annaxóots), Augustus Bean, "Thlan-Tech" [Tlanteech], Rudolph Walton, Daniel Bensen, and Mrs. James Fitzgerald wrote to Governor Brady to complain that the Marine Corps sentry was not allowing the Tlingit on the wharf when steamships were in port. Brady pursued the matter and received a testy reply from Captain Joseph Pendleton, the head of the U.S. Marine Barracks in Sitka (Fig. 67), prompting a lengthier correspondence which

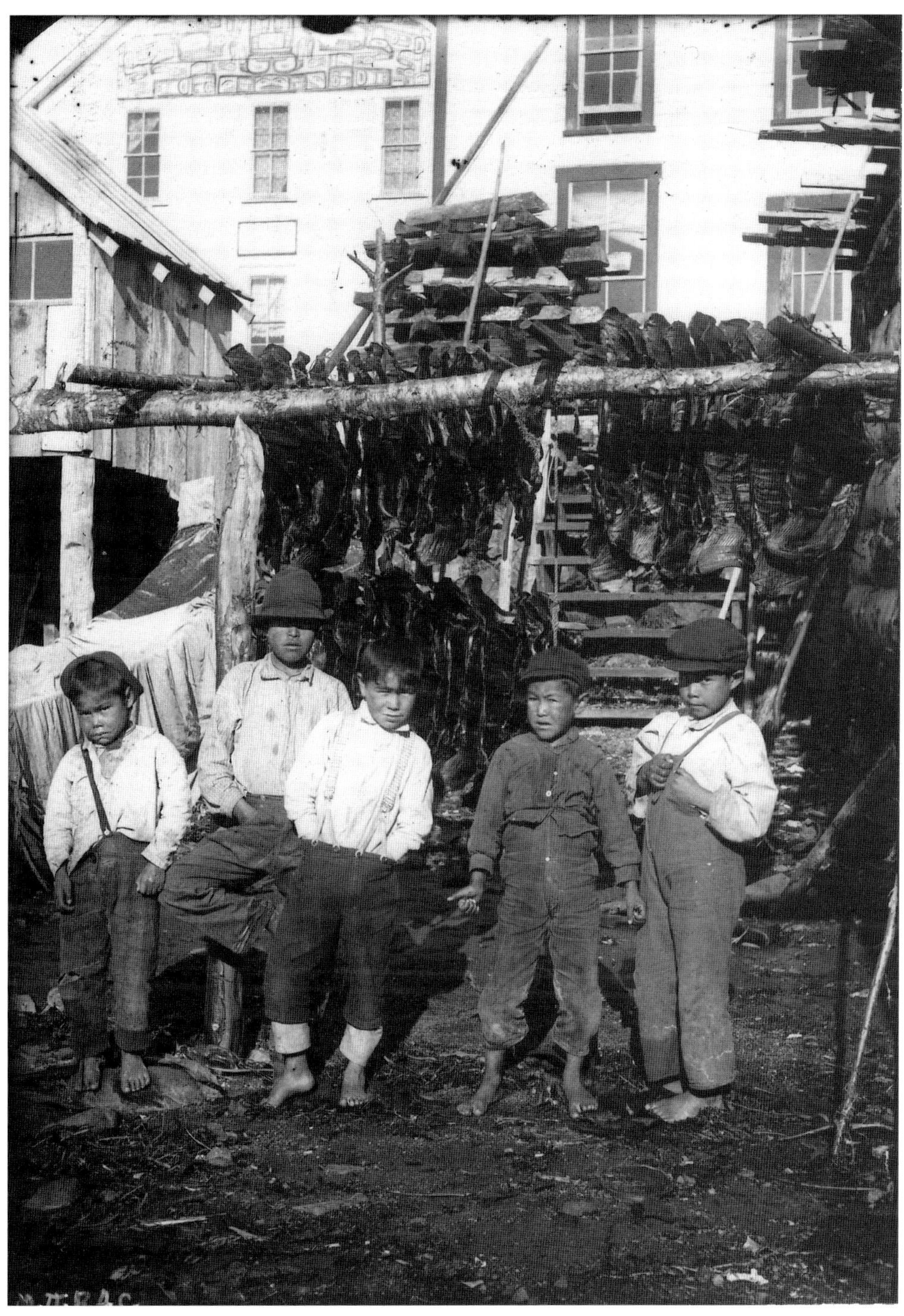

Figure 68
Village children on beach in front of drying racks, Sitka. Left to right: unknown, Dick Hallis, unknown, Charles Dick, and unknown. Photograph by E. W. Merrill. Courtesy of Stratton Library, Sheldon Jackson College, Sitka, AK. (M II B4c)

eventually involved the Commandant of the Marine Corps, the Secretary of the Navy, and the Secretary of the Interior. Not that many years before, a group of young Tlingit had "rioted" on Sitka's Parade Grounds and threatened to burn the barracks down in protest over the habit of the Collector of Customs shooting their dogs from his window on the third floor. Only when the Marines pointed howitzers at the village were the Tlingit forced to back down.

After 1906 Sitka's public schools were segregated, with No. 1 for Whites and Creoles and No. 2 for the Tlingit. Other Tlingit children attended the Sitka Industrial Training School. Sitka elders still vividly remember the name calling, rock throwing, and fist fighting that erupted between children of the two groups as they walked to and from school or ran across each other while out berry picking and at virtually any other opportunity. Historian Robert DeArmond, Jr., remembered during an interview in August 1986 feeling safe when he walked through the Tlingit village only if he had his cow or a gang of other boys with him. Tlingit children felt the same (Fig. 68). Elder Isabella Sing Brady recalled in 1986, for a somewhat later period, "We tried not to be kept after school. If we did, we'd pray for a low tide so we could run along the beach and not worry about getting beat up." Fraternal organizations like the Arctic Brotherhood and groups like the Girl Scouts did not allow Tlingit members. Tlingits and non-Natives also played on separate sports teams. Even the Presbyterian Church had separate congregations—language difficulties were only one reason for doing so—and, in 1903, separate churches were established.

Sitka's volunteer fire department was predominantly Native. City government was predominantly Euro-American, although by the 1920s prominent Tlingits like Andrew Hope and David Howard served as councilmen. Even Sitka's Pioneer Home—a Territorial retirement home for elderly Alaskans which opened in 1913—was initially whites only. Tlingit elders today remember signs in the windows of restaurants reading, "No dogs or Indians allowed."

Demeaning terms for Alaska Natives like *klootch*, *siwash*, *squaw*, *side-wheeler*, and *buck* were in common use. Some words were taken from Chinook, the contact language or trade jargon used along the Northwest Coast. *Siwash*, for example, meant "Indian" but came from the French *sauvage* (savage). *Klootch* for "woman" was derived from a Nuu-chah-nulth word. *Squaw*, also meaning woman, was originally an Algonquian word that acquired negative connotations as it spread west with early traders. A "buck" is a male deer, but the word was used as a derogatory term for male African-Americans as early as the 17th century and was then applied to Indians. *Side-wheeler* was used negatively and appears to have referred to the side-to-side gait some Alaskan Natives had as a result of illness and disability.

According to Tlingit elder Jessie Weir Price, in an interview in 1986, "The White people were very much opposed to Natives. Even the movies—they had the Natives go on the one side and the white people to the other...It was that bad. That's one of the reasons the ANB [Alaska Native Brotherhood] was organized." Leslie Yaw, a teacher who later became the superintendent of the Sitka Industrial Training School, reported in 1986 that he had been "shocked" at the prejudice he saw when he moved to Sitka in 1923: "There was not much intermarriage in that day. There were three 'squaw men,' white guys that lived with Indian women, and they were looked down on. When I came no self- respecting white girl would be seen on the street with an Indian boy or man. [But] there were mixed friendships. I learned hunting from Indian friends. And Mr. Merrill had none of this racial prejudice."

Yet Merrill was not an activist or social reformer. He was not driven like photographers Jacob Riis or Lewis Hine to use photography in an ethically evaluative way to expose social injustice and poverty and bring about change. He did not probe Sitka's back alleys or poverty-stricken homes with his camera or aim it at the drunk and

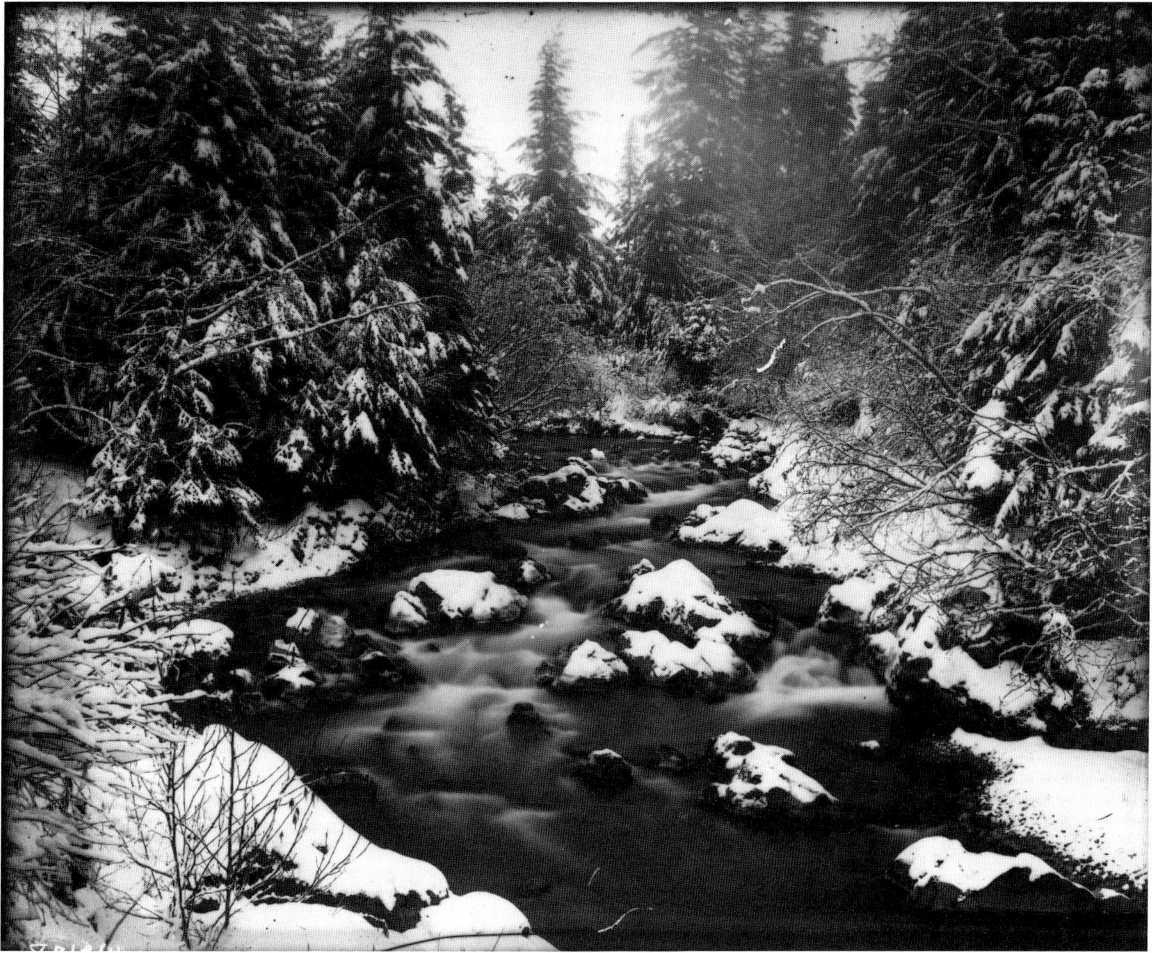

Figure 69
Indian River, Sitka, in winter. Photograph by E. W. Merrill. Courtesy of Stratton Library, Sheldon Jackson College, Sitka, AK. (M X B1e)

dissolute. He was not a well-intentioned voyeur of this sort, and his images of the Tlingit do not turn them into "facts" or objects of the viewer's compassion, pity, or condescension. Although he used a straight documentary style, his goals were primarily personal—to communicate his respect for Tlingit culture and his love of beauty and nature to those who saw his work—and most of his Tlingit work is explanatory or aesthetically evaluative, to use Barrett's classifications.

Merrill had deep feelings for nature and discussed these with like-minded people such as Robert Buchanan, Sitka's Presbyterian minister from 1916 to 1924, whose son, John Buchanan, remembered in an interview in Sitka on August 15, 1986: "Many times I recall standing being fascinated listening to them discuss philosophy... They were both very nature minded. I used to accuse my father of being a pantheist. He tied many of his sermons to something right out of nature...If Merrill had any religion at all, it was pantheism. I think that is one of the things that

   ELBRIDGE WARREN MERRILL

brought he and my father together, they both saw God in nature and liked to discuss it."

Merrill had been psychologically wounded as a child and he considered nature a healing force and his photography as a form of communication. "When we are young we all see a vision… Then we suffer, and seek desperately to get it back," he once told writer F. Barrett Willoughby. "Many of us have recovered it in the peace of Alaskan forests; but not all can stay. I like to think that my pictures will go out into the world, taking the spirit of my country to those who need it, to those who understand it" (1926:42).

Photography was also a way for him to enter into his own communion with nature, to closely observe and record its mysteries and beauty (Fig. 69). In this, Merrill was like many other Euro-American photographers and artists of the time who sought transcendent meaning in nature. Their search sprang from Romanticism, the first artistic movement to reflect modern society's distress with industry and the man-made landscape of cities. Mountains were particularly symbolic. Besides their inherent visual power, they remained largely untouched by the human hand and, as cultural observer John G. Cawelti noted, "reflected deep strains of artistic, moral and religious feeling which had long been a part of American and European culture" (Synder and Munson 1976:26). Merrill took an early view of mountains near Sitka (Fig. 70) with non-panchromatic film which imparted the same tonality to all dark colors whether black, green, brown, or gray and to all light colors, in this case snow and reflections. The idea of humans dwarfed by the scale and majesty of nature is clearly evident in Merrill's view of St. Lazaria Island in which the human figure is barely visible (Fig. 71).

Merrill often left Sitka for days at a stretch. He spent much of his time hiking, taking photographs, watching birds, and collecting specimens for his hobby, taxidermy. Taxidermy, it has been pointed out, resembles photography, except that specimens were shot with a camera and "fixed forever in the chemical emulsion of a photograph,"

rather than stuffed (Sandweiss 2002:222). In 1912 and 1913 he accompanied visiting ornithologist George Willett on birding expeditions into the mountains. According to Willett, writing in the *The Condor*, "Mr. Merrill, who is a fellow member of the Cooper Club, has taken a number of valuable specimens, and made many interesting notes on the birds of the region. He very kindly turned over to me all his notes, and the information obtained from there added materially to this paper" (1914:71). Willett's article mentions specimens taken by Merrill, including some he is said to have given to institutions like the University of Washington.

Merrill had built a cabin on the back slope of Mt. Verstovia, which he aptly named the "Hideaway." Like the Tlingit, he hunted and fished and lived off the land to a large degree. "Ferndale," his simple two-room cabin and studio on Jamestown Bay, located near the head of the present-day Verstovia trail, was one of the few dwellings on the bay at the time. It was half-hidden behind masses of ferns, foxgloves, and elderberry bushes and could be reached only by trail or by boat from town, which may explain why Merrill sometimes chose to stay in town during the winter. According to interviews with the late John Buchanan, Louise Brightman, Neill Andersen, and Afton Coon, who rented Merrill's house when he moved to Sitka in 1931, Ferndale was a simple frame cabin with wide shingle siding nailed to the studding and bare spruce floors. One room served as a bedroom, the other as combination kitchen, living room, and studio with large slanting windows in the roof to let in the southeast light. It must have been damp and cold in winter since the walls lacked interior sheathing and a potbelly stove provided the only heat. Here Merrill developed his photographs, read, and worked on his taxidermy (Fig. 72). When F. Barrett Willoughby visited him one summer in the mid-1920s, she found, besides the clutter of his photography equipment, a house decorated simply with "a few pictures of hunting dogs, a cluster of cedar cones, a rack of guns…a long, old-fashioned telescope" on the walls and a

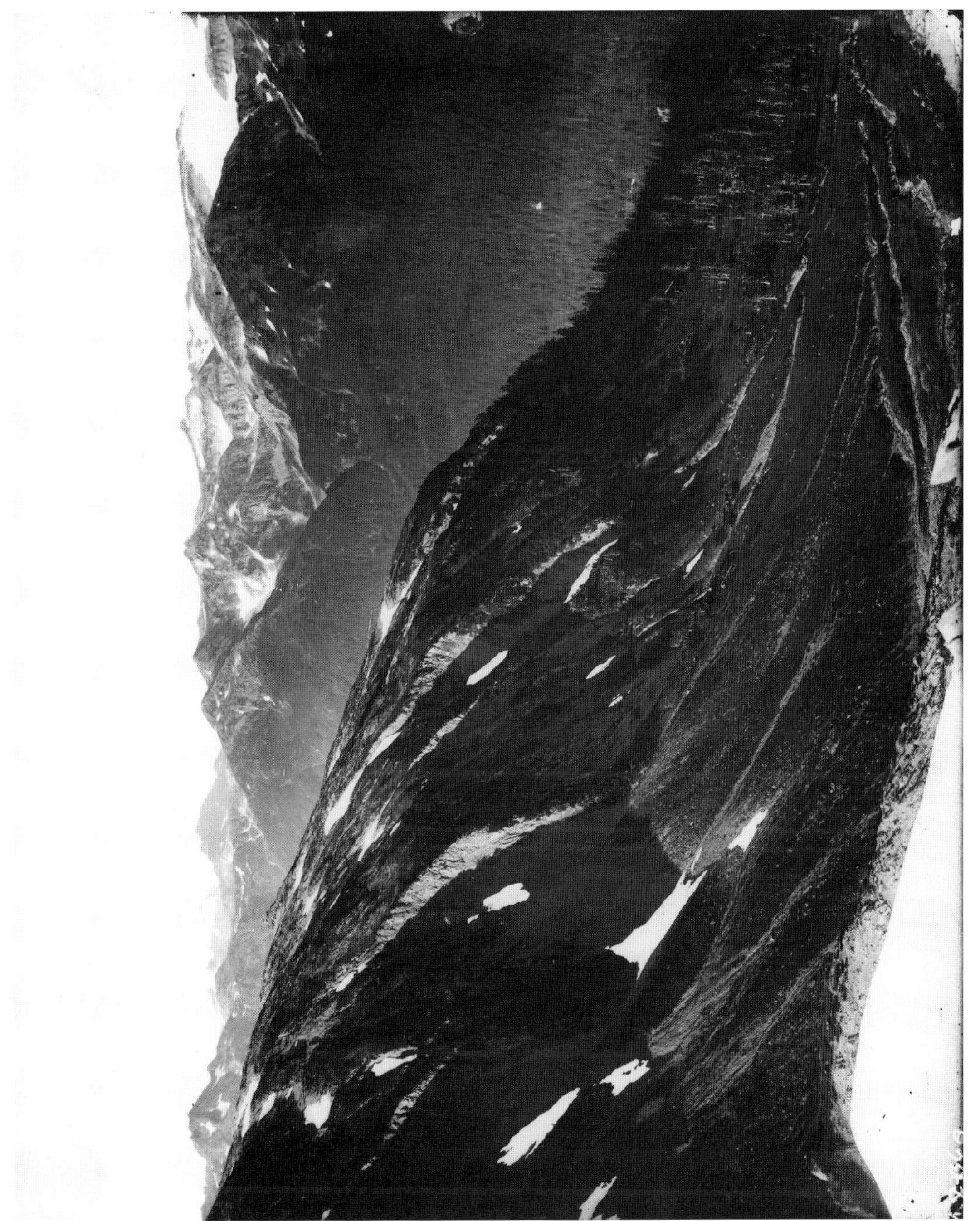

Figure 70
Mountains near Sitka, 1900. Photograph by E. W. Merrill. Courtesy of Stratton Library, Sheldon Jackson College, Sitka, AK. (M X B6e)

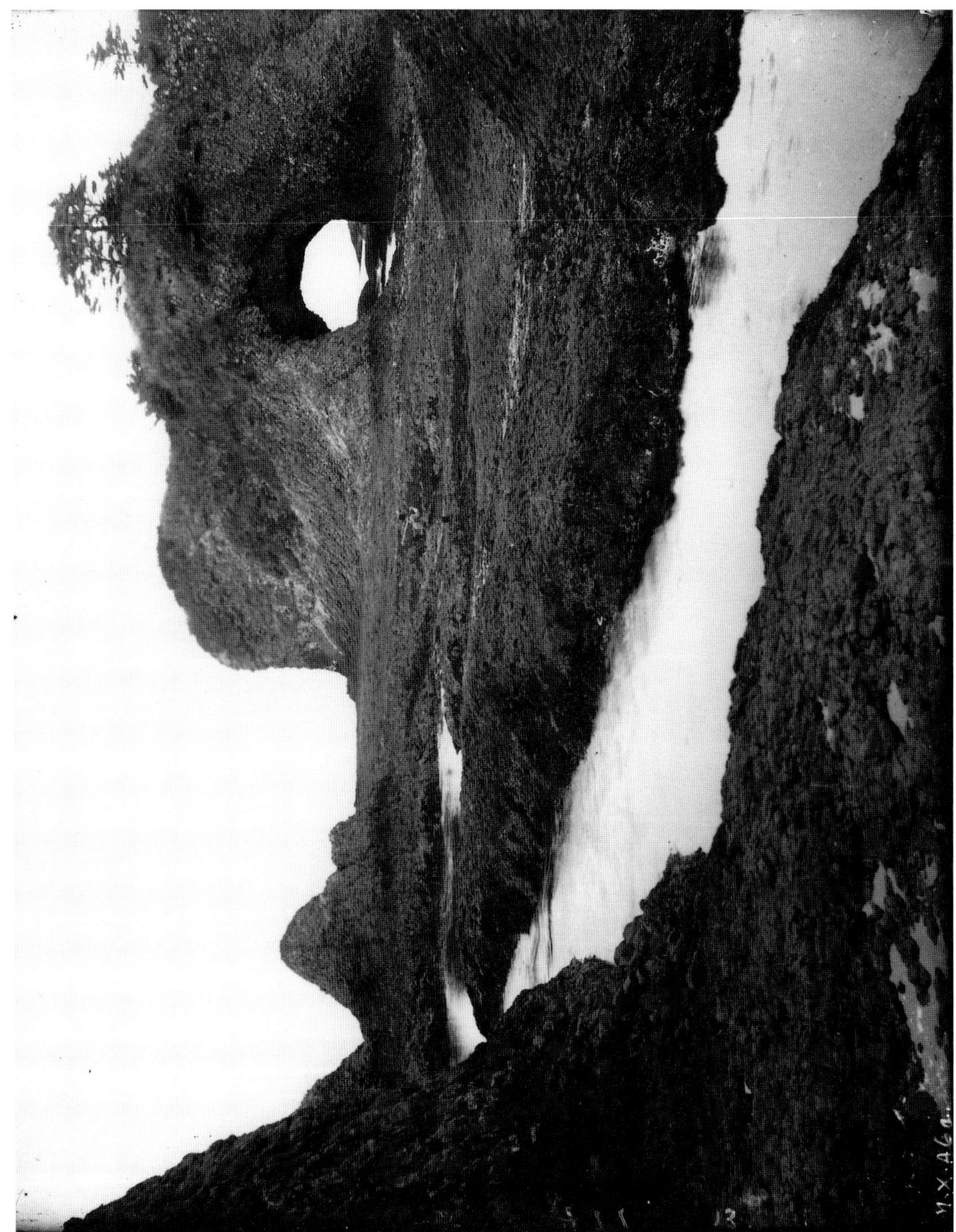

Figure 71
St. Lazaria Island, 1900. Photograph by E. W. Merrill. Courtesy of Stratton Library, Sheldon Jackson College, Sitka, AK. (M X A6a)

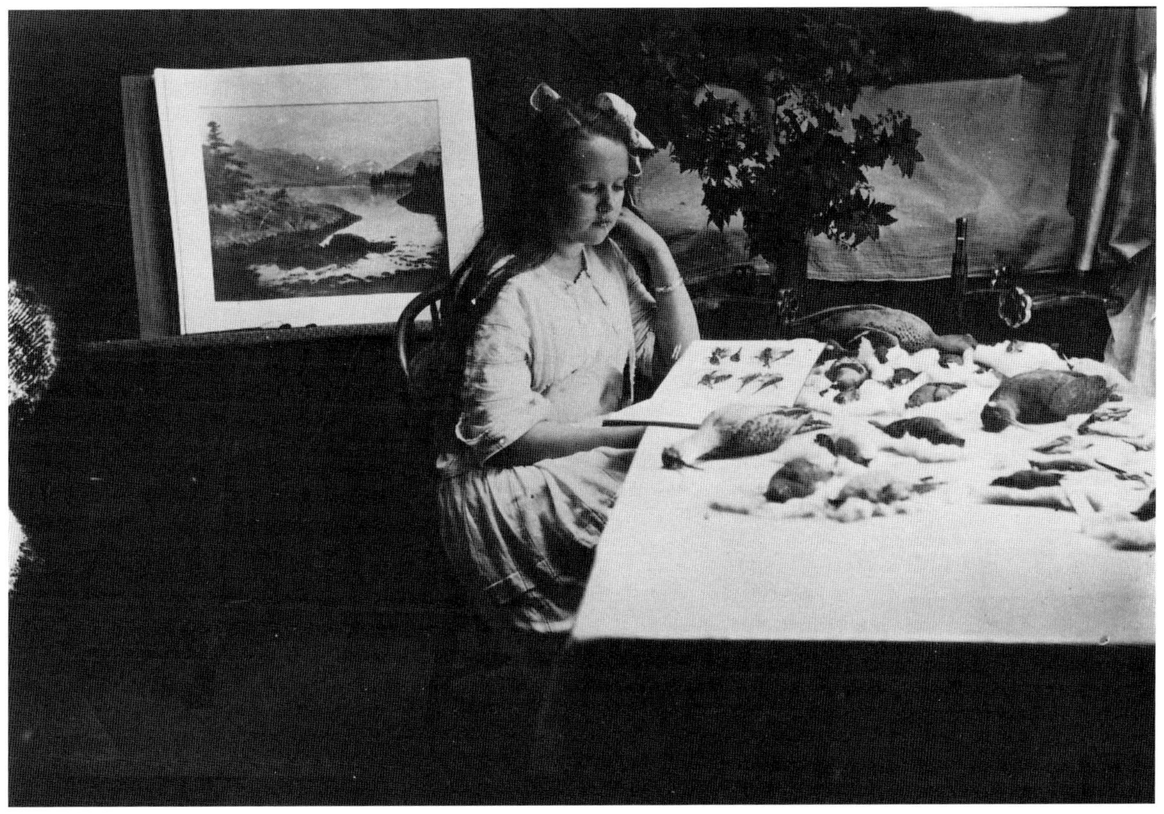

bowl of nasturtiums on the table (1926).

At 6'2" tall, with grey eyes, a square jaw, and abundant wavy black hair, Merrill cut a striking figure on Sitka's streets (Fig. 73). Older Sitkans today remember his erect posture and "stately" bearing as he strode briskly through town, often with a long black rain cape over his shoulders and a knapsack holding photography equipment and mail. People respected his photographic talent and Eastern refinement, yet he remained something of a mystery to them. He was a private person who seldom spoke of his past; all but his closest friends referred to him as "Mr. Merrill."

When he first arrived in Sitka, he shared a small house on Etolin Street in the non-Native part of town with two other bachelors, Henry Woodruff and Robert DeArmond, Sr. Woodruff and Merrill became close friends and later shared another house, but DeArmond felt that he never really knew Merrill; he "never said three sentences about himself," DeArmond's son remembered his father telling him (DeArmond 1967 and 1986).

Yet Merrill was far from a recluse. He stopped to speak to the children he passed on the sidewalks, pointing out a cloud formation or commenting on the weather, and he visited the DeArmond home every Christmas to give each child a wooden bird or whistle he had whittled. "He was lovable and he did a lot of good things for young

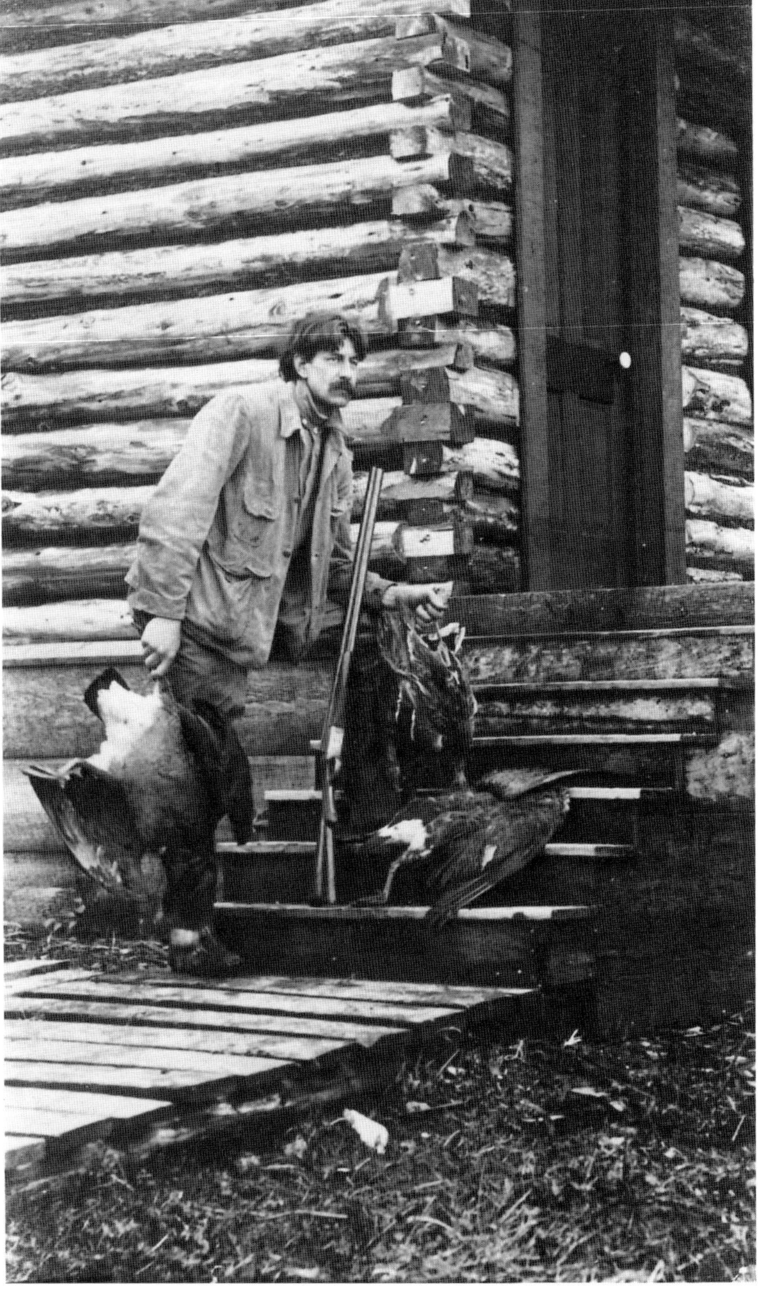

Figure 73
Merrill as a young man in
Sitka. Photographer unknown
but possibly his friend and
one-time roommate, Henry
Woodruff. Courtesy of
Stratton Library, Sheldon
Jackson College, Sitka, AK.

zation whose membership consisted of "officers and members of nearly every department of the federal, military and civil services, of doctors, lawyers, merchants, as well as miners, sailors, and other persons from ordinary walks of life" (Shoup 1909). The club prided itself on its cosmopolitan membership. One year nearly a third of its 58 members were from other countries, including Norway, Germany, Denmark, Finland, Russia, Cuba, Italy, England, and Canada. Merrill was a regular visitor at the Sitka Industrial Training School, where he took many photographs. He also participated

people," remembered the late Margaret Osbaken in an interview in Sitka on August 20, 1986: "He...taught a lot about the beauty of the land. He taught some people in Sitka photography."

Merrill also joined the Arctic Brotherhood, an ethnically mixed yet all-white fraternal organi-

in town affairs, working on Sitka's Memorial and Independence Day celebrations and serving on its Election Board several times during the 1920s, per the Minutes of the Common Council of Sitka (1900:29).

Merrill's closest personal relationships were with the non-Native community. Although he never married, he was emotionally linked to two women—both non-Natives. The first was Julia Haley, the lively and attractive daughter of a local miner and a life-long resident of Sitka. She clerked in his shop between 1905 and 1910, and a candid photograph taken by Merrill of Julia fishing suggests a certain intimacy. Some in town expected them to marry. For whatever reasons they did not, and in 1911 Julia opened her own curio store. According to Margaret Osbaken, who knew both Merrill and Julia, he was "very much in love with her. They were definitely fond of each other...very much so." Some claim that Julia developed into an eccentric in later years. "There was only one Julia Haley in the world and she was here in Sitka. She was a character. Every time the boat came in and there were a lot of tourists going by, she would play the piano like mad but leave the doors open so everyone could hear" (Anderson 1986).

Merrill was also a good friend of Elizabeth and George Barron, a fellow member of the Arctic Brotherhood. After George's death in 1916, Merrill remained devoted to Elizabeth and her daughter Frances who called him "Unckie Merrill." Merrill took many snapshots of Frances as a child. Some rumors circulated in Sitka that she was his daughter ("Frances" was the middle name of Merrill's sister), but Neill Andersen, a close friend of Elizabeth and Frances Barron who also knew Merrill, disagreed: "I don't think Frances was his daughter. I think he probably respected her as much as if she was. In this country there is always suspicion, but she didn't have any resemblance to him" (Anderson 1986). Although Merrill remained a bachelor and continued to live alone, he moved his shop into Elizabeth's general merchandise store and she and Frances became

his adoptive family. Merrill willed his negatives and photographs to Elizabeth Barron and appointed Frances to be the executrix of his estate.

He also remained close to his former housemate, Henry Woodruff. Another friend, James Condit, wrote in *The Alaska Weekly*, November 22, 1929, after Merrill's death that "His courtesy was founded upon a respect for others and a sympathy which over-leaped artificial boundary lines and gave him understanding. No one conversed with him for any length of time without being stimulated to better and higher thinking" (p. 7).

Merrill was a good conversationalist and interested in many subjects besides photography. Largely for this reason he was called upon to entertain important visitors such as Mrs. James Wickersham, the wife of Alaska's delegate to Congress, whom *The Verstovian*, June 1915, reported he escorted through the Indian River Park (Fig. 74). "He was a fascinating person to listen to," John Buchanan recalled in 1986, "because he had a beautiful, soft voice with a Bostonian accent [and]...[h]is choice of language was beautiful. It was low toned, something like Ronald Coleman." According to a friend, Merrill was "familiar with the best literature of the day, reveled in poetry and lived in an atmosphere of his thinking" (*The Alaska Weekly*, November 22, 1929, p. 7). One of the attractions of membership in the Arctic Brotherhood may have been its library, reputed to be "one of the best equipped libraries in the Northland" (*The Alaskan*, December 22, 1900, p. 3). Merrill once explained that part of his motivation for taking photographs was to "catch and hold for others some of the beautiful, ever-changing spirit of Alaska. Particularly do I want to give back to those who write books an equivalent of the pleasure they give to me" (Willoughby 1926:42).

Although Merrill advertised his photography and curio business in newspapers, listed it in business directories, and enjoyed talking about and showing his photographs to people, he apparently was an indifferent businessman. If a tourist displeased him by not properly appreciating his work or by balking at its price, Merrill would re-fuse to sell it. Local residents often had to wait months for a photograph they had ordered. In 1908 Merrill accepted a commission to take pho-tographs for a report on the Sitka National Mon-ument, but then was slow completing it. A letter written to the Forest Supervisor in Ketchikan by A. G. Shoup, a Deputy U.S. Marshal, reveals something of Merrill's working habits: "Mr. Mer-rill says that if the weather is at all favorable he will try to get some others [photographs] showing the beach line. If he does I will mail them un-der separate cover, but your negatives have some views which show that pretty well. I am sorry that they weren't sent with the report but Merrill was a little slow as usual" (Shoup 1908). The President of the Alaska Road Commission, in a letter writ-ten on October 2, 1922, to the Acting Director of the National Park Service, Arno B. Cammerer, discussing Merrill's possible appointment as cus-todian of Sitka's park, remarked: "Mr. Merrill is an expert photographer and taxidermist and has painted some really remarkable landscapes. There is quite a demand for his pictures and if he would pay attention to business he could make a good income...Unfortunately, Mr. Merrill has all the temperamental disabilities of an artist; inattention to regular and steady business being an outstanding characteristic. Were it not for his unreliability in this respect, he would be an ideal custodian for the Monument" (Steese 1922).

Connie Hodgkins, the widow of a younger friend, dentist Harry Hodgkins, remembered in an interview in Sitka on August 13, 1986, that Merrill "didn't care about money as long as he had something to eat. He used to pay the Doctor with pictures, but the Doctor told him to stop bringing them over."

Merrill was commissioned by individuals and by local groups and organizations such as the Sitka Industrial Training School, the Rus-sian Orthodox Church, the Alaska Native Broth-erhood, and the National Park Service to take photographs. In 1925, he worked briefly as a still photographer for the Metropolitan Pictures Cor-poration which was filming *Rocking Moon* on lo-cation in Sitka and nearby Goddard Hot Springs. The film, starring Lillian Tashman and John Bow-ers and directed by George Melford, was based on a novel by Florence Barrett Willoughby, the writer and short-term resident of Sitka, quoted earlier, who knew Merrill.

Merrill's store display also gives an idea of the kind of images he sold (Fig. 75); of the 11 photographs displayed, 3 are of Tlingit subjects, 3 of nature, and 3 of town scenes. His landscape photographs appeared in publications like the *Alaska-Yukon Magazine* and books including *Sitka, the Beautiful* (Stromstadt-Brown 1906), *The Story of Sitka* (Andrews 1981), and *From Mississippi to the Sea* (Coontz 1930). He also contributed bird photographs to *The Condor* and local views to many issues of *The Thlingit* and *The Verstovian* (both Sitka Industrial School publications). Mer-rill also produced postcards, mainly scenic views of Sitka and its surrounding mountains and coastline. *The Alaskan* for October 7, 1905, an-nounced that merchant "E. DeGroff has a fine line of souvenir postal cards. They are half-tone reproductions of photos taken by E. W. Merrill. The artist's and printer's work are alike com-mendable." The next year on February 10 it noted that "Our local artist, Merrill, has on sale some postal cards with a view of Mt. Edgecombe. The production is the finest we have ever seen of the extinct volcano and should rightly be called 'Merrill's Mount Edgecombe.'"

More frequently he took photographs for his own pleasure. Merrill seems not to have relied heavily on photographs of the Tlingit to gener-ate income. While he did sell them, they were just part of what he did. According to the late Kaagwaantaan elder Albert Davis (Aankadaxt-seen), in an interview in Sitka in August 1986, Merrill also "took it upon himself. He was a his-torian or something like that...He went through all these houses, through the village, taking pic-tures of artifacts...He came into the houses and told people what he would like to do." Merrill photographed many artifacts, sometimes to

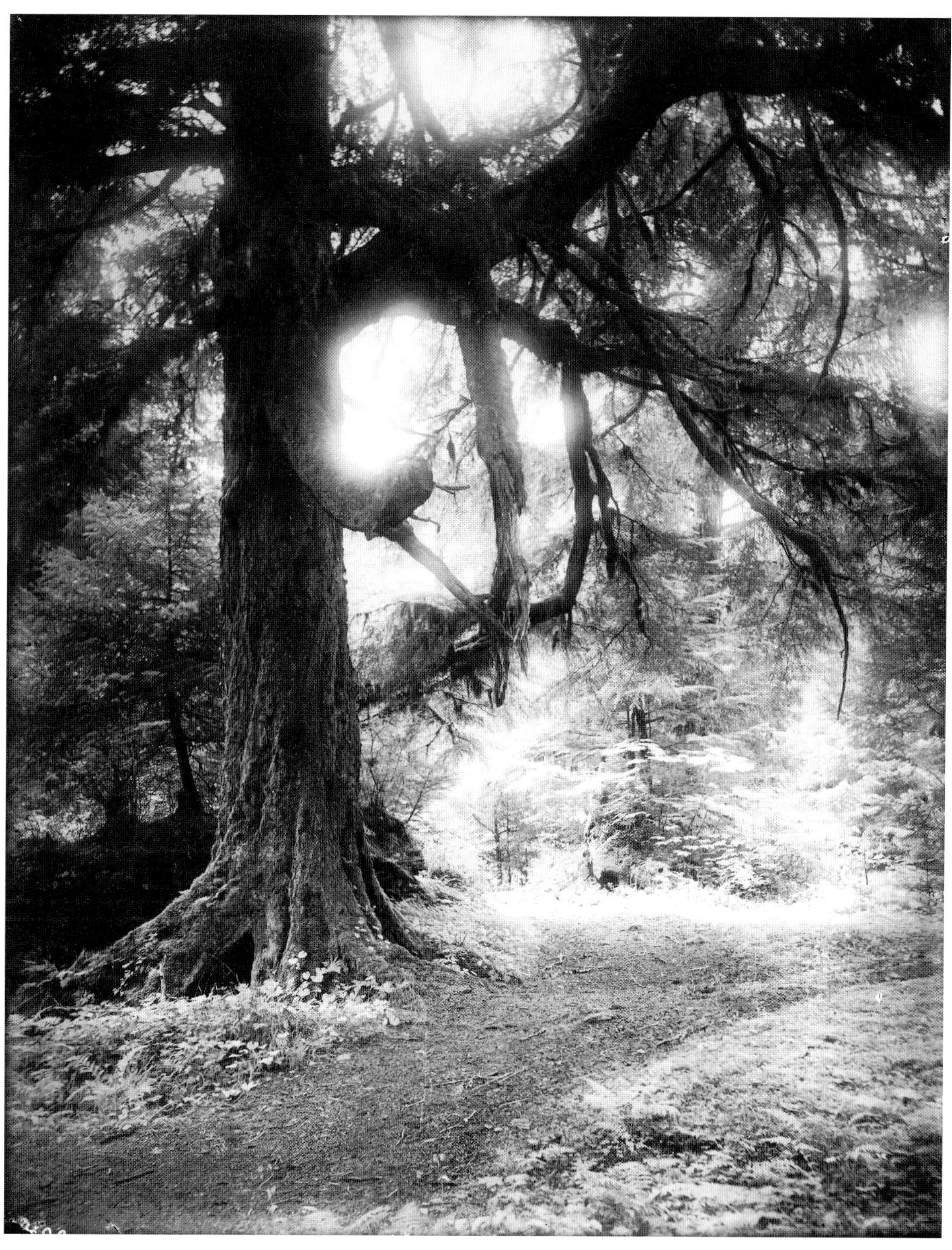

Figure 74
"Witch Tree" in Indian River Park, now gone. Photograph by E. W. Merrill. Courtesy of Stratton Library, Sheldon Jackson College, Sitka, AK.

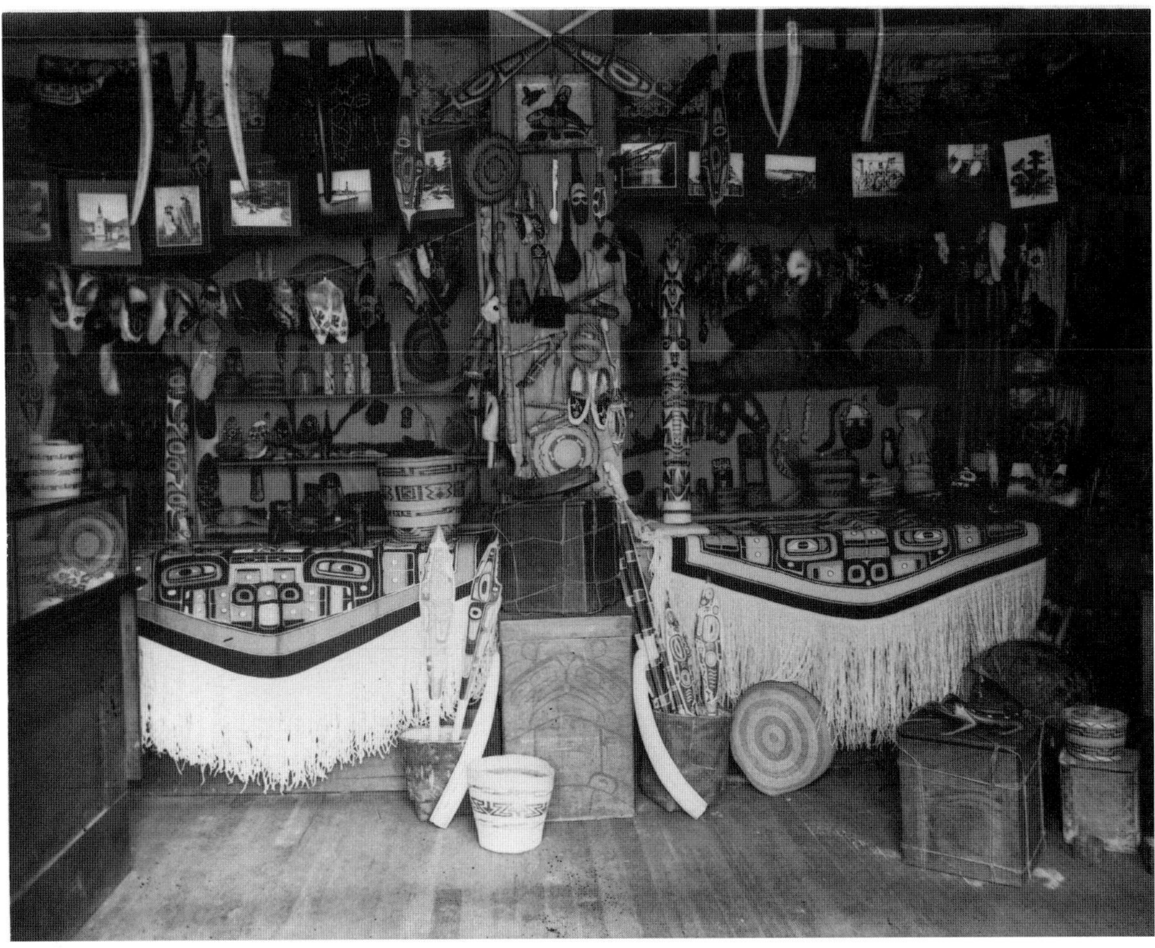

Figure 75
Merrill's curio and photography shop in Elizabeth Barron's store, Sitka, 1920. The photographs hanging from a line give an idea of the kinds of photography Merrill offered for sale. By permission of the Alaska State Library, Juneau, AK. (PC57–125)

document them and share with other collectors, more often—it seems—simply because he admired their craftsmanship and beauty, especially Chilkat blankets (Fig. 76) and spruce-root baskets with their intricate patterns representing nature: wave, tide in, tide out, fiddlehead fern, wild celery, woodworm, fish flesh, bear tracks, fireweed, butterfly, salmon berry head (Fig. 77).

Merrill used dry plate technology in a variety of formats, but mostly 8x10" glass plates.

He was an excellent technician in the opinion of Rod Slemmons, Associate Curator for Photography at the Seattle Art Museum, in a letter of January 19, 1987. He relied on natural light even for his studio portraits and used sharp lenses and small apertures, learning early that he needed to over-expose and under-develop his landscapes and deep forest scenes in order to get a long tonal range (Fig. 78). He usually made contact prints (that is, prints the same size as the nega-

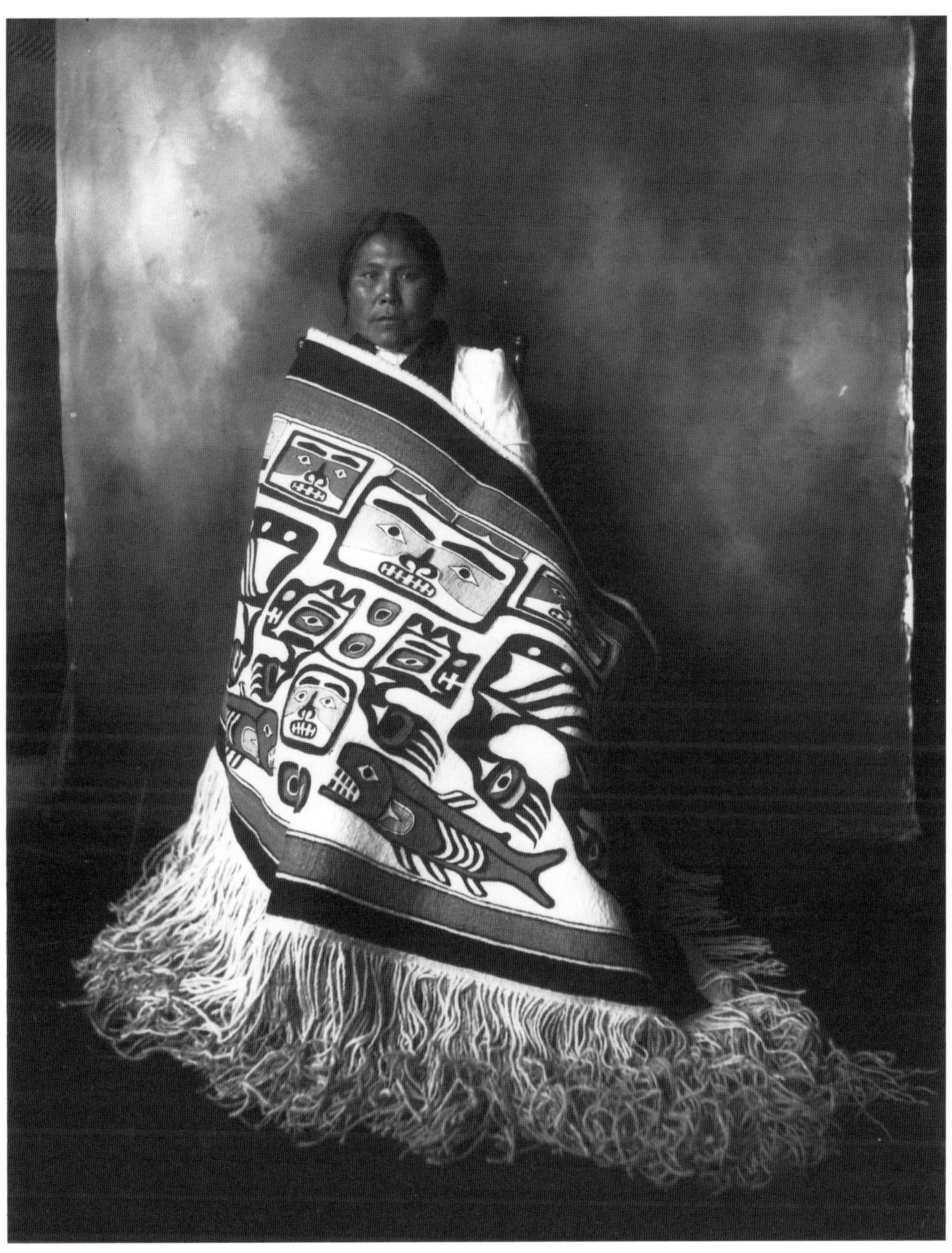

Figure 76
A<u>k</u>lé (Mary Willard) draped in the Bear Chilkat robe now owned by the Chookaneidí clan of Hoonah.
Identification by Harold Jacobs. By permission of the Alaska State Library, Juneau, AK. (P57–092)

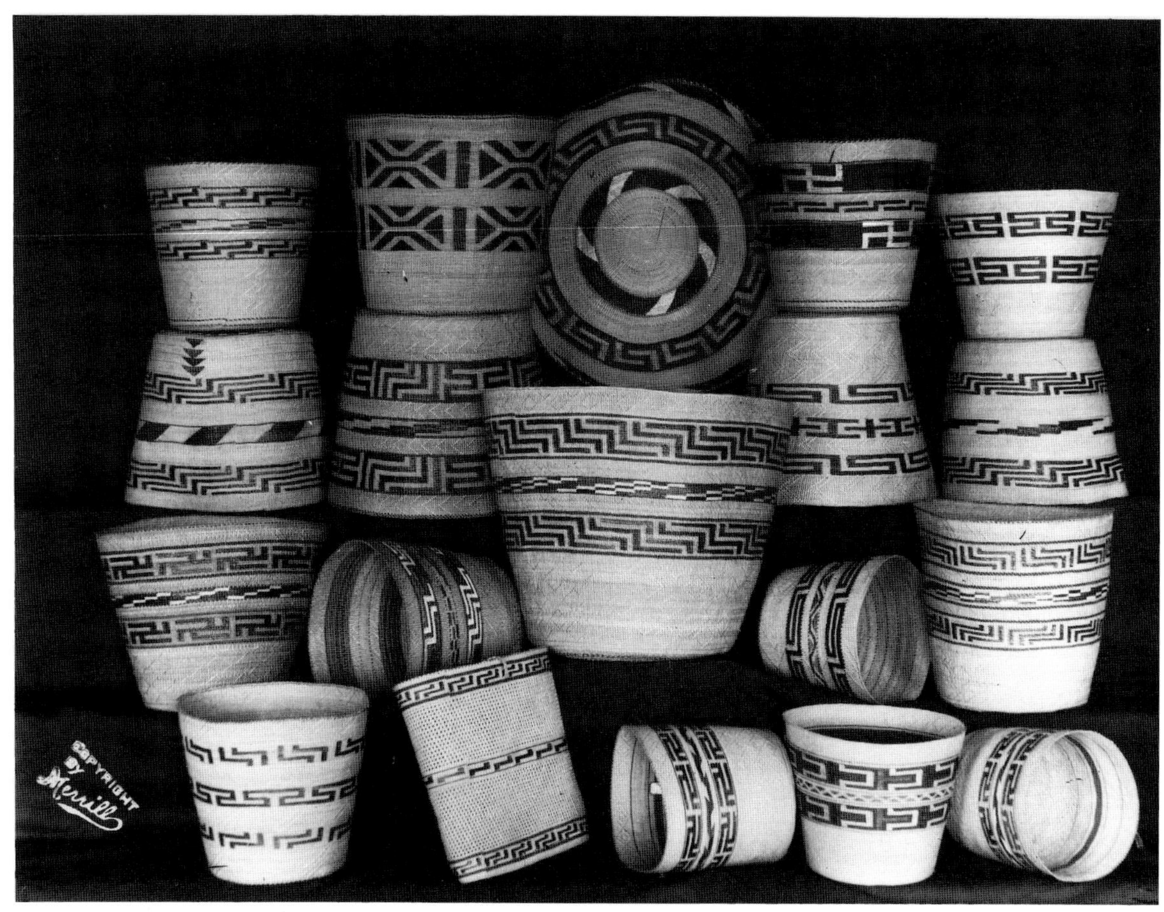

Figure 77
Part of Merrill's collection of Tlingit spruce-root baskets. Photograph by E. W. Merrill. By permission of the Alaska State Library, Juneau, AK. (P57–79)

tive), placing the glass plates on gelatin chloride printing-out paper and exposing them to light, then washing them, and sometimes hand coloring them. No chemicals were used and the process produced warm-toned images. When Merrill made enlargements, he printed on gelatine bromide/iodide developing-out paper which produced images that were colder in tone unless altered chemically. Merrill also used some cartridge roll film, although primarily for the personal snapshots he took.

At his death in 1929, Merrill had six large-format cameras. According to Henry Kyllingstad,

a photographer who printed from many of Merrill's glass plates in the 1980s, Merrill's 8x10" camera had a convertible lens which gave him three focal lengths. The appraised value of Merrill's six cameras at the time of his death in 1929 was $250 ($3,026 in 2007). Unfortunately, the cameras are not described in the appraisal, and the only one of his known cameras remaining today is an Eastman Kodak Bullet No. 2 (1896 model). His other possessions included an enlarging camera (appraised at $50), 1,500 8x10" glass negatives ($500), 693 framed and unframed prints ($642), 800 postcards ($25), 37 5x16"

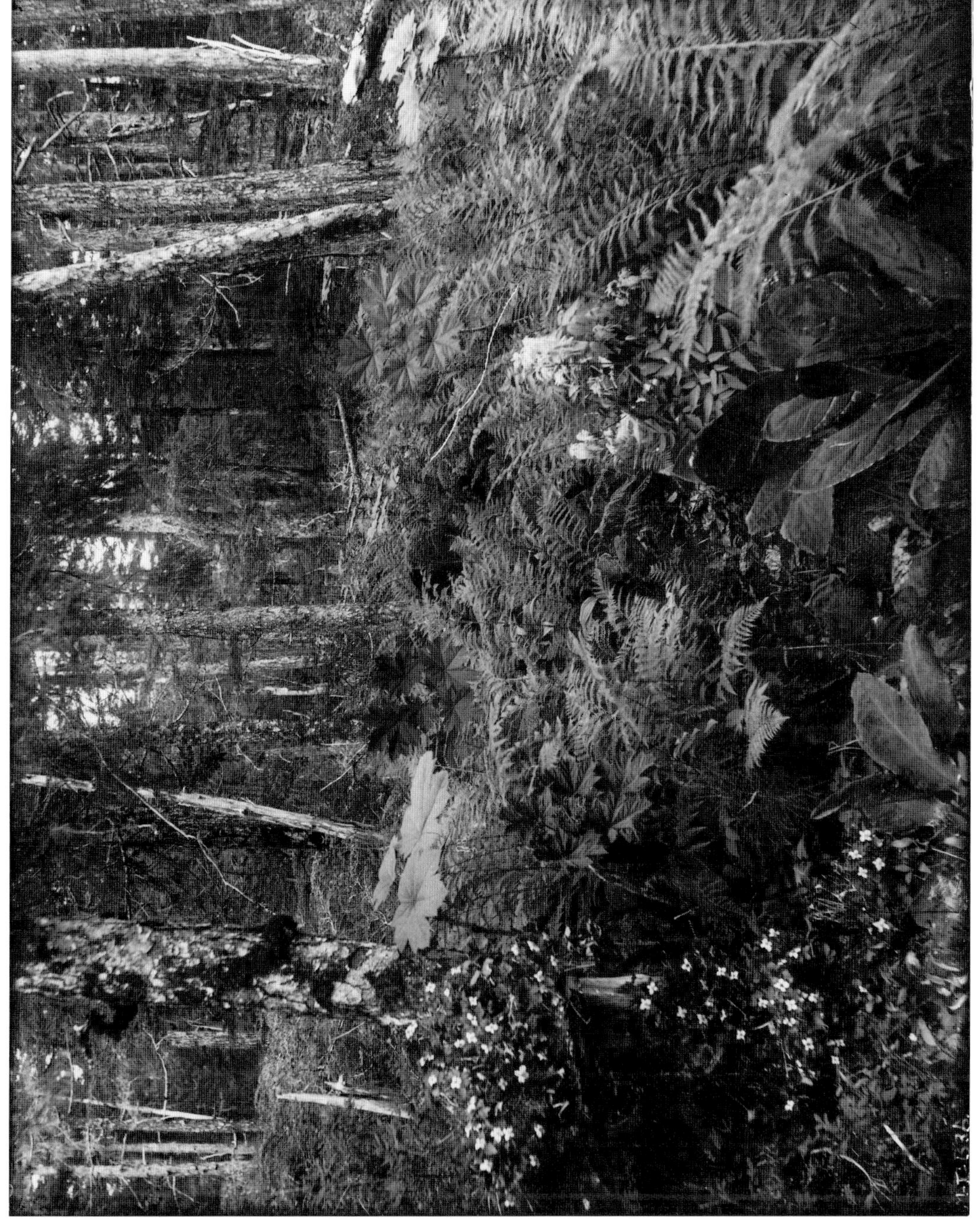

Figure 78
Forest scene. Photograph by E. W. Merrill. Courtesy of Stratton Library, Sheldon Jackson College. Sitka, AK. (M I B3b)

photographic panels ($75), and miscellaneous equipment including tripods, frames, chemicals, blocking, trays, and plate holders ($110). Their total value in 2007 purchasing power was just under $20,000.

The largest collection of Merrill's photographs until 2007—approximately 900 glass plates as well as black and white prints—was located in the Stratton Library of the Sheldon Jackson College in Sitka which is now closed. (At the time of writing they were being cared for by the Sitka National Historical Park under a temporary loan arrangement.) An additional 203 glass plate negatives are in the Sitka National Historical Park collection for a total of 1,103 glass negatives known to remain in Sitka. This represents about 73 percent of the plates inventoried after Merrill's death. In 1978 the Alaska State Library, Stratton Library, and Sitka National Historical Park jointly produced two sets of copy negatives from these plates. Today, digital images of Merrill's photographs are available on-line through the Alaska State Library; about 50 can be found on the Sitka National Historical Park website. Small numbers of prints can also be found in the Isabel Miller Museum and the Kettleson Library in Sitka, the Tongass Historical Society in Ketchikan, the Suzzallo Library at the University of Washington in Seattle, the Bancroft Library at the University of California, Berkeley, the National Anthropological Archives at the National Museum of Natural History in Washington, DC, and in private hands in Sitka, including those of many Tlingit residents.

Merrill only occasionally copied other photographers' work. Former Sitka customs agent C. L. Andrews notes in his journal, now in the Rasmuson Library at the University of Alaska, Fairbanks, that Merrill had asked him to send his photograph of the lower Russian blockhouse in Sitka. Merrill also copied a photograph taken by Alexander Phiele of a shaman's mummy found in a cave near Sitka, but indicated clearly on his glass plate negative that it was a copy.

Barrett Willoughby (1926) reported that Merrill made trips into the interior of Baranof Island to excavate and that he returned with artifacts and photographs of mummies he had found in a hidden valley (for a description of such a find see de Laguna 1933). However, no mention of such activities emerged in my many interviews with Sitkans about Merrill or in any other written document.

Other photographers at the time often put their own imprint on another person's work, and over the years many images in archives have been misattributed, including some of Merrill's Tlingit photographs. Some of his potlatch pictures, for example, have been attributed to W. C. Chase (see de Laguna 1972:1,137). The following example gives a sense of what sometimes happened. Alfred A. Hart, official photographer for the Central Pacific Railroad between 1865 and 1869, sold his negatives to photographer Carleton Watkins in 1869, who published them in the early 1880s without crediting Hart. Watkins's negatives, in turn, were seized in 1871 for nonpayment of debt by photographer I. W. Taber, who then issued a stereograph series without credit to either Watkins or Hart. In 1876, Taber also acquired Watkins's gallery and then issued Watkins's prints without credit as well.

Merrill viewed himself as an artist, and many of his nature studies and portraits can be classified as aesthetically evaluative in that they capture the beauty of form and are artistically photographed in terms of composition and light. Most people would also consider them "art" in that they evoke feeling, reflect his personal vision, and clearly entail more than mere photographic description. The Sitka Industrial Training School newspaper, *The Thlingit*, printed the following effusive assessment in December 1909: "Mr. E. W. Merrill, Sitka's artistic photographer, has recently turned out some pieces of scenic photography that are surely masterpieces in this art. Never was old Edgecombe [Mt. Edgecumbe on nearby Kruzof Island] printed in such stately grandeur, and various pictures setting forth mountain and channel, and bay and island

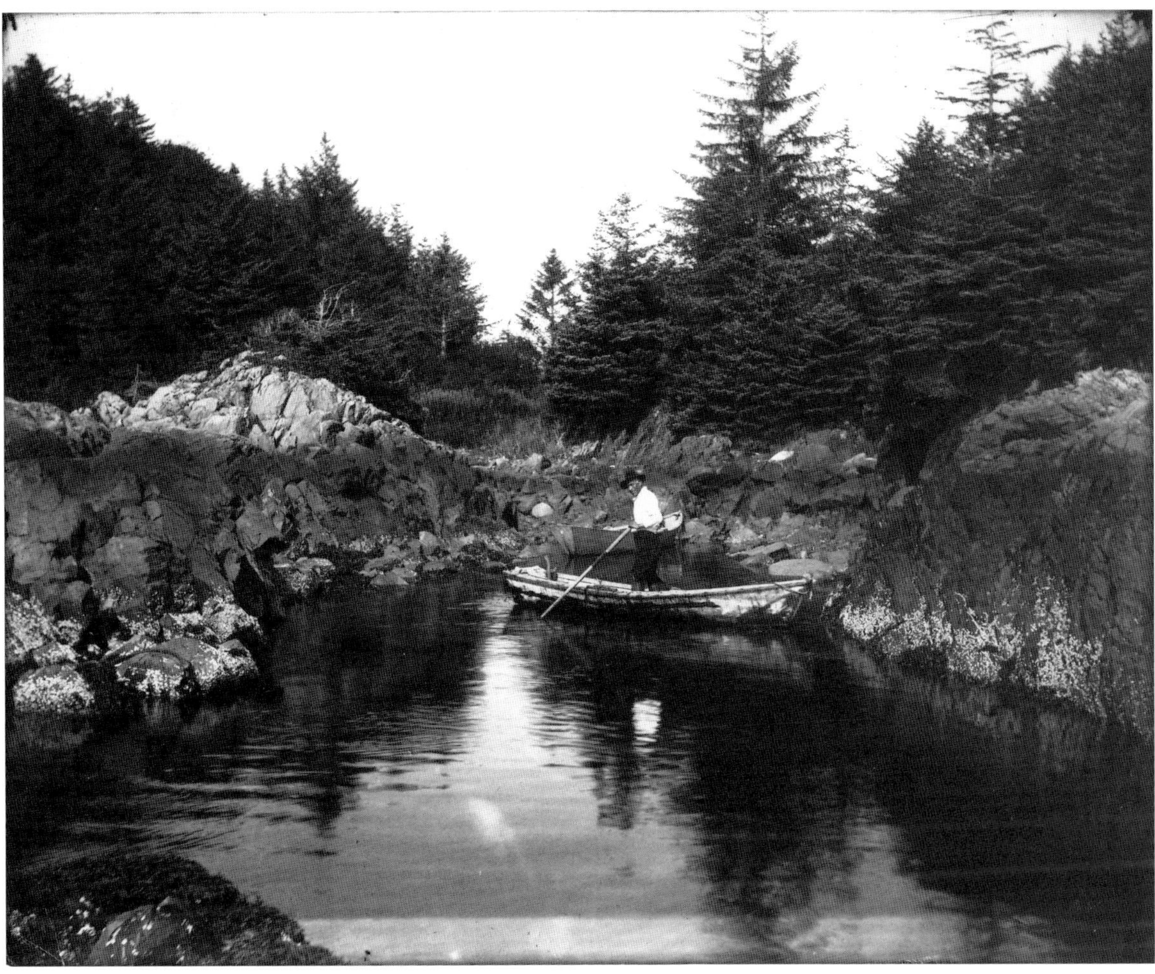

Figure 79
Tlingit man in canoe, near Sitka. Photograph by E. W. Merrill. Courtesy of Stratton Library, Sheldon Jackson College, Sitka, AK. (M II B10g)

are marvelous in their beauty" (p. 3).

The hallmark of artistic photography at the time was the individuality of style expressed in a unique print. Photographers who considered their work "art" would use their fingers, brushes, and etching tools to introduce highlights or to obscure or remove details that seemed too descriptive or factual. They often printed using bichromated gelatin and carbon, oil pigments, and art papers. As a result, no print was an exact replica of its negative. Merrill, in contrast, adopted a straight style characterized by sharp focus, detail, a broad tonal range, and minimal, if any, manipulation in the photographic process. According to art historian David Ogawa (2007) Merrill's work is reminiscent of German photographer August Sander's modernist documentary style. He may also have been influenced by French realism (Fig. 79). The Boston museum and art scene which Merrill would have been exposed to before he moved west was heavily influenced by French realism; the Boston Museum of Fine Arts, for example, had been the first American museum to acquire paintings by Courbet from

the artist in the 1850s.

Sitkans respected Merrill's commitment to his work. "He worshiped what he was doing as if that was the only thing in life," recalled Neill Andersen in an interview in Sitka in August 1986. "He might stay up two or three days just to get one picture sometimes. I heard him talk about that. Everything has to be just right—the sun, the clouds. He would spot something that he would want, but he had to take great precautions and be very careful. I remember that." During an interview in Sitka, August 17, 1986, Leslie Yaw recalled Merrill's description of how he had photographed a deer: "He spent the night on the mountain between Verstovia and Arrowhead. There's a saddle that leans over, kind of broad in one place. Mr. Merrill's up there early in the morning like five o'clock of a summer morning, and the deer is out feeding, and he very cautiously and carefully waits to get that picture with the mountain top and in the distance, Silver Bay."

Robert DeArmond, Jr., who always regarded Merrill as "a bit of a poser," remembered in an interview in August 1986 in Juneau listening to Merrill describe his photographs to a group of tourists in Elizabeth Barron's store: "He would point in an arty way to a photograph of two Tlingits and say, 'See that fine Roman nose,'

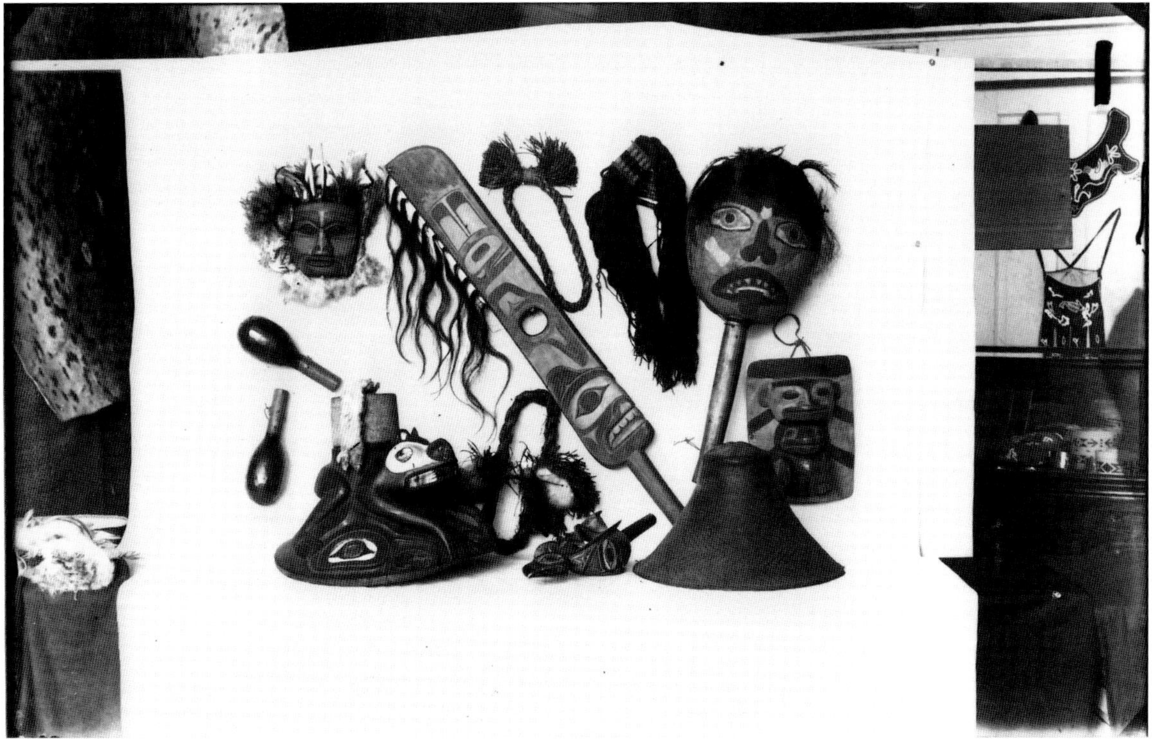

Figure 80
Part of Merrill's collection of Tlingit material culture, which he left to the Alaska Historical Library and Museum, Juneau, photographed inside his studio/shop. Two rattles (left), red cedar frog hat (left front), bird-holding-frog chief's rattle (center, front), spruce-root work hat (right, front), large rattle with face (right), dance leader's wooden staff with human hair, ceremonial cedar bark rope. Identifications by Lynn Wallen. Photograph by E. W. Merrill. Courtesy of Stratton Library, Sheldon Jackson College, Sitka, AK.

then to another photograph, 'The light had to be just right to get that.'"

What was Merrill's relationship to the Tlingit? His most compelling images, at least to this non-Native observer, are of Sitka's Tlingit residents. Merrill regarded these photographs as important works; he registered the copyright of only four photographs with the Library of Congress and all are of the Tlingit. According to elder Albert Davis (Aankadaxtseen), in an interview in Sitka in August 1986, Merrill "took pictures, all these pictures, telling people that he would put them in the world. That he was going to make compensation to them. That he was going to pay them for taking the pictures which never came about...People had a name for him. I'm sorry. I'm not going to say it. It was something like thief or something like that...People don't tell the truth now. They'll say, 'Yes, I guess so' [in response to questions about whether people liked Merrill]. [But] not all people liked him."

It would be surprising if everyone had felt the same about Merrill or Emmons or DeGroff or Andrews or Soboleff or Kayamori or any other photographer. The issue of remuneration for photographs (as for information) is always a sensitive one, and the potential for cultural misunderstandings is great. The Tlingit expected compensation for the services they performed as well as for the property and rights they "owned." Services rendered by one clan to a clan in the opposite moiety, for example, were always paid back in comparable services. Wrong doing, injury, even the accidental death of a member of one clan caused by the member of another was redressed with blankets or another medium of exchange in the amount the relatives of the injured party requested. Payment, and the acknowledgment of debt it implied, helped restore the harmony and balance which were central components of the Tlingit universe.

The Tlingit were also expert traders who knew the value of money and enjoyed a reputation as skilled bargainers. How much did this extend to photography? Sitka customs agent C. L.

Andrews took many photographs of the Tlingit at both his and their instigation and never mentions payment in his diaries. Elbridge Merrill's modest living circumstances and inattention to the monetary aspect of his business and his close relationship to some Tlingit, as well as the *many* images he took over a 30-year period, make it unlikely that he would have been regularly asked or expected to pay the Tlingit to pose for him.

Merrill was fascinated by the artistry of the Tlingit's material culture: their carved masks, halibut hooks, bowls, and house posts, their spruce-root baskets and ceremonial hats, and their elaborately woven Chilkat blankets. He began to collect pieces soon after his arrival in Sitka. Some items were standard tourist fare—miniature totem poles and paddles made explicitly for sale to outsiders—but others had been made by the Tlingit for their own use. These included older, finely woven spruce-root baskets and hats, Chilkat blankets, shaman's paraphernalia, carved masks and the like.

In time, Merrill became a knowledgeable collector. He corresponded with collector and ethnographer George Thornton Emmons, who retired from the Navy and left Sitka soon after Merrill arrived, but returned frequently to visit. Merrill willed a portion of his collection to Emmons; the remainder went to the Alaska State Museum in Juneau whose director, the Reverend Kashevaroff, he also knew (Fig. 80). The best piece in this collection, according to Museum staff members Lynn Wallen and Judy Hauck, is a beautifully carved and painted shaman's medicine box circa 1900 (not shown in the photograph). Peter Corey, Director of the Sheldon Jackson Museum in Sitka, observed in an interview in August 1986 that Merrill had a good eye for quality spruce-root baskets and "that meant good rapport with the makers, probably meaning he paid a fairer price [than many other collectors] for them." Merrill also apparently knew the cultural meaning of most items in his collection; he was interested in Tlingit history and beliefs. "Drowning, you know, is the worst death that can befall a

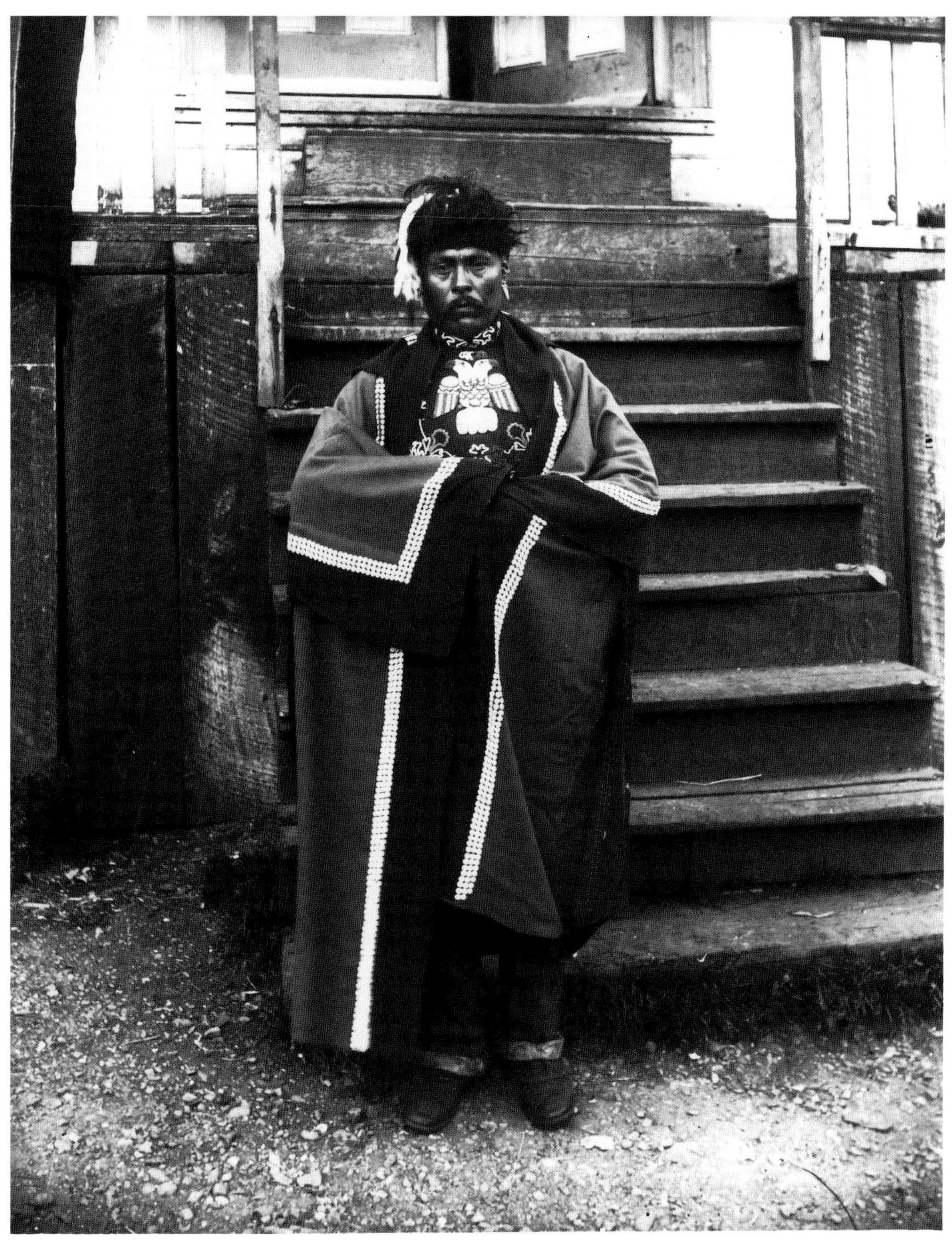

Figure 81
Chief L.aanteech, Sitka, 1905. The Kaagwaantaan clan adopted the double-headed eagle from the Russians.
L.aanteech wears the Raven headdress. Photograph by E. W. Merrill. By permission of the Alaska State
Library, Juneau, AK. (P57–150)

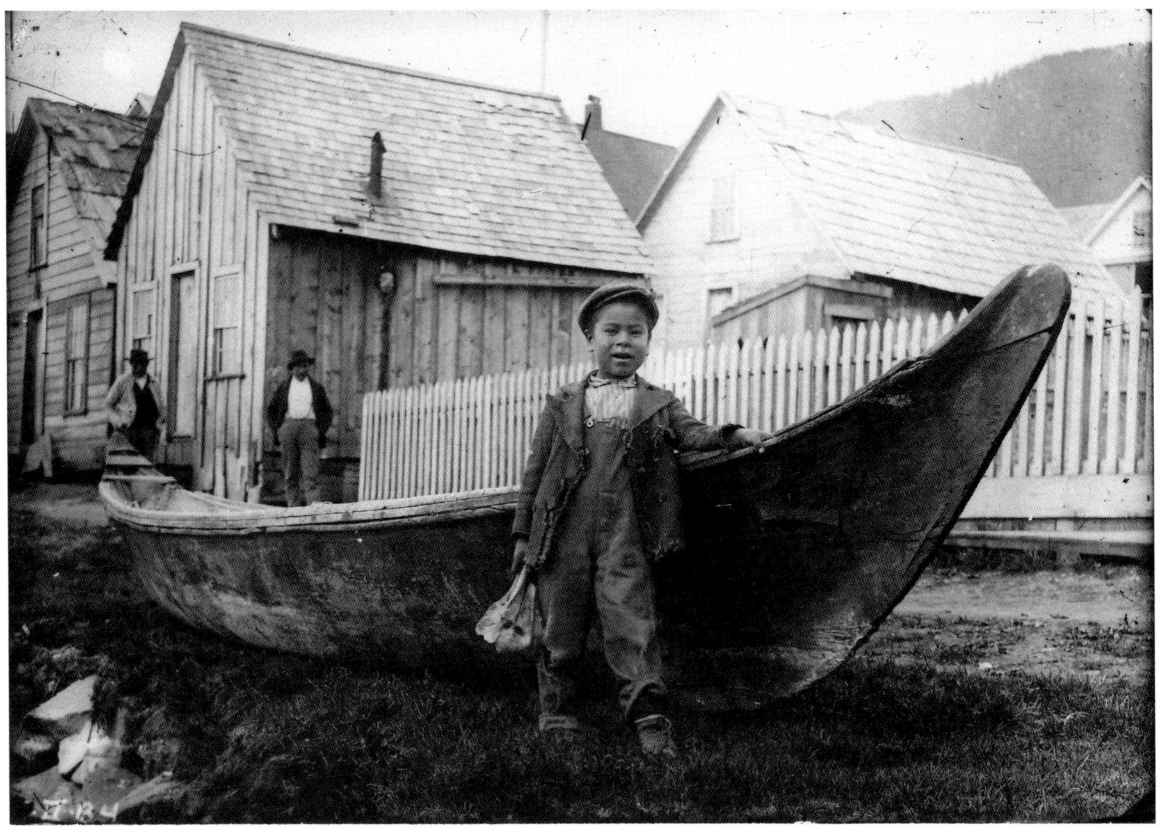

Figure 82
Unidentified Tlingit boy, Sitka, 1910. Photograph by E. W. Merrill. Courtesy of Stratton Library, Sheldon Jackson
College, Sitka, AK. (M II B4a)

Thlinget, especially if the body is not recovered," he once explained to F. Barrett Willoughby. "His spirit is believed to be captured by a land-otter, who turns it into a Kus-ta-ka [Kooshdakaa], or otter-man, a fearful woods ghost that haunts the forest along streams and lakes" (1926:68).

Merrill did not try to romanticize the Tlingit in his photographs or make them correspond to a set of preconceived stereotypes. The portrait in Figure 81 shows respectful eye-level contact with the subject, whose placement in the frame provides just enough context to ground him spatially and temporally. The costume the subject wears projects his social self, while the no-nonsense composition Merrill employed signals

that he was taking an "official portrait," not constructing an image that portrayed his own view of Tlingit culture.

Figure 64 at the beginning of the chapter, which shows one of Sitka's three Wolf clan houses with its new house post and Chilkat blankets raised high above the doorway, juxtaposes and balances these Native cultural signifiers with the building's non-traditional Western architecture. Merrill seems very aware of the visual and symbolic interplay between the Western-style building—with its strong texture—and the carving and blankets of Native tradition. The canoe in the foreground is included for depth of field and composition, but it is not fetishized as a "Native"

     ELBRIDGE WARREN MERRILL

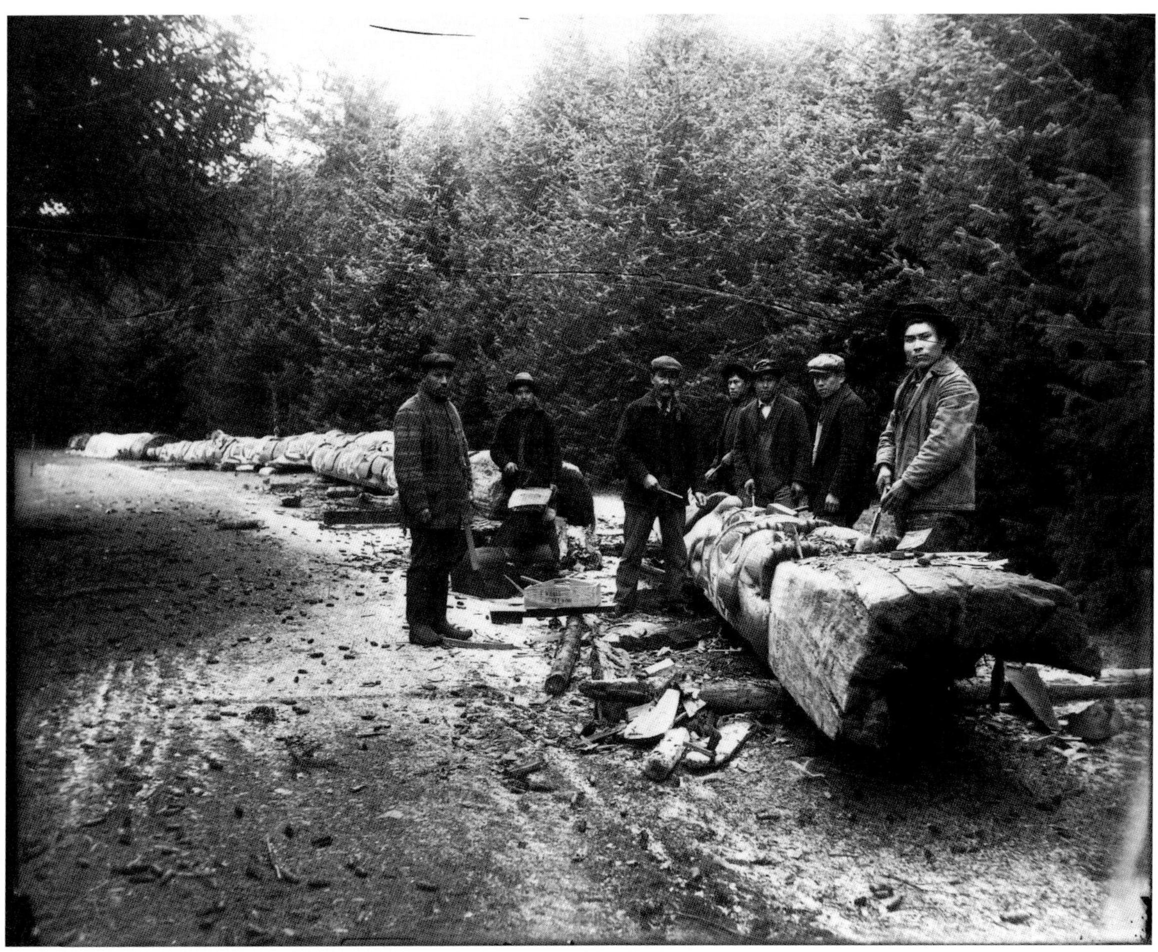

Figure 83
Tlingit craftsmen, with whom Merrill worked, repair the mostly Haida totem poles returned to Sitka following their display at the Louisiana Purchase Exposition in St. Louis and the Lewis and Clark Exposition in Portland. Left to right: John Willard, Garfield Bailey, Thomas Cook, Thomas Willis, Ray James, Albert James, and Don Cameron. Photograph by E. W. Merrill. Courtesy of the Sitka National Historical Park, Sitka, AK. (3816)

cultural object. It is there incidentally, and it could just as easily have been a wall or fence. The result is a powerful triangular arrangement, juxtaposing the ceremonial with the everyday. Figure 82 also displays an informed set of composition ideas; the Tlingit boy is dwarfed by the sweeping curve of the canoe but monumentalized by the low viewpoint from which Merrill photographed the scene. Merrill's Tlingit work, on the whole, reflects a dedication to his art, not to what might interest non-Native customers.

Although Merrill's closest connections were to the non-Native community, he knew many Tlingit and did more than just admire and photograph their culture. When the totem poles that Governor John G. Brady had collected for the Alaska Exhibits at the Louisiana Purchase Exposition in 1904 and Lewis and Clark Exposition in 1905 were returned to Sitka for permanent display, Merrill accompanied Brady and his sons

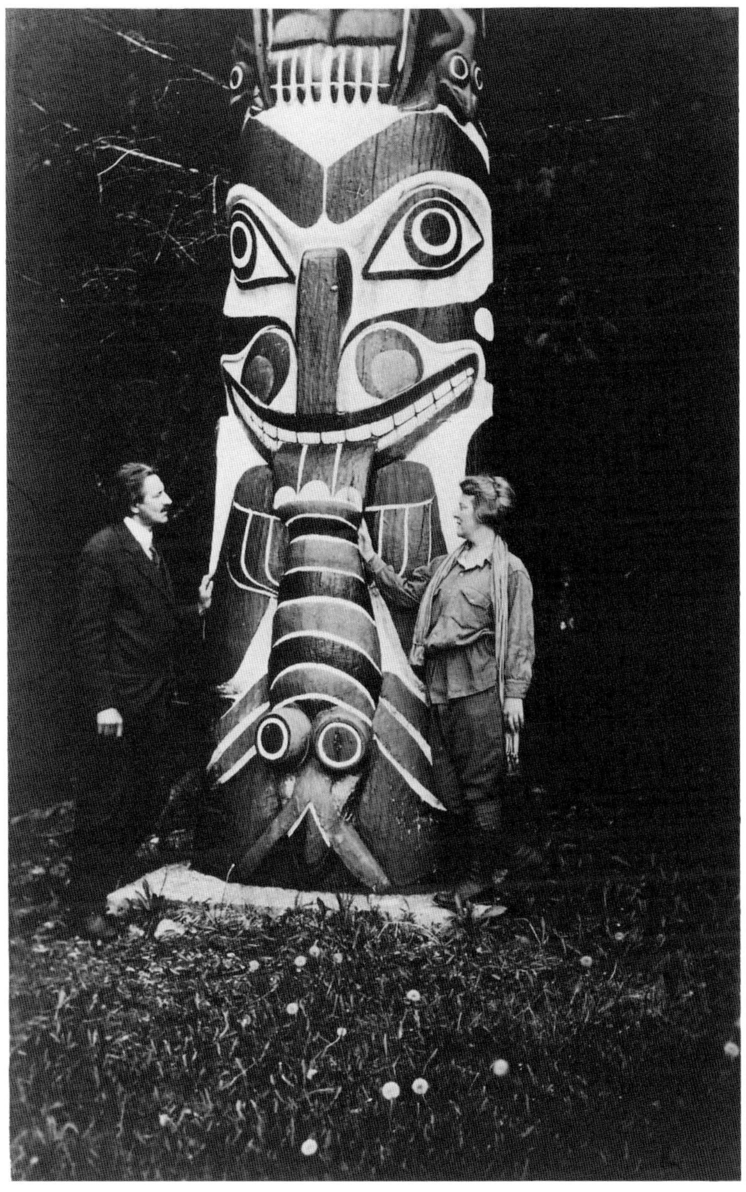

Cyrus Beck, Albert James, Garfield Bailey, George Bartlett, Thomas Willis, John Patton, Easton Hunter, Howard Patton—and "Haida Daniel"—to repair and paint the poles (Fig. 83). The men worked nearly a month at the rate of $.30 an hour; Merrill worked twenty days at $3.50 a day (or, roughly $.44 an hour). They were paid for their materials and labor by the Department of the Interior (J. Brady 1906).

Merrill spent weeks learning how to make authentic Tlingit paints, creating white from lime, vermilion from cinnabar, and green-blue from copper ore mixed with salmon egg oil. "Each totem is a record in wood of a different legend or a different family history," he explained. "That is why it took me so many weeks to select the sites for them. I tried to preserve the spirit of the old order, which is passing. The white man had educated the Thlinget of to-day to be scornful of the totem art of his

John and Hugh on a walk through the Indian River Park to discuss where they should be placed (Brady 1980). He then made the final site selections and organized their restoration. For nearly a month, he worked with 13 Tlingit craftsmen, most of whom had connections to the Sitka Industrial Training School—John Willard, Peter Jacobs, Thomas Cook, Don Cameron, Ray James,

     ELBRIDGE WARREN MERRILL

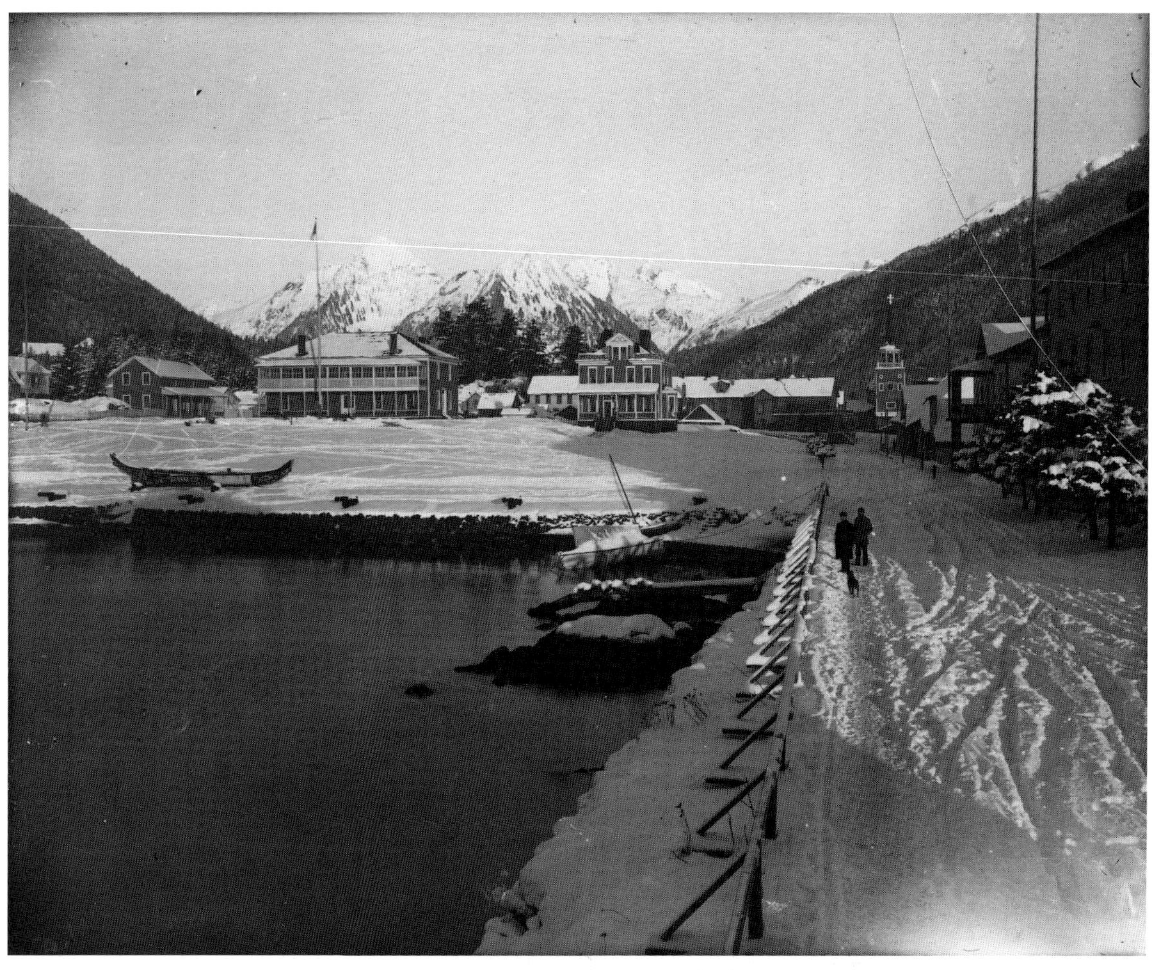

Figure 85
Sitka's Parade Ground in winter with Haida canoe on display. Photograph by E. W. Merrill. Courtesy of Stratton Library, Sheldon Jackson College, Sitka, AK.

forefathers. Soon, I fear, these will be the only specimens left in Alaska" (Willoughby 1926:41).

Largely through the efforts of the Arctic Brotherhood, to which Merrill belonged, the Indian River Park and its collection of totem poles as well as the Kiks.ádi fort site, scene of the 1804 battle with the Russians, were declared a National Monument in 1910. In 1918, *The Verstovia* reported that Merrill had been appointed official custodian by the National Park Service. Park Service correspondence indicates that an

agreement had been reached between Director Eather and Alaska's governor to appoint Merrill "in view of his great interest in the monument and the fine work he had done." For a short time he was the officially designated custodian of the park (Griffin 2000:39). But apparently Merrill never signed his appointment letter, and, when the Alaska Road Commission took over maintenance of the park in 1922 and Arno Cammerer, Acting Director of the National Park Service, again recommended that Merrill become custodian, his suggestion was rejected by the President of the Road Commission, who appointed Peter Trierschield instead (Cammerer 1922).

Once the poles were erected in Indian River Park (Fig. 84), Merrill acted as their unofficial and unpaid caretaker for more than 20 years: "If the raven's beak [on one of the totem poles] got rubbed off, Merrill got up there with his ladder and repainted it...He kept that park up all by himself for years" (Yaw 1986). Merrill and Tlingit Howard Patton also repaired and painted a Haida war canoe for about a week in March 1906. Merrill was paid $10.49 for materials and his labor (Fig. 85).

An article about their work in the *Sitka Cablegram*, March 5, 1906, reflects the unwitting and more subtle racism that existed alongside overt forms: "The old war canoe of mammoth proportions, which has lain beyond the fish house for a year or more, has been taken from obscurity and given a position of prominence on the sea wall in front of the marine barracks. There, under the direction of E. W. Merrill and the skill of a native artist, it is gradually assuming all of its former glory of brilliant color and weird design" (p. 4). Its designs were labeled "weird," and while Merrill is mentioned by name, Howard Patton becomes an anonymous Native craftsman.

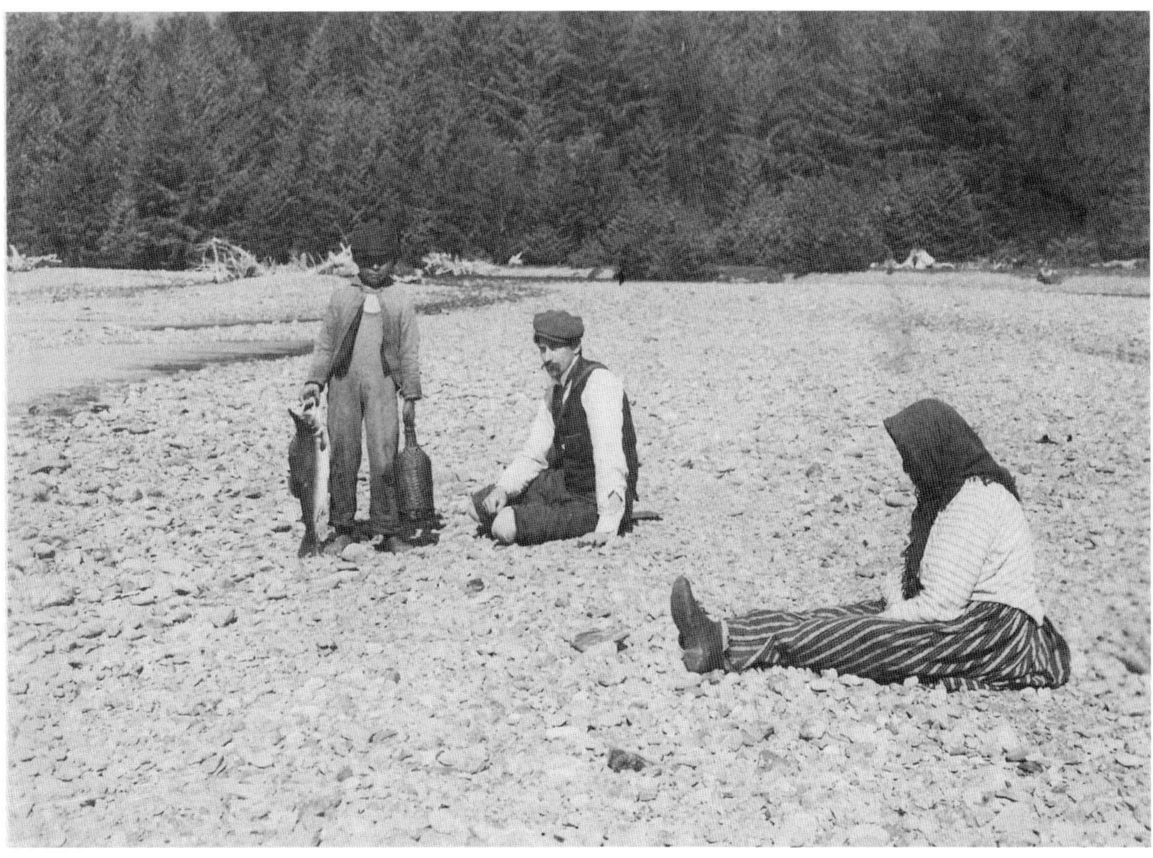

Figure 86
E. W. Merrill (seated) with unidentified Tlingit woman and boy on beach near Sitka, 1905. Photograph by "Sitka Jim" (Jim Jacobs?). Author's collection.

Merrill not only worked with Tlingit crafts-men and took an intense interest in preserving their material culture and history; he is also said to have hunted with at least one Tlingit man and to have helped his son with photography. A photograph showing Merrill sitting on a beach with a Tlingit woman and child nearby also indicates a closer relationship with at least some members of the community than mere respect and photographic access would indicate (Fig. 86). On the back of one mounted print of this image is stamped "Photograph by E. W. Merrill, Boston, Mass.," but the word "by" has been traced in ink and next to it written in "Sitka Jim, Aug 20th 1905." This photograph was taken by a Tlingit, although its composition may have been influenced by Merrill. It has a modernist and artistic sensibility; the way the stony beach forms a light, fairly neutral background with the figures silhouetted against it seems deliberate. Tension is created between the open blank space on the bottom and left, extending into the background, and the very solidly placed woman on the right. Merrill, as the principal subject, is in the middle of the image but placed between two Tlingit people with whom he seems at ease—even though all three subjects by pose are psychologically isolated from one another. The overall image has a bucolic feeling; the little boy holding the salmon comes right out of 19th century realist painting. As mentioned, Merrill's background and work in Boston would have exposed him to a heavy dose of French realist art.

Merrill's prints of the Tlingit only some-times note the subjects' names or other identifying details. He may have kept personal notebooks with such information, but they no longer exist or else remain in private hands. Merrill told F. Barrett Willoughby that some Tlingit referred to him as the "Father of Pictures," and his gravestone in Sitka is so inscribed (1926:40). Following Merrill's name on an invoice submitted by John G. Brady for payment for refurbishing Sitka's totem poles is a Tlingit name "Kirk-shr-she-tee." Unfortunately, it can not be translated

in the opinion of Tlingit speaker and historian Nora Dauenhauer because of the idiosyncratic way in which the Tlingit has been spelled. Some other white photographers also developed close relationships with the Tlingit. Lloyd Winter and Percy Pond, of Juneau, as mentioned earlier were adopted into a Chilkat Tlingit clan and received Indian names.

Merrill certainly sympathized with the stresses the Tlingit were undergoing, forced as they were to give up so much in order to adapt to a new culture. Leslie Yaw followed Merrill one day as he led a small group of tourists into his store. As Merrill took "a picture off his shelf— a picture of an Indian carver sitting on a block of wood with a blanket on his shoulders and carving a small totem pole. The chips are on the floor in this picture. Mr. Merrill used this picture to tell his little band of tourists, in not too much detail, the story of Indian culture. When he got through, he replaced the picture with this statement which I have never forgotten. He said, 'They are off in their own culture, but who can stop the march of civilization'" (Yaw 1986).

Although a few of Merrill's portraits of the Tlingit suggest a nobility of spirit that evokes the "vanishing Indian" stereotype, most of his work is totally unlike E. S. Curtis's romantic images of American Indians (Figs. 87, 88). Many employ the same frontality of posture and eye contact found in Lewis Hine's photographs of American workers or those of August Sanders of Germans. For Merrill this sprang from a democratic urge to portray the Tlingit as more than objects of the photographic gaze, to show them as proud and autonomous people. His photographs of the Tlingit are straightforward. In the view of Ron Slemmons, they are like those of Adam Clark Vrooman, D. F. Barry, Frank B. Fiske, and Fred E. Miller in their approach. They are usually posed, but there is no pretense. Merrill's sincere interest in Tlingit culture is apparent in the range of subjects he photographed: ceremonial occasions like potlatches and wakes, people engaged in everyday work (Figs. 89, 90), fish camps, formal portraits,

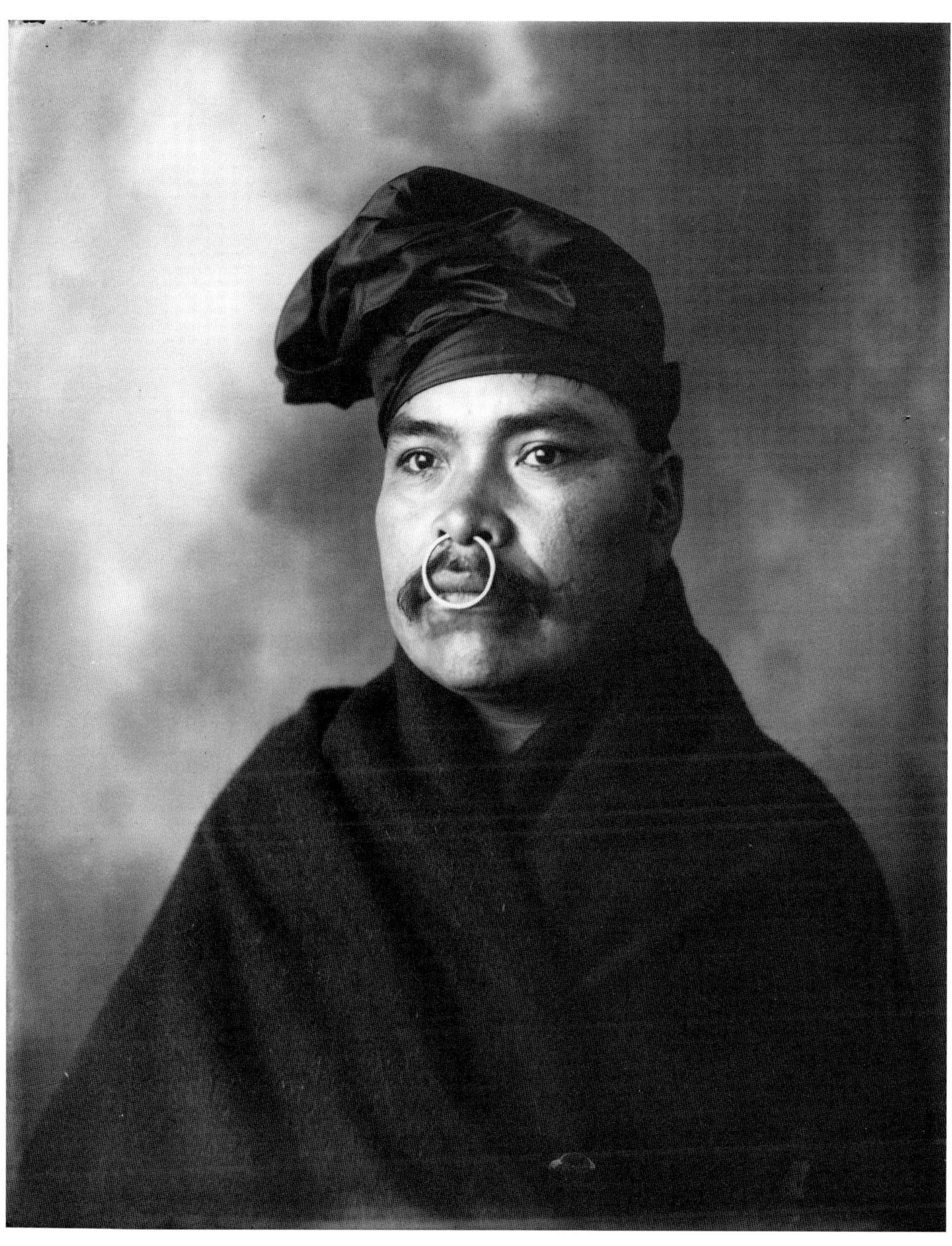

Figure 87
Studio portrait of unidentified Tlingit man. Photograph by E. W. Merrill. Courtesy of Stratton Library, Sheldon Jackson College, Sitka, AK. (M II B5g)

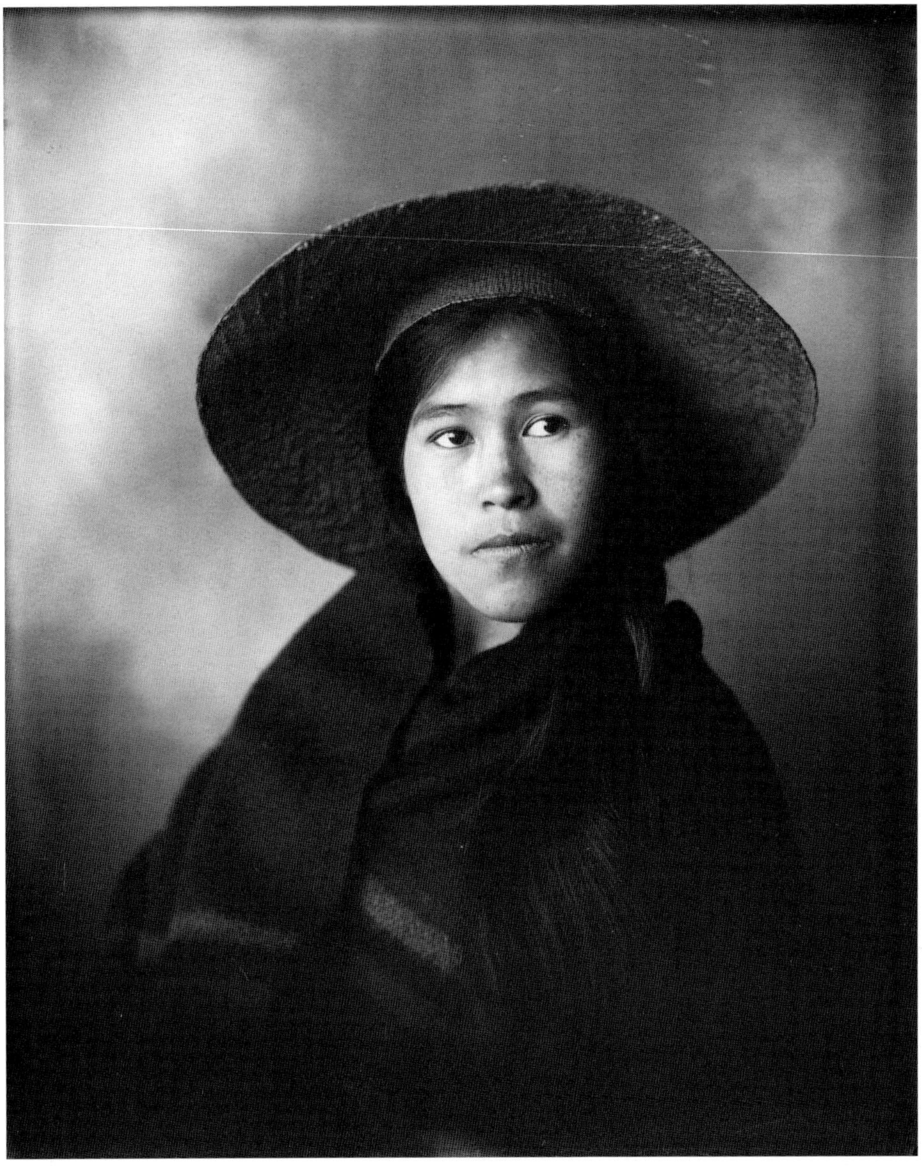

Figure 88
Studio portrait of unidentified Tlingit woman wearing spruce-root hat. Photograph by E. W.
Merrill. Courtesy of Stratton Library, Sheldon Jackson College, Sitka, AK. (M II B5d)

captured moments, and still life compositions of basketry and other artifacts.

Merrill's photographic treatment of the Tlingit and non-Natives is also evenhanded. He documented the life of Sitka's Euro-American community in the same fashion as that of the Tlingit, photographing individuals and groups, rituals and celebrations like Fourth of July parades, people at work, street scenes and architecture, and "exotic" Euro-American customs and

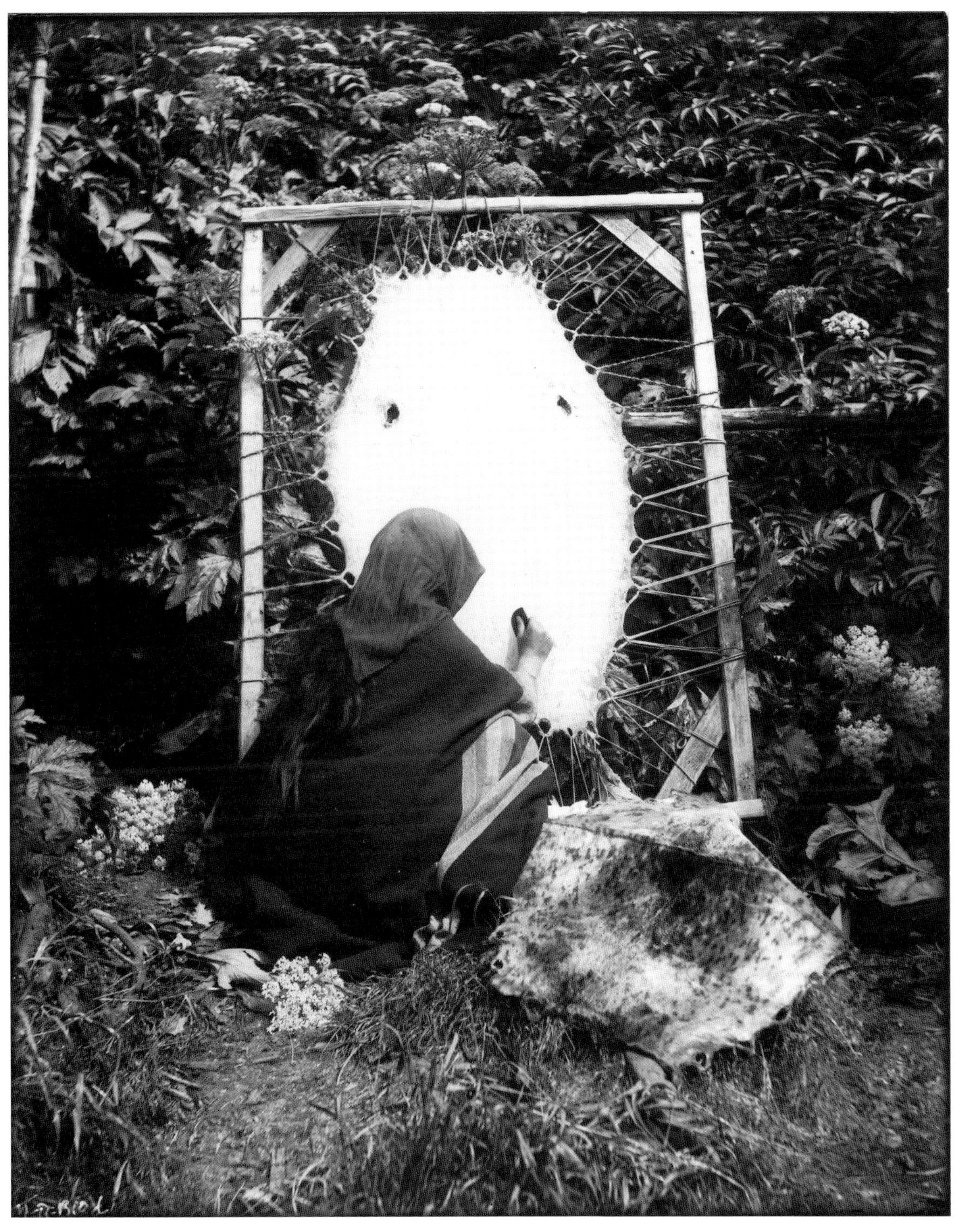

Figure 89
Tlingit woman preparing a seal skin in Sitka, 1910. Photograph by E. W. Merrill. Courtesy of Stratton Library, Sheldon Jackson College, Sitka, AK. (M II B10d)

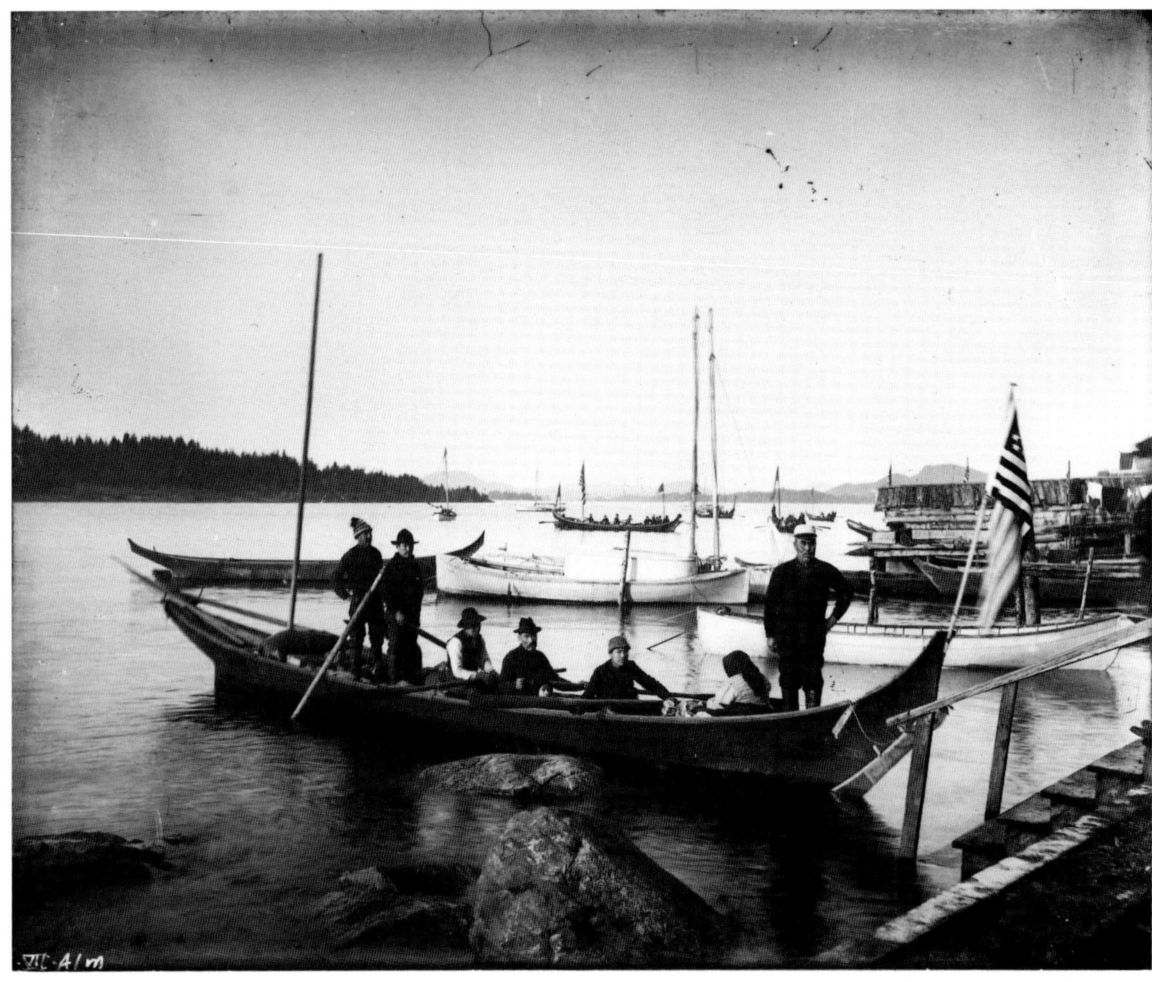

Figure 90
Potlatch canoes carrying American flags during the 1904 potlatch in Sitka. Photograph by E. W. Merrill. Courtesy of
Stratton Library, Sheldon Jackson College, Sitka, AK.

artifacts like May Pole dancing and Halloween decorations. Whether photographed in the studio or the home, it was common practice at the time for portrait sitters to pose with conventional status symbols. Merrill observed this Euro-American style of portraiture but also diverged from it. Figure 91 shows the Wirtz family at Easter inside their comfortable Sitka home amid signs of Euro-American affluence like formal clothing, lace curtains, carpeting, chandelier, china, and an elaborate wood stove; education (newspaper and book); and leisure (beer and doll).

Members of Chief Annaxoots' family likewise pose in front of the Wolf/World/Noble House on Katlian Street wearing good Western clothes (Fig. 92). Behind them is the Panting Wolf House interior house post which was being displayed on the porch for the 1904 Kaagwaantaan Wolf House potlatch. Does the fact that they are posed outside instead of inside their home

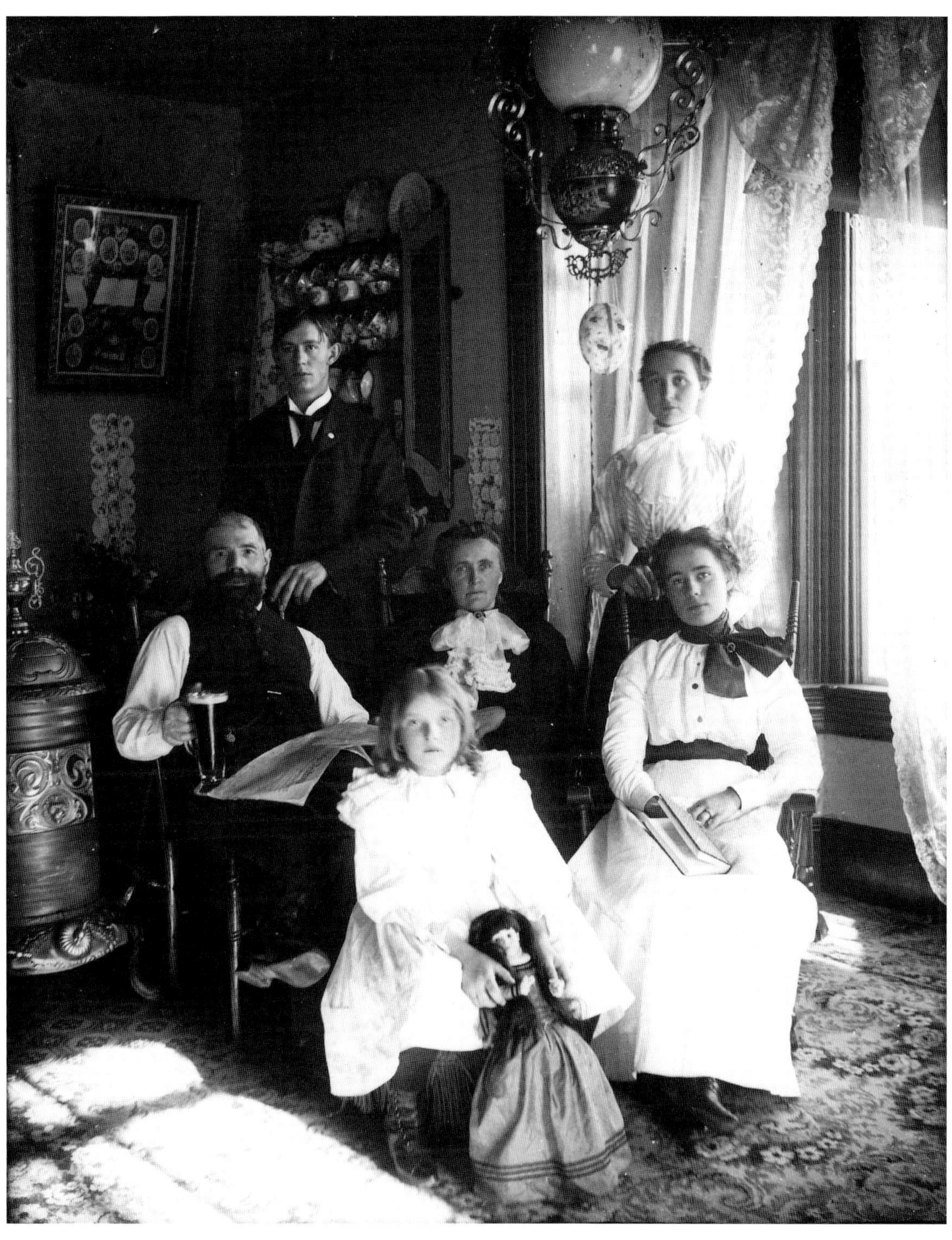

Figure 91
The Wirtz family at Easter, Sitka, 1900. Photograph E. W. Merrill. Courtesy of Stratton Library, Sheldon Jackson College, Sitka, AK. (M II A3p)

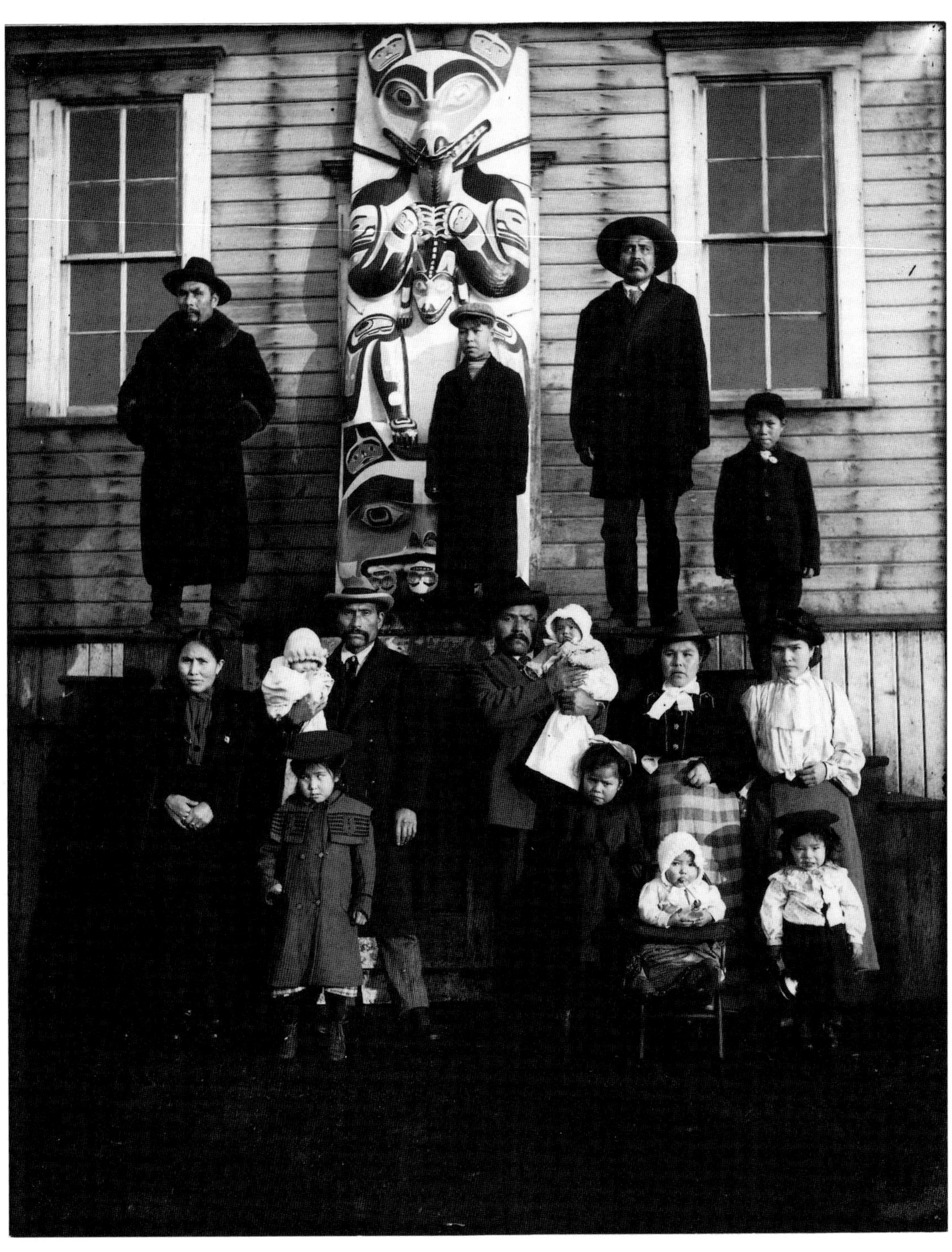

Figure 92
Annaxóots family, members of the Kaagwaantaan clan. Paddy Parker (K'axook Eesh) holds the baby on right. The formal display of the newly completed Panting Wolf interior house post was one of the main events of the 1904 potlatch. Photograph by E. W. Merrill. Courtesy of Stratton Library, Sheldon Jackson College, Sitka, AK. (M II B6e)

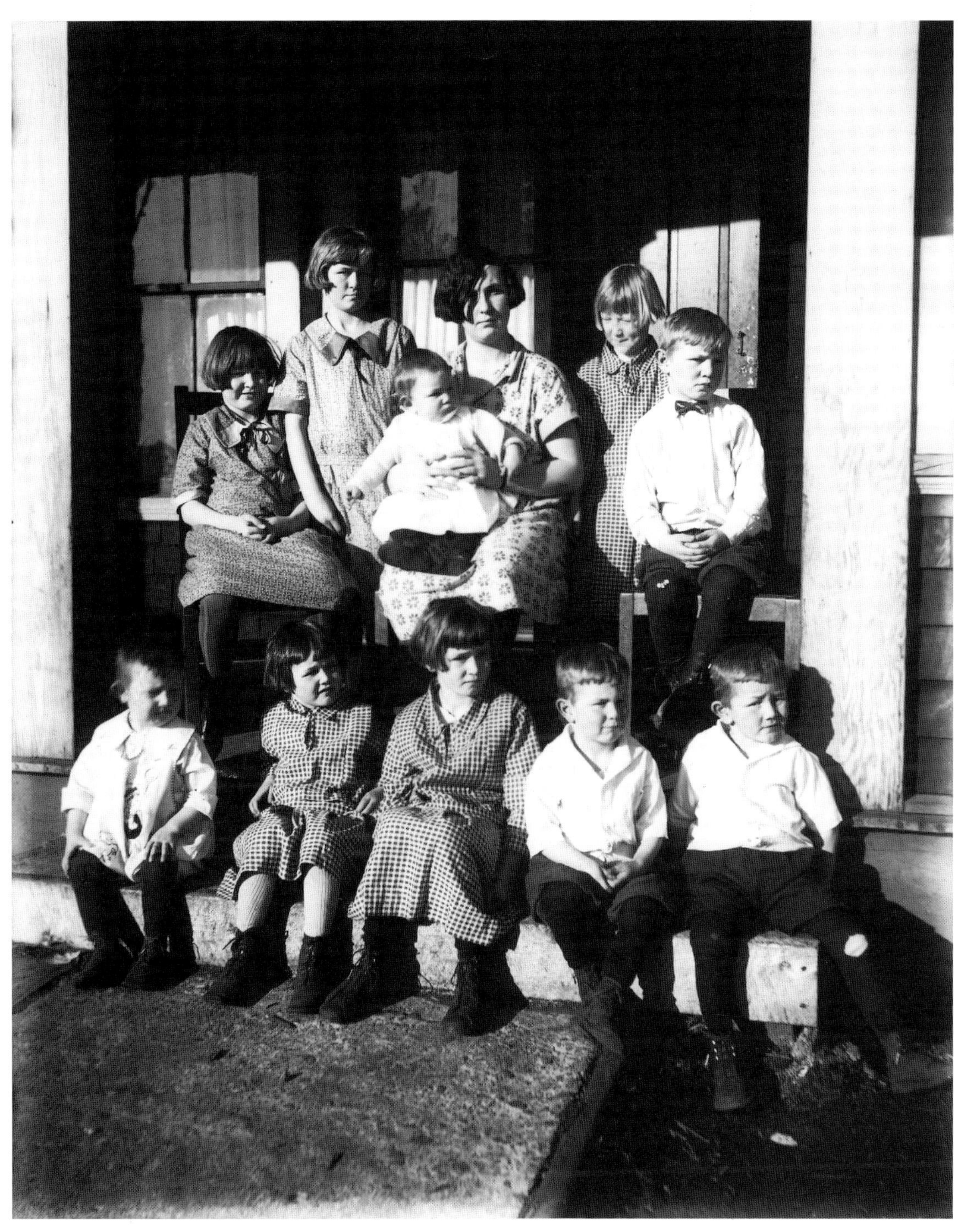

Figure 93
Mrs. McNulty and her ten children, Sitka, 1910. Photograph by E. W. Merrill. Courtesy of Stratton Library, Sheldon Jackson College, Sitka, AK. (M II A3d)

147

reveal anything about the photographer's attitude toward them, such as equating Indians with nature? Does it reflect pragmatic considerations such as wanting to take advantage of the porch for such a large group or needing to use natural light? Or does it reveal the Tlingits' own desire to pose outside with an important clan status item? In this particular case the later seems most likely, although pragmatic considerations undoubtedly played a role.

Figure 93 is one of the many images Merrill took of non-Natives, in this case Mrs. McNulty and her ten children (most of whom are dressed in homemade clothing made from the same fabrics) likewise are posed outdoors.

His choice of setting, clothing, general distance, and visual construction are fundamentally the same for both Tlingits and non-Natives.

Merrill did not manipulate his images the way some contemporary photographers of Native Americans did, costuming them in "Indian" clothing regardless of their own tribal affiliation or removing signs of Western influence in the interests of making them appear untouched by "civilization." Merrill's photographs show a proud and dignified people, wearing both Tlingit clothing and Western dress in "traditional" settings as well as those which clearly show modern intrusions. The viewer never loses sight of the fact that the Tlingit had been dramatically influenced by the outside world. The images of the Tlingit that Merrill chose to sell (as prints and postcards or to publications) were non-exploitative; he never portrayed them in a negative light—as dirty, degraded, sexualized, or savage. Merrill's respectful and dignified images of the Tlingit, his photographic access to them in both formal and informal settings, his work with Tlingit craftsmen, the opinions of most of his contemporaries, as well as the Tlingits' purchase and consumption of his images, all indicate that he was respected by them.

Today his photographs line the walls of Sitka's Alaskan Native Brotherhood hall and hang in the Sitka Tribal Association's community house. They are also used by the Sitka National Historical Park to help tell the history of the Sitka Tlingit. The Park's collection of 203 Merrill glass plate negatives of the Tlingit was originally acquired from a Kiks.ádi man. Many Sitkans, both Native and non-Native, still own Merrill prints. His images stand as a visual affirmation of the achievements of Tlingit culture. While they may evoke a sad nostalgia in some viewers for the Tlingit's lost sovereignty, their acquisition and use by community members today also expresses a new sense of empowerment as the Tlingit reclaim and use images from public archives for their own purposes. Merrill's work also reminds us that not all non-Natives, including a commercial photographer who sold most of his work to non-Natives, necessarily treated Native subjects in an exploitative way.

6

The Tlingit Response to Photography

To what extent did the power to define the Tlingit through photographs rest solely with non-Natives? What role did the Tlingit play in their image making, and what uses, if any, did they find for this new technology? When photographers moved from the studio to the field it was, in the view of Brock Silversides, "By its very nature…an invasive act, and it is amazing in retrospect that more photographers were not summarily ejected from Native communities" (1994:10). But is this necessarily so? When Frederick Dally set up his camera in the village of Ahousat, BC, in 1866, he was surrounded by Haida who milled about, watching his every movement. Their curiosity so unnerved him, however, that he packed up and left.

We do not know definitively what these Haida or the Tlingit subjects of Eadweard Muybridge's photographs taken two years later thought about the camera or about being photographed. Blackman (1982) notes that the Haida equated the camera with a mask which they called *nijangu* or "copying." Their name for camera was *k'laaga nijangwe* meaning "copying people." Linguist Jeff Leer explains that the Tlingit word for camera is *aankukdushxit'at*, meaning "that with which one draws or makes pictures of

people"; a photograph is *kaa yahaay'i*, meaning "a person's shadow, departed soul, reflection, or picture" (personal communication, August 28, 2001). The latter suggests that having a photograph taken might have induced some fear, but this is not apparent in the expressions or body language of the Tlingit in Muybridge's images. The men and women crouched along the wall of Sitka's Russian trading post look toward the camera in apparent curiosity. The faces of the Tlingit standing with two non-Natives in another of his photographs convey perplexity rather than fear (Figs. 94, 95). Had they seen the results of the camera's work yet? We do not know, although it seems unlikely at this early date and given their expressions.

Since Muybridge was working with the cumbersome wet-plate technology of the time which required using a tripod-mounted camera, composing the scene through the lens while hidden underneath a black cloth, then emerging to prepare the glass plate with chemicals, then disappearing again under the cloth to expose the image—for perhaps several minutes more depending upon the available light—it is easy to understand the bewilderment of the Tlingit watching him. Individuals may have had many reasons for

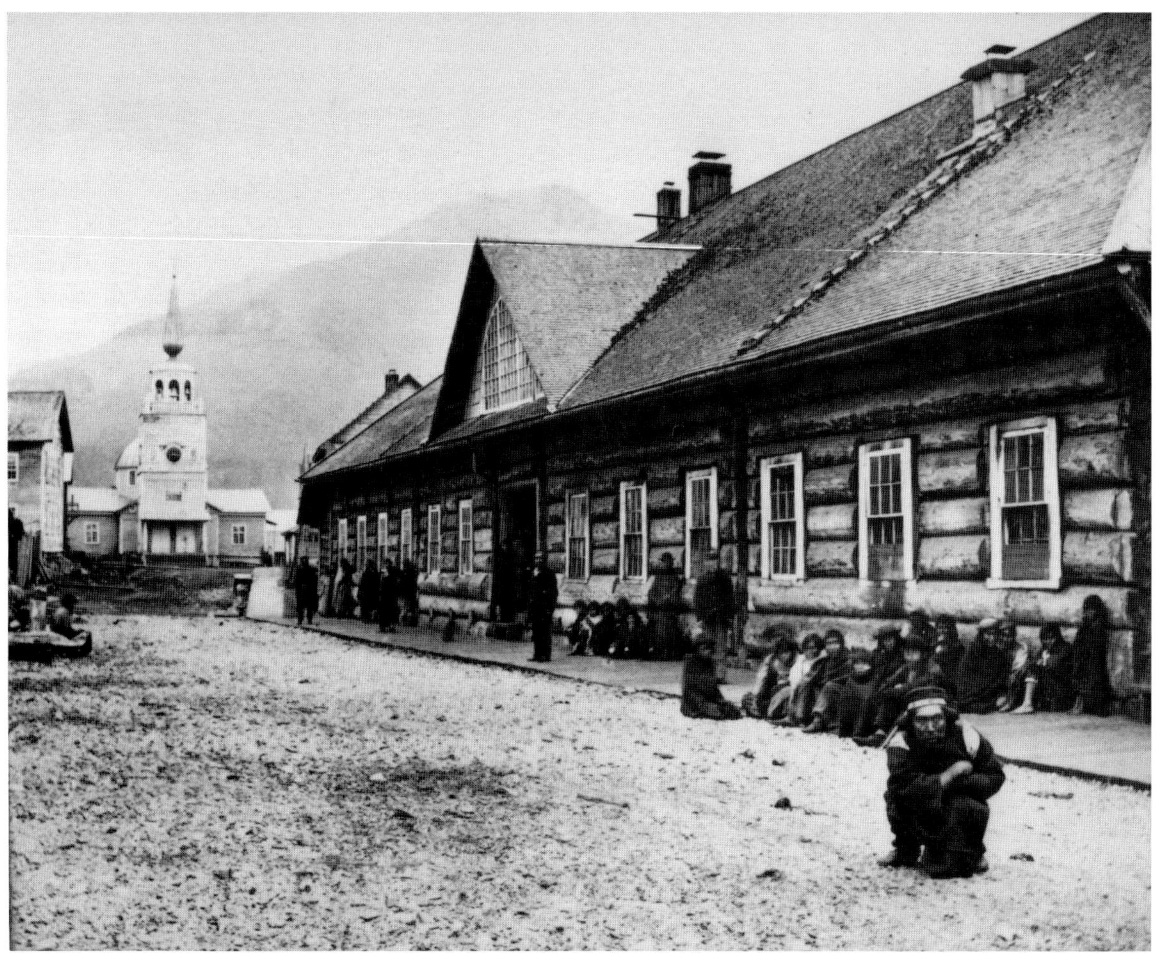

Figure 94
"Sitka—Lincoln St." Tlingit residents of Sitka line the walls of the old Russian trading post with St. Michael's Cathedral in background, 1868. Half of a stereograph by Eadweard Muybridge. By permission of the Presbyterian Historical Society, Philadelphia, PA. (RG239-17, no. 2082)

cooperating, including natural curiosity or simply no reason to object, since non-Natives were also being photographed. Some may have felt obliged to pose since the U.S. Army now controlled Sitka and had become part of the reality of everyday Tlingit life. At any rate, their assistance was vital for obtaining successful images. Another Muybridge photograph—among those he later sold as stereographs—shows them fully cooperating with the camera (Fig. 96).

Reports vary as to how Natives along the Northwest Coast and southeast Alaska reacted to photography in the following decade. When James Gilchrist Swan traveled on the U.S. Revenue Cutter *Wolcott* to southeastern Alaska in 1875 to collect ethnographic material for the Smithsonian, he watched as the ship's photographer, A. L. Broadbent, photographed several Haida, including a high-ranking chief and his family, who boarded at the village of Klinkwan. Swan notes

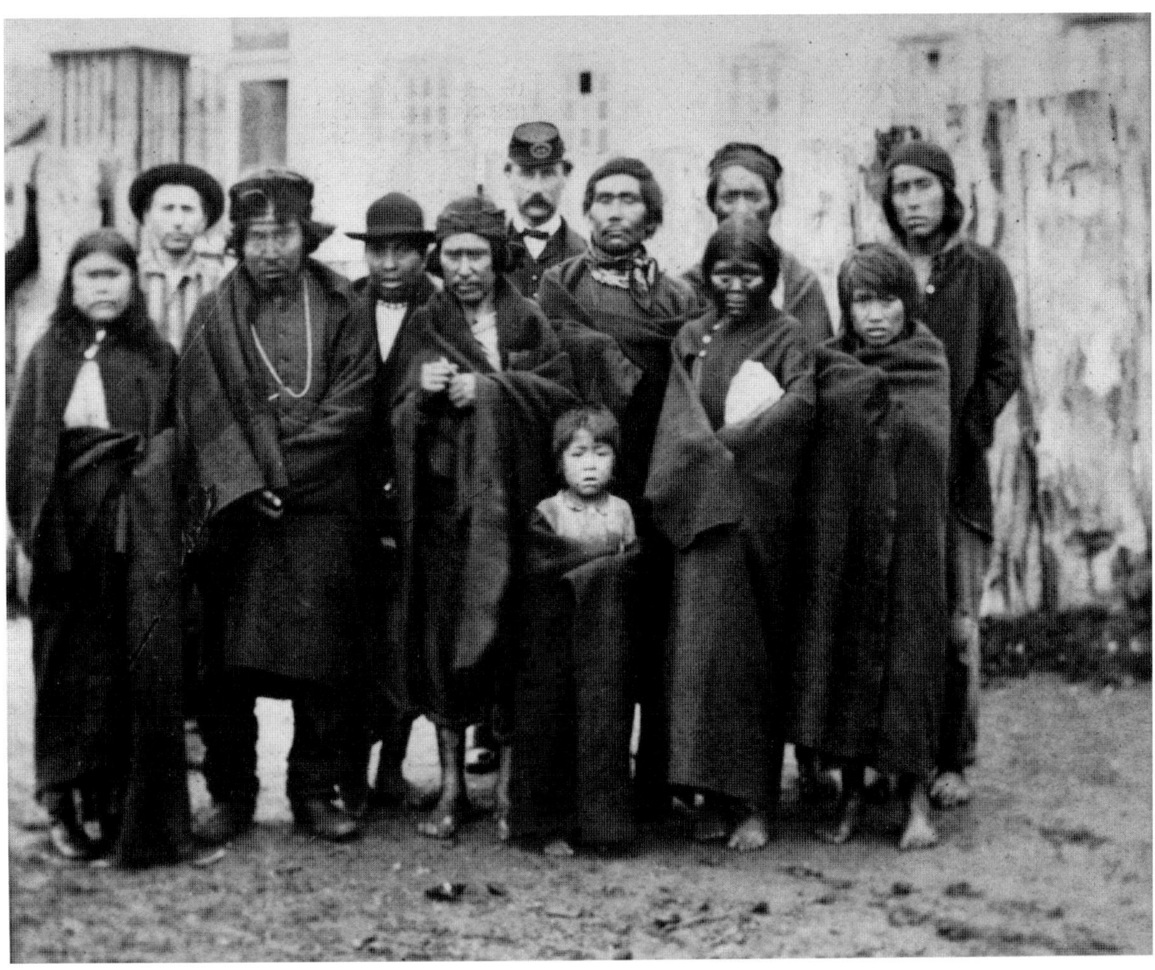

Figure 95
"Group of Indians," 1868. Photograph by Eadweard Muybridge. By permission of the Bancroft Library, University of California, Berkeley, CA. Lone Mountain College Collection of Stereographs by Eadweard Muybridge, series 2. (ID 1971.055:478–STER)

the event so casually in his journal that anthropologist Margaret Blackman concludes that we "can assume that the Klinkwan natives were neither reluctant nor fearful of being photographed" (1982:91). The men and labret-wearing women in Swan's own photograph (Fig. 20) seem willing to be photographed. The Haida chiefs encountered by George M. Dawson in 1878 were likewise ready to be photographed, but other Haida who Dawson met "disliked the idea, and especially the

women, not one of whom appeared" (Blackman 1982:92). Yet the very next year photographer Oregon Columbus Hastings, who accompanied U.S. Indian Commissioner Israel W. Powell on his official tour of Native villages, photographed two Haida women without apparent difficulty.

By the 1880s most Northwest Coast Natives, including the Tlingit, were familiar with photography and the desire of Euro-Americans to take pictures of them, having been photographed by

     THE TLINGIT RESPONSE TO PHOTOGRAPHY

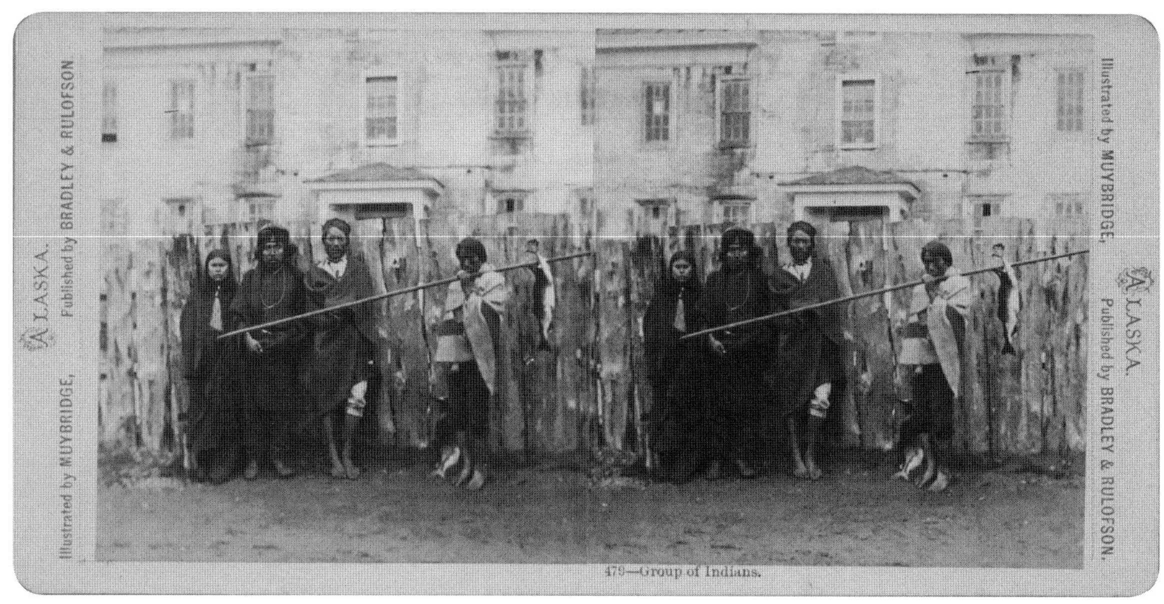

Figure 96
Tlingit Indians in Sitka, 1868. Photograph by Eadweard Muybridge. By permission of the Bancroft Library, University of California, Berkeley, CA. Lone Mountain College Collection of Stereographs by Eadweard Muybridge, series 2. (ID 1971.055:479–STER)

expedition and survey photographers, by resident and visiting military personnel and artifact collectors, by traveling commercial photographers, and increasingly by tourists. In 1885, an observer watched a Tlingit man board an Alaska Steamship Company steamer docked at Sitka's pier and strike up a pose as soon as he saw a photographer on deck; he "stiffened himself into his most rigid attitude and when the process was over could hardly be made stir from his pose" (Blackman 1980:70). This incident suggests an eagerness to be photographed on the part of some Tlingit, perhaps in hopes of receiving payment. His stiff pose may also show his familiarity with the longer exposures required by the earlier wet-plate photography.

Reactions to being photographed undoubtedly varied from one person to the next, and were based on the circumstances of the particular encounter, the relationship that existed between photographer and Native subject, and gender. Small resistances—raised blankets, dropped eyes, frowning faces, turned heads, defiant expressions—can be seen in many archival photographs. Images like these were seldom published, however, since they were dissatisfying to the photographer and deemed "poor" quality (Faris 2003, Lutz and Collins 1993).

Tlingit women displayed the most reluctance to being photographed. Visiting travel writer Septima Collis, who was in Sitka for one day in the summer of 1889, came equipped with a new Eastman Kodak box camera, as did many of her fellow passengers who enjoyed photographing each other: "The Kodak fiends were at work everywhere preserving as best they could the counterfeit presentments of each other–my party among the rest" (1890:86). She found Tlingit women vendors not as eager to be photographed.

It was wonderful what a superstitious aversion they have to the camera. When we tried our Kodaks on them they instantly enveloped

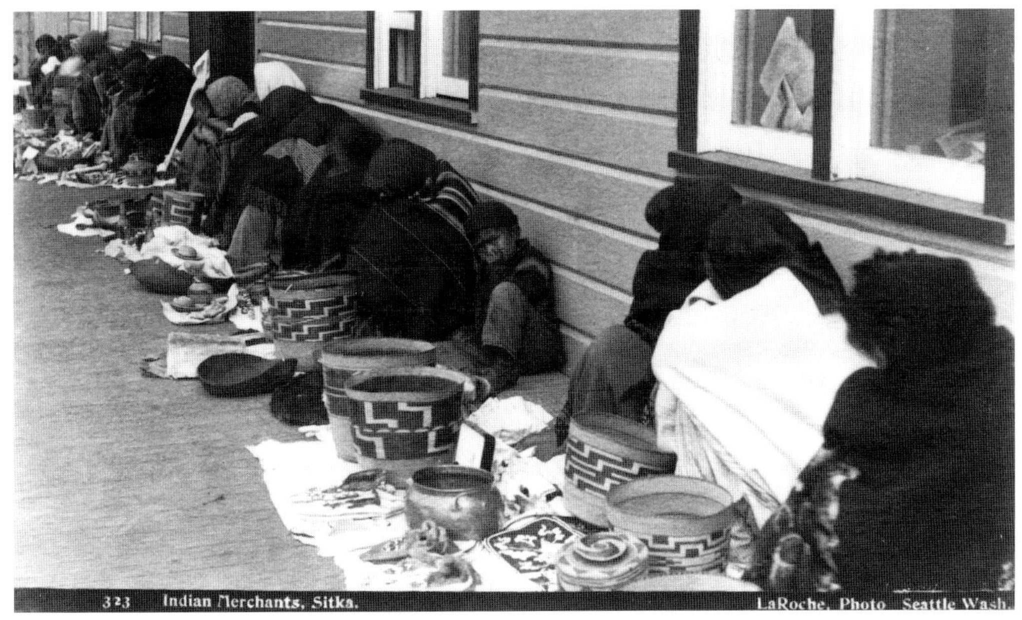

Figure 97
"Indian Merchants, Sitka," 1894. Photograph by Frank La Roche. Courtesy of the U.S. Library of Congress, Washington, DC. (Lot 12878)

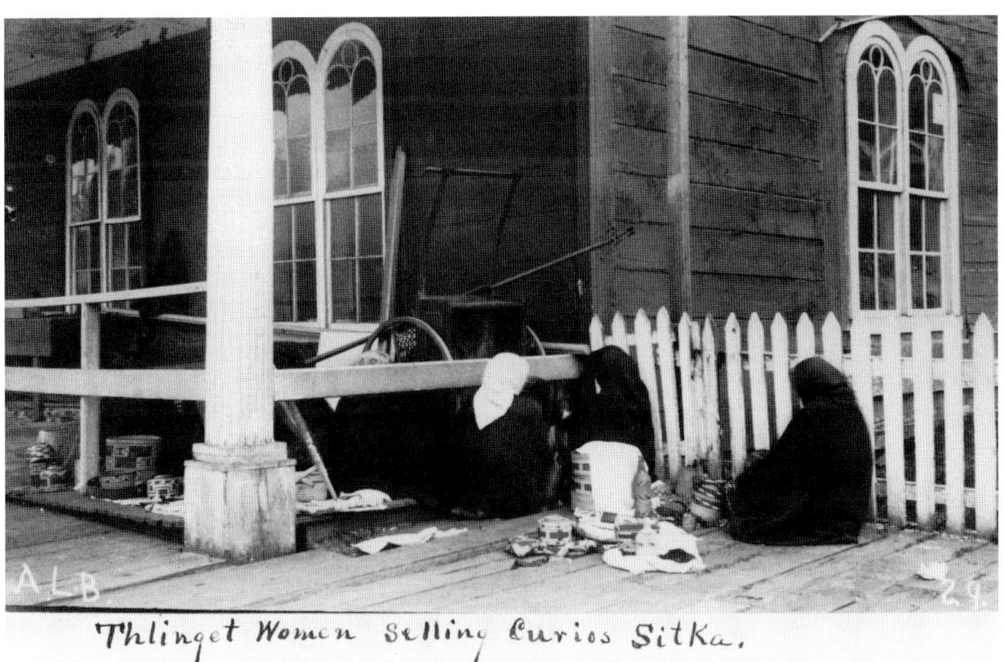

Figure 98
"Thlinget Women Selling Curios Sitka." Photographer unknown. By permission of the Presbyterian Historical Society, Philadelphia, PA.

themselves in their blankets, and would not uncover until some old crone who had an eye through a hole of her hood gave a signal. This was in fact so mysterious that we tried to reason with them, showed them pictures of ourselves, offered to send them their likenesses by the next boat, but all to no purpose, and we were about to give it up, when at the suggestion of one of the oldest inhabitants, we held aloft a silver dollar. Instantly there was a change. The superstitions simply consisted in the belief that it was not healthy to do anything without being paid for it. (1890:99–100)

The women's reluctance to be photographed at this date most likely indicates their familiarity with tourists and a pragmatic interest in profiting from the encounter, undoubtedly mixed with annoyance. According to another early tourist, some Tlingit vendors also covered up their best wares and demanded a small payment from tourists to see them (Field 1888). The Tlingit would have quickly learned that photographic images were commodities like any other. Furthermore, interactions between tourists (and most visiting photographers) and the Tlingit were impersonal. They were typically short-lived, superficial, and

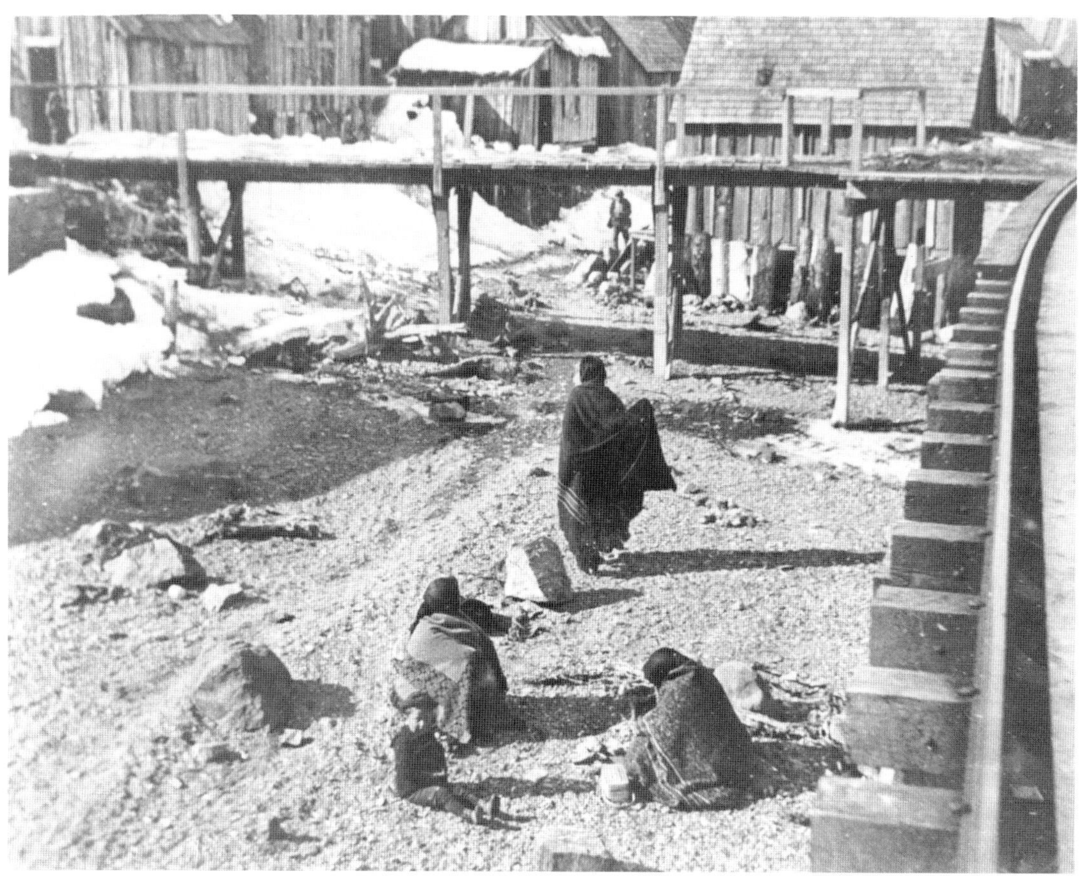

Figure 99
"Squaws at Douglas won't face the camera," 1899. The photograph also shows the elevated railway track and boardwalk. Photographer unknown. By permission of the Alaska State Library, Juneau, AK. (P01–0966)

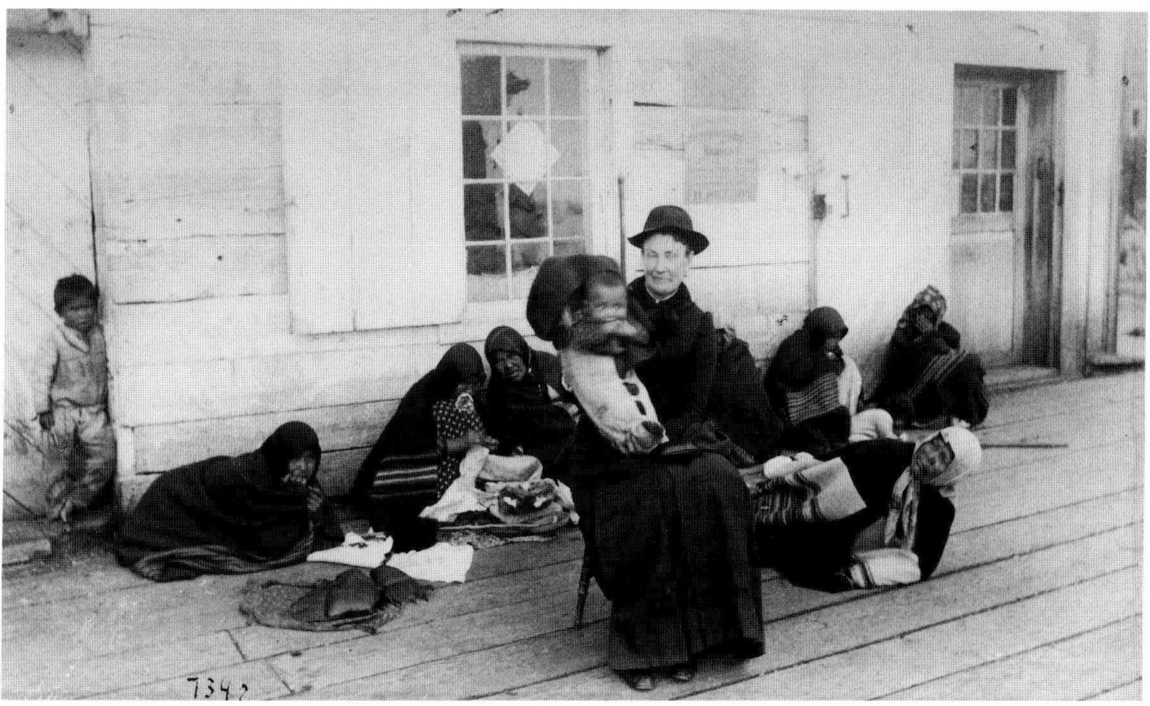

Figure 100
Woman tourist poses with a Tlingit baby on Lincoln Street in Sitka, arousing the curious and cautious looks of women vendors, 1885. Photograph by W. H. Partridge. By permission of the Presbyterian Historical Society, Philadelphia, PA. (RG 239–11, no. 212)

hampered by language differences. Many tourists haggled with the Tlingit to get them to lower their prices. Many Tlingit demanded to be paid for being photographed. "If not paid," Eliza Scidmore described an incident she witnessed, "the family seem ready to tear the camera fiend [tourist] to pieces" (1892:471).

Frank La Roche's photograph of Tlingit women vendors in Sitka hiding from the camera is very similar to many others taken in Sitka and elsewhere (Figs. 97, 98). A photograph taken by George T. Emmons shows three Tlingit women lying on the ground covering their heads with their blankets—little more than huddled blurs in the image. Emmons wrote on the back "Governor's residence, Sitka 1888. Native women lying on ground objected to having picture taken." Was their reaction directed at Emmons personally?

Was payment an issue? An unknown photographer who visited Douglas 11 years later in 1899 wrote on the back of one of his images, "Squaws at Douglas won't face the camera" (Fig. 99). Figure 100 taken by William H. Partridge, a visiting commercial photographer who spent much of the summer of 1886 in Sitka, shows some Tlingit women hiding their faces but others allowing the camera to capture them (Fig. 100). In this case, they appear to have been distracted by the white woman, apparently a tourist, who is holding one of their babies and whom they rightly thought was the main subject of the image. In 1899 John Burroughs noted that the Tlingit women the Harriman Expedition encountered near Yakutat "frowned upon our photographers and were very averse to having cameras pointed at them. It took a good deal of watching and waiting and maneu-

    THE TLINGIT RESPONSE TO PHOTOGRAPHY

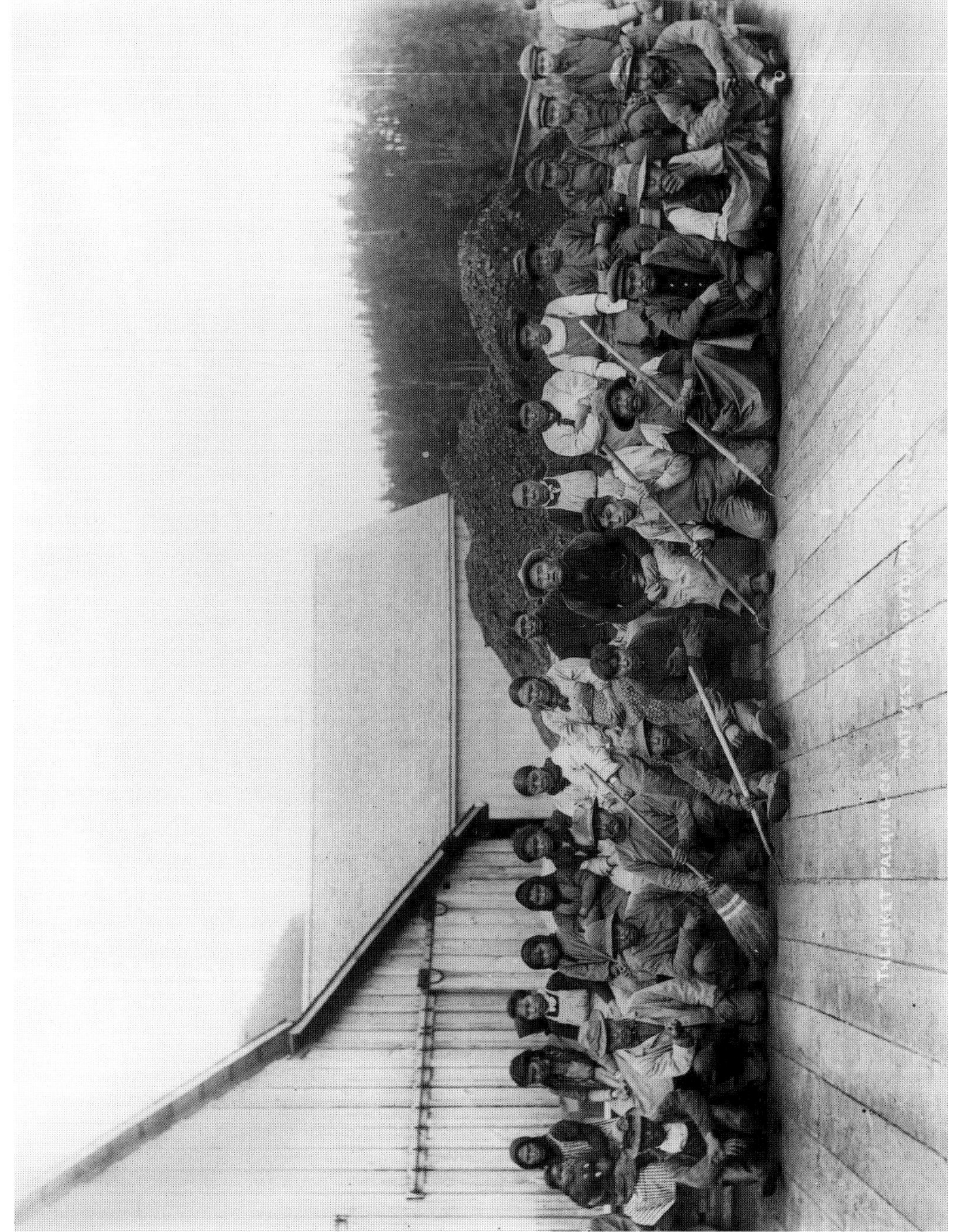

Figure 101

"Tlhinket Packing Co. Natives employed, handling fish," 1907. Photograph by Case & Draper. By permission of the University of Washington Libraries, Seattle, WA. Special Collections. (NA 2192)

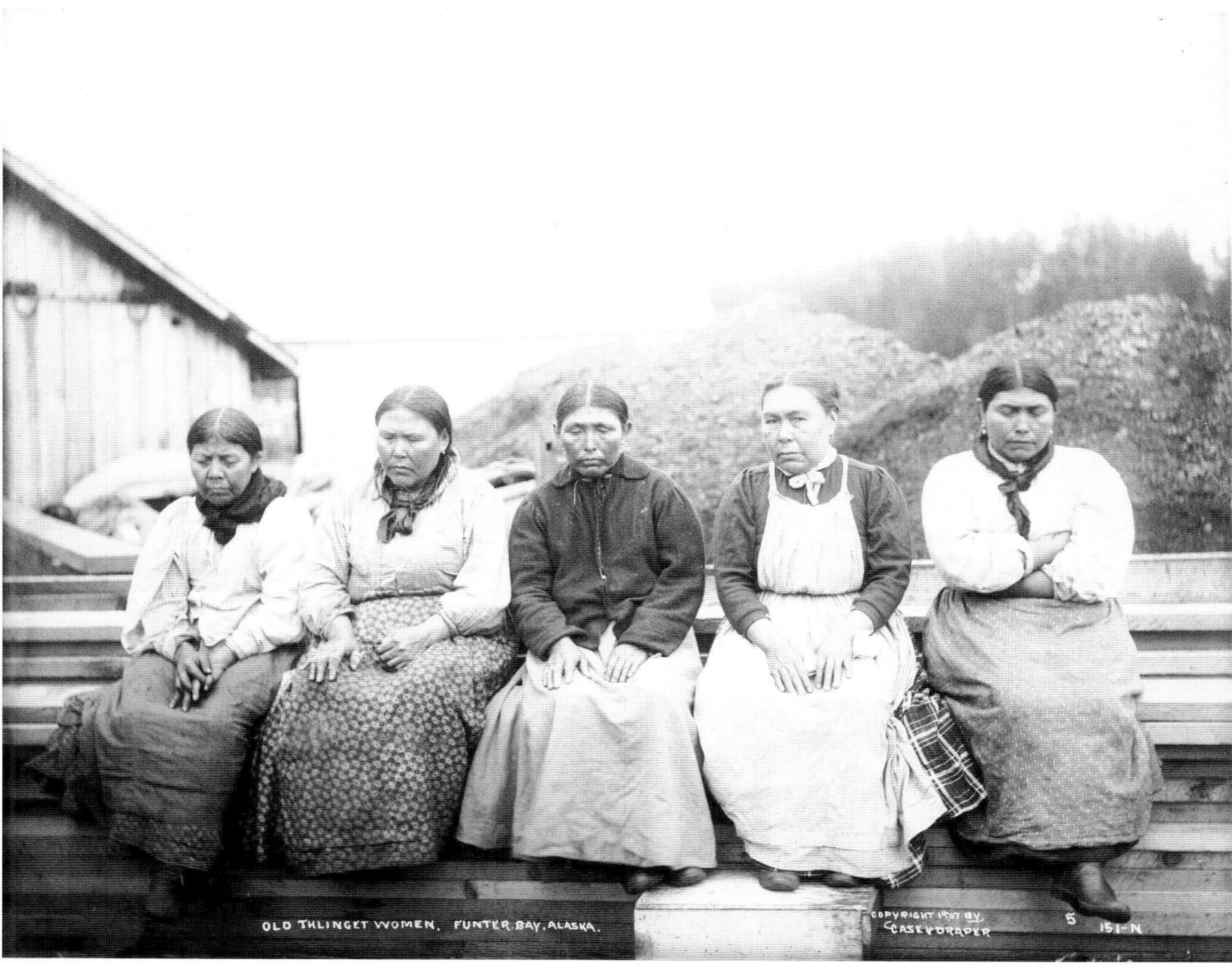

Figure 102
"Old Thlinget Women, Funter Bay, Alaska." Taken same day as Figure 101, showing the same women. Photograph by Case & Draper. By permission of the Alaska State Library, Juneau, AK. (P39–0290)

vering to get a good shot. The artists with their brushes and canvas were regarded with less suspicion" (Burroughs and Grinnel 1910:60–61).

Why this difference between the camera and the brush? Was it the opaqueness of the technology and its unseen result compared to the transparency of what the artist was doing? Two views of Tlingit cannery workers at Funter Bay taken around 1907 show a mixed-gender group and a close up of a few of the women (Figs. 101, 102). In the image of the larger grouping it is not immediately noticeable that many of the women are looking down. In the closer view, their uncooperative attitude it readily apparent: four women nod their heads and have their eyes closed; the fifth woman glares back at the camera. Were they angry at being compelled to pose for a commercial photographer from Juneau's Case and Draper Studio, especially since it is highly unlikely that any of the cannery workers were going to be paid for posing? Could they possibly have been familiar with some of the studio's other images of women such as soft porn for miners? Had the individual photographer(s) committed some gender transgression? On the other hand, a Makah elder once explained to Carolyn Marr (1989) that her aunt had never smiled for a picture because she considered it disrespectful. Do the many images of Tlingit women looking down or off to the side indicate a gendered sense of propriety or cultural conservatism?

In other places along the Northwest Coast Native people had similarly diverse reactions to photography. When anthropologist Franz Boas visited Vancouver in 1886 he encountered a Nuxalk (Bella Coola) man who had in his possession several photographs of fellow tribesmen who had traveled to Germany with Captain J. Adrian Jacobsen for a European tour and been photographed there (Cole 1985:70–71). Boas had met some of the group in Berlin. Despite this kind of intimate familiarity with photographs, other Nuxalk whom Boas met were "suspicious and unapproachable." And when he attempted to photograph a totem pole, he was asked to

pay: "naturally I refused so that I would not deprive myself of the possibility of photographing whatever I might wish" (Flemming and Luskey 1986:141). Boas's refusal to pay was pragmatically motivated, but his attitude also reflects the surprised offense many photographers (and tourists) feel even today when what they regard as their proprietary right to take pictures is challenged. Boas apparently had no difficulty photographing rituals associated with a Kwakwaka'wakw secret society, the Hómats'a, in 1894, noting in a letter to his wife: "I busied myself the whole day taking pictures. We took several of Indians and groups of Indians, from a flat rock along the shore. I took also two pictures of the purchase ceremony of the copper…[two days later] I took two pictures of this ceremony. A man also brought a copper [plate] in a ceremony of which I also took a picture. I was busy taking pictures the whole day quite successful—after some initial [technical] difficulties…Up to now we have about sixty-five good pictures" (Rohner and Rohner 1969:184–86).

On some occasions he also successfully photographed Kwakwaka'wakw women: "yesterday morning I had a few women sit for me while I took several pictures…I got a woman rocking her baby and spinning at the same time. I also got women making mats, baskets…and a woman ready to go into a canoe. If the plates turn out all right I will have really good group pictures" (Rohner and Rohner 1969:188). Yet on other occasions women resisted. Two women who approached Boas at Port Essington to get their faces cast (he was paying people to have facial casts made for later use in creating museum mannequins), refused to let him photograph them. And despite the Kwakwaka'wakw's familiarity with photography, Boas wrote his wife: "I had to laugh yesterday. The people are curious to see the pictures from the back of the camera. I was just about to photograph a woman when someone noticed that the picture was upside down, and he ran away telling everybody that her clothes had fallen over her head" (Rohner and Rohner 1969:189).

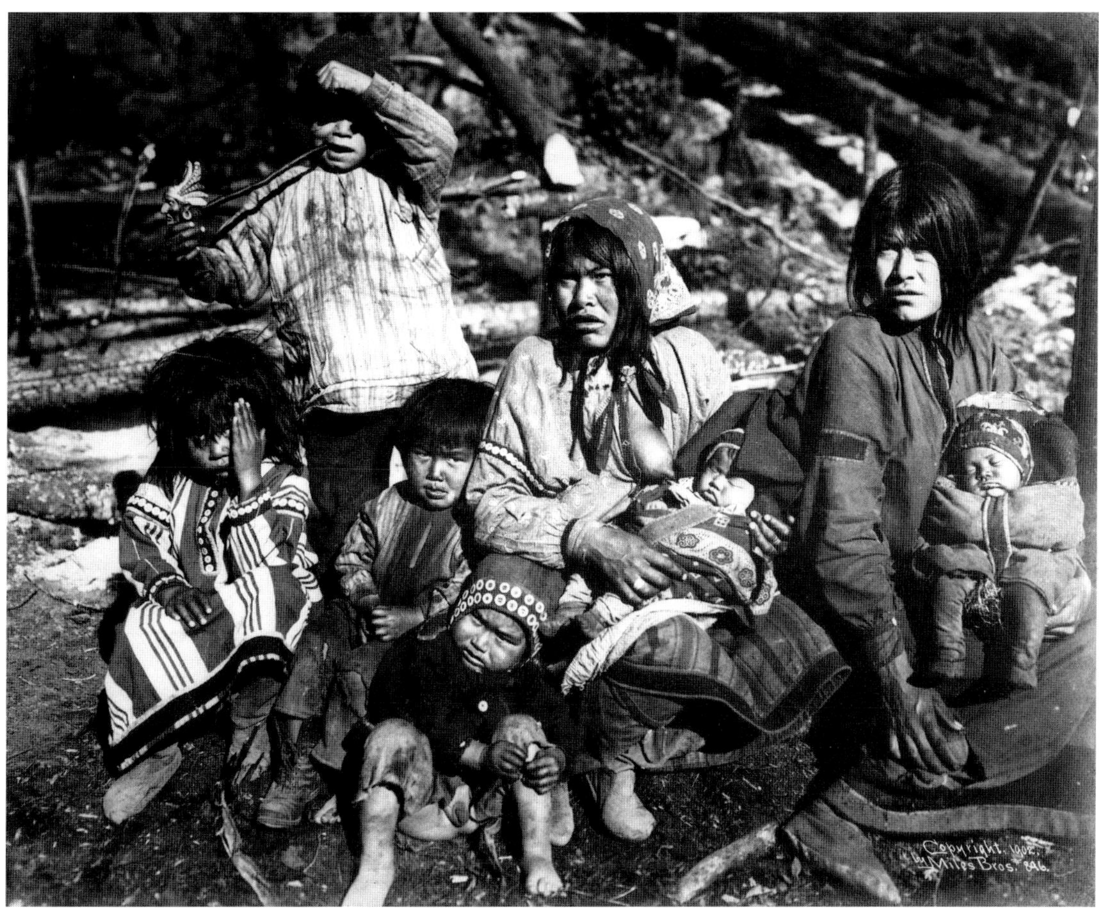

Figure 103
"Two Tlingit women with several children near the Kotsina River, Alaska," 1902. Photograph by Miles Brothers. Courtesy of the U.S. National Archives and Records Administration, Washington, DC. (524407)

Early photographers used many strategies to get the images they wanted. To overcome the objections of a Tlingit chief, commercial photographer Richard Maynard asserted during his trip to Alaska in August 1882, that he had government backing: "Took two photos—chief objected at first—saying it was his town—said I had orders from Govt. so he backed down." The photographer's alleged support of American authorities would have represented a credible threat to the Tlingit. Museum anthropologist George A. Dorsey and photographer Edward P. Allen obtained the photographs of Haida tattooing that

they wanted "by dint of much persuasion and a piece of silver" which they used to induce "a decrepit old man to leave his house long enough to enable us to carry away the photograph of his totem, which was tattooed on his breast" (Dorsey 1898:166). Visiting Seattle photographer Arthur Pillsbury, "always intent on taking new and different photographs," claimed to have hidden in the rafters of a clan house during a Tlingit potlatch in Klukwan in 1898 and "took a flash at night scaring them out of the place" (Harrison 1980:50). In other cases, subjects were simply distracted. In an image of a Tlingit family on the

     THE TLINGIT RESPONSE TO PHOTOGRAPHY

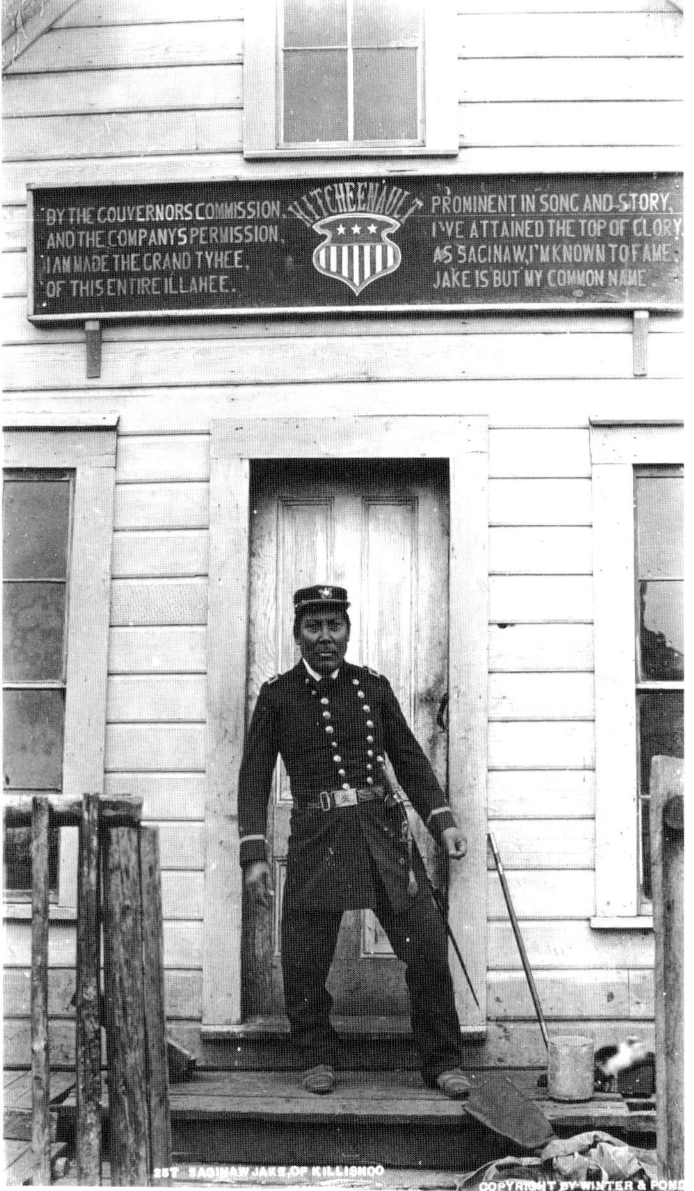

Figure 104

"Saginaw Jake of Killisnoo," 1900. Photograph by Winter & Pond. Sign reads left to right: "By the Gouvernors Commission, And the Companys Permission, I Am Made the Grand Tyhee, Of This Entire Illahee. Prominent in Song and Story, I've Attained the Top of Glory, As Saginaw, I'm know to Fame, Joe Is But My Common Name." By permission of the Alaska State Library, Juneau, AK. (P87–0224)

summer of 1888 while working with the Tsimshian on the Skeena River to go with him to a nearby island to "photograph the village while I tried to get a skull. I wanted him to do this in order to distract their attention. At low tide one can reach the island, which is about a quarter mile distant, on foot. Of course I did not tell the photographer (a stuttering idiot) what I wanted until we were there. I took a skull and the entire lower portion of the man...It is very sad that I haven't more Tsimshian skulls" (Rohner and Rohner 1969:95).

The Tlingit who were most willing to be photographed in the early years appear to have been those with high rank or chiefly status or else were successful traders or other cultural brokers (such as translators and guides) who had frequent contact with Euro-Americans and benefited from it (Figs. 104, 105). In Killisnoo, Kichnaalx (also known as Chief Jake, Saginaw Jake, and Killisnoo Jake) appears in several early photographs by Winter and Pond (Fig.

Kotsina River (Fig. 103), taken in 1902 by a photographer from the Miles Brothers Studio, only the children on the left seem to realize the photograph is being taken.

Sometimes photography was used purposely as a distraction in order to pursue other objectives. Franz Boas recorded in his diary persuading a visiting photographer he met in the

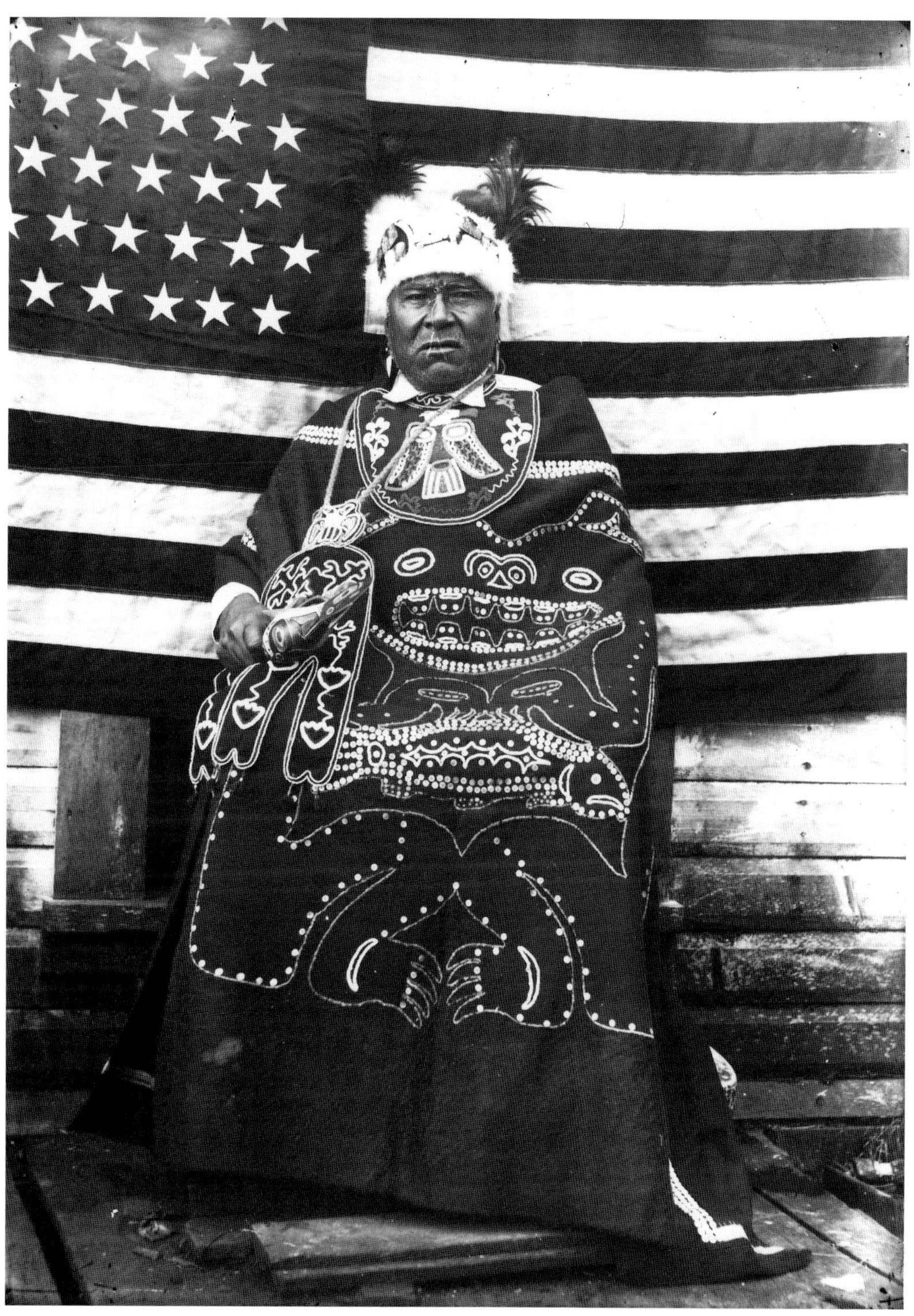

Figure 105
Deikeenaak'w, a Chichagof Island chief, poses with regalia and the American flag. Photograph by E. W. Merrill. By permission of the Alaska State Library, Juneau, AK. (P01–0895)

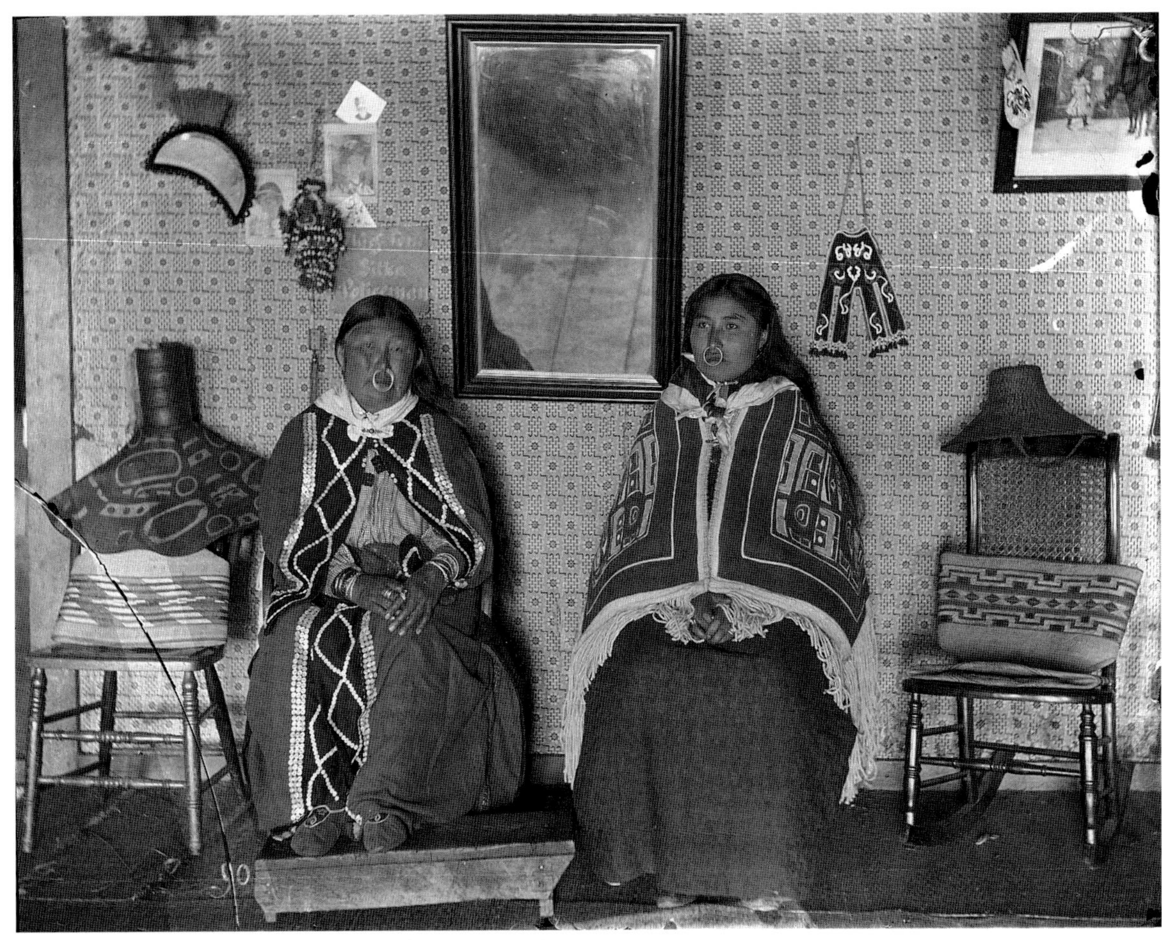

Figure 106
"Princess Thom" and "Sitka Belle," 1895. After this image was published in Knapp and Childe (1896), Princess Tom
(Thom) became part of the tourist literature of the age and a Sitka attraction in her own right. The woman on the
right is Mrs. Mausbauer. Photographer unknown. By permission of the Alaska State Library, Juneau, AK. (P–438)

104) and by Soboleff. He had intimate contact with whites. As early as 1868 he had been taken by the Navy to San Francisco aboard the U.S.S. *Saginaw*; in the late 1880s he was appointed a policeman by Governor Swineford. Chief Shakes in Wrangell, Chief Kininook in Saxman, and chiefs L.aanteech, Annaxóots, and K'alyáan in Sitka were also frequently photographed.

When commercial photographer Richard Maynard visited Wrangell in 1882, he met resistance from some Tlingit but had no difficulty photographing Chief Shakes or important pieces of Tlingit material culture, including a carved pole and a chief's grave. After photographing these as well as the interior of an Indian house and the town "in pouring rain," he went "to Chief Shakes and took the interior—then the old chief outside. Then another one of a Pole with the Chief in another dress" (Maynard 1882). According to the late Ester Littlefield, an elder of Sitka's founding Kiks.ádi clan interviewed in August 1986, photographer Elbridge Merrill "got

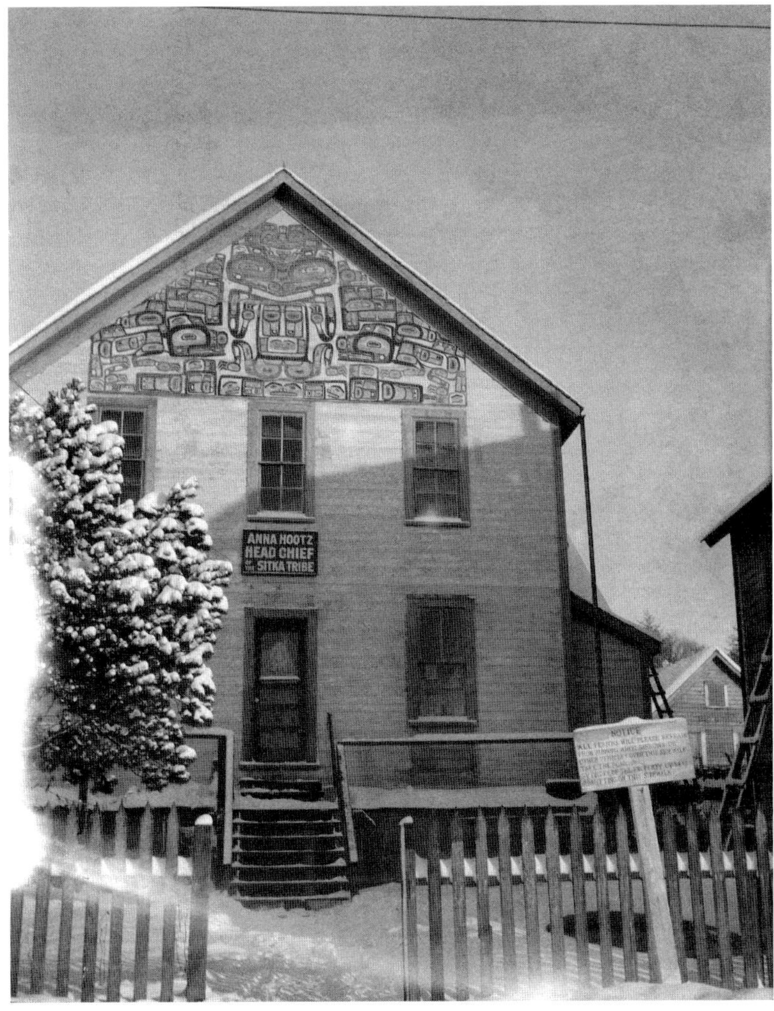

Figure 107
Clan house of "Anna Hootz [Annaxóots], Head Chief of the Sitka Tribe." Sign in right foreground reads: "All persons will please refrain from running wheelbarrows or other vehicles over this sidewalk. Take the road. By order of the property owners abutting [*sic*] on this sidewalk." Photograph by Louis Shotridge. By permission of the University of Pennsylvania Museum of Archaeology and Anthropology, Philadelphia, PA. (14808)

along real good with my family—my grandfather K'alyáan. He took lots of pictures."

Yakutat trader "Princess Tom" (sometimes spelled Thom) who moved to Sitka was also a willing subject (Fig. 106). In 1884, after Eliza R. Scidmore (1885) and some fellow tourists had met her on the roadside selling bracelets and had then visited her home in the village, she "came to the ship to be photographed by an admiring amateur" (177). Princess Tom obviously viewed doing so as an opportunity to make money. Scidmore further notes that "besides her ordinary regalia, [she had] a dozen or more pairs of bracelets tied up in a handkerchief, and we began to believe her wealth as boundless as her neighbors say it is."

Some Tlingit printed their names in English over the doorways of their homes. Princess Tom had two names printed over hers: Emeline Baker, the name given to her by missionaries, and Princess Tom, the name tourists had coined. Other residents posted signs announcing things like "Father to a large family of Orthodox Christians." House fronts were also painted with crest designs which displayed the owner's lineage and status (Fig. 107).

The Tlingit also displayed "papers," the documents or recommendation letters they had been presented with or had solicited from Euro-Americans (Krause 1956). When the U.S. Coast Survey of 1867 visited the village of Kake and its chief doubled the price of the potatoes Captain W. A. Howard wished to purchase for his crew, Howard refused to give him the "paper" he requested which would have "conferred quasi-official recognition on him as 'head chief'" (Sherwood 1959:147). The survey's head scientist George Davidson approved of the custom noting, "A very good custom prevails on this coast, in giving Indians what they term 'paper,' stating the character of the bearer; these 'papers,' particularly by the Hudson Bay Company Officers, state fairly the character of the Indian, his influence, if any, with his tribe, his prime and willingness for harm and good. One of the minor chiefs handed me a paper warning everyone to place confidence in him. These papers are highly valued and kept for years unsoiled" (Sherwood 1959:147). Thirty years later Frances Knapp and Rheta Childe found that Sitka's Tlingit cherished "a written testimonial as something priceless. Tantlatch [L.aanteech], of the Sitka ranch, has a number of such stowed away in a brass-studded chest. They have been written at his earnest request, by certain officials, and are very guarded and discreet, something after this style: 'We believe this man, Tantlatch, to be a good man. He seems very friendly and peaceable. He does not drink, so far as we know, and behaves himself very well'" (1896:104–5).

The Russians also had given documents to the Tlingit for loyalty or service, and those who possessed them had sometimes been given special rewards or gifts (Golovin 1979). Written certificates elevated the authority of the person possessing them, just as traditional Tlingit crests and acquired status items like the Russian double-headed eagle and American flag added to the social importance of the clan that possessed them (Grinev 2005:255). The importance of "paper" persists today. In 2004 to mark the centennial of the so-called Last Potlatch of 1904 and to celebrate the continuation of Tlingit culture, the

Kaagwaantaan held a large potlatch in Sitka. In addition to the many historic artifacts displayed at the event—including the Panting Wolf House Post, Multiplying Wolf House Posts, and the Multiplying Wolf House Front originally commissioned for the 1904 potlatch—a proclamation from the governor of Alaska was read commending the Tlingit for keeping their culture vibrant. This new document is now being cared for along with the historic *at.óow* mentioned above at the Sitka National Historical Park under a loan agreement with the Tlingit.

For Tlingit subjects of high rank a formal photograph may have been perceived in much the same way—as an acknowledgment or validation of their status and influence. A willingness to be photographed may also have been a way of demonstrating good will toward non-Natives and, perhaps, of currying favor. Pronouncements on the exterior of chiefs' homes and the possession of testimonial letters and photographs could work to their owner's advantage since they indicated that the individuals concerned were at least partially assimilated and accepting of Euro-American culture.

More assimilated and modernist Tlingit, such as those who had attended Sitka Industrial Training School and belonged to the Presbyterian Church, were frequently photographed. Merrill, for example, visited the school frequently and it is probable that he was personally closer to the families affiliated with it than to more traditional Russian Orthodox Tlingit. Students at the school would have had little, if any, say about whether or not their photographs were taken. Children everywhere are usually willing and unself-conscious collaborators with the camera, and students at the school were disciplined and obedient. Tlingit parents seldom if ever would have been at the school to object to photographs being taken, and even those who disliked the school's indenture agreements or the length of the school year, were undoubtedly proud of their children's familiarity with American ways and the important new skills such as literacy they were acquiring. Stu-

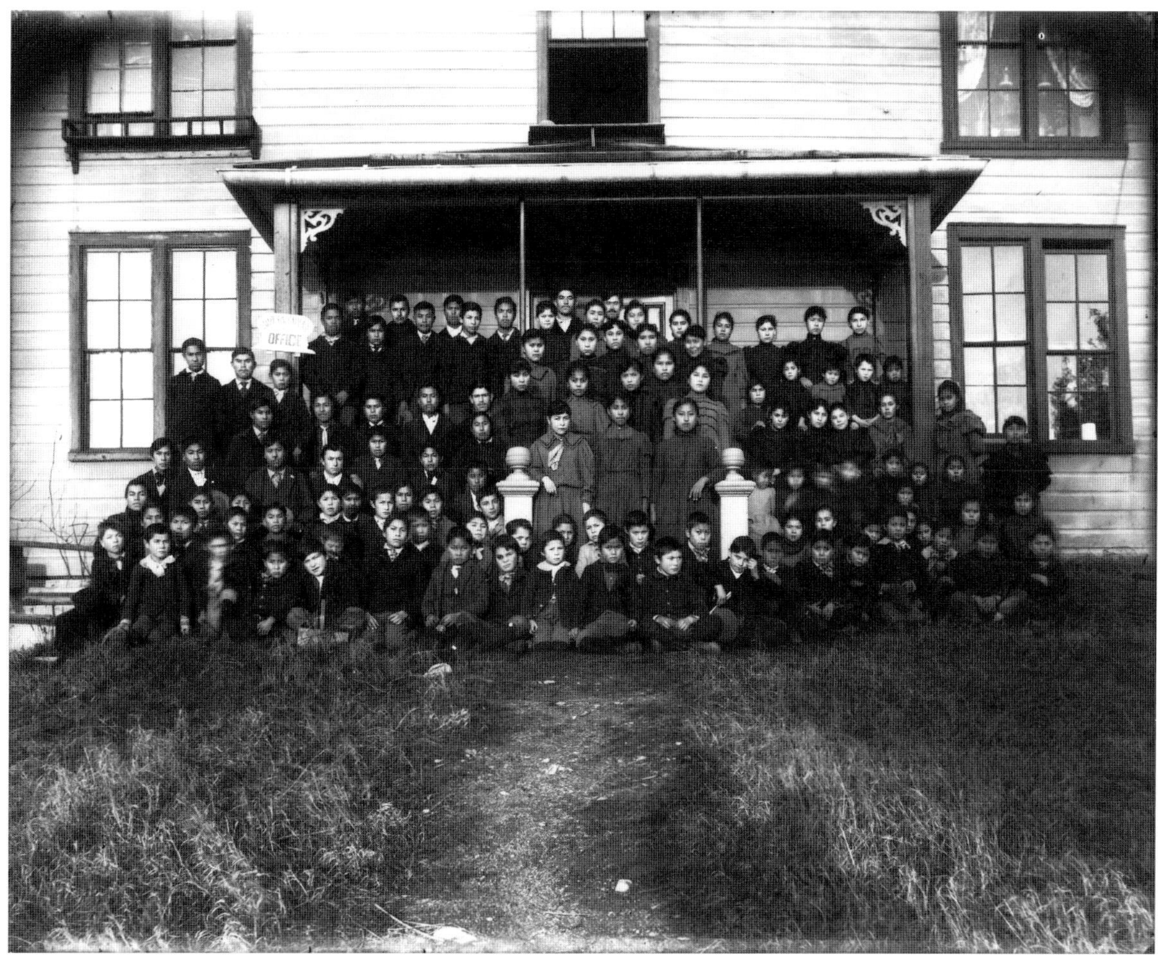

Figure 108
Sitka Industrial Training School children, 1900. Photograph by E. W. Merrill. Courtesy of Stratton Library, Sheldon
Jackson College, Sitka, AK.

dent photographs appeared regularly in Presbyterian publications to document and promote the school's work. Fundraising was much easier when people back East could see the dramatic (if only, outward) "civilizing" effect of the school on the Tlingit. The same images also promoted the government's goals and appeared in publications like the *Report on Population and Resources of Alaska at the Eleventh Census: 1890* (U.S. Department of Interior 1893) (Figs. 108, 109).

The diary and notebooks kept by amateur photographer Clarence L. Andrews, Sitka's customs agent in 1897 and 1898, throw important light on how the Tlingit reacted to and used photography at this time. Andrews notes on January 22, 1898, for example, being asked to take chief L.aanteech's portrait: "About 10 am Peter Nahns[?] came to ask me to take a picture of Klan tech. So I went." On another occasion he photographed "Father Anatoli Kamensky and the two Russian interpreters Kostromisinoff [Sergei Kostromitinoff] and Kolanpy [Kharlampii Sobolov]. Together

     THE TLINGIT RESPONSE TO PHOTOGRAPHY

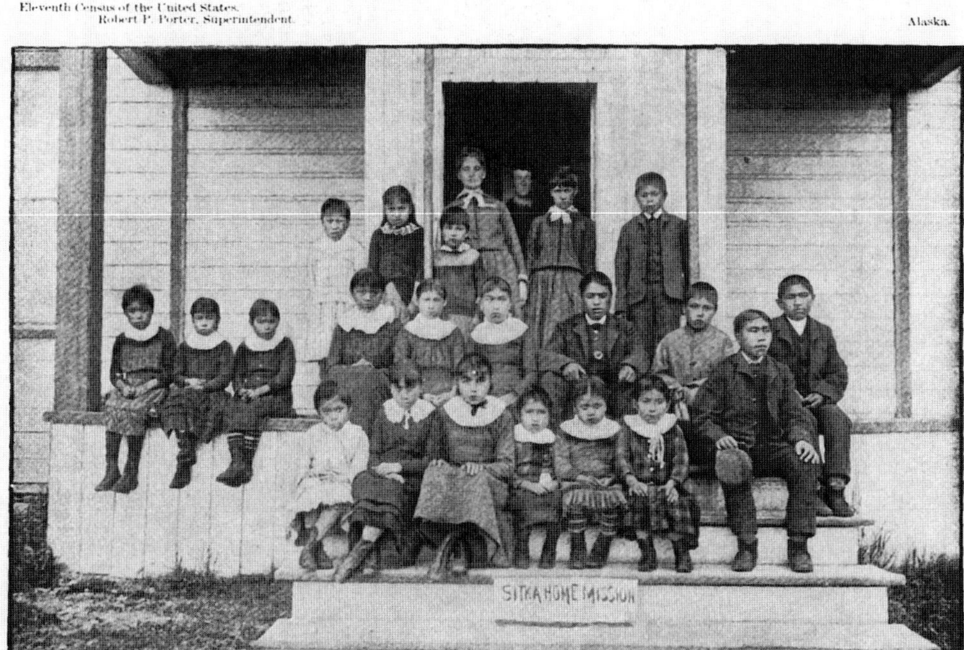

Figure 109
"Thlingit School Children" at "Sitka Home Mission," 1890. This image was published as part of the 11th census report (U.S. Department of Interior 1893).

with 5 Indian chiefs Klan-Tech [L.aanteech], Katlean [K'alyáan], Wauk, and two others."

Besides asking to be photographed, it is also clear that many Tlingit subjects selected the clothing they wore and the poses they adopted. On one occasion L.aanteech "arranged himself in his best black suit with Prince Albert coat, silk hat, cane, and gold watch chain. With a large seat [?] and posed before his house with all the dignity belonging to his station. Over his door is the inscription 'Klan Tech, Chief of the Kog-wantan [Kaagwaantaan]' clan." Yet when Andrews arrived to photograph him on February 25, L.aanteech chose to wear "Indian costume" which showed the crests to which his rank entitled him.

Andrews also photographed Jim Jacobs. "Two weeks ago last Sunday," he wrote on March 14, "I went down to the Silversmith's house. Jim dressed himself in Chilkat Blanket and Hydah [Haida] dance hat and sat, or stood for his photograph."

Isaac W. Taber captioned a photograph he took around 1890 of a Chilkat family inside their home "An Indian family 'dressed for a picture',", indicating that they wanted their portrait taken and had dressed for the occasion (Fig. 110).

In early March 1898 Andrews "tried a picture of an Indian child and unfortunately made a double exposure and spoiled both. Regretted it much as they were both good subjects and would have been good pictures. The Indians have a great notion of having their pictures taken since I have been taking some." With the arrival of resident photographers—both amateurs like Andrews and professionals—the Tlingit became

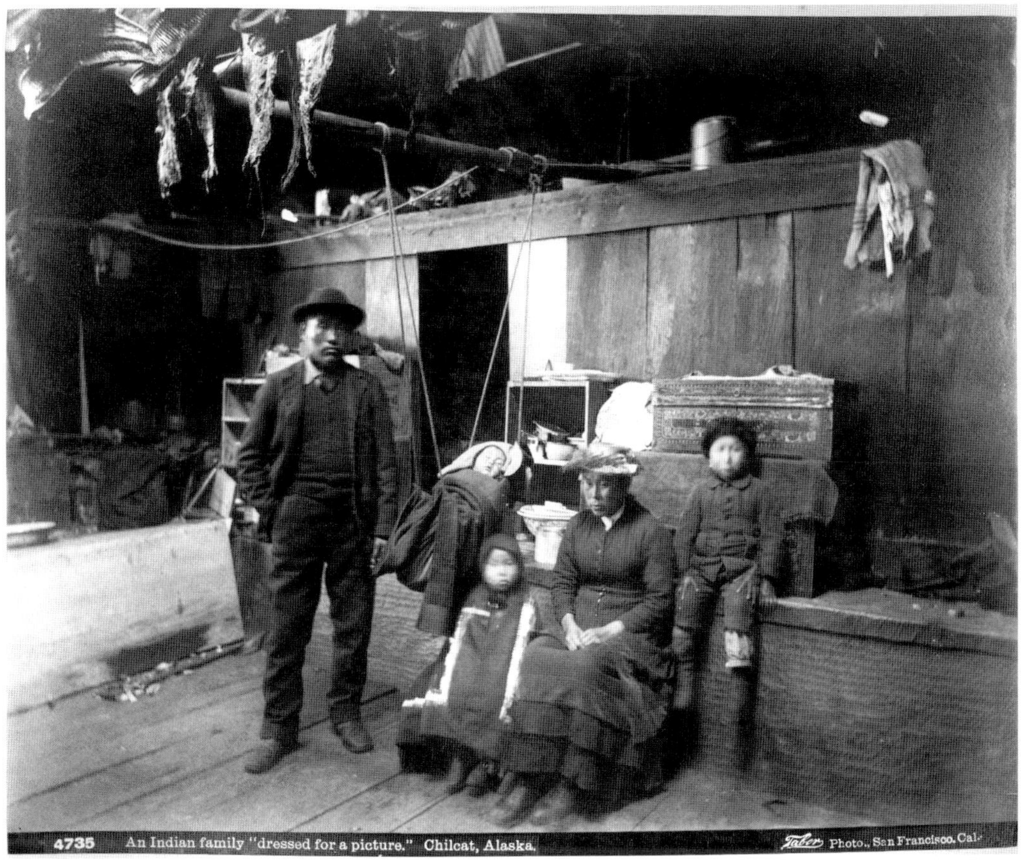

Figure 110
"An Indian family 'dressed for a picture.' Chilcat [Chilkat], Alaska," 1890. Photograph by Isaac W. Taber.
By permission of the Alaska State Library, Juneau, AK. (P438–40)

more familiar with photography and also had access to it with the result that many now became consumers.

Although Tlingit sitters frequently chose the clothing and pose they wanted to be photographed in, this was not always the case. When people are shown in photographs with Chilkat blankets artistically draped over them in ways they would never have worn them, we know that the photographer has "made" the image. Most—but not all—group poses would also have been orchestrated by the photographer. Merrill's image of the Sitka's Alaska Native Brotherhood basketball team is a clear example (Fig. 111). Reenactments

also were staged at the request of the photographer. Case and Draper's 1906 studio photograph of an "Indian witch doctor (or sha-man) healing a sick woman" (Figure 44), which was copied and further disseminated by other photographers, is an obvious example.

Many Tlingit ceremonial events were open to outsiders. On December 5, 1897, Andrews noted casually, "Today I intended taking pictures of potlatch boats but the rain came down all day." Later he did manage to photograph some leaving for Killisnoo, noting: "I indulged in some plates at their expense. Two canoes had the Russian flag. The rest the American." The words "at their

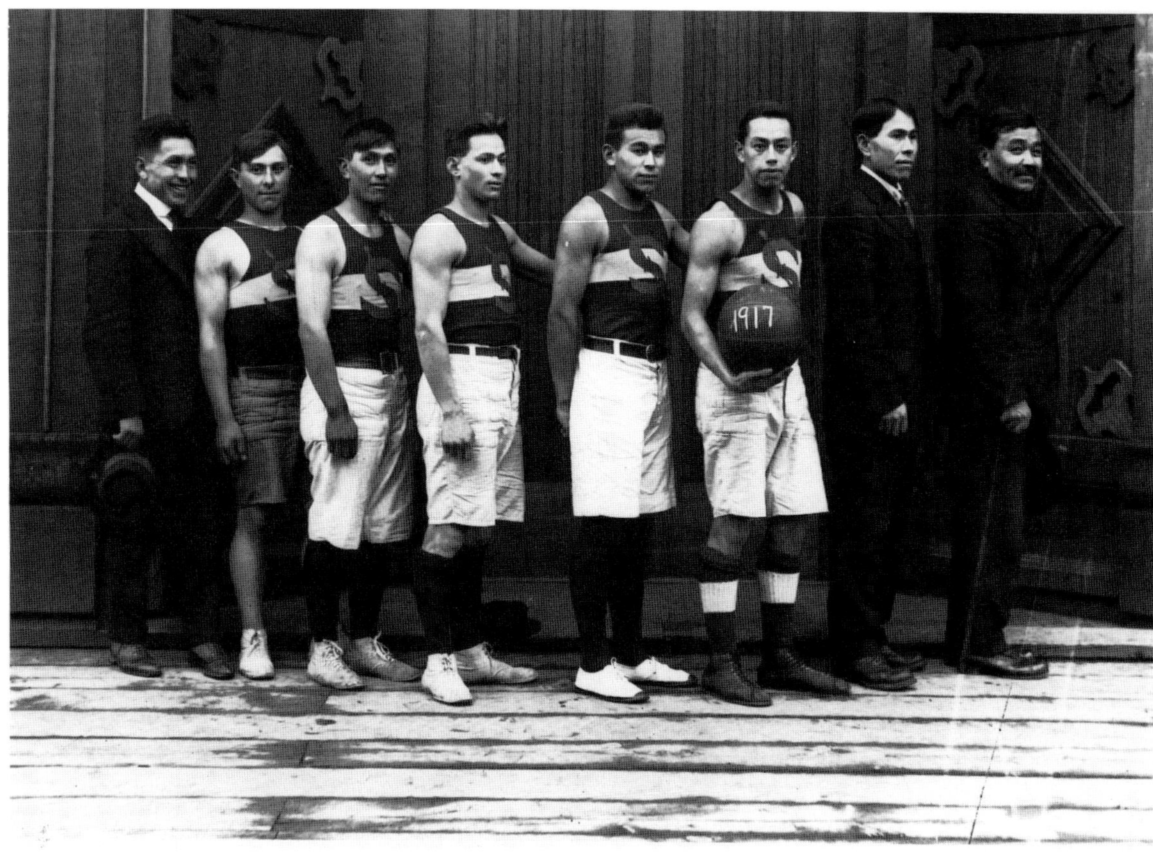

Figure 111
Sitka's Alaska Native Brotherhood basketball team, 1917. The team logo is "S" for Sitka with an ANB arrow running through it. Left to right: Tom Phillips, Howard Gray, Charlie Daniels, Thomas Williams, Louis Simpson, David Howard, Ray James, and Peter Simpson. Photograph by E. W. Merrill. Courtesy of Sitka National Historical Park, Sitka, AK. (3794)

expense" could indicate that the Tlingit had commissioned Andrews to take these photographs, but it is also possible that he was using the phrase colloquially. Nowhere in Andrews's diary or notebooks does he mention money exchanging hands for his photographs, either the Tlingit paying him to take a portrait or to document an event or their demanding payment from him for the privilege. Andrews also freely photographed Tlingit dances in Sitka in 1897 and 1898 as did cannery worker and amateur photographer Fhoki Kayamori in Yakutat between 1910 and 1941. Figure 112 shows Tlingit dancers performing inside Billy Jackson's

house in Yakutat in 1921.

Angoon resident Vincent Soboleff also photographed ceremonials. Yet, when Sitka merchant Edward DeGroff attempted to photograph a Tlingit dance he was denied permission after he refused to pay. Sitka's newspaper, *The Alaskan*, reported the incident on April 2, 1897: "Recently an Indian dance was going on in the ranch and our enterprising artist, deGroff, rushed over with his instrument all cocked and primed to take in the situation. On his arrival at the scene of action he was informed…that he must pay for the privilege of taking their picture for the reason that

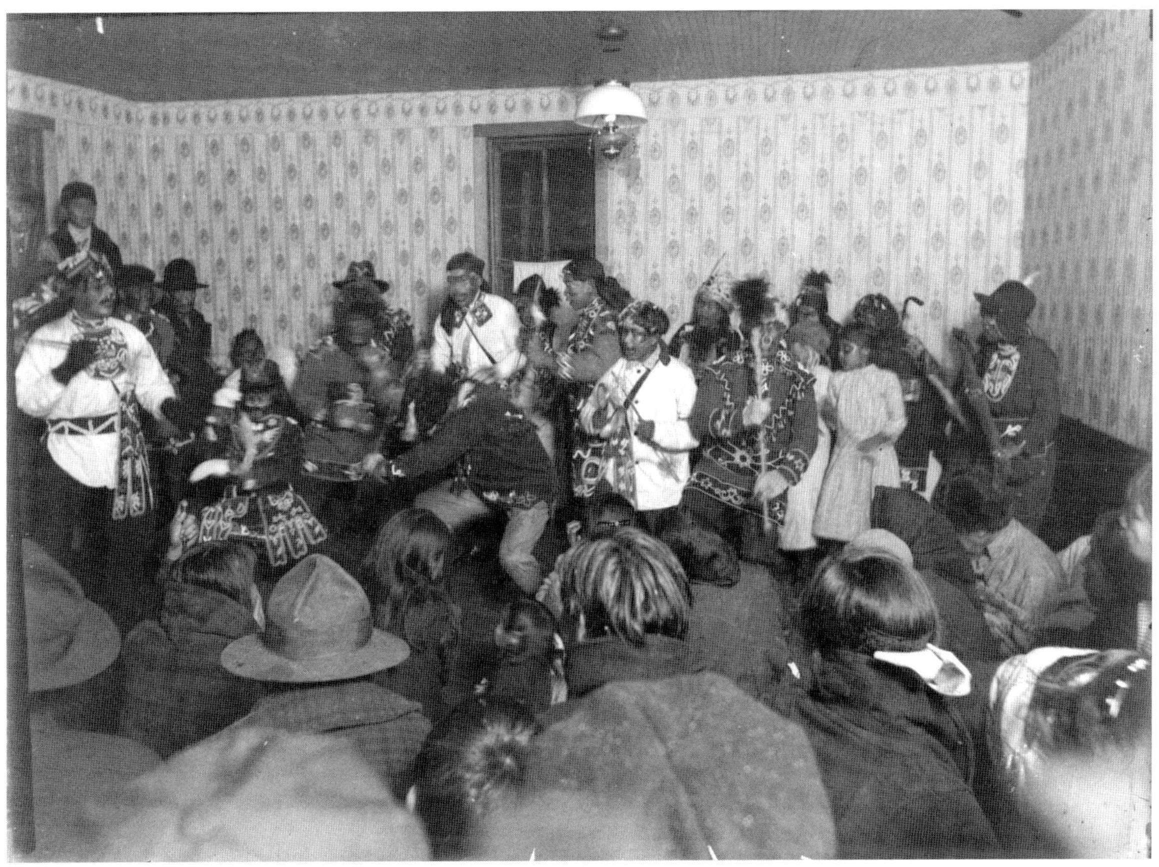

when they go to his place [his store] he charges them for taking their picture, and as he has come to their place he must pay them." DeGroff owned the Northwest Trading Company in Sitka from the 1880s to 1911. He photographed paying customers there, including the Tlingit as the news article cited above indicates, and also sold photographic prints, stereographs, and postcards of the Tlingit that he and other photographers had taken. The Tlingit were simply demanding fair play.

Further evidence for the Tlingits' consumption of photographs can be found by looking carefully at the internal content of images. Many photographs of the Tlingit reveal framed photographs hanging on the walls, such as Figures 113 and 114 taken in Yakutat by Fhoki Kayamori. It is very likely that these portraits of Sheldon and Annie James on their wedding day and of Emma and Jack Ellis (wearing his ANB sash) would soon join their other photographs on the wall.

A postmortem photograph taken by W. H. Partridge in Wrangell in 1887 also reveals photographs on the walls as do similar lying-in-state images taken by E. W. Merrill and other photographers. Vincent Soboleff's image of grave dancers from Angoon in 1899 shows two framed photographs of deceased relatives wrapped in

   THE TLINGIT RESPONSE TO PHOTOGRAPHY

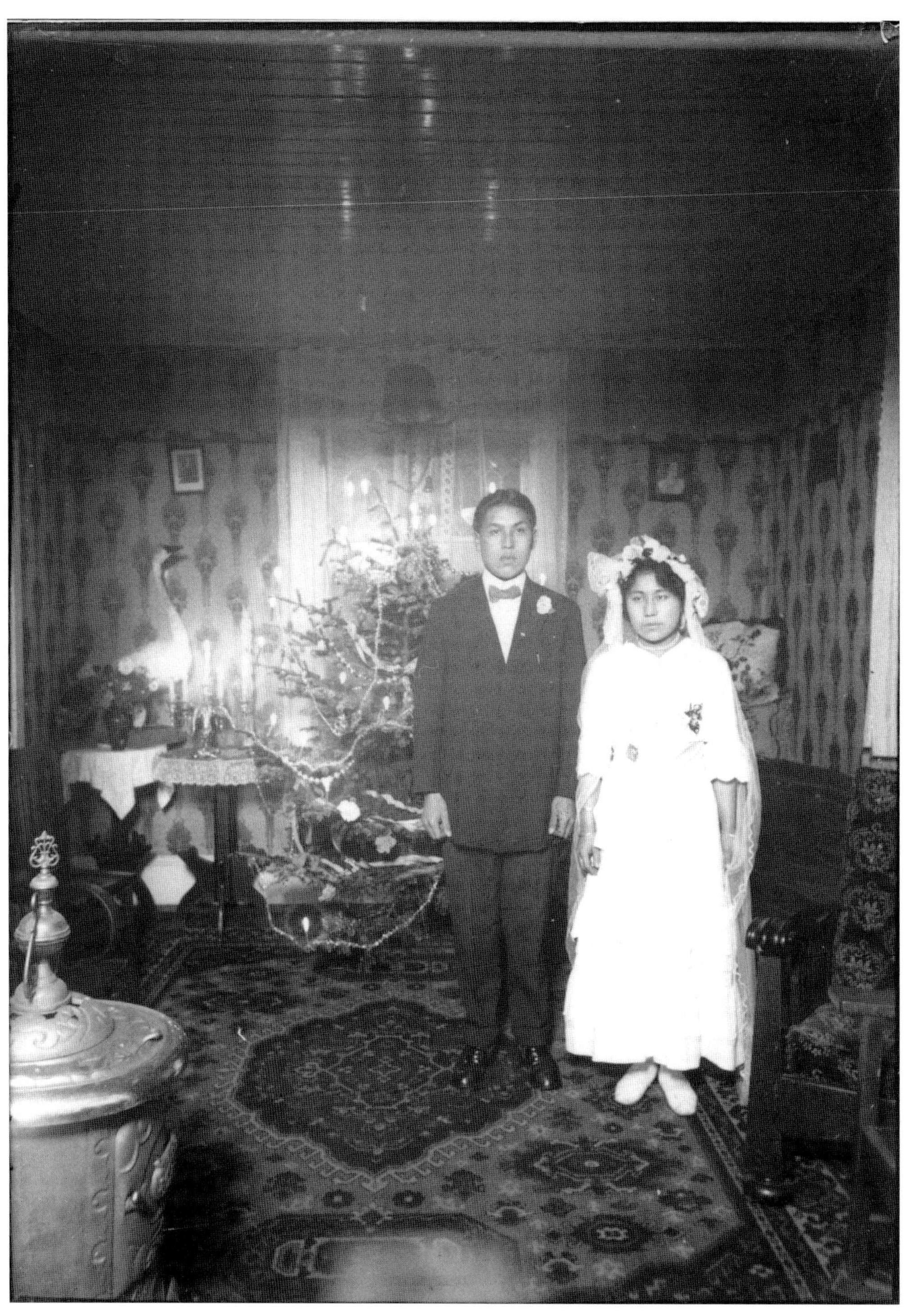

Figure 113
Sheldon and Annie James pose for their wedding portrait, Yakutat. Photograph by Fhoki Kayamori. By permission of the Alaska State Library, Juneau, AK. (P55–514)

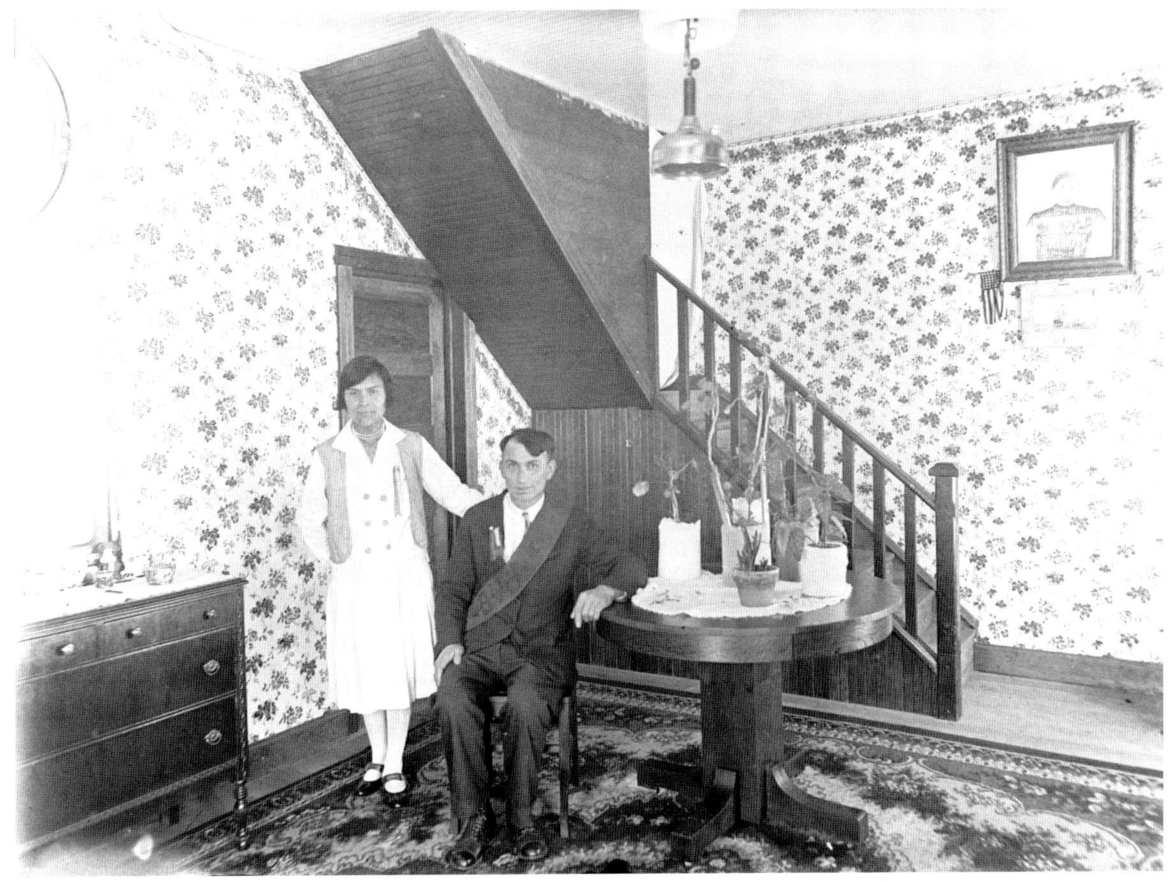

Figure 114
Emma and Jack Ellis pose for a formal portrait in their Yakutat home. He wears his ANB sash, 1925. Photograph by Fhoki Kayamori. By permission of the Alaska State Library, Juneau, AK. (PCA-55–599)

American flags or bunting prominently displayed as part of the ceremony (Fig. 115).

Written accounts also refer to the Tlingit ownership of photographs. Sophia Cracroft spent a month in Sitka in May and June 1870 while accompanying her aunt on a futile search for her husband, the arctic explorer Sir John Franklin. Together they toured the Tlingit village: "In the principal chiefs house, his apartment at the upper side, was raised above the floor of the house, & had chairs in it & a small table, with pictures on the walls. In another house, the principal apartment had the wall covered partly with playing cards stuck upon it, besides

pictures" (DeArmond 1981:25). The "pictures" she mentions are photographs; if they had been paintings, she would have been referred to them as such. At the time, the word "picture" was commonly used to refer to photographs and still is. As Cracroft's account indicates, some Tlingit in Sitka—most likely chiefs and wealthy traders— had become photography consumers as early as 1870, only two years after Muybridge's earliest images. Other Natives on the Northwest Coast, who had been exposed to photography earlier, had begun acquiring images as early as 1862 (Williams 2003).

Many postmortem photographs were taken

     THE TLINGIT RESPONSE TO PHOTOGRAPHY

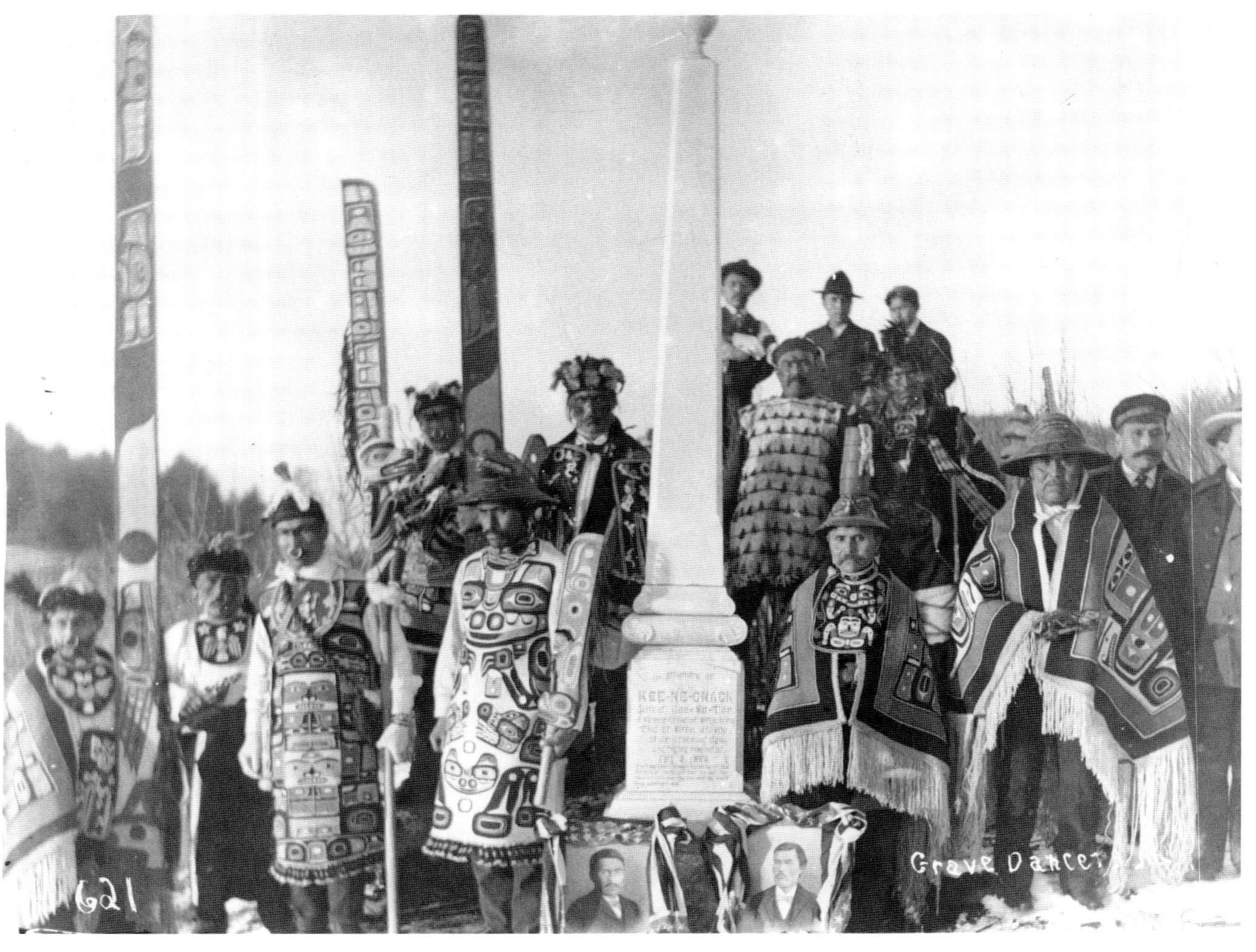

Figure 115
Grave dancers. According to de Laguna, the persons in Tlingit regalia are "chiefs and song leaders invited to the dedication of the monument; the hosts, in ordinary clothing, stand behind them" (Emmons 1991:311). The grave marker reads: "In memory of Kee-Ne-Gnack wife of Kaa _____, former chief of Sitka Tribe. Died at Sitka, at an advanced age and highly respected, 1899," 1900. Photograph by Vincent Soboleff. By permission of the Alaska State Library, Juneau, AK. (PI–031)

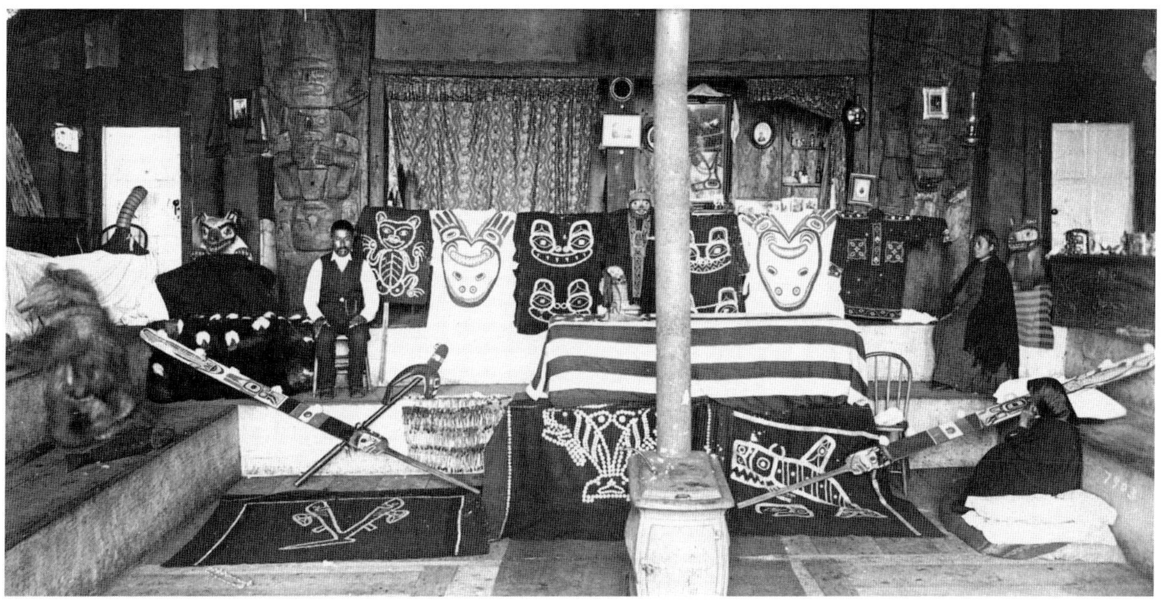

Figure 116
Chief Shakes lying in state at Wrangell, 1880s. Note the framed and unframed photographs on the wall. This image
was reproduced in the U.S. Department of the Interior 1890 census (1893). Photograph attributed to W. E. Styles. By
permission of the Glenbow Museum, Alberta. (NA 1807-39)

of the Tlingit by both amateur and professional photographers. These could not have been taken without the full cooperation, and most likely the direct invitation, of the Tlingit. When photography was still in its infancy in the 1840s Russian geologist Ilia Gavrilovich Voznesenskii had attended Tlingit lying-in-state ceremonies in Sitka and had made drawings of them (Vaughan and Holm 1982:247). The close similarity of these mid-19th century drawings to later photographs indicates that the Tlingit controlled the arrangement of clan objects and mourners. From the 1840s until the turn of the century postmortem photography was common in the Euro-American community as well with some professional photographers advertising their "readiness to make pictures from corpses if desired" (West 2000:139, Ruby 1995). Such images helped the living remember the dead with a degree of reality impossible before the advent of photography. They also documented an accepted part of life: death as a normal rite of passage even when it was photographically portrayed as sleep.

Among non-Natives, postmortem photographs seldom attempted to convey anything about the deceased as an individual. One purpose of Tlingit lying-in-state photographs, in contrast, was to document the deceased's individual identity and to validate his status by showing the body surrounded by lineage crests and important clan regalia—Chilkat blankets, dance staffs, headdresses, and even American flags that had become *at.óow* after being brought out at a potlatch. Figure 116 shows Chief Shakes lying in state at Wrangell. He is surrounded by the clan property of which he was the custodian; note also the photographs on the wall. This image was reproduced in the *Report on Population and Resources of Alaska at the Eleventh Census: 1890* (U.S. Department of Interior 1893).

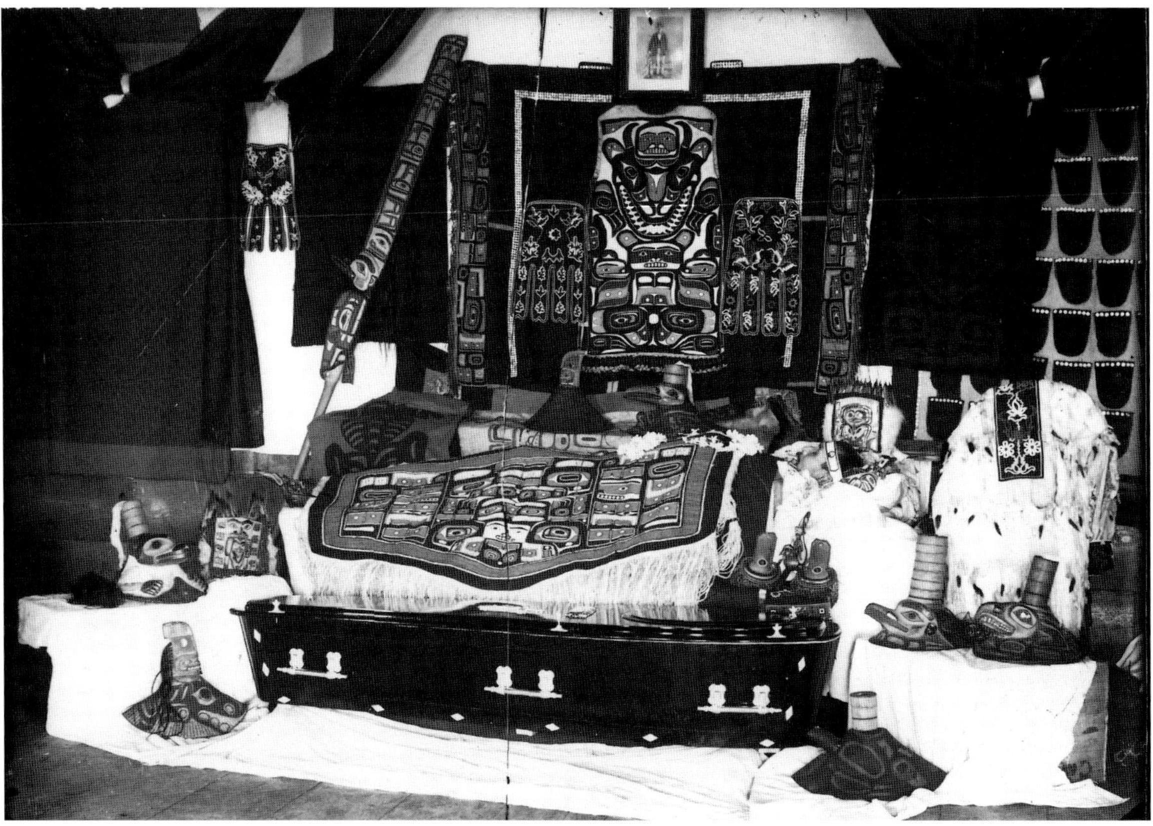

Figure 117
A photograph is positioned as part of the lying-in-state display. Photograph by E. W. Merrill. Courtesy of Stratton Library, Sheldon Jackson College, Sitka, AK.

Sometimes a photograph of the deceased was displayed along with their regalia, as in Figure 117 by E. W. Merrill. The period of lying-in-state showed respect for the departed, united mourners in their common grief, and gave people an opportunity to assess the "social career of the deceased" (Kan 1986).

Post mortem photographs began to function as visual "proof" of a clan's claim to the ownership of particular crest and ceremonial objects. According to Sergei Kan, "the relatives of the deceased requested that a photograph of the coffin and the crests be taken...It seems that the picture became an additional form of validating the claims of matrilineal groups to particular crests and demonstrating their wealth and prestige. This validation became particularly important in an era of increased disputes over the ownership of crests and the efforts of some of the more Americanized natives to sell them" (1985:21).

Photographs were also specifically commissioned to validate ownership as when Sitka's L'uknax̱.ádi clan claimed the frog as one of its emblems. Their ownership was disputed by Sitka's Kiks.ádi clan which also claimed the frog as one of its clan crests. In a Merrill image now in the Sitka National Historical Park five members of the L'uknax̱.ádi clan pose with their newly carved frog crest. The photograph, with an American flag hanging on the wall in the background, vi-

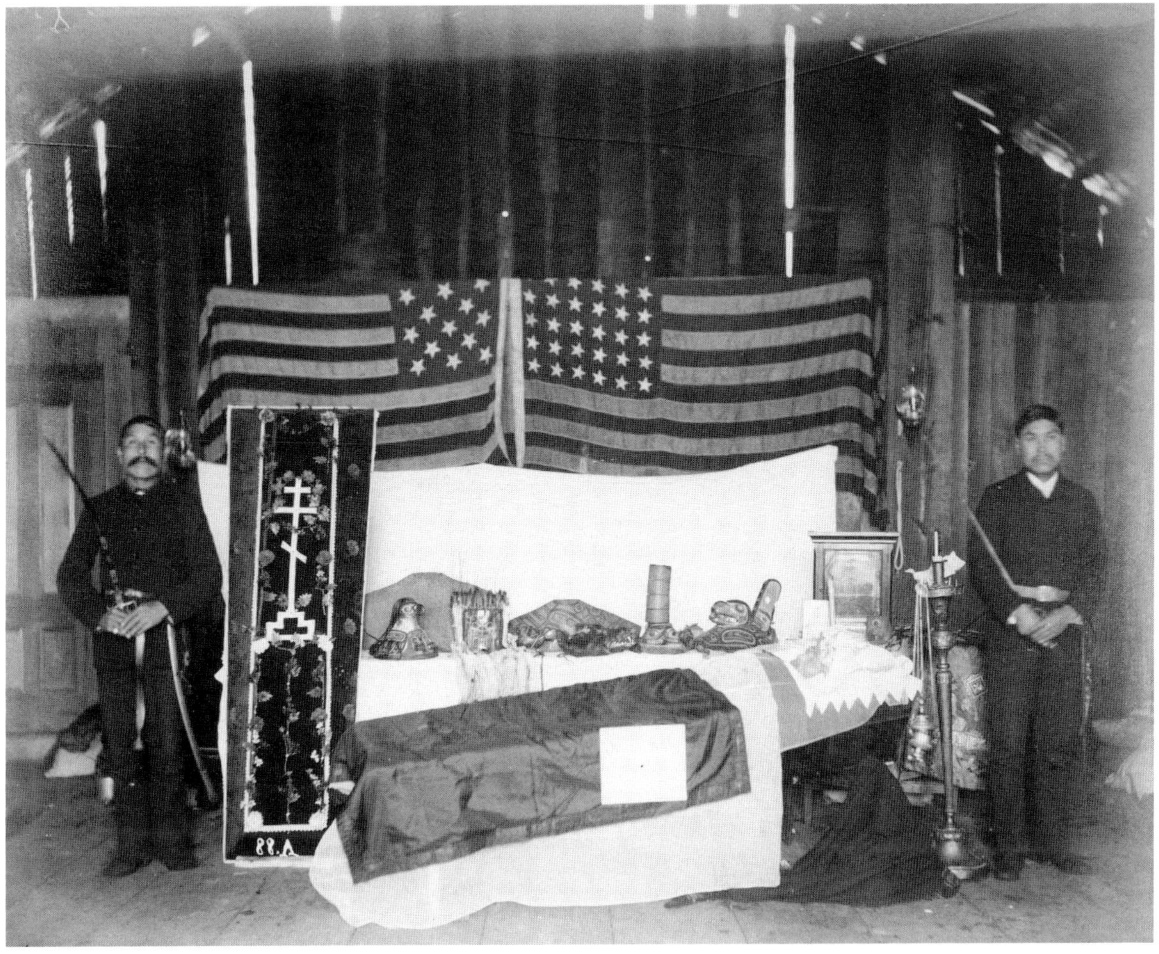

Figure 118
"Annahoots [Annaxóots] funeral," 1890s. Photographer unknown. By permission of the Alaska State Library, Juneau, AK. (P438–17)

sually asserted their ownership and implied that they had the backing of American authority. The frog dispute caused a major rift in Sitka's Tlingit community especially after nine Kiks.ádi men went to the L'uknax̱.ádi clan house where the frog carving was being displayed early one February morning in 1901 and chopped it to pieces. The issue remains sensitive, and Merrill's image is not reproduced here for this reason.

American flags are visible in many photographs of the Tlingit. In a postmortem photograph taken by Victor Soboleff at Killisnoo one American flag hangs behind the mourners and another is draped over a railing. A non-Native viewer of this image might assume that it was the photographer who had provided these props, but that was not the case. The flag—whether it was Russian or American—was recognized by the Tlingit as a powerful symbol, and it was their decision to pose with it. The caption to a postmortem photograph taken by amateur photographer O. M. Salisbury in the 1920s reads: "The mourners

    THE TLINGIT RESPONSE TO PHOTOGRAPHY

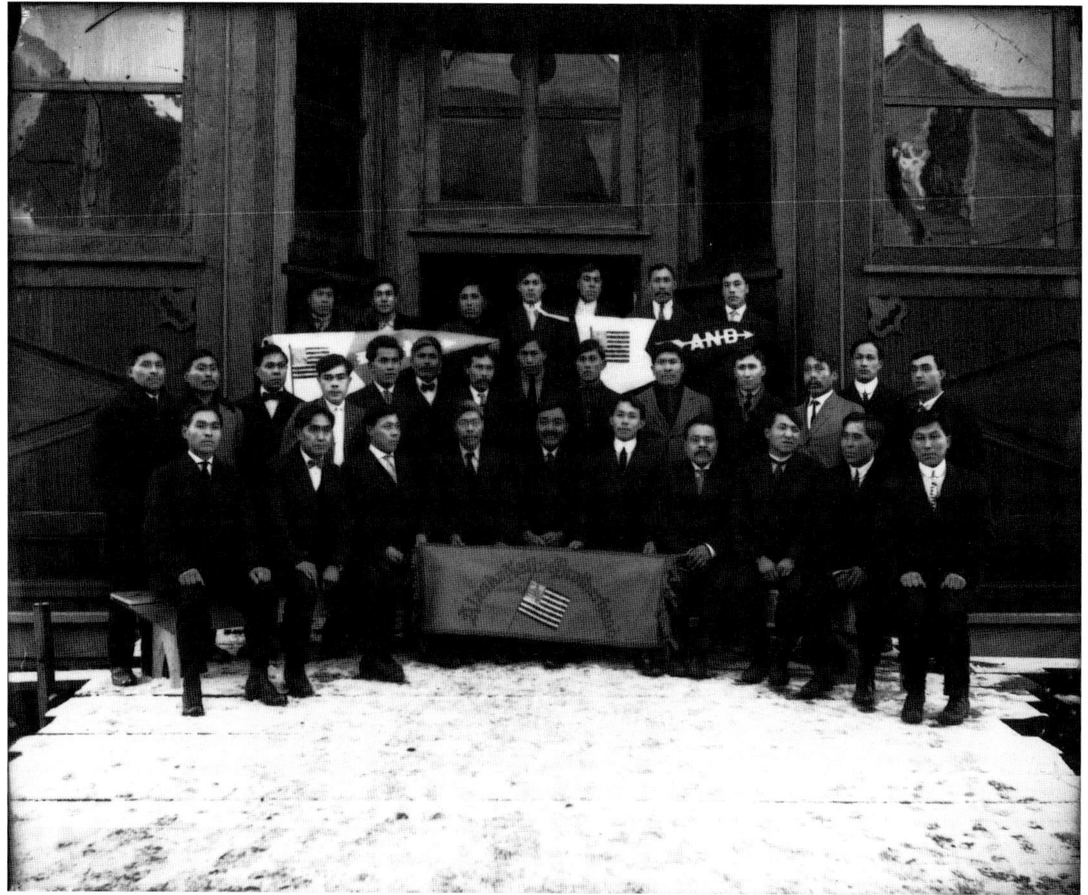

Figure 119

Founding members and delegates to the Alaska Native Brotherhood's Grand Lodge meeting held at Sitka's new ANB hall, November 1914. Left to right, front row: James Watson, Frank Mercer, Herbert Murchison, Chester Worthington, Peter Simpson (Grand President), Paul Liberty (Aanyáanáx), Edward Marsden, Haines DeWitt, Mark Jacobs, Sr. (possibly Peter K. Williams?), Charlie Newton. Middle row: John Willard, John Johnson, Seward Kunz, Stephen Nicholas, Donald Austin, George McKay, Cyrus Peck, James Morrison, Charlie Daniels, Don Cameron, Ralph Young, Rudolph Walton, William Jackson, Frank Price. Back row: James Gordon, Andrew Hope, George Bartlett, Thomas Williams, John Williams, George Lewis, Sergius (?)Williams. Twenty-four of the 31 men pictured were former pupils of the Sitka Industrial Training School. Nine lived in the school's cottage settlement. Identification from Dauenhauer and Dauenhauer (1994:461–68). Photograph by E. W. Merrill. Courtesy of Stratton Library, Sheldon Jackson College, Sitka, AK. (M II 339)

would have liked to hold the American flag behind the coffin, but [I would not let them since] it would have hidden the people" (1962:181). The Tlingit flew flags from potlatch canoes, posed in front of them in photographs which substantiated claims to status objects, and displayed those that had become *at.óow* at lying-in-state ceremonies. In a postmortem photograph of Annaxóots taken in the 1890s (Figure 118) two flags that had become *at.óow* hang behind the coffin: one has 13 stars

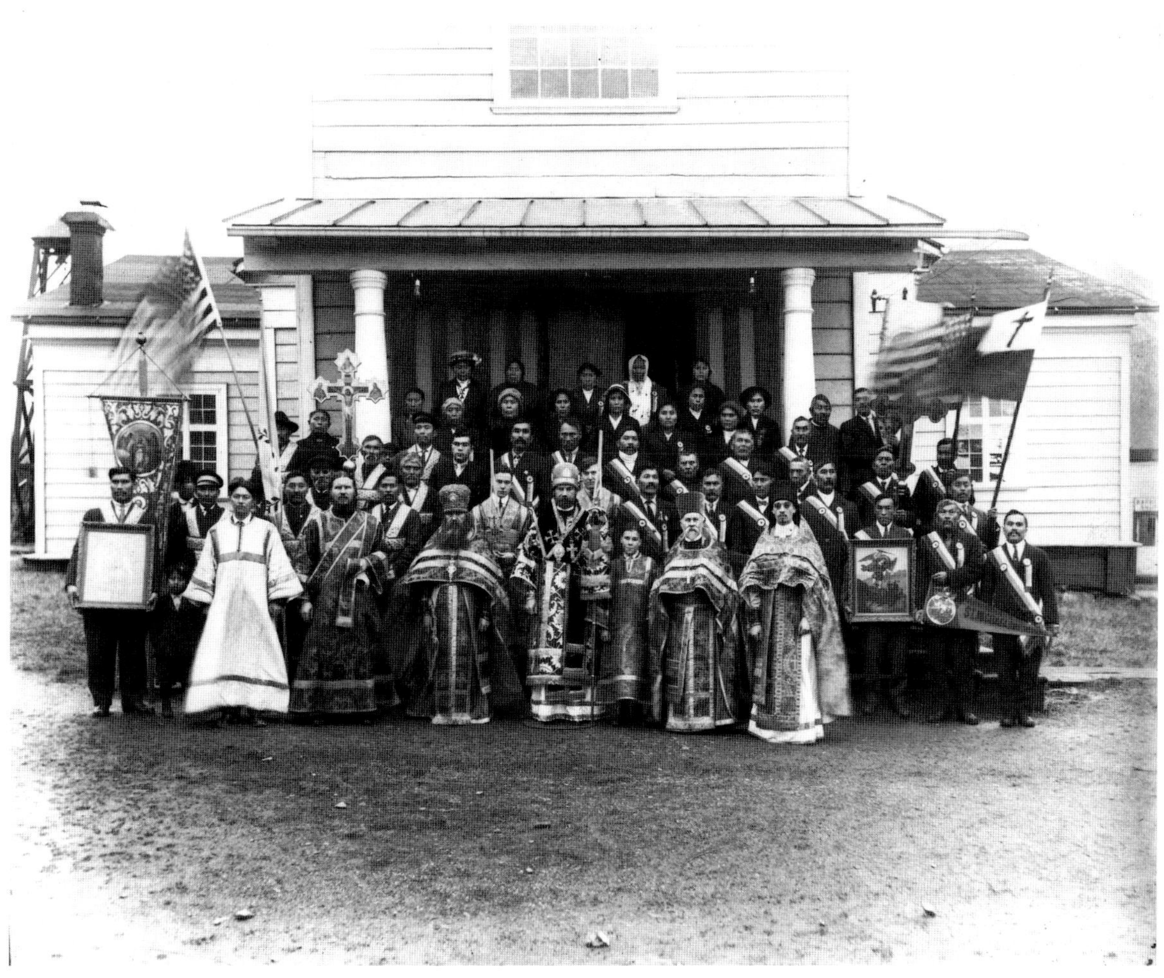

Figure 120

Members of the Russian Orthodox Brotherhoods in front of St. Michael's Cathedral, after 1904. The Russian Orthodox St. Gabriel Brotherhood (comprised mainly of members of the Kiks.ádi clan) is on the left, and the St. Michael's Brotherhood (comprised primarily of L'uknax.ádi clan members) is on the right. Front row left to right: Scotty James, Peter James (little boy), Vladimir Deiker (Decker?), Deacon Antonii, Archmandrite Amphilokhii, Bishop Philip, unidentified altar boy, Fr. Andrei Kashevarov, unidentified priest, Charlie Dick, unidentified Kookhittaan man, and Frank Joseph. See Kan (1999:331) for a complete identification. Photograph by E. W. Merrill. Courtesy of Sitka National Historical Park, Sitka, AK. (3803)

which date it to the late 18th century (1777–95), the other has 30, dating it to the mid-19th (1848–51). The flag was also adopted by other Native American groups. The Lakota incorporated it as an appealing design element on horse masks and other objects they made, but they also believed their use of the American flag would help curry favor with the military men and other government employees they had to deal with, especially those living on reservations.

When taking portraits photographers required the full cooperation of their subjects, and it is likely that the Tlingit commissioned many of these images. Organizations such as the Alaska

     THE TLINGIT RESPONSE TO PHOTOGRAPHY

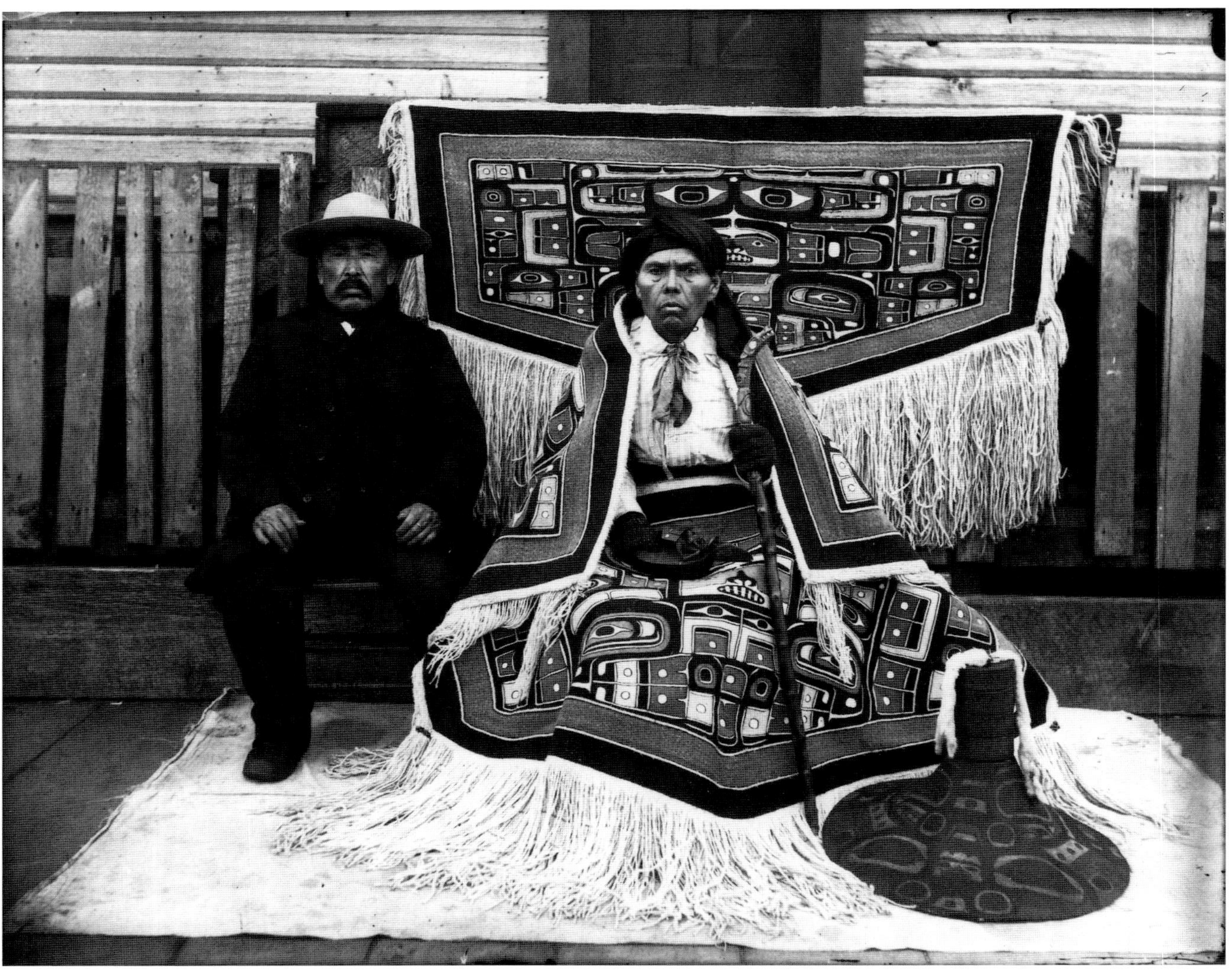

Figure 121
Identified by some as Jack Watson, an Ahtna Athabascan from Copper Center, and Mary James ("Sheep Creek Mary"), an Auk Tlingit from the L'eeneidí clan. She was a prominent Auk leader and well known among tourists in Juneau. The hat on the lower right is Lingít Aaní S'aax̱w (World Hat) of G̱ooch Hit (Wolf House, also known as Lingít Aaní Hit [World House] and Aanyédi Hit [High Caste House]), a hat captured in a battle around 1853. Identification by Harold Jacobs. Photograph taken in Sitka, 1915. Photograph by E. W. Merrill. By permission of the Alaska State Library, Juneau, AK. (P57–090)

Native Brotherhood and the Russian Orthodox Church's St. Michael and St. Gabriel brotherhoods—whose members came from the Raven and Eagle moieties, respectively—paid to have portraits taken of their memberships (Figs. 119, 120).

Most of Merrill's photographs of these groups show careful composition, including the arrangement of people by height. They were taken outside largely for practical reasons: namely, to take advantage of the natural light and to have enough room to accommodate a large group. But doing so also allowed Merrill to include visual indicators of their membership: in these examples, they are posed in front of the Alaska Native Brotherhood Hall and St. Michael's Cathedral. Portraits of individuals and small groups also reveal Tlingit cooperation. Those taken outside are often carefully posed in front of studio backdrops or Chilkat blankets suspended from an outdoor wall (Fig. 121).

Potlatches were and remain ceremonial events of great importance to the Tlingit. They acknowledge and commemorate significant events such as the dedication of a new clan house or the memorial of an important clan member when guests from the opposite moiety are formally thanked for having handled the deceased's funeral. Based on the principles of reciprocity and balance, the hosts of a potlatch regale their guests in the opposite moiety with songs, dances, oratory, food, and gifts, including money, and, in the past, blankets and valued delicacies like candlefish oil. Most of the potlatch photographs taken by Merrill in Sitka show the large potlatch given by the Wolf House lineage of the Kaagwaantaan clan in late December 1904—100 years after the Russian re-occupation of Sitka. Sitka's three Wolf Houses co-sponsored the event and commissioned monumental carvings to commemorate it. The Wolf/World/Noble House, led by Jacob "Jake" Yarkon (Yaakwaan), commissioned carver and silversmith Jim Jacobs to create the "Panting Wolf" house post (Figs. 64, 92). Augustus Bean (Keitxt'ch) of the Wolf/Eagle House commissioned Rudolph Walton to carve the "Wolf House" posts. James

Jackson (Annaxóots), then head of the Kaagwaantaan clan and leader of the Wolf/Bear House, commissioned the "Multiplying Wolf" house posts and house front. These leaders were joined by a fourth, Paddy Parker (K'axook Eesh) of the Wolf/World/Noble House, in sponsoring the event and in commissioning its *at.óow*.

All four leaders were educated Christians who had served on the Indian police force and belonged to the New Covenant League which later evolved into the Alaska Native Brotherhood. The League favored ending such traditional "vices" as polygyny, inter-clan indemnity claims, and uncle-nephew inheritance. From the American government's point of view, this potlatch was meant to be the Tlingits' last. Governor John G. Brady reported that Sitka's leaders had agreed to pay off all their debts and end obligations to sponsor future potlatchs. For some Tlingit, the potlatch was viewed as a way to heal old wounds (like the frog dispute) so the clans could begin working together to protect their interests. Sitka's Kaagwaantaan clan (Eagle moiety) invited Raven moiety guests from the L'uknax.ádi and Kiks.ádi clans of Sitka, the Deisheetaan clan of Angoon, the T'akdeintaan of Hoonah, and the Gaanaxteidi' of Klukwan. The potlatch lasted four days, during which the six commissioned wood carvings were dedicated. Despite the hosts' own assimilationist leanings and whatever understanding Governor Brady may have thought had been reached, the 1904 potlatch was treated by more traditional Tlingit as an opportunity to educate the young and impress upon them the importance of maintaining their traditions. After 1904, Tlingit potlatches were "officially" over yet they continued to be held and to be photographed.

The careful arrangement of people and poses evident in potlatch photographs, especially those take by Merrill, took time to set up and patience on the part of the both photographer and subjects, once again indicating that the Tlingit were actively involved in their creation. Merrill's group portrait of guests from Angoon, members

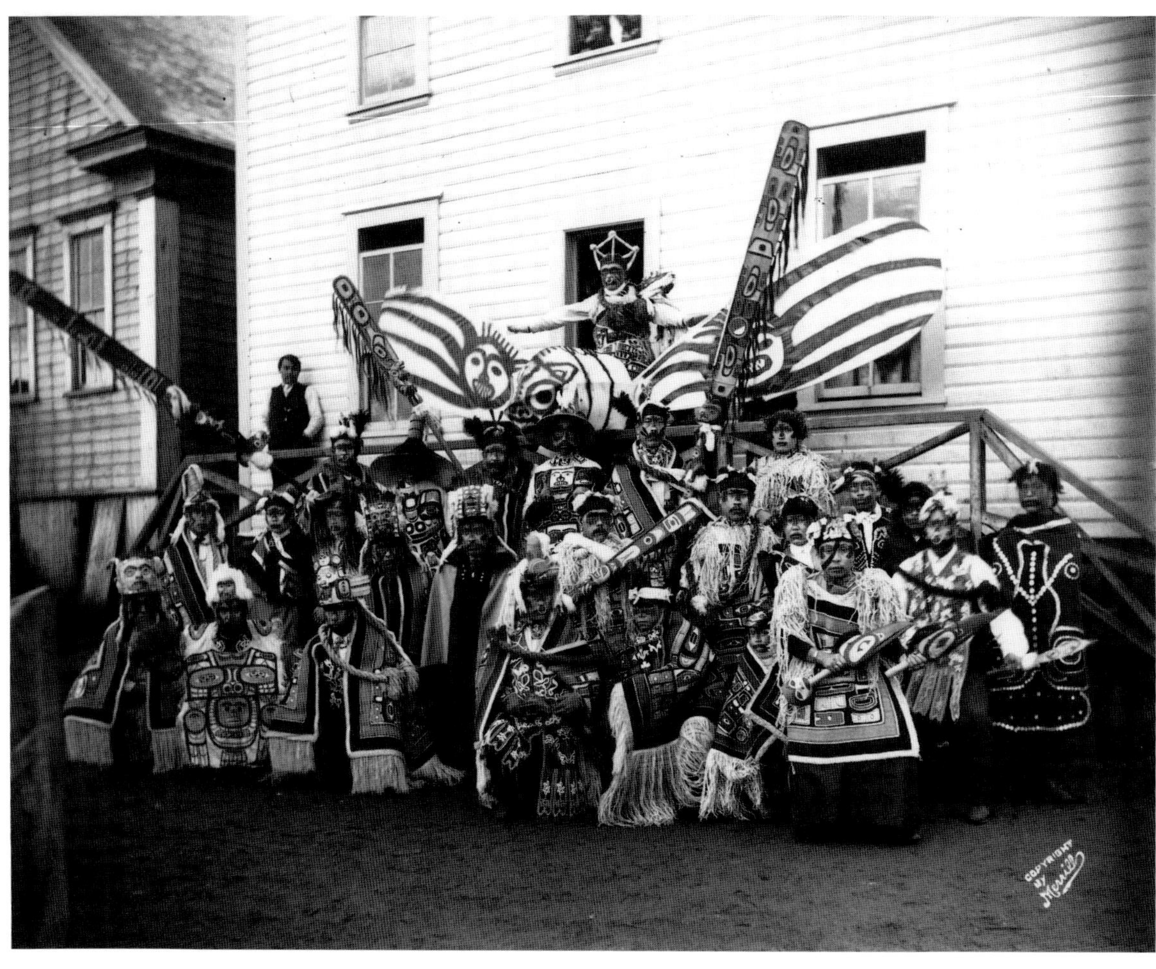

Figure 122

Kaagwaantaan Wolf House potlatch, Sitka, 1904. Thirty Tlingit, mainly Angoon guests belonging to the Deisheetaan clan, pose for a group portrait. Front row left to right: Kashaaxaaw (George Johnson), Kaatéenaa (Peter Dick), Kwaal Eésh (Jimmy Hanson), Woolshoox' (Little Jack), unknown, Keelt' (Larry Jack), and Yaxlahaat (Annie Jack). Second row left to right: Deiyiktaa (Tom Philips), Tsaakáak'w (Elsie Bell Phillips), Kaajeeskaawugáa (Mary Jones), Áaycax (Sam Johnson), Yeilk', unknown, Daalkuwoox' Éesh?, Kaachúks, and Kooĺa.áa (John Fred). Back row left to right: L.aangooshú (Billy Jones), Kichnaalx (Killisnoo Jake), Kaa Tlein (John Paul, Jr.), Yeilnaawú (Dick Yetlna), Laxkeikw (Jimmy Albert, Sr.), Shaawat Goox (Mary Albert), Kaaxoowát'ch, Sikéin, and Took' (Charlie John) . Standing on the porch is Aanx'isxaa (Pete Johnson). Identification by Harold Jacobs. Captioned photograph in the Alaska Native Brotherhood Hall, Sitka, contains further information. Photograph by E. W. Merrill. Courtesy of the Sitka National Historical Park, Sitka, AK. (3775)

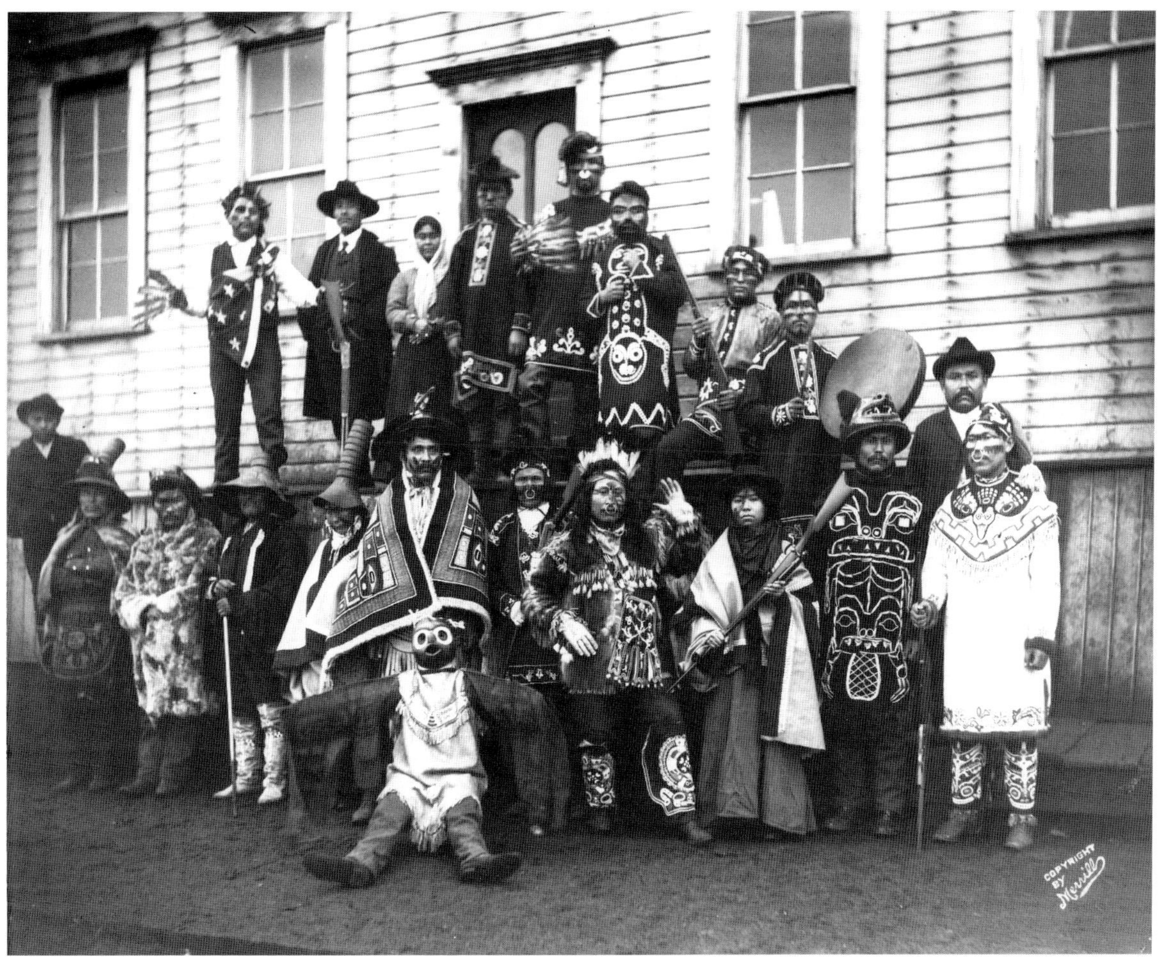

Figure 123
<u>G</u>aana<u>x</u>teidí clan guests from Klukwan at the Kaagwaantaan Wolf House potlatch, Sitka, 1904. The event was co-sponsored by Jacob "Jake" Yarkon [Yaakwaan] of the Wolf/World/Noble House, Augustus Bean [Keitxt'ch] of the Wolf/Eagle House, James Jackson [Annaxóots] of the Wolf/Bear House, and Paddy Parker (also known as James or Henry) [K'axook Eesh] from the Wolf/World/Noble House. Raven in dummy form leans against the front row. The man wearing the Chilkat robe is Yéil Gooxú (George Shotridge), father of Louis. Identification by Harold Jacobs. Photograph by E. W. Merrill. Courtesy of Sitka National Historical Park, Sitka, AK. (3769)

of the Deisheetaan clan, includes 30 people (Fig. 122). His other potlatch images also show careful composition and cooperation on the part of the Tlingit (Fig. 123). While it is possible that a resident photographer like Merrill went down to the village of his own volition and once there gained the consent and cooperation of potlatch participants, it is more likely that the Tlingit asked him

to come since they would have wanted this important event memorialized.

Photographers from other communities, on the other hand, like W. C. Chase from Juneau probably came on their own. The similarities in pose evident in images taken by different photographers—aggressive gestures, kneeling, mock fighting stances, and the dance staffs held up

    THE TLINGIT RESPONSE TO PHOTOGRAPHY

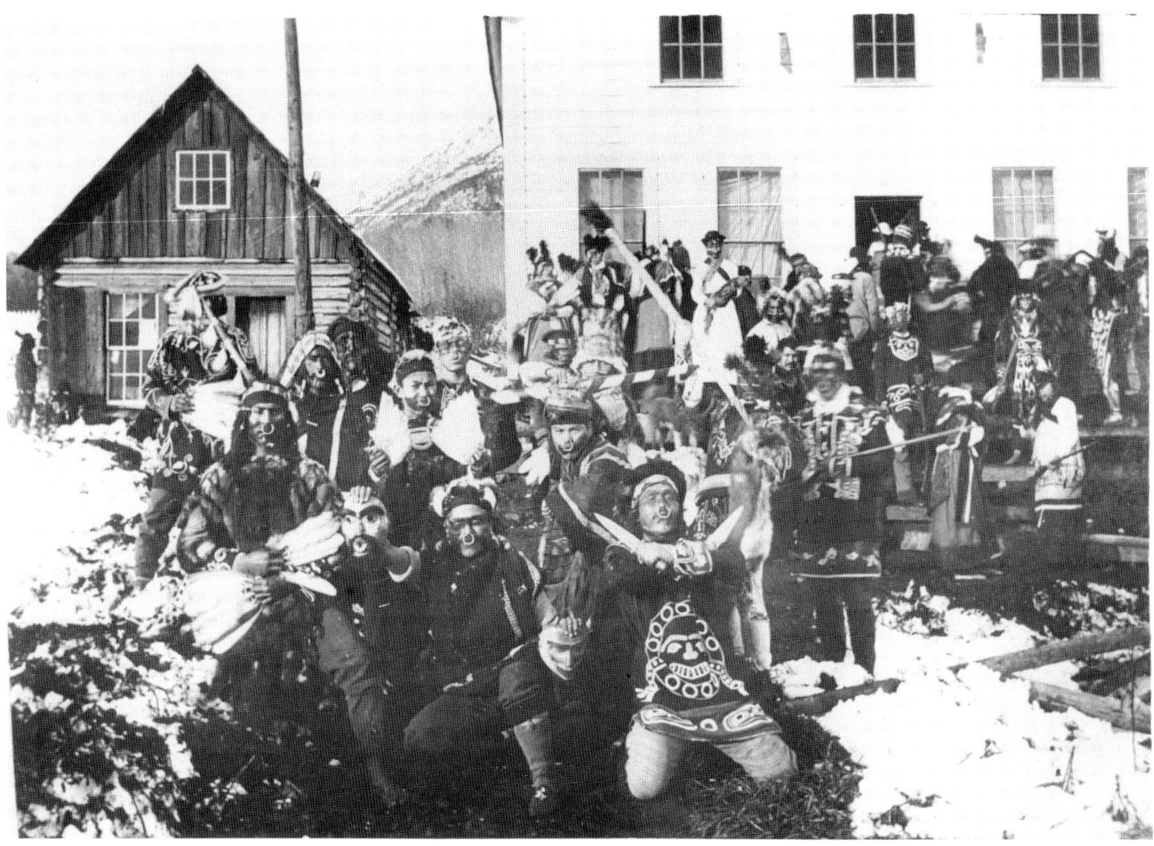

Figure 124
Chilkat potlatch dancers, Klukwan, 1895. Photographer unknown. By permission of the Alaska State Library, Juneau, AK. (PO1–0989)

dramatically—suggest that the Tlingit controlled key aspects of how they posed (as with lying-in-state photographs). The potlatch participants in the front row of Figure 124, taken in Klukwan around 1895, pose and display items of clan regalia for the camera in aggressive fashion. Figure 125, taken at Sitka in 1904, shows a man with a raised club and another aiming a pistol.

Other Natives in the region used photographs to document ceremonial events and also as part of the event. Anthropologist Homer Barnett (1955) described the Coast Salish's use in 1900 of the photograph of a deceased relative wrapped in a blanket in place of one of the effigies that were typically used during commemora-

tive potlatchs to represent deceased relatives of the host. When the host of this potlatch died two years later, his widow held a potlatch at which a large framed photograph of her husband was carried around and publicly displayed. As part of the property distribution and gifts given at this potlatch, each male attendee, including the photographer, received 50 cents; the two men who had carried her husband's photograph each received a blanket in addition.

Soboleff's photograph of Tlingit grave dancers in 1899 (Fig. 115) shows a similar ceremonial use of photographs of the deceased. According to the late Frederica de Laguna, the photographs are probably of men also being memorialized at

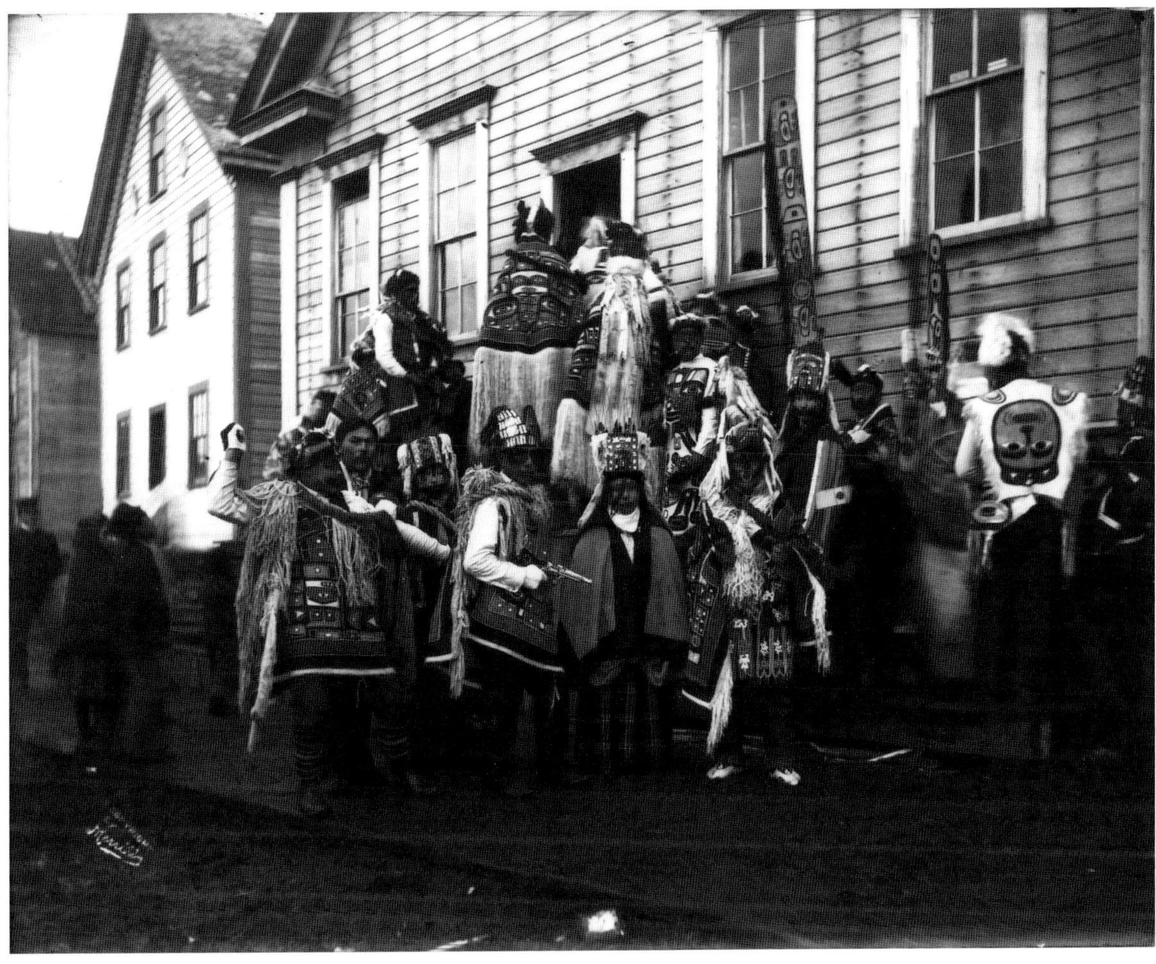

Figure 125
Kaagwaantaan Wolf House potlatch, Sitka, 1904. Two men hold mock battle poses. Photograph by E. W. Merrill.
Courtesy of Sitka National Historical Park, Sitka, AK. (3774)

the potlatch (Emmons 1991:331). Photographs were also used by Salish Indians at a formal naming ceremony in 1913. A year after birth infants were given prestigious ancestral names, usually those of a grandparent, at a public ceremony during which property was distributed. The emphasis was on keeping names alive. "A name was in reality a status which had been occupied and was to be occupied by an indefinite succession of lineally related incumbents" (Barnett 1955:134). The photograph showed the ancestor whose name and status was being passed on.

Those Tlingit who could afford to do so also bought photographs for their aesthetic appeal, as art and home decoration. The late elder Jessie Weir Price's husband Frank gave her a hand-tinted Merrill photograph of Sitka Sound as a wedding present in 1927 (Fig. 126). The Prices were educated Tlingit with strong ties to the Presbyterian Church and the Alaska Native Brotherhood (Frank Price was a founding member) and were very familiar with Merrill's work.

    THE TLINGIT RESPONSE TO PHOTOGRAPHY

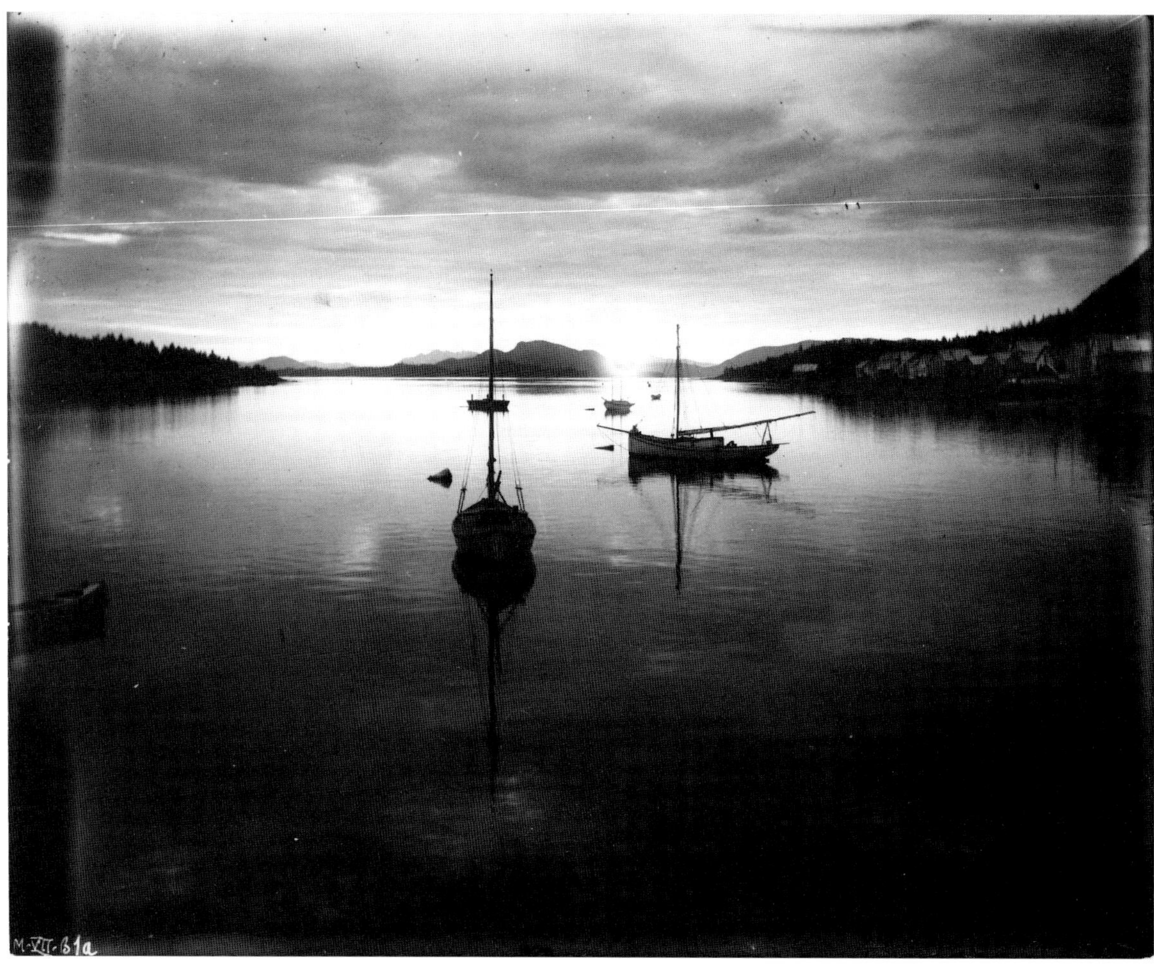

Figure 126
Sitka Sound, 1910. Photograph by E. W. Merrill. Courtesy of Stratton Library, Sheldon Jackson College, Sitka, AK. (M VII B1a)

"Frank asked me if I wanted a string of pearls or [the picture]," she recalled in an interview in August 1986, "and I wanted the picture. We valued that, both of us did. Other people felt the same way. My husband chose that one because of the Indian canoe in it...[But] I don't know why we didn't have our [wedding] picture made by him. I always felt sorry." Since Frank Price spent $50 ($597 in 2007) on Merrill's nature scene, they could well have afforded to pay for a portrait sitting.

Eventually some Tlingit acquired cameras. Merrill mentored at least one Tlingit resident of Sitka in photography, possibly as early as 1905. Louis Shotridge began taking photographs for today's University of Pennsylvania Museum of Archaeology and Anthropology in 1915. His personal photographs display the casual intimacy found in any American album: a wedding party leaving the church, children at play, informal family portraits, himself fishing on a lake (most likely taken by a Tlingit relative or friend). Figure 127 shows

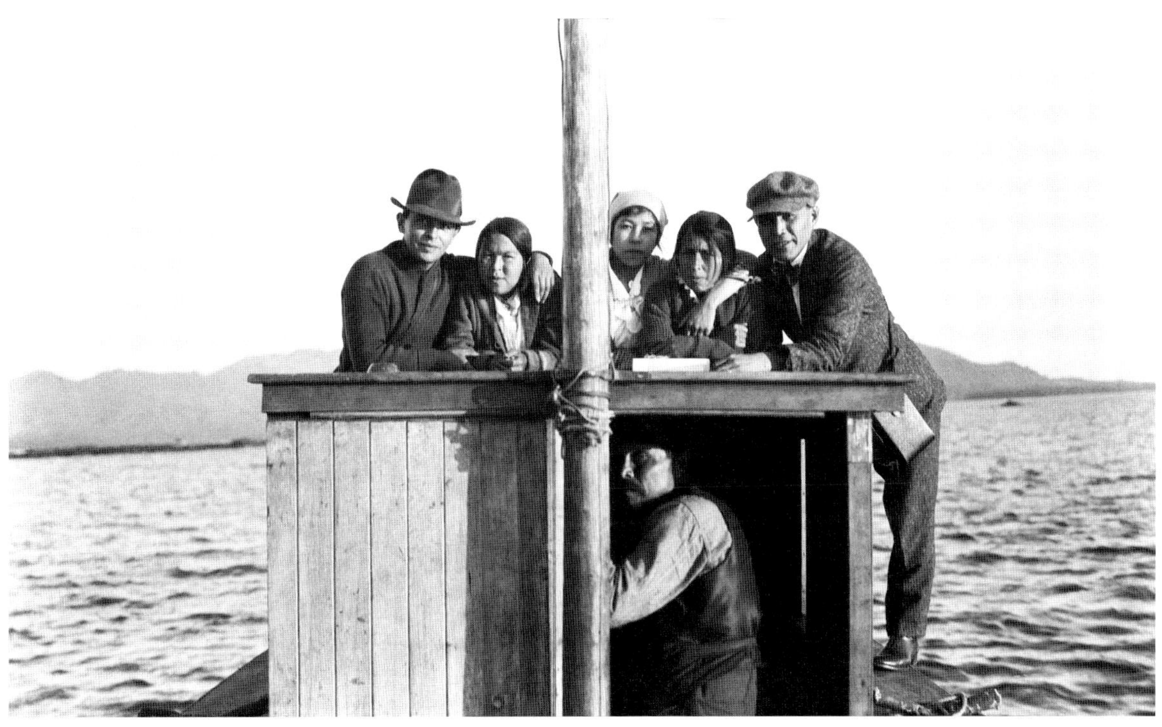

Figure 127
"A visit to the fishing camps. Couples on deck of boat, Aug. 1918." Photograph by Louis Shotridge. By permission of the University of Pennsylvania Museum of Archaeology and Anthropology. (S5, NC35, 14899)

several Tlingit traveling to their fishing grounds, arms draped across each other's shoulders as they lean against the cabin roof of their boat. George Johnston, a Canadian Tlingit from Teslin in the Yukon, began taking photographs in the mid-to-late 1920s and continued through World War II. His images display a similar casual intimacy and provide an important insider's glimpse of inland Tlingit life during this later period (Geddes 1996, Thornton 2000). Someday a sufficient corpus of early photographs taken by Tlingit photographers may be available to allow an in-depth analysis and comparison with those taken by non-Native photographers during the same period.

The camera has often been likened to a weapon which gives its user power. Who "aims," "shoots," and "captures" the image to a large extent defines how the subjects of photographs are seen

from then on. During the late 19th and early 20th centuries, non-Natives dominated photography and are responsible for most of the images of the Tlingit that were taken, disseminated, and then became part of the public record. Although the simple Eastman Kodak box camera became available in 1888, followed by the inexpensive Kodak Brownie in 1900, more non-Natives than Tlingits during the time period covered by this book had the disposable income to spend on photography.

Most photographs taken by the Tlingit at this time remain in private hands; Louis Shotridge's images are among the few to have entered the archival record. Just as not all Euro-Americans, simply by being non-Natives, took photographs that depicted the Tlingit in essentialist or stereotypic ways, so not all Tlingits, simply by being Tlingit, always respected Tlingit sensibilities.

     THE TLINGIT RESPONSE TO PHOTOGRAPHY

Shotridge ignored Native custom when pursuing the photographs he wanted. While visiting the Tsimshian village of Kitwancool, for example, he wandered off during a feast to make "some photographs of the old section of the town which is strictly prohibited, as I was informed by my host" (Dean 1998).

Were the Tlingit colonized or victimized by Euro-American photography? In some respects. Many photographs were taken without the Tlingits' knowledge or consent. Tourists, for example, seldom sought permission and often photographed people surreptitiously. The tourist gaze is authorized by the discourses of education and play: tourists travel to broaden their horizons, see the sights, and enjoy themselves, and they find nothing wrong with also "capturing" the view. Most think that it is legitimate and harmless for them to watch and to photograph the peoples they visit. Fortunately for the Tlingit at this early period, most tourists arrived in their communities by ship, did not stay long, and were generally satisfied with snapping a few standard shots. Professional photographers, collectors, and scientists sometimes used subterfuge to divert the Tlingits' attention in order to get the images (or objects) they wanted or else claimed to have the authority of the government backing them. Others simply took the photographs they wanted despite any objections.

After the very earliest years, the Tlingit exerted considerable control over the activities of Euro-American photographers and also found their own uses for photography. When they were photographed, they frequently controlled their poses, the clothes they wore, and the objects they appeared with. Chiefs and persons of high rank as well as traders and other cultural brokers used photography intentionally to assert their status or to demonstrate their connections to American culture. Photography was also used by the Tlingit to validate their ownership of clan crests and valuable regalia, to immortalize important events and people, to remember the dead, to create personal keepsakes, and sometimes to make money, as when they became paid sitters—for a shaman's re-enactment and some studio portraits—or demanded money from tourists and from local photographers they knew but did not particularly like.

But the Tlingit could not control the circulation or meaning of the images taken of them once they reached outside audiences. Few Tlingit at the time probably thought deeply about how their images would be used, how widely they would circulate, and even less about how they might be interpreted. They could not always know if they were going to be kept by the photographer or purchaser as a personal memento of a unique experience or if they would be sold and used for publicity—perhaps by steamship companies attempting to lure more tourists to the "wild" frontier—or as propaganda designed to show the positive changes brought about through control and education. Photographs taken by commercial photographers could have many lives: as illustrations in government reports, newspapers, popular magazines, and books; as postcards or souvenir prints; as publicity or propaganda; as art objects displayed in individual homes or at international exhibitions. In most cases the Tlingit could not know whether their images would paint a flattering or a negative picture of them among the audiences who received them. Case and Draper's studio portraits of semi-nude Tlingit women look especially exploitative today, regardless of whether or not their models had been paid and had fully understood the men to whom the images were being marketed. Furthermore, no one can control how a particular image is interpreted by an individual viewer. Time, as we know, also alters meaning.

Portrayed in the earliest decades of the photographic encounter as superstitious and primitive—with quizzical stares, blackened faces, blankets, bare feet, labrets, nose rings, and sometimes tattoos—the Tlingit, nevertheless, were perceived as different from and "better" than Indians in the rest of the United States (Fig. 128). They were hunters, fishers, and traders

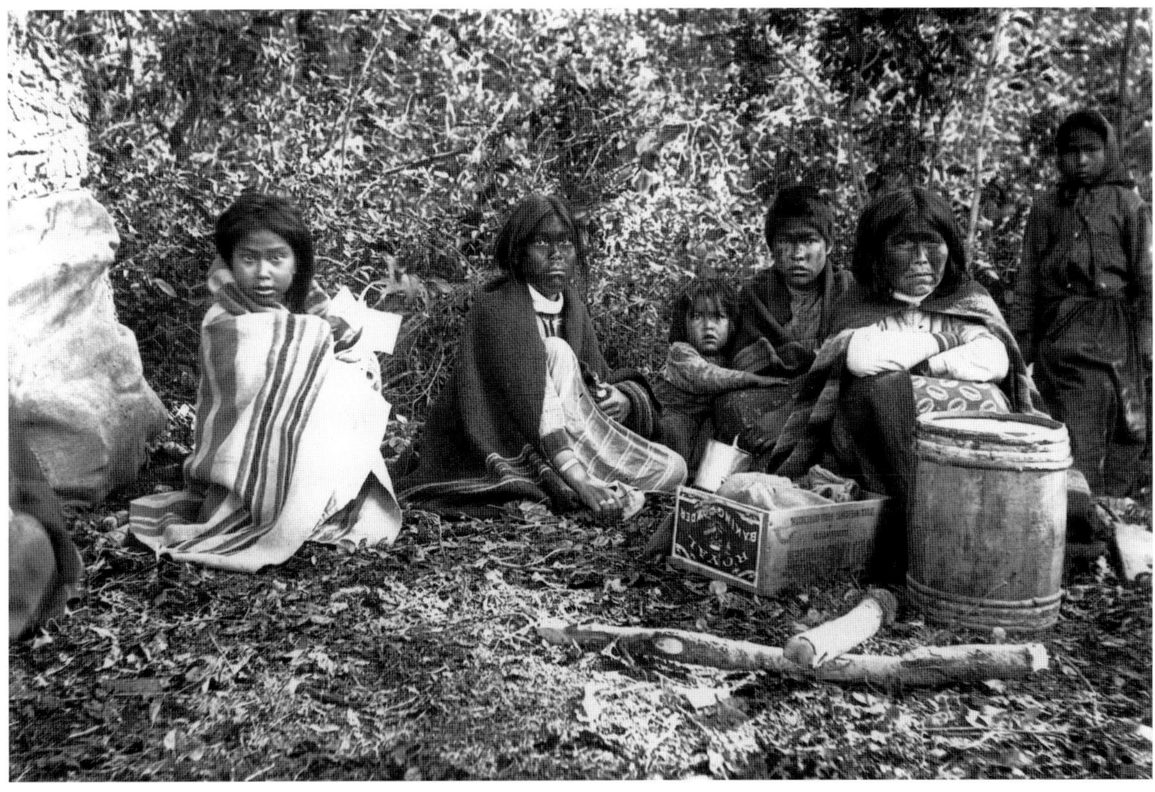

Figure 128
Chilkat women and children with supplies and barrel, Kluken, Alaska, 1884. Photographed by John Francis Pratt.
By permission of the University of Washington Libraries, Seattle, WA. Special Collections. (NA 3090)

who lived in impressive clan houses in permanent villages and who carved sea-going canoes and monumental art. Alaska, too, was different. While it drew its share of outsiders seeking to exploit its resource wealth of minerals, fish, and timber, it did not draw land-hungry settlers in the same numbers as did the rest of the country. The Tlingit resisted colonization, and even though they lost their sovereignty and much of their land, they were not faced with extermination or reservation polices as Native Americans were farther south. The impulse to demonize the Tlingit through photography in order to justify their exploitation or extermination or to depict them solely as the "vanishing race" in order to defend concerted efforts to "save" them

through missionization, reservations, or boarding schools before it was too late did not exist to the same extent it did with Indians to the south. Instead, photography was used by outsiders more to "exoticize" the fast-changing Tlingit for the purposes of tourism and to depict them as "tamed"—intelligent, skilled, under control, amenable to acculturation—in the interests of public support for their religious education and future citizenship.

Over all, the Tlingit encounter with photography was relatively benign. While there was clearly exploitation at times, with some photographers and their sponsors profiting financially and in other ways from their images of the Tlingit, the Tlingit quite quickly found ways to even

187   THE TLINGIT RESPONSE TO PHOTOGRAPHY

the exchange—demanding payment, denying photographic access, and to a large extent controlling how they were shown. Well before the turn of the 20th century they had become photographic consumers who commissioned and purchased photographs for a variety of cultural and personal purposes. Although by no means exhaustive, these included asserting or validating their status and ownership claims, documenting clan events and group memberships, expressing cultural pride and connections, celebrating and commemorating life's transitions, and enjoying—as anyone would—the memories and beauty captured by the camera.

⚜ Bibliography ⚜

Afonsky, Bishop Gregory. 1977. *A History of the Orthodox Church in Alaska (1794–1917)*. Kodiak, AK: St. Herman's Theological Seminary.

Alison, Jane, ed. 1998. *Native Nations: Journeys in American Photography*. London: Barbican Art Gallery.

Anderson, Neill. 1986. Interview, August. Sitka, AK.

Andrews, Clarence Leroy. 1898–99. Diaries. Boxes 2 and 3, Folders 17 and 25. Clarence L. Andrews Papers. Fairbanks, AK: Rasmuson Library, University of Alaska.

—— 1981 [1922]. *The Story of Sitka*. Seattle, WA: Shorey Publications.

Anonymous. "A Merrill Memorial: An Account of the Descendants of Nathaniel Merrill, 1917–28." Manuscript. Boston: Boston Public Library.

Anonymous. 1879. "The Troubles in Alaska. How the Excitement Was Created…" *New York Times* May 1, p. 2.

Baldwin, Gordon. 1991. *Looking at Photographs: A Guide to Technical Terms*. London: British Museum Press.

Barnett, Homer. 1955. *The Coast Salish of British Columbia*. Eugene, OR: University of Oregon Press.

Barrett, Terry. 2006. *Criticizing Photographs*. 4th ed. Boston: McGraw-Hill.

Barrett Willoughby, F. 1926. "'Father of Pictures' Captures the Spell of Alaska." *The American Magazine* (Jan.): 40–42, 68–70.

—— 1930. *Sitka: To Know Alaska, One Must First Know Sitka*. London: Hodder and Stoughton.

—— 1930. *Sitka: Portal to Romance*. Boston: Houghton Mifflin.

Barthes, Roland. 1964. "Rhetoric of the Image." In *Image–Music–Text*, ed. Roland Barthes, pp. 32–51. New York: Hill and Wang.

Bates, Elizabeth Katharine. 1889. *Kaleidoscope: Shifting Scenes from East to West*. London: Ward and Downey.

Beardslee, Lester A. 1882. *Reports Relative to Affairs in Alaska and the Operation of the U.S.S. Jamestown under His command, while in the Waters of that Territory*. S. Exec. Doc.71, 47th Cong., 1st sess., vol. 4. Washington, DC: USGPO.

Beattie, William Gilbert. 1907. "The Sitka Industrial Training School." *Alaska-Yukon Magazine* 4(2): 117–21.

—— 1955. *Marsden of Alaska: A Modern Indian Minister, Missionary, Musician, Engineer, Pilot, Boat Builder, and Church Builder*. New York: Vantage.

Blackman, Margaret B. 1980. "Posing the American Indian." *Natural History* 89:69–74.

—— 1982. "Copying People: Northwest Coast Native Response to Early Photography." *BC Studies* 52:86–112.

—— 1986. "Studio Indians: Cartes de Visite of Native People in British Columbia, 1862–1872." *Archivaria* 21:68–86.

Bloodgood, C. Delevan. 1869. "Eight Months at

Sitka." *The Overland Monthly* 2:175–86.

Boas, Franz. 1897. *The Social Organization and Secret Societies of the Kwakiutl Indians.* United States National Museum Annual Report for 1895. Washington, DC: USGPO.

—— 1909. *The Kwakiutl of Vancouver Island.* New York: G. E. Stechert.

Bol, Marsh. 1999. "Defining Lakota Tourist Art, 1880–1915." In *Unpacking Culture,* ed. R. Phillips and C. Steiner, pp. 1214–28. Berkeley: University of California Press.

Bolt, Christine. 1987. *American Indian Policy and American Reform.* London: Allen and Unwin.

Brady, John G. 1905. Letter to Thomas Ryan. RG48, Alaska. Box 21. Washington, DC: National Archives.

—— 1906. Letter to William L. Distin. RG 48, Secretary of the Interior Patents and Miscellaneous Division, Territorial Papers, Alaska, Box 23A. Washington, DC: National Archives.

Brady, Hugh. 1980. Letter to Marilyn Knapp, May 30. E. W. Merrill File. Sitka, AK: Sitka National Historical Park.

Brady, Isabella Sing. 1986. Interview, August. Sitka, AK.

Brady, William. 1986. Interview, August. Sitka, AK.

Brann, Harrison. 1952. "A Bibliography of the Sheldon Jackson Collection in the Presbyterian Historical Society." *Journal of the Presbyterian Historical Society* 30:139–64.

Breitbart, Eric. 1997. *A World on Display 1904: Photographs from the St. Louis World's Fair.* Albuquerque, NM: University of New Mexico Press.

Brightman, Louise. 1986. Interview, August 21. Sitka, AK.

Bromberg, Nicolette A. 1976. "Clarence Leroy Andrews and Alaska." *Alaska Journal* 6(2): 66–77.

Brown, Julie. 1994. *Contesting Images: Photography and the World's Columbian Exposition.* Tucson, AZ: University of Arizona Press.

Brumbaugh, Lee P. 1996. "Shadow Catchers or Shadow Snatchers? Ethnic Issues for Photographers of Contemporary Native Americans." *American Indian Culture and Research Journal* 20(3): 33–49.

Buchanan, John. 1986. Interview, August. Sitka, AK.

Buckland, Gail. 1980. *First Photographs.* New York: Macmillan.

Burroughs, John. 1904. *The Writings of John Burroughs: Far and Near* 8. Boston: Houghton Mifflin.

Burroughs, John, John Muir, and George Bird Grinnell. 1910. *Harriman Alaska Series.* Vol. 1, *Narrative, Glaciers, Natives.* Washington, DC: Smithsonian Institution. First published 1902, New York: Double Day, Page.

Cammerer, Arno. 1922. Correspondence with Colonel James Steese. September 18, October 2 and 12. E. W. Merrill File. Sitka, AK: Sitka National Historical Park.

Carlson, L. H. 1947. "The First Mining Season at Nome, Alaska 1899." *The Pacific Historical Review* 16(2): 163–75.

Carlton, Rosemary. 1999. *Sheldon Jackson, The Collector.* Juneau, AK: Alaska State Museums.

Coe, Brian, and Paul Gates. 1977. *The Snapshot Photography: The Rise of Popular Photography, 1888–1939.* London: Ash and Grant.

Cole, Douglas. 1985. *Captured Heritage: The Scramble for Northwest Coast Artifacts.* Seattle, WA: University of Washington Press.

Coleman, Marnie C. 1995. "Frank La Roche: A Guide to the Klondike." *History of Photography* 19(2): 143–49.

Collis, Septima M. 1890. *A Woman's Trip to Alaska.* New York: Cassell.

Colyer, Vincent. 1869. "Report of the Hon. Vincent Colyer, U.S. Special Indian Commissioner, on the Indian tribes and their surroundings in Alaska Territory, from personal observation and inspection in 1869." In *Report of the Secretary of the Interior 1869,* pp. 975–1058. Washington, DC: USGPO.

Common Council of Sitka. 1900–29. Minutes of the Common Council of Sitka. Sitka, AK.

Condit, James. 1922. Personal Papers, October 22, 26, and 28. Box 2, Folder 11. James Condit Collection. Fairbanks, AK: Rasmuson Library, University of Alaska.

—— 1923. Personal Papers, March 7 and 8. Box 2, Folder 11. James Condit Collection. Fairbanks, AK: Rasmuson Library, University of Alaska.

—— 1926. "Woman's Place in Alaska's Development." *Women and Missions* 3:257–59, 265. New York: Women's Commission of the Boards of Mission of the Presbyterian Church.

Condon, Richard. 1989. "The History and Development of Arctic Photography." *Arctic Anthropology* 26:46–87.

Coontz, Robert E. 1930. *From the Mississippi to the Sea*. Philadelphia: Dorrance.

a'Court, H. Holmes. 1879. "The Situation at Sitka." *The Alaska Appeal* 1(2): 2–3.

Corbey, Raymond. 1993. "Ethnographic Showcases, 1870–1930." *Cultural Anthropology* 8(3): 338–69.

Corey, Peter. 1986. Interview, August. Sitka, AK.

Crosby, Rev. Thomas. 1914. *Up and Down the North Pacific Coast by Canoe and Mission Ship*. Toronto, ON: Missionary Society of the Methodist Church.

Dall, William Henry. 1870. *Alaska and Its Resources*. Boston: Lee and Shepard.

Darrah, William Culp. 1951. *Powell of the Colorado*. Princeton, NJ: Princeton University Press.

—— 1964. *Stereo Views*. Gettysburg, PA: Times & News Publishing.

Dauenhauer, Nora, and Richard Dauenhauer, eds. 1987. *Haá Shuka, Our Ancestors: Tlingit Oral Narratives*. Seattle, WA: University of Washington Press.

—— 1990. *Haa Tuwunaagu Yis, For Healing Our Spirit: Tlingit Oratory*. Seattle, WA: University of Washington Press.

—— 1994. *Haa Kusteeyí, Our Culture: Tlingit Life Stories*. Seattle, WA: University of Washington Press.

Davidson, George. 1869. *The Coast Pilot of Alaska: From Southern Boundary to Cook's Inlet*. Washington, DC: USGPO.

—— 1903. *The Alaska Boundary*. Washington, DC: USGPO.

Davis, Albert. 1990. Interview, July. Sitka, AK.

Davis, Barbara. 1985. *Edward Curtis: The Life and Times of a Shadow Catcher*. San Francisco: Chronicle Books.

Dean, Jonathan. 1998. "Louis Shotridge, Museum Man: A 1918 Visit to the Naas and Skeena Rivers." *Pacific Northwest Quarterly* 89:202–10.

—— 2004. "'Their Nature and Qualities Remain Unchanged': Russian Occupation and Tlingit Resistance, 1802–1867." *Alaska History* 9(1): 1–18.

DeArmond, Robert N. 1967. Letter to Louise Brightman, July 14. E. W. Merrill File. Sitka, AK: Sitka National Historical Park.

DeArmond, R. N., ed. 1978. *Early Visitors to Southeastern Alaska: Nine Accounts*. Anchorage, AK: Alaska Northwest Publishing.

—— 1981. *Lady Franklin Visits Sitka, Alaska 1870: The Journal of Sophia Cracroft, Sir John Franklin's Niece*. Anchorage, AK: Alaska Historical Society.

—— 1986. Interview, August. Juneau, AK.

—— 1993. *A Sitka Chronology: 1867–87*. Sitka, AK: Sitka Historical Society.

—— 1998. Interview, September. Sitka, AK.

de Laguna, Frederica. 1933. "Mummified Heads from Alaska." *American Anthropologist* 35:742–44.

—— 1972. *Under Mount Saint Elias: The History and Culture of the Yakutat*. Washington, DC: Smithsonian Institution Press.

—— 1988. "Tlingit: People of the Wolf and Raven." In *Crossroads of Continents*, ed. W. Fitzhugh and A. Crowell, pp. 58–63. Washington, DC: Smithsonian Institution Press.

—— 1991. "George Thornton Emmons as Ethnographer." In *The Tlingit Indians*, ed. Frederica de Laguna, pp. xvii–xxii. Seattle, WA: University of Washington Press.

de Laguna, Frederica, ed. 1991. *The Tlingit Indians*. Seattle, WA: University of Washington Press.

Dippie, Brian W. 1992. "Representing the Other: The North American Indian." In *Anthropology and Photography*, ed. Elizabeth Edwards, pp. 132–36. London: Royal Anthropological Institute.

Dominguez, Virginia. 1986. "The Marketing of Heritage." *American Ethnologist* 13(3): 546–55.

Dorsey, George A. 1898. "A Cruise among the Haida and Tlingit Villages about Dixon's Entrance." *Appleton's Popular Science Monthly* (June):1–15.

Drinnon, Richard. 1980. *Facing West: The Metaphysics of Indian Hating and Empire Building*. Minneapolis, MI: University of Minnesota Press.

Drucker, Philip. 1958. *The Native Brotherhoods: Modern Intertribal Organization on the Northwest Coast*. Washington, DC: USGPO.

Drabek, Christopher. 1994. "The Lewis and Clark Exposition, 1905." *Pacific Northwest Forum* 7(1): 57–61.

Durlach, Theresa Mayer. 1928. *The Relationship Systems of the Tlingit, Haida and Tsimshian*. New York: American Ethnological Society.

Dykstra, Natalie A. 2002. "The Violence of Reform." *American Quarterly* 54(3): 515–20.

Eaton, Gen. John. 1899. "Sheldon Jackson." *Alaska and Northwest Quarterly* 1(2): 137–42.

Edelstein, Susan F., ed. 1980. *Carved History: The Totem Poles and House Posts of Sitka National Historical Park*. Anchorage, AK: Alaska Natural History Association.

Edwards, Elizabeth. 1996. "Postcards—Greetings from Another World." In *Tourist Image*, ed. T. Selwyn, pp. 197–221. New York: Wiley.

—— 1998. "The Resonance of Anthropology." In *Native Nations: Journeys in American Photography*, ed. J. Alison, pp. 186–203. London: Barbican Art Gallery.

Edwards, Elizabeth, ed. 1992. *Anthropology and Photography, 1860–1920*. New Haven, CT: Yale University Press.

Emmons, George T. 1904a. "The Basketry of the Tlingit." *Memoirs of the American Museum of Natural History* 3:229–77.

—— 1904b. "The Chilkat Blanket." *Memoirs of the American Museum of Natural History* 3:329–400.

—— 1910. "The Potlatch of the North Pacific Coast." *American Museum Journal* 10:229–37.

—— 1911. "Native Account of the Meeting Between La Perouse and the Tlingit." *American Anthropologist* 13:294–98.

—— 1914. "Portraiture among the North Pacific Coast Tribes." *American Anthropologist* 16:59–67.

—— 1982 [1916]. "The Whale House of Chilkat." In *Raven's Bones*, ed. A. Hope, pp. 68–90. Sitka, AK: Sitka Community Association.

—— 1991. *The Tlingit Indians*, ed. Frederica de Laguna, with a biography by Jean Low. Seattle, WA: University of Washington Press.

Entienne, Mona, and Eleanor Leacock, eds. 1980. *Women and Colonialism: Anthropological Perspectives*. New York: Praeger.

Enyeart, James L., Robert D. Monroe, and Philip Stokes. 1982. *Three Classic American Photographs: Texts and Contexts*. Exeter: University of Exeter, American Arts Documentation Centre.

Faris, James C. 1992. "A Political Primer on Anthropology/Photography." In *Anthropology and Photography, 1860–1920*, ed. Elizabeth Edwards, pp. 253–63. New Haven, CT: Yale University Press.

—— 1993. "The Navajo Photography of Edward S. Curtis." *The History of Photography* 17(4): 377–87.

—— 1996. *Navajo and Photography: A Critical History of Representation of an American People*.

Albuquerque, NM: University of New Mexico Press.

—— 2003. "Navajo and Photography." In *Photography's Other Histories*, ed. C. Pinney and N. Peterson, pp. 85–99. Durham, NC: Duke University Press.

Fast, Edward G. 1869. *Catalogue of Antiquities and Curiosities Collected in the Territory of Alaska*. New York: Leavitt, Strebeigh.

Fern, Alan. 1992. *Arnold Newman's Americans*. Boston: Bulfinch Press.

Ferrell, Nancy. 1994. *Barrett Willoughby: Alaska's Forgotten Lady*. Fairbanks, AK: University of Alaska Press.

Fey, Harold. 1955. "Alaska Native Brotherhood." *Christian Century* 72:1521–23.

Field, Kate. 1888. "A Trip to Southeastern Alaska." *Harper's Weekly* (Sept. 8).

Fine-Dare, Kathleen. 2002. *Grave Injustice: The American Indian Repatriation Movement and NAGPRA*. Lincoln, NE: University of Nebraska Press.

Fisher, Robin. 1996. "The Northwest from the Beginning of Trade with Europeans to the 1880s." In *The Cambridge History of the Native Peoples of the Americas*, ed. B. Trigger and W. Washburn, pp. 117–82. Cambridge: Cambridge University Press.

Fitzgerald, Emily McCorkle. 1986. *An Army Doctor's Wife on the Frontier: The Letters of Emily McCorkle Fitzgerald from Alaska and the Far West, 1874–1878*, ed. Abe Laufe. Lincoln, NE: University of Nebraska Press.

Fitzhugh, William W. 1998. "The Alaska Photography of Edward W. Nelson, 1877–1881." In *Imagining the Arctic*, ed. J. C. H. King and H. Lidchi, pp. 125–42. Seattle, WA: University of Washington Press.

Fitzhugh, William, and Aron Crowell, eds. 1988. *Crossroads of Continents*. Washington, DC: Smithsonian Institution Press.

Fleming, Paula R., and Judith Luskey. 1986. *The North American Indians in Early Photographs*. New York: Harper & Row.

Fortuine, Robert. 1989. *Chills and Fever: Health and Disease in the Early History of Alaska*. Fairbanks, AK: University of Alaska Press.

Frankenstein, Ellen, and Sharon Gmelch. 1992. *A Matter of Respect: Modern Alaska Natives Balancing the Past and Present*. Video. Hottokus, NJ: New Day Films.

Geddes, Carol. 1997. *Picturing People: George Johnston, Tlingit Photographer*. Video. Ottawa, ON: National Film Board of Canada.

Gibson, James R. 1987. "Russian Dependence upon the Natives of Alaska." In *Russia's American Colony*, ed. S. F. Starr, pp. 77–104. Durham, NC: Duke University Press.

Gidley, Mick. 1979. *With One Sky Above Us: Life on an Indian Reservation at the Turn of the Century*. Seattle, WA: University of Washington Press.

—— 1985. "American Indian Photographs/Images" (review essay). *American Indian Culture and Research Journal* 9(3): 37–47.

—— 2003. *Edward S. Curtis and the North American Indian Project in the Field*. Lincoln, NE: University of Nebraska Press.

Glass, Henry. 1890. "Naval Administration in Alaska." *Proceedings of the United States Naval Institute* 16(1): 1–19.

Gmelch, Sharon Bohn, ed. 2004. *Tourists and Tourism*. Long Grove, IL: Waveland Press.

Gmelch, S. B. 1995. "Elbridge Warren Merrill: The Tlingit of Alaska, 1899–1929." *History of Photography* 19(2): 159–72.

Gmelch, George, and Sharon Bohn Gmelch, with Richard K. Nelson. 1985. *Resource Use in a Small Alaskan City–Sitka*. Technical Paper No. 90. Juneau, AK: Alaska Department of Fish & Game, Division of Subsistence.

Goetzmann, William H., and William N. Goetzmann. 1986. *The West of the Imagination*. New York: W. W. Norton.

Goffman, Erving. 1961. *Asylums*. New York: Doubleday, Anchor.

Goldberg, Vicki. 1991. *The Power of Photography: How Photographs Changed Our Lives*. New York: Abbeville.

—— 1996. "Western Deserts and Their Myths." *New York Times* (July 7): 26.

Goldschmidt, Walter, and Theodore Hass. 1946. "Possessory Rights of the Natives of SE Alaska." Unpublished report. Copy at Suzzallo Library, University of Washington, Seattle.

Goldschmidt, Walter, Theodore Hass, and Thomas Thornton. 1999. *Haa Aani, Our Land: Tlingit and Haida Land Rights and Use.* Seattle, WA: University of Washington Press.

Golovin, Pavel Nikolaevich. 1979. *The End of Russian America: Captain P. N. Golovin's Last Report, 1862,* trans. Basil Dmytryshyn and E. A. P. Crownhart-Vaughan. Portland, OR: Oregon Historical Society.

Golovnin, Vasilii Mikhailovich. 1979. *Around the World on the Kamchatka, 1817–1819,* trans. Ella Lury Wiswell. Honolulu, HI: University of Hawaii Press.

Goodale, Preston. 1898. "Diary of I. Preston Goodale, a Klondike Prospector of 1898." *The Historical Collections of the Danvers Historical Society* 25:4–12.

Gould, R. R. 1895. "Cremating an Alaska Chief." *Home Mission Monthly* 9(5): 108–9.

Govorlivyi, Z. 1990. *Diseases Prevalent among the Kolosh Indian Inhabitants of the Island of Sitka,* trans. Tanya DeMarsh. Kingston, ON: Limestone Press.

Graburn, Nelson. 2001. "Secular Ritual: A General Theory of Tourism." In *Hosts and Guests Revisited: Tourism Issues of the 21st Century,* ed. Valene Smith and Maryann Brent, pp. 42–50. Elmsford, NY: Cognizant Communications.

Grant, Whit M. 1888. "Confining Maidens in Alaska." *Journal of American Folklore* 1(2): 168–69.

Green, Lewis. 1981. *The Boundary Hunters: Surveying 141st Meridian and the Alaska Panhandle.* Vancouver, BC: University of British Columbia Press.

Green, Nancy. 2005. "Twice-told Tales: Photographs and Their Stories from Alumni Collections." Exhibit. Ithaca, NY: Cornell University.

Green, Rayna. 1988. "The Tribe Called Wannabee: Playing Indian in America and Europe." *Folklore* 99(1): 30–55.

Griffin, Kristen. 2000. *Early Views: Historical Vignettes of Sitka National Historical Park.* Anchorage, AK: U.S. Department of the Interior.

Griffiths, Alison. 2002. *Wondrous Difference: Cinema, Anthropology, and Turn-of-the-century Visual Culture.* New York: Columbia University Press.

Grinev, Andrei Val Terovich. 2005. *The Tlingit Indians in Russian America, 1741–1867,* trans. Richard Bland and Katerina Solovjova. Lincoln, NE: University of Nebraska Press.

Grinnell, George Bird. 1910. "The Natives of the Alaska Coast Region." In *Harriman Alaska Expedition,* ed. C. Hart Merriam. Vol. 1, pp. 137–83. Washington, DC: Smithsonian Institution. First published 1902, New York: Doubleday, Page.

Gunther, Erna. 1972. *Indian Life on the Northwest Coast of North America as Seen by the Early Explorers and Fur Traders during the Last Decades of the Eighteenth Century.* Chicago: University of Chicago Press.

Gutman, Judith Mara. 1982. *Through Indian Eyes.* New York: Oxford University Press.

Harkin, Michael. 1988. "History, Narrative, and Temporality: Examples from the Northwest Coast." *Ethnohistory* 35(2): 99–129.

Harring, Sidney L. 1989. "The Incorporation of Alaskan Natives under American Law: United States and Tlingit Sovereignty, 1867–1900." *Arizona Law Review* 31(2): 279.

Harrison, Steven. 1980. "His Camera Was His Gold Mine: The Alaska Photographs with Arthur C. Pillsbury." *The Alaska Journal* (1980): 48–53.

Hastrup, Kristen. 1992. "Writing Ethnography:

State of the Art." In *Anthropology and Autobiography*, ed. J. Okely and H. Callaway, pp. 116–33. London: Routledge.

—— 1992. *Other Histories*. London: Routledge.

Haycox, Stephen. 1984. "Races of Questionable Ethnical Type: Origins of the Jurisdiction of the United States Bureau of Education in Alaska, 1867–1885." *Pacific Northwest Quarterly* 75:156–63.

—— 1986/87. "William Paul, Sr., and the Alaska Voters' Literacy Act of 1925." *Alaska History* 2(1): 17–38.

Hinckley, Ted. 1965. "The Inside Passage: A Popular Gilded Age Tour." *Pacific Northwest Quarterly* 56:67–74.

—— 1979. "A Victorian Family in Alaska." *American West* 16:32–37, 60.

—— 1982. *Alaskan John G. Brady: Missionary, Businessman, Judge, and Governor, 1878–1918.* Columbus, OH: Ohio State University Press.

—— 1996. *The Canoe Rocks: Alaska's Tlingit and the Euroamerican Frontier, 1800–1912.* New York: University Press of America.

Hirsch, Robert. 2000. *Seizing the Light: A History of Photography*. New York: McGraw-Hill Humanities Social.

Hodgkins, Connie. 1986. Interview, August 13. Sitka, AK.

Holm, Bill. 1965. *Northwest Coast Indian Art: An Analysis of Form*. Seattle, WA: University of Washington Press.

Holm, Bill, and William Reid. 1975. *Form and Freedom: A Dialogue on Northwest Coast Indian Art.* Houston, TX: Institute for the Arts, Rice University.

Hope, Andrew, III, ed. 1982. *Raven's Bones*. Sitka, AK: Sitka Community Association.

—— n.d. Traditional Tlingit Map and Tribal List. Manuscript. Sitka, AK: Sitka National Historical Park.

Jacknis, Ira. 1984. "Franz Boas and Photography." *Studies in Visual Communication* 10:2–60.

—— 1991. "Northwest Coast Indian Culture

and the World's Columbian Exposition." In *The Spanish Borderlands in Pan-American Perspective*, ed. David H. Thomas, pp. 91–118. Washington, DC: Smithsonian Institution Press.

—— 1992. "George Hunt, Kwakiutl Photographer." In *Anthropology and Photography, 1860–1920*, ed. Elizabeth Edwards, pp. 143–52. New Haven, CT: Yale University Press.

Jackson, Sheldon. 1880. *Alaska and Missions on the North Pacific Coast*. New York: Dodd, Mead.

—— 1886. *A Statement of Facts Concerning the Difficulties at Sitka, Alaska in 1885.* Washington, DC: Thomas McGill.

—— 1903. *Facts about Alaska: Its People, Villages, Missions, Schools*. New York: Board of National Missions of the Presbyterian Church.

Jacobs, Mark, Jr. 1986. Interview, August. Sitka, AK.

—— 1990. "The Tlingits Meet the Russians." *Alaska Magazine* 34 (Oct.): 64–65.

Jacobs, Mark, Jr., and Mark Jacobs, Sr. 1982. "Southeast Alaska Native Foods." In *Raven's Bones*, ed. A. Hope, pp. 112–30. Sitka, AK: Sitka Community Association.

Jacobsen, Johan Adrian. 1977. *Alaskan Voyage, 1881–83*. Trans. Erna Gunter. Chicago: University of Chicago Press.

Johnson, Tim, ed. 1998. *Spirit Capture: Photographs from the National Museum of the American Indian*. Washington, DC: Smithsonian Institution Press.

Jojola, Ted. 1990. "American Indian Stereotypes." *Northeast Indian Quarterly* (Fall): 26–28.

Jones, Livingston F. 1914. *A Study of the Tlingets of Alaska*. New York: Fleming H. Revell.

Jonaitis, Aldona. 1978. "Land Otters and Shamans: Some Interpretations of Tlingit Charms." *American Indian Art Magazine* 4(1): 62–66.

—— 1981. *Tlingit Halibut Hooks: An Analysis of*

the Visual Symbols of a Rite of Passage 57, Part 1. New York: American Museum of Natural History.

—— 1986. *The Art of the Northern Tlingit*. Seattle, WA: University of Washington Press.

—— 1999. "Northwest Coast Totem Poles." In *Unpacking Culture*, ed. R. Phillips and C. Steiner, pp. 104–21. Berkeley: University of California Press.

Kamenskii, Fr. Anatolii. 1985 [1906]. *Tlingit Indians of Alaska*, trans. and ed. Sergei Kan. Fairbanks, AK: University of Alaska Press.

Kan, Sergei. 1985. "Russian Orthodox Brotherhoods among the Tlingit: Missionary Goals and Native Response." *Ethnohistory* 32(3): 196–223.

—— 1986. "The 19th Century Tlingit Potlatch: A New Perspective." *American Ethnologist* 13:191–212.

—— 1991. "Shamanism and Christianity: Modern-Day Tlingit Elders Look at the Past." *Ethnohistory* 38(4): 363–87.

—— 1993. *Symbolic Immortality: The Tlingit Potlatch of the Nineteenth Century*. Washington, DC: Smithsonian Institution Press.

—— 1999. *Memory Eternal: Tlingit Culture and Russian Orthodox Christianity Through Two Centuries*. Seattle, WA: University of Washington Press.

—— 2004. " 'It's Only Half a Mile from Savagery to Civilization': American Tourists and the Southeastern Alaska Natives in the Late 19th Century." In *Coming to Shore: Northwest Coast Ethnology, Traditions, and Visions*, ed. M. Mauzé, M. Harkin, and S. Kan, pp. 201–20. Lincoln, NE: University of Nebraska Press.

Kaplan, Susan, and Kristin Barsness, eds. 1986. *Raven's Journey: The World of Alaska's Native People*. Philadelphia: University of Pennsylvania Museum of Archaeology and Anthropology.

Kashavaroff, Andrew. 1927. "How the White Men Came to Lituya and What Happened to Yeahlth-kan Who Visited Them."

Alaska Magazine 1:151–53.

Katz, Adria. 1986. "The Raven Cape: A Tahitian Breastplate Collected by Louis Shotridge." In *Raven's Journey*, ed. S. Kaplan and K. Barsness, pp. 78–90. Philadelphia: University of Pennsylvania Museum of Archaeology and Anthropology.

Kendall, Laurel, Barbard Mathe, and Thomas R. Miller. 1997. *Drawing Shadows to Stone: The Photography of the Jesup North Pacific Expedition, 1897–1902*. New York: American Museum of Natural History.

Kennedy, Michael S. 1973. "Alaska's Artists: Theodore J. Richardson." *Alaska Journal* 3(1): 31–40.

Khlebnikov, Kyrill. 1976 [1835]. *Colonial Russian America: Kyrill T. Khlebnikov's Reports, 1817–1832*, trans. Basil Dmytryshyn and E. A. P. Crownhart-Vaughan. Portland, OR: Oregon Historical Society.

King, J. C. H., and Henrietta Lidchi, eds. 1998. *Imagining the Arctic*. Seattle, WA: University of Washington Press.

Klein, Laura. 1976. "She's One of Us You Know: The Public Life of Tlingit Women." *Western Canadian Journal of Anthropology* 6(3): 164–83.

—— 1978. "Demystifying the Opposition: The Hudson's Bay Company and the Tlingit." *Arctic Anthropology* 24(1): 101–14.

—— 1980. "Contending with Colonization: Tlingit Men and Women in Change." In *Women and Colonization: Anthropological Perspectives*, ed. Mona Entienne and Eleanor Leacock, pp. 88–108. New York: Praeger.

—— 1995. "Mother as Clanswoman: Rank and Gender in Tlingit Society." In *Women and Power in Native North America*, ed. L. Klein and L. A. Ackerman, pp. 28–45. Norman, OK: University of Oklahoma Press.

Klein, Laura, and L. A. Ackerman, eds. 1995. *Women and Power in Native North America*. Norman, OK: University of Oklahoma Press.

Knapp, Frances, and Rheta L. Childe. 1896. *The*

Thlinkets of Southeastern Alaska. Chicago: Stone and Kimball.

Knapp, Lyman E. 1890. *Report of the Governor of Alaska for the Fiscal Year 1890*. U.S. Dept. of Interior. Washington, DC: USGPO.

—— 1891. "A Study upon the Legal and Political Status of the Natives of Alaska." *The American Law Register* 30:325.

—— 1892. *Report of the Governor of Alaska for the Fiscal Year 1892*. U.S. Dept. of Interior. Washington, DC: USGPO.

Knight, Rolf. 1978. *Indians at Work: An Informal History of Native Indian Labour in British Columbia*. Vancouver, BC: New Star Books.

Koven, Seth. 1997. "Dr. Barnardo's 'Artisitic Fictions': Photography, Sexuality, and the Ragged Child in Victorian London." *Radical History Review* 69:6–43.

Krause, Aurel. 1956 [1885]. *The Tlingit Indians: Results of a Trip to the Northwest Coast of America and the Bering Straits*, trans. Erna Gunther. Seattle, WA: University of Washington Press.

Krause, Aurel, and Arthur Krause. 1993 [1881–82]. *To the Chuchi Peninsula and to the Tlingit Indians 1881/82: Journals and Letters by Aurel and Arthur Krause*, trans. Margo Krause McCaffrey. Fairbanks, AK: University of Alaska Press.

Krauss, Michael. 1980. *Alaska Native Languages: Past, Present and Future*. Research Papers 4. Fairbanks, AK: Alaska Native Language Center.

Langdon, Stephen John. 1979. "Comparative Tlingit and Haida Adaption to the West Coast of the Prince of Wales Archipelago." *Ethnology* 18(2): 101.

La Pérouse, J. F. G. de. 1799. *A Voyage Around the World Performed in the Years 1785, 1786, 1787, 1788, by the Boussole and Astrolate*. 2 vols. Amsterdam: N. Israel. Reprint, New York: DaCapo Press, 1968.

La Roche, Frank. 1898. *En Route to the Klondike: A Series of Photographic Views of the Picturesque Land of Gold and Glaciers*. Chicago: W. B. Conkey.

Lee, Molly. 1991. "Appropriating the Primitive: Turn-of-the-Century Collection and Display of Native Alaskan Art." In "Art and Material Culture of the North American Subarctic and Adjacent Regions/Collecting in the North," special issue, *Arctic Anthropology* 28(1): 6–15.

—— 1999. "Tourism and Taste Cultures: Collecting Native Art in Alaska at the Turn of the Twentieth Century." In *Unpacking Culture*, ed. R. Phillips and C. Steiner, pp. 267–81. Berkeley: University of California Press.

Lesy, Michael. 1972. *Wisconsin Death Trip*. Madison, WI: University of Wisconsin Press.

Liapunova, R. G. 1987. "Relations with the Natives of Russian America." In *Russia's American Colony*, ed. S. Frederick Starr, pp. 105–46. Durham, NC: Duke University Press.

Litke, F. P. 1987. *A Voyage Around the World 1826–1829*, trans. Renee Marshall and ed. Richard A. Pierce. Kingston, ON: Limestone Press.

Littlefield, Ester. 1986. Interview, July. Sitka, AK.

Lofgren, Orvar. 2004. "Narrating the Tourist Experience." In *Tourists and Tourism*, ed. Sharon Gmelch, pp. 91–110. Long Grove, IL: Waveland Press.

Low, Jean. 1977. "George Thornton Emmons." *The Alaska Journal* 7(1): 2–11.

Lukens, Matilda Barns. 1889. *The Inland Passage: A Journal of a Trip to Alaska*. New Haven, CT: Beinecke Library, Yale University.

Lutz, Catherine, and Jane Collins. 1993. *Reading National Geographic*. Chicago: University of Chicago Press.

—— 1994. "The Photograph as an Intersection of Gazes: The Example of National Geographic." In *Visualizing Theory*, ed. Lucien Taylor, pp. 363–84. New York: Routledge.

Lydon, Jane. 2005. *Eye Contact: Photographing Indigenous Australians*. Durham, NC: Duke

University Press.

Lyman, Christopher. 1982. *The Vanishing Race and Other Illusions: Photographs of Indians by Edward S. Curtis.* Washington, DC: Smithsonian Institution Press.

Maher, T. J. 2006. "The Coast Survey on the Pacific Coast." Washington, DC: NOAA. *http://www.history.noaa.gov* (accessed April 24, 2008).

Mahood, Ruth I., ed. 1961. *Photographer of the Southwest: Adam Clark Vroman, 1856–1916,* introduction by Beaumont Newhall. Los Angeles: Ward Ritchie Press.

Malmsheimer, Lonna. 1985. "Imitation White Man: Images of Transformation at the Carlisle Indian School." *Studies in Visual Communication* 11(4): 54–75.

—— 1987. "Photographic Analysis as Ethnohistory: Interpretive Strategies." *Visual Anthropology* 1(1): 21–36.

Margolis, Eric. 2004. "Looking at Discipline, Looking at Labour: Photographic Representations of Indian Boarding Schools." *Visual Studies* 19(1): 72–96.

Marien, Mary Warner. 2002. *Photography: A Cultural History.* New York: Prentice-Hall.

Marr, Carolyn J. 1982. "Photographers and Their Subjects on the Southern Northwest Coast: Motivations and Responses." *Arctic Anthropology* 27(2): 13–26.

—— 1989. "Taken Pictures: On Interpreting Native American Photographs of the Southern Northwest Coast." *Pacific Northwest Quarterly* 80:59–61.

Mason, J. Alden. 1960. "Louis Shotridge." *Expedition* 2(2): 10–16.

Masson, Jack, and Donald Guimary. 1981. "Asian Labor Contractors in the Alaskan Canned Salmon Industry: 1880–1937." *Labor History* 22(3): 377.

Mattison, David. 1982. "British Columbia Photographers of the Nineteenth Century: An Annotated, Select Bibliography." *BC Studies* 52 (Winter): 166–70.

—— 1985. "Richard Maynard: Photographs of Victoria, B.C." *History of Photography* 9(2): 109–29.

—— 1999–2007. *Camera Workers: The British Columbia Photographic Directory, 1858–1950.* Online: *http://members.shaw.ca/bchistorian/cw1858-1950.html* (last accessed July 2008).

Mattison, David, and Daniel Savard. 1992. "The North-west Pacific Coast: Photographic Voyages 1866–81." *History of Photography* 16(3): 269–88.

Mauzé, Marie, Michael Harkin, and Sergei Kan, eds. 2004. *Coming to Shore: Northwest Coast Ethnology, Traditions, and Visions.* Lincoln, NE: University of Nebraska Press.

Mayberry, Genevieve. 1953. *Sheldon Jackson Junior College: An Intimate History.* New York: Board of National Missions of the Presbyterian Church.

Maynard, Richard. 1882. Diary Entries. Box 2, Folder "Trip to Alaska, August 7–26, 1882." Victoria, BC: British Columbia Archives.

McCurdy, H. W. 1966. *Marine History of the Pacific Northwest.* Seattle, WA: Superior Publishing.

Meek, Henry M. 1890. *Naumkeag Directory for Salem, Beverly, Danvers, Marblehead, Peabody, Essex, and Manchester.* Salem, MA: H. M. Meek.

Milburn, Maureen. 1986. "Louis Shotridge and the Objects of Everlasting Esteem." In *Raven's Journey,* ed. Susan Kaplan and Kristin Barsness, pp. 54–77. Philadelphia: University of Pennsylvania Museum of Archaeology and Anthropology.

—— 1994. "Weaving the Tina' Blanket: The Journey of Florence and Louis Shotridge." In *Haa Kusteeyi', Our Culture: Tlingit Life Stories,* ed. Nora Dauenhauer and Richard Dauenhauer, pp. 548–64. Seattle, WA: University of Washington Press.

Miller, Polly, and Leon Gordon Miller. 1967. *Lost Heritage of Alaska.* New York: World.

MOHAI (Museum of History and Industry).

2008. Photo ID SHS 1,679. *http://www. seattlehistory.org/photo_database/photo. preview.cfm?photoid=7336* (accessed March 2008).

Monroe, Robert D. 1982. "The Earliest Pacific Northwest Indian Photograph (1860)." In *Three Classic American Photographs: Texts and Contexts*, by J. L. Enyeart, R. D. Monroe, and P. Stokes, pp. 13–20. Exeter: University of Exeter, American Arts Documentation Centre.

Moser, Jefferson F. 1899. "The Salmon and Salmon Fisheries of Alaska." *Bulletin of the United States Fish Commission 18, 1898.* Washington, DC: USGPO.

—— 1902. *Alaska Salmon Investigations in 1900 and 1901.* Washington, DC: USGPO.

Moses, L. G. 1996. *Wild West Shows and the Images of American Indians, 1883–1933.* Albuquerque, NM: University of New Mexico Press.

Muir, John. 1979. *Travels in Alaska.* Boston: Houghton Mifflin.

Niblack, Albert Parker. 1890. *The Coast Indians to Southern Alaska and Northern British Columbia.* Annual Report for the U.S. National Museum for 1888, pp. 225–386. Washington, DC: USGPO. Reprint, New York: Johnson Reprint, 1970.

Oberg, Kalervo. 1973. *The Social Economy of the Tlingit Indians.* Seattle, WA: University of Washington Press.

O'Connor, Nancy Fields. 1985. *Fred E. Miller: Photographer of the Crows.* Boise, MT: University of Montana.

Ogawa, David. 2007. Interview, June. Albany, NY.

Okely, J., and H. Callaway, eds. 1992. *Anthropology and Autobiography.* London: Routledge.

Okun, S. B. 1979. *The Russian-American Company,* ed. B. D. Grekov and trans. Carl Ginsburg. New York: Octagon.

Oleksa, Michael J. 1992. *Orthodox Alaska: A Theology of Mission.* Crestwood, NY: St. Vladimir's Seminary Press.

Olson, Ronald L. 1961. "Tlingit Shamanism and Sorcery." *Kroeber Anthropological Society Papers* 25:207–22.

—— 1967. "Social Structure and Social Life of the Tlingit in Alaska." *Anthropological Papers* 26. Berkeley: University of California Press.

Orvell, Miles. 2003. *American Photography.* Oxford: Oxford University Press.

Osbaken, Margaret. 1986. Interview, August 20. Sitka, AK.

Pagh, Nancy. 1999. "An Indescribable Sea: Discourse of Women Traveling the Northwest Coast by Boat." *Frontiers: A Journal of Women's Studies* 20(3): 1–26.

Patrick, Andrew. 2002. *The Most Striking of Objects: The Totem Poles of Sitka National Historical Park.* Anchorage, AK: National Park Service and Sitka National Historical Park.

Paul, Frances. 1944. *Spruce Root Basketry of the Alaska Tlingit.* Lawrence, KS: Haskell Institute.

Paul, William L. 1939. "Historical and Legal Materials Relative to the Tlingit and Haida Claims Act of 1935." Research Paper, Law 198 (mimeograph copy). Seattle, WA: University of Washington.

Peabody Museum. 1873. *Sixth Annual Report of the Peabody Museum of American Archaeology and Ethnology.* Salem, MA: Salem Press.

Peirce, Benjamin. 1869. *Report of the Superintendent of the United States Coast Survey Showing the Progress of the Survey during the Year 1867.* Washington, DC: USGPO.

Peterson, Nicolas. 1984. "The Changing Photographic Contract: Aborigines and Image Ethics." In *Photography's Other Histories,* ed. C. Pinney and N. Peterson, pp. 119–45. Durham, NC: Duke University Press.

Petrov, Ivan. 1884. *Report on the Population, Industries and Resources of Alaska, 10th Census of the United States, 1880.* U.S. Dept. of Interior, 8. Washington, DC: USGPO.

Phillips, Ruth. 1995. "Why Not Tourist Art? Significant Silences in Native American Museum Representations." In *After Colonialism: Imperial Histories and Postcolonial*

Displacements, ed. Gyan Prakash, pp. 98–125. Princeton, NJ: Princeton University Press.

Phillips, Ruth, and C. Steiner, eds. 1999. *Unpacking Culture*. Berkeley: University of California Press.

Pierce, Richard. 1977. "Eadweard Muybridge: Alaska's First Photographer." *The Alaska Journal* 7(4): 202–10.

Pilsbury, David. 1898. *The Pillsbury Family: Being a History of William and Dorothy Pillsbury of Newburg in New England*. Everett, MA: Massachusetts Publishing.

Pinney, Christopher. 2003. "Introduction." In *Photography's Other Histories*, ed. C. Pinney and N. Peterson, pp. 1–16. Durham, NC: Duke University Press.

Pinney, Christopher, and Nicolas Peterson, eds. 2003. *Photography's Other Histories*. Durham, NC: Duke University Press.

Polk, Ralph Lane. 1900–15. *Alaska-Yukon Gazetteer and Business Directory*. Detroit, MI: R. L. Polk.

Poole, Deborah. 1997. *Vision, Race and Modernity*. Princeton, NJ: Princeton University Press.

Powers, Willow R., and Richard Hill. 1996. "Images across Boundaries: History, Use and Ethics of Photographs of American Indian." *American Indian Cultural and Research Journal* 20(3): 129–36.

Prakash, Gyan, ed. 1995. *After Colonialism: Imperial Histories and Postcolonial Displacements*. Princeton, NJ: Princeton University Press.

Preucel, Robert W., and Lucy Williams. 2005. "The Centennial Potlatch." *Expedition* 47(2): 9–19

Price, Derrick. 1997. "Surveyors and Surveyed." In *Photography: A Critical Introduction*, ed. Liz Wells, pp. 55–102. London: Routledge.

Price, Jessie. 1986. Interview, August. Sitka, AK.

Price, Robert. 1990. *The Great Father in Alaska: The Case of the Tlingit and Haida Salmon Industry*. Douglas, AK: First Street Press.

Rohner, Ronald, and Evelyn C. Rohner. 1969. *The Kwakiutl Indians of British Columbia*.

Florence, KY: Thomson Learning.

Roppel, Patricia. 1975. "Loring." *The Alaska Journal* 5(3): 169–78.

Rosenblum, Naomi. 1997. *A World History of Photography*. 3rd ed. New York: Abbeville.

Royal Anthropological Institute. 1899. *Notes and Queries on Anthropology*. 3rd ed. London: Edward Stanford.

Ruby, Jay. 1995. *Secure the Shadow: Death and Photography in America*. Cambridge, MA: MIT Press.

Russell, Lewis. 1890. "Two Expeditions to Mount St. Elias." *The Century Magazine* 41:865–84.

Russell, Nigel. 1998. "Processes and Pictures: The Beginning of Photography and Photographing American Indians." In *Spirit Capture*, ed. T. Johnson, pp. 113–34. Washington, DC: Smithsonian Institution Press.

Rydell, Robert. 1984. *All the World's Fair: Visions of Empire at American International Expositions, 1876–1916*. Chicago: University of Chicago Press.

Salisbury, O. M. 1962. *Quoth the Raven*. Seattle, WA: Superior Publishing.

Sandweiss, Martha A. 2002. *Print the Legend: Photography and the American West*. New Haven, CT: Yale University Press.

Scherer, Joanna C. 1975. "You Can't Believe Your Eyes: Inaccuracies in Photographs of North American Indians." *Studies in the Anthropology of Visual Communication* 2(2): 67–79.

—— 1990. *Picturing Cultures: Historical Photographs in Anthropological Inquiry*. New York: Routledge.

—— 1983. "The Photographic Document: Photographs as Primary Data in Anthropological Enquiry." In *Anthropology and Photography, 1860–1920*, ed. Elizabeth Edwards, pp. 32–41. New Haven, CT: Yale University Press.

Scidmore, Eliza Ruhamah. 1885. *Alaska: Its Southern Coast and the Sitka Archipelago*.

Boston: D. Lothrop.

—— 1893 *Appleton's Guide-Book to Alaska and the Northwest Coast.* New York: D. Appleton.

Sexton, Thomas. 1982. "The Images of Charles H. Ryder." *Alaska Journal* 12(3): 32–41.

Shalkop, Antoinette. 1987. "The Russian Orthodox Church in Alaska." In *Russia's American Colony,* ed. S. Frederick Starr, pp. 196–217. Durham, NC: Duke University Press.

Shepard, Isabel S. 1889. *The Cruise of the U.S. Steamer 'Rush' in Behring* [sic] *Sea Summer of 1889.* Boston: D. Lothrop.

Sherwood, Morgan B. 1959. "George Davidson and the Acquisition of Alaska." *Pacific Historical Review* 28(2): 141–54.

—— 1965a. "Ardent Spirits: Hooch and the Osprey Affair at Sitka." *Journal of the West* 4:312–13.

—— 1965b. *Exploration of Alaska: 1865–1900.* New Haven, CT: Yale University Press.

Shotridge, Florence. 1913. "The Life of a Chilkat Indian Girl." *Museum Journal* 4(3):101–3.

Shotridge, Florence, and Louis Shotridge. 1913a. "Indians of the Northwest." *Museum Journal* 4(3):71–80.

—— 1913b. "Chilkat Houses." *Museum Journal* 4(3):81–100.

Shotridge, Louis. 1917. "My Northland Revisited." *Museum Journal* 8:105–15.

—— 1919a. "War Helmets and Clan Hats of the Tlingit Indians." *Museum Journal* 10:43–48.

—— 1919b. "A Visit to the *Tsimshian* Indians." *Museum Journal* 10:49–67, 117–48.

—— 1920. "Ghost of Courageous Adventurer." *Museum Journal* 11:11–26.

—— 1922a. "Land Otter-Man." *Museum Journal* 18:55–59.

—— 1922b. Letter to George B. Gordon, October 14. Shotridge Collection. University of Pennsylvania Museum of Archaeology and Anthropology.

—— 1924. Letter to George B. Gordon, January 7. Shotridge Collection. University of

Pennsylvania Museum of Archaeology and Anthropology.

—— 1928. "The Emblems of Tlingit Culture." *Museum Journal* 19:350–77.

—— 1929. "The Kaguanton Shark Helmet." *Museum Journal* 20:339–43.

—— 1932. Letter to Horace Jayne, January 18. Shotridge Collection. Box 1/6–Correspondence, 1930–37. University of Pennsylvania Museum of Archaeology and Anthropology.

Shoup, A. G. 1908. Letter to W. A. Langille, November 22. E. W. Merrill File. Sitka, AK: Sitka National Historical Park.

—— 1909. *History of Camp Sitka No. 6* (pamphlet prepared for the Alaska-Yukon Exposition in Seattle). Sitka, AK: Kettleson Library.

Silversides, Brock. 1994. *The Face Pullers: Photographing Native Canadians 1871–1939.* Saskatoon, SK: Fifth House.

Sinclair, Jane, and Richard Engeman. 1991. "Professional Surveyor, Amateur Photographer: John F. Pratt on the Chilkat River, 1884." *Pacific Northwest Quarterly* 82(2): 51–58.

Sitka Presbyterian Church. 1885–1929. Session Records of the Sitka Presbyterian Church. Sitka, AK: Stratton Library, Sheldon Jackson College.

Smith, Liz. 1998. *Photography: A Critical Introduction.* London: Routledge.

—— 2002. *The Photography Reader.* London: Routledge.

Smith, Paul Chaat. 1995. "Ghost in the Machine." In *Strong Hearts: Native American Visions and Voices,* Aperture Foundation staff, pp. 6–9. New York: Aperture.

Snyder, J., and D. Munson. 1976. *The Documentary Photograph as a Work of Art: American Photographs, 1860–1876.* Chicago: David and Alfred Smart Gallery.

Solnit, Rebecca. 2003. *Rivers of Shadows: Eadweard Muybridge and the Technological Wild West.* Minneapolis, MN: University of Minnesota Press.

Sontag, Susan. 1977. *On Photography*. New York: Farrar, Straus and Giroux.

Stafford, Maria. 1997. "Think Again: The Intellectual Side of Images." *Chronicle of Higher Education* 20 (June 20): B6.

Starr, S. Frederick, ed. 1987. *Russia's American Colony*. Durham, NC: Duke University Press.

Steese, James G. 1922. Letter to Arno B. Cammerer, October 2. E. W. Merrill File. Sitka, AK: Sitka National Historical Park.

Steiger, Ricabeth, and Martin Tuareg. 1987. "Sleeping Beauties: On the Use of Ethnographic Photographs 1880-1920." In *Visual Explorations of the World*, ed. M. Tuareg and J. Ruby, pp. 316-41. Aachen: Edition Herodot.

Stern, Pamela. 1998. "The History of Canadian Arctic Photography: Issues of Territorial and Cultural Sovereignty." In *Imagining the Arctic*, ed. J. C. H. King and H. Lidchi, pp. 46-52. Seattle, WA: University of Washington Press.

Stevenson, John J. 1893. "Some Notes on South-Eastern Alaska and Its People." *Scottish Geographical Magazine* 9:66-83.

Stewart, Susan. 1984. *On Longing: Narratives of the Miniature, the Gigantic, the Souvenir, the Collection*. Baltimore, MD: Johns Hopkins University Press.

Strobridge, Truman, and Dennis Noble. 1999. *Alaska and the U.S. Revenue Cutter Service 1867-1915*. Annapolis, MD: Naval Institute Press.

Stromstadt-Brown, Dazie M. 1906. *Sitka, the Beautiful*. Seattle, WA: Homer M. Hill.

Swanton, John R. 1908. "Social Conditions, Beliefs, and Linguistic Relationship of the Tlingit Indians." In *Twenty-sixth Annual Report of the Bureau of American Ethnology, 1904-05*, pp. 391-501, Washington, DC: USGPO.

—— 1909. *Tlingit Myths and Texts*. Smithsonian Bureau of American Ethnology Bulletin 39. Washington, DC: USGPO.

Szarkowski, John. 1963. *The Photographer and the American Landscape*. New York: Museum of Modern Art.

—— 1966. *The Photographer's Eye*. New York: Doubleday.

—— 1997. *Looking at Photographs*. New York: Bulfinch.

Tagg, John. 1988. *The Burden of Representation: Essays on Photographies and Histories*. Amherst, MA: University of Massachusetts Press.

—— 2001. "Evidence, Truth and Order: Photographic Records and the Growth of the State." In *The Photography Reader*, ed. Liz Wells, pp. 257-60. New York: Routledge.

Taylor, Lucien, ed. 1994. *Visualizing Theory*. New York: Routledge.

Teichmann, Emil. 1963. *A Journey to Alaska in the Year 1868 Being a Diary of the Late Emil Teichmann*. New York: Argosy-Antiquarian.

Thomas, Alan. 1982. *Time in a Frame: Photography and the Nineteenth-Century Mind*. New York: Schocken.

Thomas, David H., ed. 1991. *The Spanish Borderlands in Pan-American Perspective*. Washington, DC: Smithsonian Institution Press.

Thompson, Jerry. 2003. *Truth and Photography: Notes on Looking and Photographing*. Chicago: Ivan R. Dee.

Thornton, Thomas F. 1998a. *Traditional Tlingit Use of Sitka National Historical Park: Final Report*. Sitka, AK: Sitka National Historical Park.

—— 1998b. "Introduction: Who Owned Southeast Alaska? Answers in Goldschmidt and Haas." In *Haa Aani, Our Land: Tlingit and Haida Land Rights and Use*, ed. W. Goldschmidt, T. Haas, and T. Thornton, pp. xvii-xxii. Seattle, WA: University of Washington Press.

—— 2000. "Picturing a People: Tlingit Photographer George Johnston" (film review). *American Anthropologist* 102(1): 155-56.

Tikhmenev, Petr A. 1979 [1861-63]. *A History of*

the Russian-American Company, trans. and ed. Richard A. Pierce and Alton Donnelly. Seattle, WA: University of Washington Press.

Tollefson, Kenneth. 1996. "From Localized Clans to Regional Corporation: The Acculturation of the Tlingit." *Western Canadian Journal of Anthropology* 8(1): 1–20.

—— 1995. "Tlingit Acculturation: An Institutional Perspective." *Ethnology* 23:229–47.

Trigger, Bruce, and Wilcomb Washburn, eds. 1996. *The Cambridge History of the Native Peoples of the Americas.* Cambridge: Cambridge University Press.

Tsinhnahjinnie, Hulleah J. 1994. "When Is a Photograph Worth a Thousand Words?" In *Photography's Other Histories*, ed. C. Pinney and N. Peterson, pp. 40–52. Durham, NC: Duke University Press.

Tuareg, Martin, and Jay Ruby, eds. 1987. *Visual Explorations of the World.* Aachen: Edition Herodot.

Turner, Victor, and Edith Turner. 1976. *Image and Pilgrimage in Christian Culture.* New York: Columbia University Press.

Underwood, John J. 2003 [1913]. *Alaska: An Empire in the Making.* Whitefish, MT: Kessinger.

Urry, John. 1990. *The Tourist Gaze.* London: Sage.

U.S. Copyright Office. 1951. *Motion Pictures 1912–30.* Washington, DC: USGPO.

U.S. Department of the Interior. 1870. *Report of the Board of Indian Commissioners.* Washington, DC: USGPO.

U.S. Department of the Interior, Census Office. 1893. *Report on Population and Resources of Alaska at the Eleventh Census: 1890.* Washington, DC: USGPO.

Vaughan, Thomas, and Bill Holm. 1982. *Soft Gold: The Fur Trade and Cultural Exchange on the Northwest Coast of America.* Portland, OR: Oregon Historical Society.

Venn, George. 2006. *Soldier to Advocate: C. E. S. Wood's 1877 Diary of Alaska and the Nez Perce Conflict.* Portland, OR: Wordcraft of Oregon.

Vogel, Susan. 1988. "Introduction." In *ART/ artifact*, ed. Center for African Art, pp. 11–17. New York: Center for African Art.

Wamsley, Douglas, and William Barr. 1998. "Early Photographers of the Canadian Arctic and Greenland." In *Imagining the Arctic*, ed. J. C. H. King and H. Lidchi, pp. 36–45. Seattle, WA: University of Washington Press.

Watkins, Thomas H. 1965. "The Americanization of Sitka." *American West* 2:54.

Wells, Liz, ed. 1997. *Photography: A Critical Introduction.* London: Routledge.

—— 2002. *The Photography Reader.* London: Routledge.

West, Nancy M. 2000. *Kodak and the Lens of Nostalgia.* Charlottesville, VA: University Press of Virginia.

Whymper, Frederick. 1868. *Travel and Adventure in the Territory of Alaska.* London: John Murray.

Wilbur, Bertrand K. 1979. "J.A.M. (Just About Me): Bertrand K. Wilbur, Medical Missionary to Sitka, Alaska 1894–1901." Manuscript. Sitka, AK: Stratton Library, Sheldon Jackson College.

Willard, Carolyn McCoy. 1884. *Life in Alaska: Letters of Mrs. Eugene S. Willard*, ed. Eva McClintock. Philadelphia: Presbyterian Board of Publication.

Willett, George. 1914. "Birds of Sitka and Vicinity, Southeastern Alaska." *The Condor* 16:71–91.

Williams, Carol J. 1999. "Photographic Portraiture of Aboriginal Women on Canada's Northwest Coast circa 1862–1880." *SIGHTS: Visual Anthropology Forum. http:// cc.joensuu.fi/sights/index.html* (accessed April 6, 2008).

—— 2003. *Framing the West: Race, Gender, and the Photographic Frontier in the Pacific Northwest.* New York: Oxford University Press.

Willinsky, John. 1998. *Learning to Divide the*

World: Education at Empire's End. Minneapolis, MN: University of Minnesota Press.

Wood, C. E. S. 1882. "Among the Thlinkits in Alaska." *The Century Magazine* 24(3): 323-39.

Worl, Rosita. 1982. "Spiritual Food for the Dead: Tlingit Potlatch Bowls." *Alaska Native News* (May/June): 43.

—— 1990. "History of Southeastern Alaska since 1867." In *The Handbook of North American Indians* 7, ed. Wayne Suttles, pp. 149-58. Washington, DC: Smithsonian Institution Press.

Wright, Julia McNair. 1883. *Among the Alaskans*. Philadelphia: Philadelphia Board of Education.

Wright, Terence. 1992. "Photography: Theories of Realism and Convention." In *Anthropology and Photography*, ed. Elizabeth Edwards, pp. 18-31. New Haven, CT: Yale University Press.

Wyatt, Victoria. 1986. "A Unique Attraction: The Alaska Totem Poles at St. Louis Exposition of 1904." *The Alaska Journal* 16:14-23.

—— 1987. "Alaskan Indian Wage Earners in the 19th Century." *Pacific Northwest Quarterly* 78(1-2): 43.

—— 1989. *Images from the Inside Passage: An Alaskan Portrait by Winter and Pond*. Seattle, WA: University of Washington Press.

—— 1992. "Interpreting the Balance of Power: A Case Study of Photographer and Subject in Images of Native Americans." *Exposure* 28(3): 21-31.

Yaw, W. Leslie. 1932. Letter to Katherine Gladfelter, April 15. RG 301.18, Box 18. Philadelphia: Presbyterian Historical Society.

—— 1985. *Sixty Years in Sitka: With Sheldon Jackson School and College*. Sitka, AK: Sheldon Jackson College Press.

—— 1986. Interview, August 18. Sitka, AK.

Young, Ralph, Frank Price, and Stephen Nicholas. 1920. "The Alaska Native Brotherhood." *The Pathfinder* 1(12): 5.

Young, S. Hall. 1915. *Alaska Days with John Muir*. New York: Fleming H. Revell.

—— 1927. *Hall Young: "The Mushing Parson."* New York: Fleming H. Revell.